A Civil War Gunboat in Pacific Waters

New Perspectives on Maritime History and Nautical Archaeology

UNIVERSITY PRESS OF FLORIDA

Florida A&M University, Tallahassee
Florida Atlantic University, Boca Raton
Florida Gulf Coast University, Ft. Myers
Florida International University, Miami
Florida State University, Tallahassee
New College of Florida, Sarasota
University of Central Florida, Orlando
University of Florida, Gainesville
University of North Florida, Jacksonville
University of South Florida, Tampa
University of West Florida, Pensacola

A Civil War Gunboat in Pacific Waters

Life on Board USS *Saginaw*

Hans Konrad Van Tilburg

Foreword by James C. Bradford and Gene Allen Smith

University Press of Florida
Gainesville | Tallahassee | Tampa | Boca Raton
Pensacola | Orlando | Miami | Jacksonville | Ft. Myers | Sarasota

First cloth printing, 2010
First paperback printing, 2023

28   27   26   25   24   23   6   5   4   3   2   1

Library of Congress Cataloging-in-Publication Data
Van Tilburg, Hans.
A Civil War gunboat in Pacific waters : life on board USS Saginaw / Hans
Konrad Van Tilburg ; foreword by James C. Bradford and Gene Allen Smith.
p. cm.
Includes bibliographical references and index.
ISBN 978-0-8130-3516-1 (cloth) | ISBN 978-0-8130-8017-8 (pbk.)
1. Saginaw (Steamer) 2. Pacific Area—History, Naval—19th century. 3.
Seafaring life—Pacific Area—History—19th century. 4. United States.
Navy—History—19th century. I. Title.
VA65.S227V36 2010
359.3'25—dc22   2010020781

The University Press of Florida is the scholarly publishing agency for the State
University System of Florida, comprising Florida A&M University, Florida
Atlantic University, Florida Gulf Coast University, Florida International Univer-
sity, Florida State University, New College of Florida, University of Central
Florida, University of Florida, University of North Florida, University of South
Florida, and University of West Florida.

University Press of Florida
2046 NE Waldo Road
Suite 2100
Gainesville, FL 32609
http://upress.ufl.edu

To my original mentor in maritime history,
Dr. William N. Still Jr., who told me,
"You've got to get out there in the Pacific—it's wide open!"
It still is.

Contents

List of Figures ix

Foreword xi

Acknowledgments xiii

———————

Introduction 1

1. A New Ship for a New Ocean 9

2. Seasoning on the China Station 37

3. The Civil War on the Pacific Coast 80

4. Hard Times on Coastal Patrol 121

5. Exploring Seward's Icebox 147

6. Hawai`i and the End of the Archipelago 179

7. The Castaways of Ocean Island 218

8. Afterword: Legacy and Shipwrecks 280

———————

Notes 325

References 343

Index 349

Figures

1. The Pacific cruising areas of USS *Saginaw*   7

2. Rare photo of USS *Saginaw*   17

3. *Saginaw* waterlines and internal details, 1859   21

4. *Saginaw* sail plan and elevation drawing, 1863   22

5. *Saginaw* deck plans, 1863   23

6. Mare Island Navy Yard, ca. 1850s   26

7. Mare Island and the town of Vallejo, 1870   26

8. Receiving ship USS *Independence* at Mare Island   27

9. Lieutenant Commander Montgomery Sicard, ca. 1870   180

10. Rear Admiral Montgomery Sicard, 1890s   180

11. The Northwestern Hawaiian Island chain   206

12. The shacks at Midway Island, 1870   209

13. Details of the cut surveyed by Sicard, 1870   212

14. Townsend's patented rock-drilling machine, 1869   214

15. Sketch of USS *Saginaw* hard aground at Kure Atoll   226

16. Satellite image of Kure Atoll, eastern reef crest   230

17. Island rats swarming the wing holes in the dunes   233

18. Sicard's tent on the beach, Ocean Island   235

19. Sketch of the stern breaking apart on the reef   236

20. Donkey boiler condensing freshwater, Ocean Island   236

21. Crew laying out sails for the gig   241

22. Sketch of the captain's gig ready for sea   241

23. Executive Officer John Gunnel Talbot   245

24. Gunner's Mate William Halford   245

25. Building the schooner *Deliverance*, Ocean Island   257

26. Sketch of castaway camp, Ocean Island   258

27. Photo of Green Island today   258

28. Photo of the gig at Honolulu Harbor   269

29. Headstone at Nu`uanu Cemetery, Honolulu   285

30. Beach-built sextant at the Naval Academy   297

31. Memorial tablet at the Naval Academy chapel   297

32. *Saginaw*'s gig on display in Saginaw, Michigan   298

33. Names of J. Andrews and J. Muir etched into gig's hatch   298

34. *Saginaw*'s anchors near the impact site   307

35. An encrusted 24-pdr broadside cannon   308

36. Author near the boiler face on the reef   310

37. Diver searching the surge channels   314

38. Brass and bronze steam engine components   315

39. Ship's bell discovered after 136 years underwater   316

40. One of the Parrott rifled pivot guns found by divers   317

41. Distribution of artifacts at the wreck site   318

42. The 2006 site survey team   319

Foreword

Water is unquestionably the most important natural feature on earth. By volume, the world's oceans compose 99 percent of the planet's living space; in fact, the surface of the Pacific Ocean alone is larger than that of the total land bodies. Water is as vital to life as air. Indeed, to test whether the moon or other planets can sustain life, NASA looks for signs of water. The story of human development is inextricably linked to the oceans, seas, lakes, and rivers that dominate the earth's surface. The University Press of Florida's series New Perspectives on Maritime History and Nautical Archaeology is devoted to exploring the significance of the earth's water while providing lively and important books that cover the spectrum of maritime history and nautical archaeology broadly defined. The series includes works that focus on the role of canals, rivers, lakes, and oceans in history; on the economic, military, and political use of those waters; and upon the people, communities, and industries that support maritime endeavors. Limited by neither geography nor time, volumes in the series contribute to the overall understanding of maritime history and can be read with profit by both general readers and specialists.

This volume epitomizes the goals of the series. It combines nautical archaeology and documentary research to chronicle the construction, service career, wreck, and survey of artifacts from the wreck site to tell the story of the USS *Saginaw*, the first U.S. naval vessel constructed on the west coast. The gunboat *Saginaw* played a supporting role in the great events of its decade of service, the 1860s. Assigned first to the East India Squadron, *Saginaw* cruised the coast of China to suppress piracy and protect American lives and property. In June 1861, *Saginaw* was searching for survivors from the merchant ship *Myrtle* when the local Chinese commander ordered a battery at the entrance to Qui Nhon Bay to fire on the *Saginaw* for violating Chinese territorial waters. James F. Schenck, commander of the *Saginaw*, responded by bombarding the battery in a confrontation typical of many confrontations between Western navies and Chinese authorities during the mid-nineteenth century.

In poor condition, *Saginaw* was decommissioned in Hong Kong in January 1862 and returned to Mare Island for extensive repairs before being recommissioned in March 1863. During the last two years of the Civil War, *Saginaw* patrolled the west coast from Central America to British Columbia watching for Confederate activity; to counter potential European intervention in Mexico; and to protect American lives and property during the conflict between supporters of Maximilian and Benito Juarez. Particularly important was the protection of shipments of gold from California to Panama. In 1866, *Saginaw* was assigned to support the laying of a telegraph cable by Western Union Company. Following the U.S. purchase of Alaska the following year, *Saginaw* was dispatched to the area to chart portions of its coast and enforce stability and order during the transition from Russian to American rule. In 1870, *Saginaw* was sent to Midway Island to support the development of a coaling station for trans-Pacific liners. When the Pacific Mail Steamship Company abandoned its attempt to blast a ship channel through the reef, *Saginaw* evacuated the company's remaining employs in October 1870. En route to San Francisco, *Saginaw* struck and grounded. The ship's crew made it to shore before the pounding serf destroyed the ship. One hundred and thirty years later, divers found the remains of the *Saginaw*, and a team of nautical archeologist led by Hans Van Tilburg began recording artifacts at the site.

This volume describes the side-wheel steamer *Saginaw* and its construction; traces its service in a secondary theater of the Civil War at a time when the young United States, still an Atlantic-oriented nation, was only beginning to expand its interests in the Pacific (illustrated by the purchase of Alaska and the government's backing of the Pacific Mail Steamship Company) and describes the discovery and survey of its wreck. Always, the focus is on the men and mission of the *Saginaw*. The result is a work that puts a human face on events encircling the North Pacific that laid the basis for American rise to power in the region a half century later.

James C. Bradford and Gene Allen Smith, Series Editors

Acknowledgments

The project of compiling the historic narrative of USS *Saginaw* has stretched slowly over the last six years; this account was written on various weekends, certain vacation days, and after work hours. During that time, I have had the personal pleasure of seeking out the details of *Saginaw*'s story that only those who have become completely obsessed with historical research can know. It is always exciting to come across shipboard events associated with great moments in history, with rebellions and wars and action at sea. But who is also excited about the other parts of the narrative? Who turns the pages of the logbook to read more about the 75 pounds of salted pork coming on board for the crew's mess? Or the surgeon's mustard plasters and opium pills? Or the pickles and soap brushes and tar and shoes and the hundreds of other smaller items carried abroad, the minor comforts on a vast ocean? Only those afflicted with an unexplainable urge—and granted the opportunity one way or another to indulge themselves in the historical narrative—do this work willingly. If it's that enjoyable, it simply cannot be a chore.

During the past six years, I have had the pleasure to work with and learn from a number of special people, only a few of whom I can briefly acknowledge here: Rebecca Livingston, reference archivist at the National Archives and Records Administration, Washington, D.C., for her insight into the Naval Records Collection; Robert Schwemmer, maritime heritage coordinator for NOAA's Office of Marine Sanctuaries West Coast Region, for his unceasing assistance with online research; Paul Nitchman, fellow *Saginaw* researcher, for his complete dedication to detail, his knowledge of the tragedy on Kaua'i and his review of this manuscript; Dr. William Dudley, former director of the Naval Historical Center, for his support of the initial wreck-site survey; Bill Crozier, for information about his grandfather Arthur H. Parsons, ensign on board

USS *Saginaw*; fellow divers on the 2003 shipwreck survey team, Kelly Gleason, Tony Sarabia, Brad Rodgers, Don Moses, and Andy Lydecker; fellow divers on the 2006 shipwreck survey team, Lindsey Thomas, Kelly Gleason, Tane Casserley, Brenda Altmeier, and Robert Schwemmer; and, finally, Dr. William N. Still Jr., for his consistent and unfailing outspoken and unspoken encouragement in all this historical business.

Introduction

Sometimes the biggest stories begin with the smallest discoveries. In 2003, research divers with the Office of Marine Sanctuaries of the National Oceanic and Atmospheric Administration (NOAA) came across a small and almost insignificant accumulation of brass sheathing tacks, a few nails grouped together in a cuplike hole in the reef. This might have seemed relatively unimportant were it not for their location. These first traces of a possible shipwreck site were near Green Island at Kure Atoll, the most remote coral reef on the planet, in the geographic middle of the North Pacific Ocean and 1,200 miles across open ocean from the nearest port—Honolulu, Hawai`i. After the nails came the discovery of anchors and cannon and steam-engine equipment; in fact, a whole trail of historic destruction lay beneath the breaking surf. The wreck turned out to be the remains of the navy gunboat USS *Saginaw*, a wooden side-wheel steamer that was lost at this tiny atoll on October 29, 1870, her bones resting underwater for more than 130 years. The survey of the physical artifacts and the history associated with the ten-year service of USS *Saginaw* open a window onto one of the unique maritime narratives of the Pacific Ocean.

The importance of finding such artifacts underwater goes beyond the initial excitement of discovery. The survey of shipwreck sites like *Saginaw*'s, with the application of a little historical and archaeological imagination, is actually a form of time travel. Archaeologists do not see just the encrusted iron or bronze shapes, but watch in their mind's eye the cannons sliding wildly across the deck in the final moments of destruction. They feel the stout wooden hulls being broken apart by the ocean, dropping the copper fasteners onto the reef, and hear the rigging and topmasts crashing down into the waves. Shipwreck sites are often tragic in nature. Over time the artifacts become a unique record of the historic event. So even at the moment of discovery, with a little imagination, it is possible to look into the past more directly than through any document. The primary physical evidence is a kind of frozen time capsule, slowly becoming part of the reef.

In 2003, I had the good luck to be the lead investigator with the NOAA team diving at Kure, having been inexplicably taken up with the story of USS *Saginaw* a few years earlier. My involvement with the maritime world has something of an obsessive quality, beginning with sailing on my father's boat *Brunhilde* as a young child and continuing through a professional diving and academic career in underwater archaeology and history (indebted to Lloyd Bridges and the old black-and-white television series *Sea Hunt*). I am fascinated with the fluid and ever-changing maritime world, where so many mysteries remain below, typically unseen beyond the flat expanse of the ocean's surface. And I am amazed at how all mariners have struggled to survive on and relate to the sea, for we evolved toward the land and, unlike certain other species, never went back. This relationship between people and the sea is of central importance, for our planet is mostly water, and our connection to and understanding of the ocean is the single most important environmental issue that we face today.

I don't know what it is specifically about USS *Saginaw* that first captured my imagination, but it may have been just the existence of Civil War artifacts there in the middle of the vast Pacific Ocean. The Civil War, after all, had been fought exclusively in the eastern and southern states, had it not? What was the navy doing in the Pacific? What were these sailors doing on a remote coral atoll in 1870? What explained the footprint of this site? What was the whole story behind it?

The history of great events is often told only from the narratives of famous admirals during major naval engagements or the movements of large and powerful fleets of capital ships across the world's stage. But even the smallest ships can occasionally do great service in the vast ocean, and history is more than just the combined biographies of famous leaders. The enlisted men serving before the mast tell their own tales, as do the young ensigns and lieutenants just setting out on their first commands at the very beginning of their careers. The daily drills and common sights, and the sounds and even the smells capture the common realities of life at sea that are lost in the grander narratives. And this is particularly true for the maritime history of the Pacific during the mid-nineteenth century for the United States had no great fleet or powerful flagships, or anything more than a handful of young former Civil War officers, to chart our nation's path in that ocean. Frankly, the Pacific Squadron consisted of whatever the east coast could spare. Throughout *Saginaw*'s service career, spanning

1860 to 1870, America was decidedly an Atlantic nation, but was also just as decidedly making its way slowly westward, one stepping-stone at a time—a shipyard here, a port there, a lonely American flag far overseas. The wreck of USS *Saginaw* at Kure Atoll, the location of her last mission in the middle of the Pacific, is literally one of those stepping-stones.

The Pacific Ocean one hundred years ago was not the cruising ground of great fleets, but the arena for the humblest of vessels. And the men who served on board those small ships were witness to some of the most important world-shaping historical events in the nineteenth century. It made no difference that they walked the foredeck of a fourth-rate gunboat and not a powerful ship of the line. They saw a Pacific that held vast potential for a young nation.

This is the ten-year story of a small side-wheel steamer, the first vessel built at the Mare Island Naval Shipyard in California, America's first navy yard on the west coast. USS *Saginaw* was launched in the days before the American Civil War, receiving her commission in 1860 and setting out for East Asia and the China seas. There the gunboat played a unique role protecting American citizens and property during the incredible turmoil of the Second Opium War (also known as the Arrow War) and the massive internal social upheaval of the Chinese Taiping Rebellion. During her service on the China Station, *Saginaw* called at numerous ports in Japan as well, an empire recently opened to Westerners by Admiral Matthew Calbraith Perry. Conditions in Japan were uneasy at best. Loyal samurai naturally resisted the incursion of foreign merchants and outside powers. *Saginaw* was the nation's new player on the international scene, though with so few ships and men, America was a relatively minor member of the foreign coalition in East Asia at the time.

With the outbreak of the Civil War in 1861, *Saginaw* returned to the United States, with the crew and officers in such haste to join the action that they managed to arrive before their own ship, which they had abandoned overseas to the great surprise of their superiors. Rescued from that fate, *Saginaw* stood wartime duty in the Pacific, an ocean often considered a peaceful backwater compared to the naval engagements and blockade duties on the southeast coast. However, the Pacific included a huge stretch of coastal territory, guarded only by a handful of Union vessels. And the treasure-laden Pacific Mail Company steamers carried a continuous stream of gold from San Francisco to the Bay of Panama, from there headed east over the mountains by rail and then onward to New York. This was the critical Pacific communication route, the marine highway to the Atlantic.

Confederate soldiers shaped their plans to cross the isthmus and capture those steamers, and ships like the tiny *Saginaw* cruised to foil them. And there were other troubles along the coast as well. In France, Napoleon III took the opportunity during the American Civil War to intervene in Mexico, establishing military support for the puppet regime of Austrian emperor Maximilian I, hoping to end the struggle with the Mexican revolutionaries and create a permanent foothold of European empire in the new world. Naval service on the west coast was not easy.

Following the war, *Saginaw* ventured north. The 1867 purchase of Alaska from Russia by the American secretary of state, William Henry Seward, though ridiculed by some at the time as an immense waste of funds, ultimately had enormous consequences for the United States. *Saginaw* headed to the inside passage in 1868 to assist in the early military administration of the new territory and to survey for anchorages and new sources of coal. The land was beautiful but rugged, and the jagged channels, with their treacherous rocks and strong currents, formed a maze of passages. Merchant captains took advantage of the departure of the Russian America Company, leading to a booming smuggling trade in weapons and liquor. *Saginaw* found herself amidst the winter gales and incessant cold rains, and the drunken and disorderly garrison life at Sitka. During the transition from Russian to American administration, conflicts between the new military occupation forces and the native inhabitants were not infrequent, and *Saginaw* was (unfortunately) a part of those as well.

The ship's final Pacific service in 1870 took her far into the vast emptiness, to the end of an uninhabited and remote archipelago. The assignment involved supporting a team of Boston hard-hat divers in their efforts to blast open a channel into the lagoon at Midway Atoll, a strategic but isolated island claimed by the U.S. government only a few years earlier in 1867. It was clear that the nation's government, even back then, recognized the potential of Midway Atoll. At that time, the creation of a coal depot there would have bolstered all of the country's maritime activities in East Asia. It would have fueled coal-hungry ships in their lonely and difficult passages across the largest ocean in the world. Of course, the islands at Midway were later developed into a crucial naval air facility and submarine base, central to offensive operations in the Pacific during World War II, and later on the front line of the distant early-warning system of the subsequent Cold War. In 1870, however, the Boston engineers, experienced in breaking apart solid rock but completely unfamiliar with the realities of coral reefs, soon gave up their futile battle with the sea and packed up their gear in defeat. The channel was not to be created in 1870. *Saginaw* embarked the sunburned divers and turned her bow for San Francisco, for home. But the ship never arrived at port.

If you had served for ten years on the deck of USS *Saginaw*, the ship would have taken you all the way around the rim of the Pacific Ocean, encountering Taiping rebels, Confederate spies, Mexican revolutionaries, Alaskan natives—and, finally, the clacking gooney birds and oily monk seals of a distant and uninhabited barren island, Midway Atoll. *Saginaw's* service, her life on the Pacific, is a slice of history taken at the eventful and exciting midcentury point. The ship's end is one of the great tragic tales of maritime lore.

While transporting the working party home to San Francisco, *Saginaw* ran aground in the middle of the night, October 29, 1870, on nearby Ocean Island (as Green Island at Kure Atoll was then called). The ship was making only two knots at the time. It is possibly the world's slowest shipwreck, but it was inevitable, nonetheless. At the moment the lookout spotted the surf, the ship was beyond the point of turning back. And once on the reef, the sea turned the ocean swells into crashing breakers, and the dark and quiet night into a chaotic fight for survival. The ship's battered crew salvaged what they could from the disaster and spent two very difficult months on the low sand spit of Ocean Island, while five volunteers made their way in one of the ship's boats across more than 1,500 nautical miles of open ocean in search of rescue. When they finally did manage to come ashore, four died in the surf, leaving the sole survivor to carry word of his castaway shipmates to the local American minister and His Majesty Kamehameha V of the Kingdom of Hawai`i. One hundred and thirty-six years later, the underwater survey of the shipwreck site was completed, capturing new aspects of this story and our maritime heritage that can be discovered in no other way.

The sea was the highway that brought the world to the doorstep of the United States with each and every port touched by USS *Saginaw*. San Francisco was an isolated town on a distant and undeveloped coast, but the wharves of the city were literally the gateway to Hong Kong and Nagasaki, to La Paz and Sitka and Honolulu. And that highway was (and is) an ever-changing passage, one often fraught with hazards. Mariners know that the ocean at all times provides a challenge to the vessels that plough its surface. And, as sailors know, the ocean is consistently intolerant of the smallest of mistakes. The bottom of the sea has become a literal museum of these tragedies, historic shipwrecks unseen until discovered, interpreted, and shared.

The navy has always rated its most powerful front-line ships as first-rate, second-rate, and so on. The fourth-rate USS *Saginaw* was the humblest of vessels on that longest of all marine highways. Yet, in more ways than one, the side-wheeler was a unique part of the westward vision of America, an instrument in the creation of our national presence overseas. Today the U.S. Pacific Fleet is unchallenged, a status that some might have thought inevitable. But America was not that power in the nineteenth century; this outcome was not assured. What are the origins of the nation's present-day naval strength? What was the grand strategy in the Pacific? No combined fleets or powerful dreadnoughts laid the path toward naval domination in that ocean. The navy did not concentrate its forces there, but dispersed them thinly across a broad swath. The country supported a cruising navy, and solitary vessels led the way in the nineteenth century, many of them aging and in need of repair. Lone commanders and oftentimes ambivalent and mixed crews served under canvas sails and inefficient steam engines on distant foreign shores, exposed to the worst of circumstances of tropical climate and disease. Instructions from their superiors took months to reach them, if they arrived at all. Single ships and individual officers and crewmen set the stage for our current footprint in the Pacific. It was a different age.

What was it like to serve on USS *Saginaw*, to enlist in the East Indies Squadron or the Pacific Station from 1860 to 1870? What did the crew eat, where did they sleep, what kind of trouble did they get into when they went ashore? No single author recorded the service career of this ship, but a plethora of naval documents capture the experience of many. The logs and letters of those who lived on board fill in the details as seen from the captain's cabin, and from the slung hammocks of the berth deck, on board this small gunboat of the old steam navy. A Union vessel on the west coast during the war; a side-wheeler in a time of emerging screw propulsion; a small workhorse on a huge ocean—this is the life (and sometimes the death) of the men as seen from the deck of the ship in Mexico and Alaska, in China and Japan, in Panama and Hawai`i, in Washington and California set amidst all of the changes of the mid-nineteenth century. And it is the beginning and the end of the ship's own service career. Like all nautical tales, the story of USS *Saginaw* touches upon many shores (see fig. 1). And

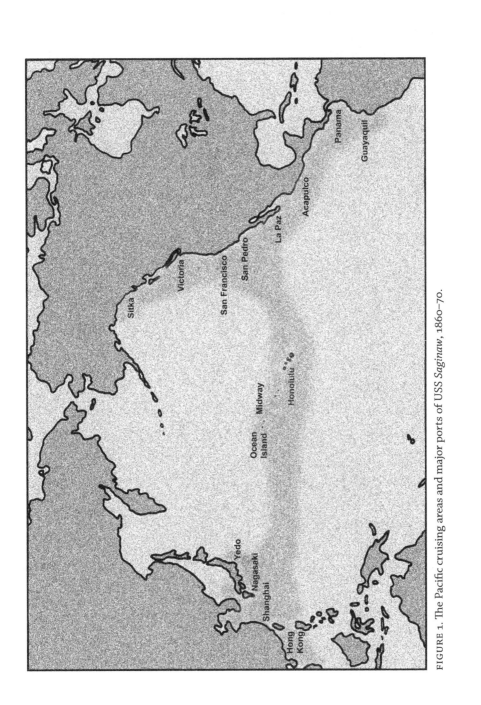

FIGURE 1. The Pacific cruising areas and major ports of USS *Saginaw*, 1860–70.

the ship remains the single physical reality around which all blue water tales must be told.

USS *Saginaw* was our small, self-confident, impetuous tool in a remote ocean, assigned the unique role of initiating our national vision on the Pacific. And she boldly began to carry out that mission far ahead of schedule, long before we really had the ability to see the job through to completion.

1

A New Ship for a New Ocean

[W]e in accord with the laws of progress—are destined to civilize and control those nations. . . . [I]t is here . . . upon this [Pacific] sea . . . the ocean bride of America, that the East and West will join hands and the great circle of civilization will be complete.

Robert Schufeldt, 1870

Hardly any of us today would remember—though their grandparents may once have told them of it—a time when California and the west coast seemed as distant to most Americans as the moon. America was an east coast nation, and few initially felt themselves hardy enough to attempt the trek to, let alone survive, the distant and uncivilized western frontier. The west coast, and the Pacific beyond it, was therefore born late into the American public consciousness, and it took major events like the gold rush of 1848 to accomplish this. Freshly minted cities like San Francisco, therefore, traced their earliest roots to these few eventful decades in the mid-nineteenth century. Everyone heard the stories of the Wild West, but it all lay thousands of miles from the familiar world, and the boundaries of East Coast civilization.

The origins of USS *Saginaw* lie with this great westward movement, with the need for America to project power, to sail in support of commerce, and to show the flag in new and remote corners of the globe. And at the midpoint of the nineteenth century, any location on the Pacific was truly remote. No easy passage between the coasts existed for travelers to San Francisco or the gold fields, no transcontinental railway blazed its trail across the mountains and deserts. Ships had been sailing down the South Atlantic and rounding Cape Horn amidst the mountainous seas and gales of the "roaring '40s" for hundreds of years, and they typically received a tremendous beating on the route. To enter the Pacific they pushed westward, against the prevailing winds and seas of the circumpolar ocean, straining the rigging and spars. Ice and Antarctic waves swept their decks, breaking equipment and sailors alike. But there was no major shipyard established anywhere in that distant ocean, and no permanent naval presence.

Prior to 1849, San Francisco (or Yerba Buena, as it was known) was a sleepy little town consisting of a few dwellings, a supply store, and a church. The non-native population at the time numbered fewer than four hundred people. Going overland, travelers usually left from either St. Joseph, Missouri, or Council Bluffs, Iowa, on covered-wagon treks lasting from two to three months. And "if the emigrants conduct themselves properly, no danger need be feared from any Indian tribes through which the road passes."[1] Of course, if one preferred to rely on the proven 'round-the-Horn sailing route, passage could be made by clipper ship from New York to California, a distance of roughly 14,700 miles around the Cape, in three to four months. Slower (less expensive) merchant ships that did not feature the sleek lines and tall masts of the fastest clipper designs could add two more months to that estimate.

Shorter and safer means were pursued as competition arose for facilitating passage between the coasts. This meant going by ship but still avoiding the Cape route—in other words, paying more and crossing to the Pacific over the mountains of Nicaragua or Panama. The Nicaragua Company's route, as advertised by railroad magnate and shipping-line owner Cornelius Vanderbilt, consisted of a 2,000-mile steamship passage from New York to San Juan del Norte, and thence onto river steamers for a 52-mile ascent up the San Juan River to the Castillian Rapids, where passengers left their vessel to climb above the roaring obstacle and make another 27 miles on the river to Lake Nicaragua. After transiting 42 miles more on this lake, they arrived at Virgin Bay, where a 13-mile land crossing on a plank road brought them to San Juan del Sud on the Pacific Coast. Reboarding a steamship there left them with only a 2,800-mile leg up the coast to San Francisco. By modern standards, this was a hellishly long and dangerous journey.

The Panama Route advertised passage from New York to Colón in Panama via either Kingston, Jamaica, or Havana, Cuba. Colón was soon renamed Aspinwall after Baltimore businessman William Henry Aspinwall, who in 1848 organized with partners the Pacific Mail Steamship Company (PMSS) for "the purpose of building, equipping, furnishing, purchasing, chartering, and owning vessels, to be propelled solely by steam or other expansive fluid or motive power, to be run and propelled in navigating the Pacific Ocean."[2] Passengers and freight were then shipped by rail car from there to Panama, some 49 miles distant across the isthmus. Rail lines were completed in 1855, the project managing to overcome extreme obstacles and costly overruns. This was a large improvement on the mule-and-canoe-through-the-tropical-jungle method. From Panama, passengers stopped at Acapulco, San Diego, and Monterey during the transit north. Three wooden side-wheel Pacific Mail Steamship Company vessels bore these travelers and their goods to San Francisco. The establishment of such important lines of communication was spurred by congressional approval of ocean-mail contracts, direct government subsidies, in 1845. There was money to be made by heading west, and in many more ways than working the gold fields. And with these lines of maritime communication came the need to protect American passage through the Pacific ports in Central America, for U.S. citizens and their property moved on these routes between their own east and west coasts only through thousands of miles of foreign territory.

Generally, the Nicaragua or Panama routes took about thirty days from coast to coast. Voyagers might have saved time on both by embarking at New Orleans, but many preferred to avoid the potential of cholera near the Mississippi. But both of these routes also exposed passengers to malaria and yellow fever in other locations, notably on the transisthmus leg. The choice could be difficult. One could be exposed to familiar and temperate terrestrial hazards for months, or one could choose to cut the transit time in half and risk briefer exposure to more unfamiliar tropical diseases. American development of the Pacific region might have seemed difficult at the time, but despite these obstacles, the Pacific would be drawn inexorably closer to New York, Boston, and Washington, D.C.

There was no doubt that the United States had clear interests in an expansive role in the Pacific and needed to establish more reliable communication. Secretary of State William Henry Seward's speech to the United States Senate on July 29, 1852, made clear the necessity and needs of commerce on the Pacific Ocean. He spoke at length of mariners the world over, of Phoenicians and Portuguese and Dutch and English sailors. But most of all, he spoke of American mariners, and in particular whalers, and the "subjugation of the monster of the seas to the uses of man," meaning the great profitability of the whaling industry. Seward aimed wisely at the pocketbook. The heart of the matter was, after all, economic gain and national greatness. At the time of his address, the American whaling fleet in New England stood at more than seven hundred vessels. These were the days described by Herman Melville in *Moby Dick*, the days when the profit-bent Quaker captains of New Bedford and Nantucket pursued their liquid gold—whale oil. Whaling was big business, and the early to mid-nineteenth century was the high point of the industry for America, particularly in regard to the sperm whale fishery and the catch in the Pacific. This was no accident. In 1838, the U.S. government had committed to that vast ocean a six-ship exploring expedition, under the somewhat contentious command of Lieutenant Charles Wilkes. For four years, the expedition charted the unknown reefs and shoals, the hidden dangers to the nation's whaling fleet—and the secret locations of the whales. America was committed to the Pacific and had been for decades, for reasons far beyond a sense of adventure or protecting miners on their way to the gold fields.

The Pacific was a tantalizing vision of change, and the shapers of the American presence in that ocean foresaw great commercial opportunities. In 1842, ports in China, offering the wealth of Asia but notoriously difficult for foreign merchants, had been forced open to direct Western contact and trade as a result of the first Opium War, wherein the British secured the right to more equitable trade privileges (and the ability to more easily import illegal opium into China). The Honorable East India Company for hundreds of years had sent ships from England to China to carry away the wealth of the Orient. China had what the West wanted: silks, porcelains, spices, and especially tea. England was a nation addicted to the drink. The problem was that the West had very little that the Chinese would actually accept in trade. Woolens did not make much sense in the heat of the South China Coast. The British had to pay cash, or find a substitute. The poppy fields of British India supplied the answer. The crowded coastal provinces in China were shaped by the foreign merchants into a huge market of opium addicts.

This opium smuggling on board foreign ships, illegal in China, brought the trade issue to a head. The imperial Confucian bureaucrats banned the drug and confiscated hundreds of chests from the foreign warehouses, to be destroyed in pits filled with lye and cast out to sea. The Western merchants clamored for a response to this affront to their deeply held beliefs in property and free trade, and the Royal Navy obliged. Virtually unopposed, ships-of-the-line ultimately threatened the supply routes of grain to the northern imperial capital, and the war was over. The military defeat of imperial Chinese armies opened the empire to foreigners at five "treaty ports": Guangzhou, Xiamen, Ningpo, Fuzhou, and Shanghai. The Treaty of Nanjing spoke of trade and access, and yet, ironically, remained silent on the importation of opium.

But the Western merchants still did not realize the kinds of profits they saw as possible in China. They had no access to the interior, to the hinterlands, and soon felt that the greater volume of trade was occurring elsewhere. Not satisfied with the five ports, the British began the Arrow War, or Second Opium War, in 1856, ostensibly in response to the illegal search and seizure of a British-registered Chinese lorcha. The Arrow War was somewhat a repeat of the first experience, ending in imperial defeat. This further eroded the sovereign capacity of the Chinese government. More coastal ports were opened, and routes into the hinterlands and particularly into the interior of the country along the marine highway of the Yangzi (also spelled Yangtze) River were added. Western merchants paused at the brink of entering these new domains. Who would be their escort? For nothing could quell the growing economic and social unrest that swept the country, and it seemed that China really had no response to the very real threat of being cut apart by foreign powers.

This lesson did not go unobserved by others. As a result of Admiral Matthew Calbraith Perry's visits and a combination of diplomatic and military restraint on both the Japanese and American sides, the formerly closed empire had been "peacefully" forced open to Western trade in 1853 following some 250 years of near complete isolation from foreigners. Diplomacy, coupled with modern cannon and the U.S. Navy steam frigates *Mississippi* and *Susquehanna* standing off in Tokyo Bay, made a powerful argument. Several treaty ports soon opened in Japan, and a timetable was created for the opening of others. These agreements are referred to today, for obvious reasons, as the "unequal treaties." Although America positioned herself as the protector of Japan during an era of Western-induced change, the Japanese needed only to look across the narrow sea to witness the results of foreign encroachment by the allies of the Americans in China, and the consequences of conducting an unequal naval confrontation. Traditional technologies—the war junks and marine police force of the daimyos, or war lords—could not withstand the test. Resistance, as they say, was futile. Japan would have to adapt to excel, and adapt quickly. Traditional sentiments and culture, though, could not be so easily changed, and resentment and violence against foreigners during the transition became a common problem.

East Asia was undergoing massive change. Furthermore, with the decline of the established trade monopolies like the British East India Company, and the changing fortunes of Old World Spanish colonies in South America, the Pacific as a whole entered a new phase of upheaval. In the eyes of many, this meant economic potential, brimming with commercial opportunity for the West. Seward was right about the critical nature of whaling in the Pacific, but there was much more happening in that ocean. Trade and profits were growing by leaps and bounds for distant powers who could maintain a presence there.

Sometimes these nineteenth-century American hopes and dreams took on elements of the mythic and symbolic realm. Pacific expansion wore an easy cloak of manifest destiny, of predestined cultural uplift. Many commentators felt strongly about this and voiced their observations in broad terms; naval officer Robert Wilson Schufeldt stated: "the Pacific Ocean, with its long swell and gentle breezes lies waiting for the American flag. . . . A recent cruise of three years in China and Japan—has imparted to me the full conviction—that we in accord with the laws of progress— are destined to civilize and control those nations. . . . [I]t is here . . . upon this [Pacific] sea . . . the ocean bride of America, that the East and West will join hands and the great circle of civilization will be complete."[3]

This kind of implied racial preeminence was actually a reflection of even older bias. Georg Wilhelm Friedrich Hegel had contrasted the importance of other (lesser) nations to the inevitable progress of the West. He identified the East as being at the beginning of the evolution of civilizations, yet stalled somehow and unable to move forward. The true divisions between men, for Hegel, were based clearly on moral principles: "The course of the sun is a symbol of the course of the human spirit; and as the light of the physical sun travels from the east to the west, so does the light of the sun of the self-consciousness. Asia is the determinate east or absolute beginning, and Europe the determinate west or end of history."[4] Others, like Leopold von Ranke, the founder of modern historical science, held similar views, interpreting civilizations in the light of social Darwinism: "The British rule the whole world with their trade; they have opened East India and China to Europe, and all these empires are almost submitting to the European spirit."[5] During the nineteenth century, this theory worked compatibly with Adam Smith's understanding of market forces. And America was not going to fail to claim its slice of the Pacific pie.

For all these reasons, the United States saw a need for Pacific expansion, whether it was the development of its own California coast or support for its whaling industry or building its presence in profitable East Asian waters. The question remained, though, how was this to be done? American businessmen were already profiting overseas, but protection came from the warships of other countries. American whalermen were exploring the vast ocean, but often found themselves alone and shipwrecked on hostile shores and imprisoned in foreign jails. And the distances involved in maintaining communication across the ocean meant that supplies of coal needed to be developed. There were clear opportunities in the Pacific and East Asia, a critical if somewhat remote arena. But if the United States was to be guaranteed a part of the economic action and national standing in what was, for lack of a better term, the "spoils" of the Pacific, if the country were truly going to be a player in this arena, how was it to protect its assets and routes across the largest ocean on the planet? The U.S. Navy was left to define a peacetime commercial role for itself, and to define a peacetime vessel in the service of Pacific expansion.

The Right Tool for the Job

In 1857, the U.S. Navy was in the process of redefining its needs for different types of ships, and handy coastal vessels in particular. Achieving a steamship design that was of shallow draft, yet narrow enough for speed and of large enough displacement to carry the weight of effective ordnance was a matter of exacting compromise to which naval architects like William L. Hanscom and John W. Griffiths (famous for his clipper ship designs) applied themselves. Isaac Toucey, a lawyer and former governor of Connecticut appointed as the civilian secretary of the navy by his friend President James Buchanan that very year, had requested $2.3 million for ten navy ships, emphasizing shallow-draft vessels as better for coastal work, designs featuring light draft, high speed, and heavy guns. Toucey was doing what he could to update a navy that was out-of-date and in poor condition. Buchanan agreed, and in his annual message to Congress set forth the plan for the shallow-draft armed steamers. Congress approved the Department's request, though paring the order to eight vessels and specifying one of them as a side-wheel steamer for services in the East India Squadron. Seven of these ships would be screw (propeller)–armed sloops: USS *Mohican*, *Iroquois*, *Wyoming*, *Dacotah*, *Pawnee*, *Narragansett*, and *Seminole*. The requirement for ordnance on the screw sloops would be met by one or two heavy shell cannon, typically 11-inch Dahlgrens mounted on centerline as pivot guns, and up to six smaller cannon for broadside batteries.[6] The appropriation for seven armed sloops and, almost as an afterthought, a single side-wheel steamer was passed by an act of Congress, June 2, 1858.

The United States was at peace in 1858, and during this period was certainly not committed to the full-time projection of power abroad. It was, after all, a time when authors of naval history wrote about only Britain or France as having the capability of ruling the waves. The U.S. Navy usually did not warrant treatment beyond simply being lumped in with countries like Sweden, relegated to the ambiguous category of "other." The United States sought to bring its navy (slowly) into the nineteenth century, though, given the stringent peacetime limitations in funding and its chosen role as protector of American merchantmen overseas, rather than the projection of powerful fleets abroad. It simply made economic sense not to focus on expensive capital ships that could challenge an opposing fleet, but to emphasize the need for something more along the lines of a maritime border police—swift, shallow-draft vessels capable of efficient coastal work. And as for that afterthought of the eighth vessel in the appropriation, what was better for going on and coming off river shoals than a paddle-wheel steamer? The *Report to the Secretary of the Navy* in 1858 highlighted these needs, remaining somehow optimistic on the chances of a better budget.

All our past experience has evinced the necessity of an increase of the navy. It is impossible with our present naval force to give adequate protection to the persons and property of American citizens pursuing their various avocations by land and sea in all parts of the world. What we more especially need in time of peace is a larger number of vessels capable of entering the rivers and harbors of all foreign countries as well as our own. Such is the condition of Mexico and of the Central and South American States that it is indispensably necessary that we should be able to approach them frequently, and at every accessible point. There is no other mode of extending effectual protection to American interests in that or any other quarter of the globe where the existing governments lack stability, or, for other causes, cannot be relied on for the performance of international duties. The frequent presence of a ship-of-war, though not of the largest class, exerts a powerful restraining influence, and will generally save our citizens from the infliction of gross injustice.[7]

During peacetime, the business of the navy was to protect the business of American businessmen, among other things.

An "Earnest" Paddle Wheeler

The original intentions for a vessel dedicated to the coastal Pacific featured something on a larger scale; say the size of the other seven steam sloops in the appropriation. Engineer William Norris of Philadelphia and John W. Griffiths of New York petitioned Secretary Toucey for what they saw as the most appropriate ship for peacetime duties in the Pacific: "First of a steamer for China, on the earnest principle of side wheel propulsion to be not less than eleven hundred (1100) tons custom house measurement, pierced with four gun ports on each side, two forward and two aft of the wheels, carrying four ten inch shell guns, and two nine inch pivot guns, the latter to be used either for battery guns, or in chasing, or being chased."[8]

The earnest principle of side-wheel propulsion would remain, but all other dimensions of the vessel's build were reduced (see fig. 2). USS *Saginaw* would be built as a third-class steamer, fourth-rate naval vessel. It was clear that the Navy Department would save the most money by having the ship built on the west coast, and construction was accordingly assigned to the brand-new Mare Island Naval Shipyard under Commandant Robert B. Cunningham, who had assumed the post following Admiral Farragut. The

FIGURE 2. A rare photograph of USS *Saginaw*, broadside to the camera (*right*). From Read, *Last Cruise of the* Saginaw.

choice of the new shipyard, of carpenters and engineers so far removed from established facilities on the east coast, was unprecedented, and it placed the burden of accomplishment and the chance for nautical reputation squarely on California and the citizens of San Francisco.

> The Department having decided that the side wheel steamer . . . intended for service in the China Seas, whose greatest draft of water shall not exceed eight feet, shall be built at the yard under your command. You will please instruct the naval constructor to prepare a plan substantially to agree with the requirements herewith given. . . .
>
> When on her station it is proposed the vessel shall have 90 days provisions and 18 days water for 50 persons; shall be armed with a 32 pd. gun on a pivot and two boat guns; the steam machinery including water in the boilers is estimated to weigh 80 tons, and to stow 100 tons of coal.[9]

Cunningham received instructions issued by John Lenthall, chief of the Bureau of Construction, dated July 17, 1858, but plans for the ship herself were not provided. Instead, Lenthall instructed Cunningham to have his own civilian chief naval constructor, Isaiah Hanscom, superintendent of Mare Island's dry-dock facilities, draw up the required plans and send copies back to Washington, D.C.[10] The vessel was, therefore, of a unique and western class. *Saginaw*, as built, was 155 feet in length and 26 feet in beam, with a light draft of 4½ feet. At 453 tons (gross), the ship was small, and lightly rigged as a two-masted brig. As originally designed, she carried a single 32-pounder pivot gun forward, and two 24-pounder broadside cannon.[11] The vessel was designed for a complement of fifty-nine crew members.

Saginaw's machinery was somewhat more unique. The ship had installed two steam engines or cylinders, two main boilers, and one auxiliary boiler. Also, two surface condensers would be capable of distilling 150 gallons of freshwater into her internal tanks daily. The paddle wheels were iron, 20 feet in diameter, with floats, or "paddles," 6 feet in length and 18 inches wide, all of the finest construction. Following a month-long open-bid period, Mare Island awarded the machinery contract on January 10, 1859, to the Union Iron Works in San Francisco, a firm owned by Peter Donahue. The Union Foundry, as it was known then, had begun operations in 1849; it was the oldest establishment of its kind on the west coast, located in three large brick buildings at First and Mission streets. The work itself was placed under the supervision of Chief Engineer George Sewell, and completion of the contract was set for August 10, or, pending delays in the ship's hull, six weeks from the date of launching. *Saginaw* was constructed for a total cost of $188,666.69.[12]

The machinery was somewhat untried. Plans called for two oscillating cylinders, both with bores 39 inches in diameter and 48 inches stroke, and two three-furnace water-tube boilers. Boiler tubes were to be of seamless brass. The boilers, once installed in the wooden ship, had to be insulated. They were covered with 1½ inches of felt, then flax canvas, and sealed, or "lagged," with kiln-dried tongue-and-groove boards, all wrapped with iron straps.[13] This was only the second time that a U.S. Navy vessel would employ the inclined oscillating steam cylinder engines. The other vessel with oscillating cylinders was the storeship *John Hancock* of 1850.[14] The design was chosen for its compactness and simplicity. The machinery space on *Saginaw* was 23 feet long and only 16 feet wide. In 1858, marine steam propulsion was still in its relative infancy. Transitional designs operated at low steam pressure (plans called for *Saginaw*'s engines to be tested at 40 psi, and to operate at 30 psi—not quite enough pressure to fill a modern car tire). Typical marine engines were large, slow, and heavy. Inclined oscillating cylinders were a solution to some of these obstacles. The large trunnioned cylinders, positioned fore and aft in the machinery space on the heavy iron A-frame, connected directly to the overhanging paddle-wheel, or waterwheel, shafts, both cylinders rocking back and forth in hypnotic synchronicity as the shaft rotated. This must have been quite a sight in the confined spaces of the ship's engine room. Was it ideal to have such wild motion on such a small vessel? It had worked on larger ones. Steamship designer Isambard Kingdom Brunel's famous *Great Eastern* had four such oscillating cylinders, but that famous passenger ship, capable of carrying four thousand paying passengers or ten thousand troops, was far larger than *Saginaw*. In fact, Brunel's ship at that time was actually too large to be operated efficiently, and did not make a profit for her owners.

USS *Saginaw*, referred to as a "United States Steamer," was nonetheless a sailing vessel as well. This was the era of the sail-assisted steamship, or rather the steam-assisted sailing ship, for it would be a long while before shipbuilders would trust steam machinery completely, and before steam engines were fuel-efficient enough, for vessels to do away with masts and rigging completely. Admittedly, a sailing ship hull designed for shallow-draft paddle-wheel operation was a hydrodynamic compromise, and *Saginaw*'s sailing properties would suffer in proportion. But this early steam propulsion, as coal-hungry and inefficient as it was, proved a marked advantage when necessity demanded. The ship was able to get up steam and get into action when called upon, as long as operations did not take her far beyond the vicinity of available coal supplies. The majority of *Saginaw*'s long-distance cruising would be conducted under sail.

The building instructions sent by the Bureau in July 1858 were at least four weeks in transit, and the keel was laid down four weeks after that, on September 16. Notably, Lenthall urged Commodore Cunningham to use "the opportunity of showing how expeditiously you can complete the vessel for service," though acknowledging that time pressure might influence the quality of the construction, such as in the choice of wood to use in the ship's framing.[15] The easterners waited to see what the Californians could do.

Saginaw was a sleek and narrow vessel (see figs. 3–5). And, as with all ships, her construction reflected more than just the technical and hydrodynamic requirements of marine sail and steam; it also reflected the social organization of the navy. *Saginaw* was comprised of three distinct areas. The forward third of the vessel belonged to the enlisted men. The 32-pounder pivot gun, foremast, forward hatches, and capstan were the only significant features on the weather deck. Below, the berth deck, or forecastle, was comprised of an open space surrounded by lockers lining the port and starboard bulkheads. This was the area where the majority of *Saginaw*'s crew lived, where hammocks swung from the overhead beams at night, packed closely enough to resemble a single sheet of living canvas. As the forecastle encountered the largest seas, and was also pierced by the hawse pipes for the anchor chains, it was usually the wettest part of the ship. With slightly less than 6 feet between the deck and the overhead beams, the berth deck would seem low by modern standards, but back then most could still stand upright with ease. The muster rolls from *Saginaw* reveal a commonly known phenomenon: nineteenth-century sailors were short, most ranging between five feet two inches and five feet six inches. (This is likely due to socioeconomic and physiological factors. The low between-decks made shortness an advantage.) The ship's small galley was set in the middle of the crew's berthing space, providing a source of heat in colder climes. Beneath the forecastle was the fore hold, storage for the water tanks and casks, sail room, paymaster's stores, block room, and chain locker.

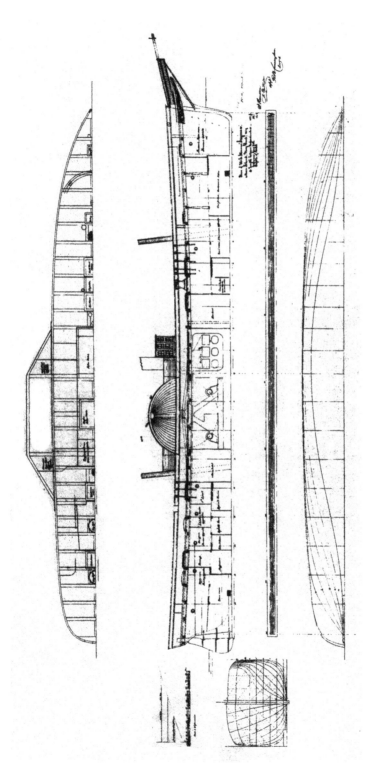

FIGURE 3. Naval constructor Isaiah Hanscom's drawing of *Saginaw*'s waterlines and internal details, 1859. Courtesy of National Archives and Records Administration, College Park, Maryland.

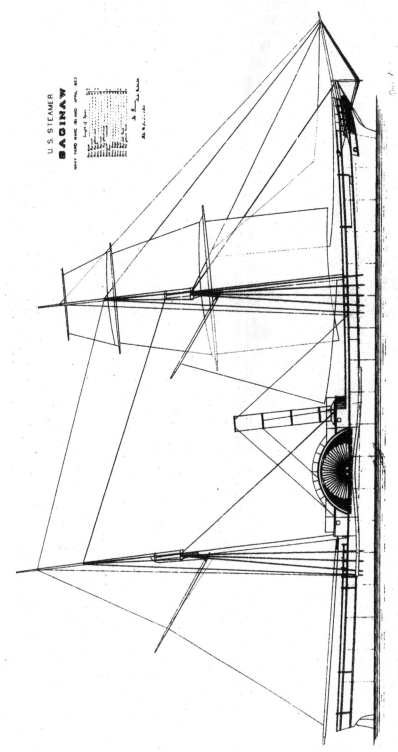

FIGURE 4. USS *Saginaw*'s sail plan and elevation drawing, 1863, following the ship's service in East Asia and subsequent refit. Courtesy of National Archives and Records Administration, College Park, Maryland.

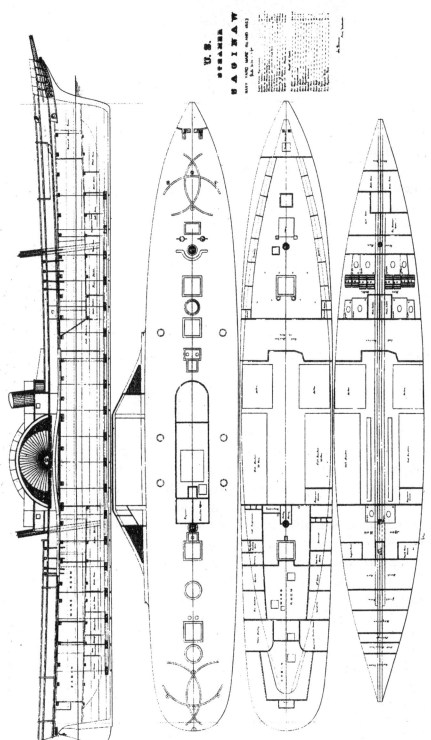

FIGURE 5. USS *Saginaw*'s deck plans, 1863. Courtesy of National Archives and Records Administration, College Park, Maryland.

Officers' cabins were at the stern, the aft third of the vessel. The weather, or hurricane, deck featured skylights over the interior spaces. (The 1863 refit would add a pivot gun on the aft weather deck.) Below, the berth deck was divided into individual cabins for the surgeon, paymaster, engineer, and lieutenants. Smaller spaces were partitioned for the wardroom pantry, dispensary, and paymaster's issuing room. The largest cabins at the extreme aft end of the vessel belonged, of course, to the captain, whose stateroom and pantry enclosed his own sitting area at the transom of the vessel, allowing him ports overlooking the ocean. All of these cabins surrounded the common space of the wardroom, where the officers dined and spent many of their spare hours. Below the aft berth deck lay the after hold, the bread room, surgeon's stores, wardroom stores, shell room, magazine, boat ammunition room, and captain's private storage—and the spirit room for the ship's traditionally copious supply of wines and liquors.

Separating these extremities at bow and stern, the large midsection of the ship was devoted to the steam machinery. The steam engineers, a new class of seamen among the once all-sail navy, worked somewhere between the officer's quarters and the crew's forecastle, a metaphor perhaps for their newfound social standing. *Saginaw*'s narrow deckhouse was located on the centerline of the weather deck, with the large paddle-wheel boxes extending outboard from the port and starboard gunwale. At the forward end of the port paddle box was the crew's "head," the marine toilet that consisted simply of an open-air bench on the deck grating above the ocean. At the aft end of the port box was the captain's "head," and officers used a similar space aft of the waterwheel on the starboard side. Below, the midship machinery space was entirely dominated by the large, iron A-frame and engine bed, which supported the paddle-wheel shafts and the trunnioned steam cylinders, and the two boilers and three coal bunkers with a capacity of over 100 tons. The bulky mid-nineteenth-century steam machinery and coal bunkers created a significant separation between the forecastle and the wardroom. And this was a good thing. The efficient operation of ships in the U.S. Navy depended on a carefully maintained hierarchy, and the social and physical distance between the officers and the enlisted men (and even between the captain and his own officers) was a necessity, a reality of life at sea.

Mare Island's First Job

By 1854, the United States finally had a naval shipyard on the Pacific Ocean. Mare Island itself was (and is again today) a beautiful and quiet location on San Pablo Bay to the north of San Francisco, the rolling oak and grassland hills bordered by tule or reed marshes and thousands of waterfowl of many species. Cold rain from the Pacific marked the winters, and fog stood a chance of extending up the bay any time of the year, but for the most part, temperate and pleasant California weather predominated. The new shipyard was a testament to the emerging political and economic interests in the Pacific, and to the fact that almost the entire ability to reinforce the sparse regiments guarding the length of America's west coast lay in maritime and naval transport.

Mare Island lay across the water from the small settlement of Vallejo, the one-time capital of California turned sleepy hamlet. The shipyard would prove a boon to the town, which soon expanded in size to rival nearby Benicia, whose citizens grew envious of Vallejo's naval yard connection. The yard would provide the vibrant economic base for Vallejo for more than one hundred years. Mare Island took its name from the story of a mare that had been swept to the island, exhausted but alive, by the swift current of the Sacramento River. This particular animal was a favorite of the cavalry commander General Mariano Guadalupe Vallejo, a Mexican leader in Alta California. As a lieutenant in the Mexican Army, Vallejo had mapped the entire San Francisco region.

By 1850, the United States had taken a serious interest in developing a naval facility in the remote West, and Congress appropriated construction funds in 1851. Commodore John D. Sloat recommended the location of Mare Island to the Navy Department. Surveying missions were conducted, and the location selected by committee as having "ample space for all the buildings required . . . with good anchorage for ships of war. We consider it the most eligible location near San Francisco." The island was purchased in January 1853 for $83,491 from George W. P. Bissel of San Francisco, and William Henry Aspinwall and Mary S. MacArthur of Baltimore.[16]

David G. Farragut was the first to take command at Mare Island. He arrived with his wife, Virginia, and his son, Loyall, in 1854 via the Nicaragua Route.[17] Farragut, of course, already had some forty years of navy service behind him, having enlisted at the age of ten on the U.S. frigate *Essex*. He would later gain lasting fame at the Battle of Mobile Bay during the Civil War. Buildings soon began to spring up on the barren island, temporary

FIGURE 6. An early poster of the Mare Island Navy Yard, ca. 1850s, showing the floating dry dock. Courtesy of National Archives and Records Administration, Pacific Region.

FIGURE 7. Mare Island and the town of Vallejo across the straits, 1870. Courtesy of National Archives and Records Administration, Pacific Region.

FIGURE 8. The receiving ship USS *Independence* at Mare Island, temporary home to sailors of the Pacific Fleet. Courtesy of National Archives and Records Administration, Pacific Region.

housing at first, but then the row of beautiful homes for officers of the yard, and long, 65 × 400 foot brick structures for the naval storehouse, molding loft, timber shed and joiner's shop, blacksmith building, brass foundry, etc.—all the necessary trades for a full shipyard. The contract for the construction of a marine railway and basin was given to a company from New York. Later work saw the completion of the marine barracks, naval hospital, and the Mare Island cemetery.

And what is a shipyard without ships? The first naval vessel to arrive at Mare Island was the frigate USS *Independence*, the first ship-of-the-line commissioned in the U.S. Navy in 1814. Soon after this, the old sloop-of-war supply ship USS *Warren* came in under tow from Sausalito to the new yard. In a short time, a variety of vessels, steamers, ferries, and surveying schooners lined the stone quay. The 3,270-ton razee *Independence* (the frigate's upper works were removed in 1846) would remain at Mare Island as the station and receiving ship, home to thousands of transiting sailors at the yard for many years (see figs. 6–8).

The ships were, of course, ubiquitous in the yard, but the most important feature at Mare Island at the time was the floating dry dock, built in New York and disassembled for transport by sailing vessel around Cape

Horn. Sections of the heavy oak timber and iron floating dry dock began to arrive in 1853. Once completed, the ingenious structure measured 100 feet wide × 325 feet long. Sliding up and down on fixed posts, watertight tanks adjusted by steam pumps allowed the dock to sink and vessels to gain access. After landing her guns, the *Independence* was the first vessel to test the dock. This was the only such repair facility in the Pacific Ocean.

A Small Ship on a Large Sea

USS *Saginaw* was to inaugurate Mare Island's long history of shipbuilding as the first vessel launched by the newest shipyard on the west coast. Her keel was laid down on September 16, 1858. At the time, Mare Island's wood sheds were filled with pine and fir from the Puget Sound, suitable for spars and masts, and the upper works of the ship. Sugar pine, along with maple and redwood for finishing the cabins, came from the Coast Ranges and the Sierra Nevada Mountains to the east. California live oak suited shipbuilders for the frames of vessels; found in abundance in the coastal areas, live oak was declared "as durable and in every way as suitable as that which can be found in the Atlantic States."[18] Cedar from Port Orford was used for the planking of small boats. And native laurel was also mentioned as being "extensively used for boat timbers."[19] This use of laurel was not included in Bureau Chief Lenthall's instructions to the shipyard, which specified that the ship's keelsons, frames, and counter timbers, and garboard strake, bilge strake, and clamps be shaped from white oak; apron, breast hooks, main transom, and knight heads of live oak; and beams, deck planks, and waterways of yellow pine. The instructions mentioned nothing about laurel. Had there been enough of the specified woods on hand and well seasoned for the construction? Delays were frowned upon. Some of the other native Californian species available in the vicinity of Mare Island were also unfamiliar to the officers so recently arrived from the east coast. Shipwrights there had never heard of laurel being used in construction.

Through the winter from September 1858 and until March 1859, the wood chips flew, and every day the work bell rang the shifts, and carpenters, caulkers, riggers, laborers, blacksmiths, machinists, painters, and sail makers from Vallejo would drag themselves out of their warm houses, ride the ferry across the quarter-mile strait, and toil away on the vessel taking shape on the ways. USS *Saginaw* was launched on March 3, 1859, christened initially as USS *Toucey* (her original name, after the secretary of the navy) by Commandant Cunningham's daughter. Yet there was still much work to be done, and attention continued to her fittings, rig, boilers and engine, etc., extending right through the remainder of the year.

The ship received her navy commission on January 5, 1860. Though she had been launched as *Toucey*, which had seemed a politically savvy decision at the time, the ship had already been referred to as *Saginaw* (or "*Saganaw*") during the previous year, at least as early as Peter Donahue's contract with the navy for the construction of the boilers and machinery. By the time the ship was put into commission, *Toucey* had officially become USS *Saginaw*. Perhaps not everyone was truly pleased with Toucey's performance as secretary of the navy, or with his political views. The nation was quickly moving toward an open break with the southern secessionists, and Toucey, as some noted, "has always rested under the imputation of sympathizing, if not actually cooperating with them, and no attempt appears to have been made to relieve him from the charge."[20] With the elections in 1860, President Lincoln's administration brought about the expected and necessary cabinet changes to the Department. Toucey would soon turn his office and position over to Gideon Welles, the avowed antislavery Republican from Toucey's own home state. Welles, the former candidate for the governorship of Connecticut and editor of the Hartford newspaper, would thus inherit the pending and difficult task of leading the Navy Department throughout the entire American Civil War.

More immediate to *Saginaw*, Commander James Findlay Schenck had been ordered by the Department to assume command of the ship just two days prior to her commissioning. Schenck, born in 1807 in Franklin, Ohio, had the distinction of being the first person from that state to enter the U.S. Navy. He had been appointed midshipman in the navy in 1825. He then served on a number of vessels in the West Indies, the Mediterranean, Brazil, and Pacific squadrons. Schenck was an experienced veteran of the Mexican-American War and had served as a lieutenant under Commodore Stockton. He was actually the first person to raise the American flag at Santa Barbara, and was also instrumental in the capture of Los Angeles (raising the flag there as well), the bombardment and capture of Guaymas, and the taking of Mazatlan, all towns on the Mexican Pacific coast. He had obviously distinguished himself as an officer of some renown in the old sailing navy. Following the war with Mexico, Schenck then served as a captain of the Pacific Steamship Company's fast liner *Ohio* on the New

York-to-Aspinwall run. In 1860, though, the venerable and stately fifty-three-year-old naval commander would have to be satisfied with serving on the distant Pacific station, on board a much smaller fourth-rate vessel. These were the things commanders had to accept during peacetime if they sought a return to duty at sea. And in 1860, with gathering storm clouds on the horizon, Schenck sought exactly that, and used his influence to gain the deck. Officers could sometimes despise peacetime service. Schenck was such an officer of the "old school" and was a respectable choice for the new small steamer.

USS *Saginaw* was officially handed over by the commandant to her new commander at 10:00 a.m. The day was gray and rainy, with a light breeze blowing from the north, and Mare Island's band protected their cherished instruments as they waited. Guests from Vallejo and San Francisco were seated along the quay overlooking the affair due to the limited space on board. The order "commission USS *Saginaw*" made the rounds through the officers, and Schenck then issued his first command—"set the watch!"—immediately followed by the officer on deck taking his station. With the piping of the boatswain's call, the ship commenced her naval service. Commandant Cunningham's short and predictable speech was, naturally, full of good wishes for both the ship and his shipyard. Following the ceremony, the men at Mare Island returned to work, bringing on board shells, solid shot, grapeshot, and sea stores in general. Riggers and carpenters were hurriedly employed in a variety of small jobs. The officers drank toasts into the night.

Saginaw's sea trials soon got under way following some unexpected delays in getting the final anchors, cables, and galley equipment on board, items that arrived very late. The ship completed only five days of the planned week, a gale cutting her trials short. Most reviews, however, were glowingly positive: "The engines worked with as much ease and regularity as though they had performed for years. After . . . receiving the customary salutes when passing other steamers, not to say anything about the salutes of white cambric by the fair hands of ladies, she returned to the yard, having performed in a most satisfactory manner."[21] The new vessel was not only an object of pride for the U.S. Navy, but an achievement closely monitored and commented upon by the entire maritime community in San Francisco, something of which they rightfully claimed a part. And her machinery represented a major accomplishment for the west coast foundry:

The work on the engines and boilers is of the most exquisite description and finish and workmanship, and reflects the highest credit upon all who were in any way connected with its production. . . . [A]lthough this city is but ten years old, we have the necessary tools, men, and all other facilities, for producing marine steam engines of any description. . . . President Buchanan and Secretary Toucey, of the navy, are entitled to our warmest thanks for favoring this State with a chance to demonstrate that we could do our share of building war steamers.[22]

The public challenge from the distant east coast had been taken up by the California shipwrights and answered. But could they really compete with their eastern counterparts and show themselves as equals (or even better)?

It was a pleasing sight to us Californians, as everything in the way of shipbuilding helps to develop the resources of our State. . . . The Saginaw is built entirely of timber cut on this coast, and consists of live oak, white oak, pine and laurel. . . . An attempt has been made by many enemies of our State to prove that we have no wood suitable for shipbuilding; but I can assure you that such is not the case, as we have an abundance of the finest ship timber in the world up in Tularee valley.[23]

Obviously there was a great deal of pride and economic optimism behind the desire to see *Saginaw* succeed, but this simply served to make any comments to the contrary seem all the more unfair. Not all were so pleased with the ship's construction and performance during the trials. A local journalist obtained a negative review from the ubiquitous "unnamed official source":

Some days ago we published a communication alleging serious defects in the construction of the steamer Saginaw. . . . We are interested in learning whether there is room for these suspicions, and certainly have no interest whatever in proving them true. . . . As we anticipated, the publication has raised quite a storm. . . . [H]er engines and boilers were never assailed. We shall be glad to know that her hull is, after all, equally deserving of commendation; but we are not satisfied by the intemperate denunciations of a brandy-drinking officer, who did not superintend her construction. . . . Is it true that the Saginaw's hull is built of unseasoned, short-grained and brittle wood? And, if so, is that the sort of material upon which California mechanics are willing to rely, for the vindication of their skill? Are her laurel knees shrunken and warped, and any of her oak knees cracked? . . . If these green knees are warped and cracked already, will they not become much worse in the hot climate of China? . . . Is it true that one of the frames is already rotten? Is it true that Oregon pine is unfit for decks, because of its aptness to shrink? Is it true that the steamer is without sister or bilge keelsons? And if so, was it safe to put 70 tons of machinery into the vessel. Without having these keelsons to sustain the weight? . . . We shall be glad to have these queries answered, and most happy shall we be if the answers are satisfactory.[24]

The navy, of course, was not in the habit of relying on civilian accusations in the public arena, but rather on their own internal review. And they were quite capable of producing their own propaganda as well. Commandant Cunningham forwarded Commander Schenck's report to Washington, D.C.: "Commander Schenck . . . speaks in exalted terms of the superior qualities of the *Saginaw* as a sea-boat, of her judicious and comfortable accommodations for her crew and officers, and speaks in unqualified terms of her entire success . . . and of his entire faith in her ability and strength to weather in safety any gale of wind he may chance to fall in with."[25] To do anything else at this point might have bordered on blasphemy, but Schenck would shortly be of a different mind.

No matter the true status of the vessel's build, enlisted navy men did not have the option of choosing their ship, and went where they were told. Following the ship's sea trials, sailors at Mare Island, old-timers and new recruits, began to move their few possessions from the old frigate *Independence* to the more cramped quarters below on tiny *Saginaw*. The crew's complement of petty officers, seamen, landsmen, boys, apprentices, cooks, stewards, and coal heavers (but no marines) began to fill out. The many ratings of master-at-arms, boatswain's mate, gunner's mate, carpenter's mate, quartermasters, etc. provided the functional structure to the ship's crew. Officers as well began to report to Commander Schenck for duty, a fairly large list for *Saginaw*'s small size, including three lieutenants, master, surgeon, purser, four engineers, and purser's and commander's clerks. Woodhul S. Schenck, the commander's son, filled the last role on the ship's first cruise.[26]

Unlike the exclusively American naval officers, the ship's crew represented an international mixture from a variety of countries: Ireland,

England, Denmark, Germany, Jamaica, Manila (New Spain), France, Scotland, Canada, though there was, of course, a more significant representation from Maine, Massachusetts, Pennsylvania, and New York as well. Before the creation of America's new steam navy in the later decades of the nineteenth century, U.S. citizens did not, in fact, hold service on board the wooden sailing ships in high regard and did not tend to enlist en masse into their own navy. The perception that navy men were dragged from the bars and side streets and jails of harbor ports persisted. Manning the peacetime navy was a difficult issue. Though the punishment of flogging with the cat, or lash, had been abolished earlier, finding enough sailors to join what was seen by some as a floating wooden prison cell still meant offering numerous inducements, such as shorter enlistment terms. The majority of *Saginaw*'s crew signed on board for a period of two years service, and some of them were not at all averse to attempting to desert their ship and cut that service short before their time was up.

Slowly the crew grew accustomed to the inevitable repetition of U.S. Navy drills. Small-arms training, running out the broadside cannon or the larger pivot rifles, target practice at "great guns," pike and sword work, frequent inspections at quarters, setting and reefing sail, washing and drying laundry—these whistles and drills marked their days with familiar regularity. And every Sunday divine service was held on deck, providing a chance for the captain to include the Articles of War in his sermon. These were the regulations by which the United States Navy maintained control over their sailors, a detailed catechism of all the infractions and punishments to which the men were subject, so God and the Navy Department shared the quarterdeck weekly on *Saginaw*.

In the mid-nineteenth century, the single-greatest perceived common evil for sailors was alcohol, so Sundays were also opportunities to regularly chastise the men against intemperance, one of their favorite pastimes. Yet judging from the sheer number of incidences, many of the sailors honestly viewed being locked in double irons (shackled hand and foot) and placed on bread and water a fair price to pay for a long night at a tavern in Vallejo or San Francisco.

For those not on the bread and water diet, the solid and generic daily servings of beans and potatoes and salt meat, along with bread, pickled vegetables, coffee, and like fare, had to suffice. At sea, provisions were brought topside in wooden barrels from the hold of the ship. At the naval yard, the 72.5 pounds of beef and 72.5 pounds of vegetables per day came on board with staggering culinary monotony. After coaling the ship, which involved the entire crew swinging on board 100 tons of coal in dirty bags and then cleaning the ship of the sticky coating of black sooty dust afterward (always a miserable and filthy job), *Saginaw* steamed across the bay for San Francisco, and prepared to set out for the China Station.

Across the ocean, American merchants maintained a tenuous grasp on their new national presence in the empire of Japan. They sought to establish themselves at advantageous trading ports, often against the naturally hostile public and ill-concealed imperial resistance. These were dangerous times, for foreign encroachment meant social, economic, and political upheaval. Unregulated trade wreaked havoc on the tight social structures of traditional Japanese society. Admiral Perry's 1853 fleet was not solely the cause of all turmoil in the late Tokugawa Shogunate period, for there had already existed a local anti-bakufu or antimilitary government movement for a number of complex reasons. As an outward sign of modern changes, however, foreigners were obvious targets. Soon after Yokohama was opened, a Russian officer and two sailors were murdered by roving samurai, initiating a round of bloody street attacks on Westerners and their collaborating Japanese associates, traitors in the eyes of the traditionalists, who were militantly loyal to their emperor rather than the shogun ruler of Japan.

In China, riots in the northern ports broke out as part of the continuing consequences of conflict associated with the Second Opium War of 1856–58. The opening of additional harbors to Westerners beyond the initial five ports brought about greater turmoil. For one thing, foreigners on Chinese soil enjoyed their own judicial extraterritoriality—in other words, sailors committing crimes against the local populace could not be charged in Chinese courts, an outrage to many Chinese. Also, the semi-enslavement of Chinese contract laborers bound overseas on board Western ships, known as the coolie trade, sparked a number of tragic transgressions against the so-called "voluntary" migrants. And in the south, the single-largest social and military rebellion in the history of the world was taking place. Southern Chinese minority groups, such as the Hakka, rose against the Manchu officials, the rulers of the Qing Dynasty.

The leader of the southern rebellion was a failed Chinese scholar turned Christian convert named Hong Xiuquan. At first cautiously enthusiastic that their teachings had finally taken root, Western missionaries soon realized that Hong had quite a different vision of Christianity.

Hong's personal revelation confirmed to himself that he was indeed Jesus' younger brother. His own mission on earth was to slay the evil demons, the nonbelievers in China and particularly the Qing imperial government forces, the Manchu rulers, a nomadic people from north of the Great Wall and foreigners themselves in China since their conquest of the giant empire in 1644. In the end, Hong's military theocracy devolved into debauchery and authoritarian abuses. Westerners in China at the time, though, soon found themselves caught between the "evil Manchu demons" and the heretical Taiping soldiers of the "Heavenly Kingdom of Great Peace" led by the mentally unstable Hong Xiuquan.

By 1860, the Taiping armies numbered nearly 2.5 million soldiers, both men and women fighting side by side. Many were Hakka, a Chinese minority who did not abide by the traditional foot-binding practices of the Han Chinese, subjugate women, or even wear their hair in the required queue or Manchu tight braid. They were therefore known as long hairs, or changmao. The rebellion, begun in 1851, had succeeded in capturing the large coastal city of Nanjing two years after that, when the Taiping forces defeated an imperial army of thirty thousand men. Foreigners attempted (usually successfully) to stay out of the way. Though some American merchants had been in China for more than fifty years, and American government agents for more than thirty years, and American missionaries for twenty years, there was no general policy or instruction guiding American presence in the empire. America's countrymen walked a fine line of neutrality, a balancing act that became increasingly difficult as China wound deeper under rebellion and chaos.[27] These were, indeed, tumultuous times. The American minister to China, John Ward, wrote to Secretary of State Lewis Cass:

> The Chinese once aroused against foreigners will recognize no distinctions, nor will they be softened. . . . I have since my arrival in China known American women to fly from a fate worse than death to English ships of war to find that safety which their government did not furnish. These things are likely again to occur, but will the English ships be there to give their protection? With the full knowledge of our weakness in China we have been treated with a mixture of politeness and insolence. . . . I most earnestly appeal . . . to increase the squadron here without delay.[28]

The tiny two-masted side-wheel steamer *Saginaw*, proudly built by California craftsmen to protect their fellow citizens and American property in East Asia, swung peacefully at anchor for just a moment, poised on the edge of the great Pacific highway. Events across the ocean beckoned. Commander Schenck and his men took their ship out of port on March 8, 1860, and shaped a course into the setting sun.

2

Seasoning on the China Station

Commander Schenck reports to me that the number of sick
he now has (eight), his working force is so much reduced, as
to render the Saginaw inefficient and not able to weigh her
anchors.

Cornelius Stribling, 1860

The pressing need for strengthening the East India Squadron led to a fair
deal of anxiety among those waiting for *Saginaw*'s arrival in China. Secretary Toucey had envisioned a multipurpose antipiracy patrol vessel and
had communicated this to Captain Stribling, who had just replaced Flag
Officer Josiah Tattnall as commander of the squadron, regarding USS
Saginaw's future role. The broad objective made clear in Toucey's instructions was the protection of trade with China, Japan, and India, and the
enlargement of commercial intercourse, no small task for the gunboat.
The protection of American whalers was also singled out as a specific concern. The chief threat, according to the admiral, was piracy: "The East India
Squadron has heretofore been much embarrassed in its operations from
the want of suitable steamers of light draught. The *Saginaw* which has
been constructed for service in that squadron will in some measure supply
that want. While answering other purposes of the squadron, she can be
particularly useful in suppressing piracies, as her light draught will enable
her to reach the retreats of those who commit them."[1]

Fortunately, South Carolinian Cornelius Kinchiloe Stribling was an experienced officer of some accomplishment. He had entered the navy as
a midshipman in 1812, and had served in the Pacific beginning back in
1840. Like Schenck, he was also a veteran of the Mexican-American War,
having been fleet captain on board USS *Ohio*. Later, Commander Stribling
presided over the newly named United States Naval Academy as its third
superintendent, quadrupling its size and enhancing its military character

during his term there. Prior to the opening of the academy at Annapolis in 1845, midshipmen had been sent somewhat informally to a kind of sailor's home to study for their examinations, such as the naval asylum in Philadelphia. That was an institution that lacked discipline, where students either studied or not as they pleased. Before that, some candidates took their naval examinations at Barnum's Hotel in Baltimore.[2] American naval officers in those days were more likely to be self-educated, achieving the finer points of their knowledge by their own resources. Much of the strict cadence of military life now associated with the U.S. Naval Academy started with the dedicated efforts of officers like Commander Stribling.

Stribling had fought piracy in the West Indies in the 1820s, and he harbored no fanciful illusions regarding the American presence in China, for in 1860 the U.S. Navy's position there was shaped more by circumstance than by intention. At times, the East India Squadron was so small as to consist of a single vessel, though the locations for American commerce in China had increased. The Treaty of Tianjin, forced on the Chinese government by the conclusion of the Second Opium War, had been signed on June 26, 1858. The interior of China was now open to foreigners, as were more ports as well. The practice of Christianity was officially protected, and the opium trade brought by the West legalized. But the Chinese had balked at allowing foreign ambassadors to reside permanently in the northern capital of Beijing, as stipulated in the treaty. And yet the war was not truly over.

A signed piece of paper could not pacify an empire falling into chaos. The British once more had attacked the Taku Forts (also called Peiho Forts) near Tianjin, the critical entrance to the waterway leading to the Grand Canal and to the northern capital, but had been temporarily repulsed. The Chinese had reinforced the forts after their initial defeat almost twenty years earlier. Negotiators sent to the emperor in Beijing were arrested by Qing imperial forces, and some were executed.[3] British and French expeditionary forces were again gathering off northern China, and hostilities were about to begin anew. Thanks to the most-favored-nation clause, the French, Americans, and other Western noncombatants benefited equally from whatever further concessions British forces could secure.

In a letter dated February 14, the flag officer on board the 2,550-ton screw sloop USS *Hartford* at Hong Kong warned Secretary Toucey of the inadequacy of the American naval forces. *Hartford* was alone on station. Stribling petitioned for a minimum of six vessels, but would ultimately have to make do with a total of three. Of the two vessels recently ordered to China, neither USS *John Adams* nor USS *Saginaw* had yet arrived. In fact, *Saginaw* had yet to leave Mare Island at the time of his letter. Furthermore, according to the ship's commanding officer, the sloop *John Adams* had been forced into Rio de Janeiro for repairs.[4] That was no surprise, for the old training vessel had originally been built in South Carolina as a frigate in 1799. A survey, however, revealed only a moderate leak. Was the ship's captain really that anxious to serve in the East India Squadron?[5]

Stribling had other troubling news to report, and he included transcripts from American Minister Ward that detailed the attempted kidnapping of 432 coolies by "ruthless and lawless men" on board the American ship *Messenger*. During the period of contract labor migration into the Pacific (Queensland, Valparaiso, Hawai`i, etc.), there was money to be made by Chinese contractors and Western captains, and abuses were rife. Other American sailors in China were involved in the "convoy" business on the coast (a euphemism for piracy) or other forms of levying blackmail on native fishermen and traders and generally committing atrocities at sea.[6] Enforcing the rules, and following through with punishments, was difficult if not impossible. If caught, convicted murderers were being shuffled around on board any available American ship, for no prison facilities existed on shore. The American consuls in the opened treaty ports had no facilities for them. In fact, American consuls did not even receive a salary for their diplomatic services until 1856, surviving mainly on shipping fees and their own commercial interests prior to that time. In short, without many effective regulations or restrictions from their home countries, foreign sailors were quick to take advantage of any opportunities they could find amidst the deteriorating social and political situation in China. Notably, Secretary Toucey's instructions to Commander Stribling did not specify which pirates, European or Chinese, *Saginaw* was to apprehend. Part of *Saginaw*'s job would be checking on American vessels clearing Chinese ports.

But where was *Saginaw*? Stribling had been waiting anxiously since mid-February for his additional vessels, having no idea about the delays on the west coast. Word finally arrived on May 5, when the flag officer learned that *Saginaw* had been at Honolulu at the end of March. The ship had made swift passage to the Kingdom of Hawai`i in twelve days, arriving on March 22, where she crossed paths with Commander Josiah Tattnall and USS *Powhatan*, then in port at Honolulu. *Powhatan* was accompanying the Japanese steam warship *Kanrin Maru*, bearing the first Japanese embassy to the United States. Due to rough weather, the two vessels had been forced to change course and had touched at Honolulu to reprovision with coal, a surprise visit. (This was actually the second such foreign embassy to cross the Pacific; Japanese ambassadors had previously traveled to Europe via Mexico in 1614 on board the galleon *San Juan Bautista*.) The *Pacific Commercial Advertiser* devoted pages to the description of the exotic embassy and the Japanese homelands. The ambassadors were attended to ashore for almost two weeks, granted a royal reception and all the honors accorded to their status.

Saginaw was minor news in the islands compared to these visitors. However, residents in Honolulu commented soon enough on the model of the much smaller steamer, "a most beautiful one, and as a specimen of naval architecture, she reflects credit on California ship-builders."[7] Some thought that, with only her single light 32-pounder forward pivot gun and two small 24-pounder broadside cannon, she looked more like a merchantman than a war steamer. But this *was* a peacetime navy. *Saginaw* had departed Honolulu on April 9, having spent a more than adequate amount of time to provision and coal. Sailors ashore enjoyed touring the pali, or cliffs of the high mountains, and mad dashes on horseback through the dirt streets of the growing town of Honolulu, and the taverns near the waterfront. The spring whaling fleet was in, and at least forty New Bedford vessels swung at anchor alongside the steamer. There were also perhaps some forty grog shops in town, filled with thirsty sailors. During the day, the white, billowing clouds piled up against the green mountains with the trade winds, and at night the stars shone brightly above the palms.

Most of *Saginaw's* crew had an enjoyable time in the islands, however brief. Several men, though, were stricken with "Maui fever," and several more were soon under the surgeon's treatment for gonorrhea. The fever usually ran its course in five days. The venereal disease sometimes put men on the sick list for more than two weeks. The surgeon applied the tools of his nineteenth-century trade, his acetate of potash, flaxseed tea, and cold water, along with confinement to the hammock and a light diet.[8] But the most serious cases proved more difficult to diagnose. Lieutenant Bayse R. Westcott reported himself unfit for duty while in the islands. Although the ship's surgeon could find no physical abnormality, he reported in his journal that Westcott's "nervous system is shattered, that he has no appetite, does not sleep, and suffers from extreme mental depression. . . . His mind is in rather a morbid condition and he says he has been under treatment."[9] He was apparently mentally unstable. Commander Schenk allowed the lieutenant ten days shore leave. This was extended in the end to seventeen days, the surgeon underlining the word "hypochondriasis" in his notes on the Westcott case.

At Shanghai, USS *John Adams* had already arrived, provisioned, and been sent on to Fuzhou, where Americans had major business interests. The British and French recent occupation of the Chusan area at the mouth of the Yangzi River delta was seen as a provocative measure. "Humanity as well as policy requires that you should afford protection as far as possible to all foreigners. Force must not be resorted to except upon your being satisfied no other means at your command will be effective. The United States not being a party to the difficulty now existing . . . must evince our neutral position by perfect impartiality."[10]

USS *Saginaw* finally made Shanghai on May 12, 1860, thirty-two days from Hawai'i and reportedly in good condition. Steam was raised, sails furled, and the buckets rigged back onto the paddle wheels. The ship brought herself to her mooring at the bend of the Wusong River amid the throngs of junks and Chinese watercraft, flying signals from her yards to the flag ship USS *Hartford*, and Commander Schenck and his officers soon made official report of their passage. *Saginaw* was immediately surrounded by sampans of the tanjia, or boat people, selling their wares, foods, and offering services. The masts of shipping across the river from the waterfront were like a small, ragged forest. Stribling was pleased with the appearance of his new side-wheel steamer, as was Minister Ward, though her small size required that additional suitable accommodations be built somehow in order to accommodate the American minister in China and his entourage. The crew could count on becoming even more crowded on the tiny ship.

The clear skies, trade winds, and warm welcome of Honolulu were now things of the past. *Saginaw* was a wet boat, the relatively low freeboard allowing water to be shipped frequently in rough seas, and nothing could be kept dry. The ship's commander sometimes referred to this tendency as being "underwater." The oppressive heat and humidity of the southern China coastline accosted the ship's crew. Sailors, sweating it out on the berth deck below, rigged wind sails on deck in an effort to funnel some cooler air into the forecastle. These, of course, worked only when there was a breeze. The extreme heat made the tar and pitch from the seams of the deck stick to the sailors' feet, which was then tracked across the decks and below. (They had to regularly holystone the decks clean, grinding them with pumice.) And there was little chance for escape. Chaotic conditions ashore meant a curtailment of the usual amount of liberty. The twenty-four-hour watches were increased, with lookouts wary of insurgent activities on the yellowish muddy harbor, which served as the sewer of the overcrowded walled city. The complex of foreign smells was overpowering. Quinine and opium pills, chicken broth and rice supplied the sick list for the treatment of diarrhea and intermittent fever outbreaks. Hawai`i had been an inadequate prelude to this.

The Changmao, or Longhair Taiping

The old walled city of Shanghai had once been an important harbor and waypoint for Chinese coastal and ocean trading junks, which discharged their cargoes and sent them upriver to the interior markets of Suzhou and onward to other ports by way of the Grand Canal. Shanghai was ideally situated at the convergence of northern coastal shipping and southern coastal shipping, as well as the entrance to the Yangzi River leading deep into China's interior. This trade was actually enhanced following the First Opium War. British warships trained their guns on the city and forced a ransom from Shanghai of 1 million taels of silver. The Treaty of Nanjing in 1842 had then opened the city to the presence of foreign merchants and warships, and to the opium trade. The riverfront on the vast alluvial plain had bloomed into a busy international port, wharves and docks developing outward around the foreign buildings. The instant foreign-trade emporium soon made the old Chinese port seem like a sleepy little village. The road along the river, originally the towing track for grain junks, became the famous Bund of Shanghai. The French, English, and American concessions were grouped together on the river, and these were the focus of Western defensive efforts against any threats that might have been directed at the city as a whole. There the garrisons and naval depots and coaling stations and warehouses were surrounded by whitewashed walls. As long as the revenue from the trade of silks and tea continued to flow, the merchants were happy. And trade had been flowing. By 1860, more than two hundred foreign vessels nestled alongside the wharves at Shanghai, or moored in the stream. But conflict again brought disruptions.

The rebellion had changed the entire countryside around the city, and changed the city itself. Hundreds of thousands of refugees from the interior had flooded inside the protective walls, fleeing the violence wrought by the pillaging and looting by both the Taiping and Chinese imperial armies. In 1860, this disruption threatened all businesses, Chinese and Western alike. All usual trade patterns ceased. William L. G. Smith, the U.S. consul at Shanghai, painted a grim picture: "I have no doubt that the Chinese authorities and the well informed Chinese regard the Government of the United States and its citizens as friends, but in case of an outbreak, I presume the Chinese would regard all foreigners in the same category, and in such case, in my judgment, the Chinese authorities would be utterly powerless to maintain order and afford the necessary protection to the lives and property of the citizens of the United States at this port."[11]

In 1860, British and French forces were arriving in Shanghai in preparation for movement north. The city had become a large naval and military garrison. Paradoxically, the British and French forces resisted the Taiping when their pseudo-Christian rebel army, known as the "Heavenly Army," threatened foreign concessions. Thus, the Taipings actually aided the Chinese imperial forces, distracting the Western Allies while they were busy preparing to force their way past the Taku (Peiho) River Forts and threaten the imperial capital in order to force obedience to the final concessions listed in the Tianjin Treaty. This was a confusing position in a confusing time. Suzhou, a city of 2 million residents seventy miles from Shanghai, fell to the rebels in June.

American merchantmen on the river greeted USS *Saginaw* as a small but long-awaited sign of protection. The gunboat paddle wheeler, though, offered little by way of haven for their goods or for themselves in time of need. In July, Flag Officer Stribling left for Tianjin on USS *Hartford*. The summer had so far seen little serious Taiping activity in the immediate vicinity, and orders from the State Department to take Minister Ward to the Gulf of Peichili, where the Allies were preparing an attack on the Chinese capital, took priority over the direct protection of American citizens in Shanghai. Commander Schenck on *Saginaw* raised anchor and followed a few days later, having waited for the July mails. In Peichili, Ward transferred to *Saginaw*, relying on the smaller steamship as his personal conveyance for critical meetings with the Russian Plenipotentiary General Ignatieff, and with the Chinese governor general, and freeing *Hartford* to make a trip south. Though the British had requested an allied force of France, Russia, and the United States, only France had sent ships and troops to China for the war. The United States and Russia contributed representative envoys. Schenck and his crew were on a diplomatic mission of symbolic support.

At the entrance to the Peiho River, the British and French fleets stood in to anchor. *Saginaw's* crew were there amidst the hot winds and choking dust of the Peiho, and witnessed the historic event, adding their own vocal comment on the proceedings by conducting target practice with broadside and pivot gun. On August 3, Lord Elgin successfully disembarked the expeditionary forces. Ships' boats ferried 11,000 British and 6,700 French troops across ten miles of delta and shoal to the shore, while enemy Tartar horsemen could be seen riding to and fro behind their camps. The landing, however, was unopposed for the most part. Elgin's allied army would ultimately force the complete capitulation of the Chinese government. Subsequently, they would sack the imperial Summer Palace, an act of almost pure spite and greed. The Summer Palace was not just a single building, but a large number of individual palaces, all located on beautifully landscaped terrain, the unique storehouse of centuries of imperial treasures and rare gifts. Emperor Xianfeng fled for his life. The humiliation of the Manchu ruling class was complete. Had there been any doubt as to the outcome of the conflict?

For the Americans, this symbolic allegiance did not offer a clear role. Some officers on board *Saginaw* were sure their services were needed elsewhere. After all, the more immediate threat in China came from the huge and unpredictable Taiping armies. During the approaching conflict in the north, word arrived that conditions in Shanghai had deteriorated. British and French troops had left the city, followed by most of the Chinese imperial "enemy" forces, and the region then had no defense against the Taiping soldiers. Frenzied news arrived from U.S. Consul Smith in Shanghai, and Commander Schenck was soon ordered south.

The existence of the foreign community is sometimes cited as the saving grace of Shanghai, for through missionary interpreters, the Taiping rebels had been insisting that they had no argument with the Western foreigners, who were their brother Christians. By August, though, the Taiping had overrun most of the province surrounding Shanghai, and were obviously gathering forces for a final siege. Alarm spread among the foreign concessions, and American women and children from the missionary settlements sought refuge on board any available merchant ships. The rest were instructed to remain within their homes and organize all means of defense they could command. *Hartford* and *Saginaw* steamed south and returned to Shanghai as soon as possible. *Saginaw* arrived first; the attack on the city had not yet begun. The ubiquitous river traffic of junks, sampans, lighters, punts, and dinghies had vanished. Commander Schenck, lacking marines, gathered a squad of sailors and sent them to the American concession ashore, along with all the small arms, carbines, cannon, and ammunition he could spare, for use by U.S. citizens.[12] Only about one thousand Chinese troops defended the walled city, while both France and Great Britain pledged assistance. Meanwhile, refugees continued flooding through the city gates, while 150,000 residents had simultaneously fled Shanghai to Ningpo and other nearby ports.

On August 18, twelve thousand Taiping soldiers approached the walls and attempted to enter the city's south gate, but were fired upon by a detachment of British Royal Marines and Sikh auxiliaries and repulsed. The rebel army formed parallel lines to the walls, and parties commenced to probe entrances through the fortifications, searching for a way in but not firing a single shot. Alarms sounded in the night. An additional five thousand Taiping warriors then arrived from the north, completely surrounding Shanghai, yet still proclaiming no interest in engaging French or British troops. At this point, British men-of-war began firing shells from the river, over the city and into the rebel camps. Flag Officer Stribling and USS *Hartford* arrived, landing a contingent of American marines to further guard property and lives. They remained ashore for a month. With these obvious signs of foreign resistance, Taiping battle plans were reshaped. Commander Schenck retrieved *Saginaw*'s boat howitzers. Eventually the Heavenly Army dispersed, taking their wounded with them and burying their dead. Though Shanghai was not immediately threatened again, rebel parties continued to loot outer villages, simply to feed the thousands of soldiers in the vicinity.

These were extremely confusing times. Some foreigners felt that, following the defeat of Manchu forces in the north, Westerners should have greeted the Taiping with open arms, no matter their religious oddities. The Taiping warriors, laying siege to the city, were shocked when Westerners fired on their ranks. Minister Ward, returning to Shanghai on board *Saginaw*, learned that the rebels had not actually committed any acts of hostility on foreigners, and when fired upon by the Allies, they had retreated without returning fire: "It is evident that they had been deceived by foreigners who had from time to time been visiting them at Suzhou, and selling them opium, arms, and ammunition, and to ingratiate themselves with the rebels they had told them that foreigners would not object to their taking the Chinese city."[13] Ward assured Secretary of State Lewis Cass that Americans had been involved only in the protection of their own property and lives.

That may have been true, but besides the crews of *Saginaw* and *Hartford*, there were rogue Americans involved as well. The attack was repulsed with the assistance of one Frederick Townsend Ward, a small-time entrepreneur and sailor from Massachusetts who led the defense of the foreign nationals. Frederick Ward had, at various stages, been a first mate in the merchant trades, filibuster and scrap metal dealer in Mexico, and soldier in the Crimean War. In Shanghai, where he had arrived with his brother in 1860, he took charge of the armed river steamer *Confucius* and engaged in pirate suppression. Backed by the wealthy merchants of the city, Ward also employed small shallow-draft paddle-wheel steamers, armed with a 32-pounder pivot gun forward and a 12-pounder pivot aft.[14] His victorious army, Western trained and led, included many Manila men armed with Sharp's repeating rifles and Colt revolvers. He was, simply stated, a mercenary taking advantage of the situation. Later he was celebrated as a hero to the Chinese, a naturalized subject of the empire, an adopted mandarin or Chinese official. No doubt, such individuals threatened Minister Ward's precarious balancing act of neutrality.

The Taiping were incensed by what they saw as an act of treachery. Commander Li Xiucheng addressed the crews of *Hartford* and *Saginaw* and the foreign contingent in Shanghai on August 21, 1860, attempting to appeal to the commercial interests of the Westerners while drawing a line between them and the Manchu government:

> You and we alike worship Jesus, and . . . there exists between us the relationship of a common basis and common doctrines. Moreover I came to Shanghai to make a treaty in order to see us connected together by trade and commerce; I did not come for the purpose of fighting with you. Had I at once commenced to attack the city and kill the people, that would have been the same as the members of one family fighting among themselves, which would have caused the demons to ridicule us. Further, amongst the people of foreign nations at Shanghai, there must be varieties in capacity and disposition: there must be men of sense, who know the principles of right, and are well aware of what is advantageous and what is injurious. They cannot all covet the money of the demon's dynasty, and forget the general trading interests in this country.[15]

The choice between siding with heretic rebels or the crumbling dynasty, though, was a decision for civilian leaders and diplomats, not the military. Officers in the U.S. Navy followed orders. The anticipated massacre having been averted, Schenck and USS *Saginaw* were then ordered to Ningpo and Fuzhou, delivering dispatches and men, and communicating with the relatively immobile old ship *John Adams*. Following these tasks, *Saginaw* was to embark Minister Ward and his retinue and make a tour of all of the ports of commerce important to American interests, prior to Ward's six months of leave for medical reasons, desperately seeking a more temperate climate. The minister had been requesting leave for some time, and he was increasingly concerned with political developments in the United States and the growing divisions between the American North and South.

The monsoon environment and five months of service on the China Station had caught up with the crew of *Saginaw* as well. The sick list was beginning to expand. The medical journal, a daily record of diagnoses and treatments, reflected a repetitive litany of chills, fever, primary and secondary venereal diseases, and particularly diarrhea contracted from a variety of sources (contaminated drinking water, fruits purchased from the bum boats selling produce alongside, etc.). Men suffered from the heat of the deck during the day and, escaping the stifling berthing deck, from chills due to exposure at night. In October, following a brief chill, eighteen-year-old seaman Thomas Walker was found to be "almost pulseless, extremities to be very cool, in a condition which has but little hope."[16] Though he soon appeared to make a quick recovery, he subsequently died of remittent fever in the harbor of Hong Kong, due to "exposure to the cool night air after becoming overheated pulling a boat, and previous exposure to the influences of a climate which made him liable to an attack."[17] Flag Officer Stribling's instructions, nonetheless, were to keep the small side-wheeler constantly on the move.

Commander Schenck reports to me that the number of sick he now has (eight), his working force is so much reduced, as to render the Saginaw inefficient and not able to weigh her anchors. (The power of the purchases for this purpose are very defective.) I am satisfied the Saginaw with her present crew is unequal to the work requested and recommend that it be increased by an addition of four seamen and six ordinary seamen and landsmen. As there is now a large number of sick, I have authorized Commander Schenck to employ temporarily ten coolies who can go in boats, and do other duty to relieve the crew from much exposure which I believe is a principal cause of their sickness. I enclose copies of orders to Commander Schenck and Berian [USS *John Adams*].

In addition Commander Schenck has, under orders, visited Ningpo and the Chusan Islands with Mr. Ward, and followed us to the Gulf of Pe-ichili, returned to this place, and joined us with the mail at Chefoo, and then went to the mouth of the Peiho with Mr. Ward and returned to this place.[18]

This was the first time that Chinese civilians had been employed to perform shipboard duties on board a U.S. Navy vessel while on a foreign station, an act forced out of sheer necessity. This would later become much more common for American naval ships of the Yangzi patrol. The environment forced a constant struggle against sickness and disease. Sailors at the time referred to the phenomenon of "seasoning," or the period in which men contracted and then (hopefully) survived the onslaught of unfamiliar diseases, thereby increasing their own immunity. Seasoning was a consequence of military duty in unfamiliar (often tropical) locations. It was a brutal reality. In China, and particularly in crowded inner cities such as Shanghai, cholera, dysentery, smallpox, and malaria were very prevalent, and little could be done against them. After "rendering protection" at the ports of Ningpo and Fuzhou, where conditions appeared peaceful, *Saginaw* returned to Shanghai to prepare for Ward's cruise.

Unexpected delays frequently plague diplomats, and Minister Ward was not immune to them. Scheduled to leave for Kanagawa on September 1, *Saginaw* was still in Shanghai in late October. Port and starboard watches, in turn, finally received liberty ashore during the delay. The sailors found themselves lost amid thousands of returned residents, and the crowded streets of the inner city and market stalls sold everything imaginable. The Shanghai waterfront was a sailor's port, providing the objects of all vices, circulating around brothels, bars, and the opium imported from India and Pakistan, easily available to those who sought them. This was not a place for the unfamiliar foreign sailor to venture alone, so parties tended to stick together on their city trek. Even that provided no guarantee of protection, for some excessive indulgence proved too great. Upon his return to the ship, Landsman James Campbell, a painter who had enlisted in San Francisco only a couple months prior to *Saginaw*'s departure, fell overboard from a small boat and drowned. Alcohol was involved, and the death was listed as "not in the line of duty."[19]

Then, on September 26, Flag Officer Stribling received a report of an American vessel having been seized and the crew all murdered by pirates. Commander Schenck took on a river pilot, Captain Goff, and *Saginaw* quickly recalled her lost crew and got under way. The search began near the mouth of the Yangzi River, but no trace of the captured ship, the pirates, or even the source of the rumor could be located. Following a second search farther north, Schenck returned to Shanghai on October 3 with two prisoners. The truth seemed quite different from the rumor. Apparently, six deserters from American ships at a nearby port had stolen a boat and made their way south along the coast. Short of provisions, they landed and commenced to prey upon Chinese villagers in a coastal village. The villagers killed four and wounded the remaining two men, who then proceeded to report the false news of a wrecked and looted American bark. Stribling wrote, "It now appears that they were the only pirates, and deserve much greater punishment than they received at the hands of the Chinese."[20]

Japan in Transition

The East India Squadron's duties extended to America's precarious political situation in newly accessible Japan as well, and visits were planned for the fall. The flagship USS *Hartford* had gone there in advance, and the large screw frigate USS *Niagara* had then arrived in Yokohama. The mere presence of *Niagara* made a strong statement to the population and the government of Japan at a time when protection of foreigners was critical. *Niagara* also delivered gifts from the Navy Department to the emperor: four howitzers, four field carriages, four boat carriages, shrapnel, shell, shot, and canister ammunition, muskets, carbines, cartridges, tools, forge, etc.[21] Following the ship's visit, USS *Niagara* was ordered to head for Hong Kong for the sole purpose of embarking the sick and invalid sailors of the squadron. Seasoning was taking its toll on the whole station.

Commander Schenck had orders for Japan as well, taking Minister Ward to Kanagawa via Hong Kong and Guangzhou. At Kanagawa, Schenck was to communicate with American Minister Townsend Harris and offer to convey him "to Hakodadi and such other ports as he may wish to visit, for the purpose of selecting one to be opened to foreign communication instead of Neguata, which has been found undesirable for commercial purposes."[22] The port of Neguata had only nine feet of water on the bar, too shallow for deep-draft oceangoing vessels.

Given the post-Perry tensions in Japan, it was not easy for American merchants and diplomats to ascertain which ports were truly suitable for foreign trade. Minister Harris had petitioned former Flag Officer Tattnall to conduct a survey of various ports in Japan long before *Saginaw*'s arrival in China, but as of October 1860, none had been completed. His requests were then forwarded to Stribling, who then sent Commander Schenck and *Saginaw* to survey specific ports as thoroughly as time and means permitted. Furthermore, if the ship needed to purchase coal in Japan, Schenck was to find its source and make careful estimates of its abundance and steaming qualities, etc. Above all, the officers and crew of *Saginaw* were to behave themselves: "You will be careful in your intercourse with the Japanese to foster the good understanding already existing by kindness and forbearance; and be particular in requiring the same course of conduct by all under your command. Important results may depend upon the manner in which you discharge the duty now assigned to you, and I have every confidence that you will in its performance fully meet my expectations."[23] There had been complaints, after all. The officers of USS *Powhatan*, quite apart from their mission of conveying a Japanese embassy to Panama, had purchased kobang, or Japanese gold coins, with the aim of selling them in China for three times the purchase price. American merchants in China were outraged. Japanese officials were, frankly, disgusted. Minister Harris warned, "in the Japanese mind, the idea of a person bearing the military commission of a great country, like the United States, engaging in trade, is a monstrous parody . . . to the injury of our national character in the eyes of the Japanese."[24]

Saginaw arrived in Kanagawa on November 4, 1860. USS *Niagara*, which had departed New York on June 30, was then returning the Japanese embassy to Yedo (Tokyo), anchoring near where Commodore Perry had dropped anchor, following the signing of the unequal treaties. *Saginaw*, of shallower draft, moved some two miles closer to shore than *Niagara*, the better for assisting with the movement of the embassy's baggage, a poor second-place task to *Niagara*'s starring role. When the actual ambassadors disembarked onto their own boats from *Niagara*, Schenck's crew paid honors by removing their jackets and lining the yards and rails. A Prussian frigate lay nearby, seeking a treaty like the Americans had done.

The village of Kanagawa itself was of minor consequence, but it was an entry point for Yedo, the closely guarded capital of the shogun, the military leader of Japan. As in China, the right of foreign access to the capital had to be carefully negotiated. Kanagawa had been opened by treaty agreement on July 4, 1859. Permanent residence in the city of Yedo itself, though, had not yet been granted. Commander Schenck and his officers were escorted along the smoothed, clean streets by mounted guard, past the temples and gardens and fortresses with cannon (all facing seaward) to the capital, where they met with Minister Harris. Parties of American officers rode through the town, in groups of ten to fifteen, marveling at the well-kept fishponds and flowers. All wore dress uniform and swords. Yedo was unlike any other location *Saginaw*'s officer had visited, for this was the residence of some 18 greater and 342 lesser daimyos, or lords, each with thousands of retainers. Major daimyos controlled between 6,000 and 10,000 samurai, while lesser daimyos supported 2,000 to 3,000 each. In short, in Yedo, there were some 300,000 samurai, all of whom were armed. They were described by foreigners as existing in idleness, as both arrogant and aggressive, subjecting all lower classes to abuse. Harris reported that "they haunt the streets in great numbers, frequently in a state of intoxication, and, being always armed, are not only prompt in taking offense, but ready to seek it."[25] In addition, some 150,000 imperial functionaries and 200,000 nonofficial inhabitants lived and worked among the palaces of the princes and the royals.[26] Yedo was an impressive but dangerous place, for the samurai were loyal to their lords, many of whom, despite the treaties made by the shogun, were stridently anti-Western. Perhaps the military equipment given to the shogun by USS *Niagara* granted *Saginaw*'s officers some feeling of protection. Perhaps civilians, not uniformed naval officers, were perceived as more suitable targets for the roving samurai. A day after they arrived, however, Chinese staff in the employ of the British in nearby Yokohama were killed by Japanese assassins.[27]

There was no easy or immediate solution to such animosity. In January 1861, Minister Harris's own translator, Secretary of the American Legation Charles Heusken, was attacked. As he rode out at night with his mounted escorts, samurai cut down the horses and killed his guard, mortally wounding Heusken. He rode 200 more yards before he perished. The attack frightened the diplomatic corps, though, amazingly, Minister Harris did his best to calm the fears. He reported to the secretary of state: "The English and French representatives are both extremely nervous men, and for the last 16 months they have been in a chronic state of excitement. Should they succeed in impressing their respective governments with their peculiar views of affairs here, I do not see how a war with this country can be avoided."[28] In the end, Heusken's mother was compensated ten thousand dollars, and the French and British ministers returned to Japan. A month later, two Dutch sea captains were hacked to bits in the streets of Yokohama. Again, Harris avoided spreading his own dire political warnings, finding that gangs of drunken foreign sailors had behaved in a riotous and disorderly fashion earlier that day, and the attack had been a case of simple revenge. Prudently, though, he established a curfew for American citizens from sundown to sunrise, urged them to travel only with guards, and recommended they arm themselves.

USS *Saginaw*'s passage through the inland sea of Japan included calls at the ports of Yokohama and Nagasaki as well, where the same underlying potential for violence existed, but fortunately Commander Schenck and his crew managed to avoid any outright confrontations. The vast inland sea area—consisting of five large, interconnected basins filled with thousands of islands—was the birthplace of Japanese seafaring and focus of maritime activity. It had not been frequented by foreign ships until 1860, so the many islands and harbors were the subject of much comment. Local pilots were unwilling to navigate at night near so many rocky shoals and reefs, so the ship anchored. Wood and water were available at small villages, and parties of officers were allowed to walk carefully through the coastal towns, where they found themselves treated in a strictly proper and civil fashion. They did not stay long. The meeting at Yedo curtailed the ship's assignment in Japan. Minister Harris still needed the surveys of Neguata, Hioga, and other ports, but November was not the time to attempt these: "The season is now so far advanced that I do not think it would be prudent to make the voyage at this time."[29] Minister Harris feared for the safety of *Saginaw* and her crew, for fog and high seas prevailed at that time of year on the west coast, a lee shore, and the volcanic coast all along the survey area was virtually uncharted. *Saginaw* provisioned and coaled ship from U.S. naval stores at Kanagawa and sailed away from Japan. She arrived in Hong Kong on November 27, going through a rough crossing and sustaining damage to her upper works.

The crew had now been on the China Station for seven months, becoming seasoned to the foreign climate. The surgeon's medical survey revealed the effects of constant duty on station. Ordinary Seaman William Martin suffered from chronic gastritis and "long standing derangement of the liver." In Japan, he had been vomiting blood. Ordinary Seaman Charles Gaines suffered from dysentery and from syphilis and fever as well. The coal passers John Kelly and James McNamara had secondary syphilis of long standing.[30] All had little to no possibility of recovery on station; all were judged to have contracted their ailment while "not in the line of duty." Three more were sent back to Mare Island on USS *Niagara*.

The Restless Crew

Tension and confrontation on board ship were always to be expected under these sorts of conditions, and these were always handled in the navy manner. The ship had to be a world rigidly structured, for it revolved around the necessity of strict obedience in the worst of times, during conflict or great natural peril at sea. Obedience demanded a strict code of justice, doled out in measured amounts through the captain's mast for minor infractions, court-martial for formal judgments, and then the prescribed punishments.

Commander Schenck, of course, conducted his own courts of inquiry, one being convened on *Saginaw* for the purpose of investigating certain charges made against U.S. Marine Corps officers Captain Garland and Sergeant Munger. Two days earlier, a fight had broken out among four marines on board: James H. Moore, Christopher Nugent, Joseph Warren, and Dennis Sullivan. Munger, the sergeant of the guard, broke up the fight and made his report directly to USMC Captain Garland in the wardroom. The marines on board navy ships operated with a degree of autonomy, and in most cases meted out their own discipline and punishments. For some reason, though, *Saginaw*'s executive officer, Lieutenant Edward A. Barnet, took great exception to this, accusing Munger of gross negligence of duty, of failing to report promptly to the officer of the deck (Barnet) in order to send the delinquents to the mast, of disrespectful intrusion into the wardroom, etc. Garland was accused of issuing orders contrary to the discipline of the ship and conflicting with Barnet's authority as executive officer.[31] The court of inquiry found the charges baseless.

For the enlisted sailors the cruise in Japan had been scenic but disappointing, for often the potential dangers ashore prevented liberty parties, their only chance for time away from the ship. Service on the small vessel seemed endless. Tensions among the officers themselves came to a head in December when the possibly mentally unstable Lieutenant Westcott, long unhappy being trapped on board, brought official charges against Commander Schenck following the Japan cruise, accusing him of "a uniform system of persecution from the day I found the vessel at San Francisco to the present moment, with a total disregard for the laws and usages of the service, and ignoring my rank given me by the President and Senate of the United States."[32] In other words, Westcott had finally snapped. James Findlay Schenck faced four specific charges: using reproachful and obscene words unbecoming an officer; placing the lieutenant in a "degraded capacity" by deferring to others beneath his rank; disregarding the etiquette and discipline needed for a well-regulated naval vessel; and finally, being intoxicated in Yokohama and (surprisingly) exposing himself to officers on board his own ship and those of USS *Hartford*.

Flag Officer Stribling, faced with charges against one of his own commanders, ordered a court of inquiry to review the seriousness of the accusations and determine if there were sufficient grounds for a court-martial. The charge of using reproachful language was proven, for Commander Schenck admitted to saying to Westcott "You are drunk . . . you are crazy" on the quarterdeck, and also circulating the report that the lieutenant was mentally deranged.[33] The incident had occurred following *Saginaw*'s return to the China coast, near the city of Fuzhou. Commander Schenck had verbally abused the first lieutenant on deck, and then ordered the second lieutenant to move the ship from one Min River anchorage to another, thus allegedly ignoring and degrading Westcott's rank. Lieutenant Westcott, whom Schenck claimed was an inefficient and incompetent first officer, had faced an earlier summary, or deck trial, in June. He had been found guilty as charged of being intoxicated while on duty and sentenced to be dismissed from the squadron, suspended from rank and command for one year, and placed on furlough pay—just as soon as the navy was done using him on the China Station. The two officers continued to serve together on the crowded deck of *Saginaw* for months, though the breach between the first lieutenant (also known as the ship's executive officer, a critical position) and the ship's captain greatly disrupted the normal functioning of the vessel.

As to the charge of disregarding the discipline needed to manage a well-regulated ship, Commander Schenck used the occasion to do a little griping about his command and replied, "I would like to learn the secret of making a well regulated and efficient man-of-war out of a little side wheel steamer armed with two boat howitzers and a badly fitted light 32-pounder, without marines, who are so necessary . . . with only six seamen, four ordinary seamen, four landsmen or boys, and a proportionate number of petty officers, firemen and coal heavers."[34] Schenck, it seemed, found *Saginaw* somewhat beneath his rank: "The *Saginaw* is the smallest seagoing steamer in the service in command of a commander, with fewer guns and men than five others commanded by lieutenants. I am prevented from interchanging visits with foreign officers of my same grade, because my vessel does not afford the means of receiving them with the usual naval etiquette . . . at this moment there is in this harbor [Hong Kong] a ship of 18 guns and 180 men commanded by my junior, who has seen seven years less sea service."[35] Surely this stung his pride. Schenck's next command would be the old 1,708-ton ordnance storeship USS *St. Lawrence*, larger but decidedly less than dashing.

As for the charge of exposing himself in front of officers of his ship and those of USS *Hartford*, this act remained unproven, though the court of inquiry came to the conclusion that Schenck had been "manifestly" intoxicated. However, though Stribling felt that "the discipline of USS *Saginaw* has to some extent been neglected by J. Findlay Schenck . . . the charge of drunkenness on his part is confined to but a solitary instance."[36]

There may have been something of a recriminatory and malicious nature in Westcott's charges against his captain, but in any event Stribling was not going to go forward with a real trial. He simply was not in a position to convene the required number of senior officers to hold a full court-martial, nor did he consider it wise to remove a commander from his ship on the distant and almost unsupported China Station. In the end, Stribling simply recommended that a trial be held following the expiration of Commander Schenck's current cruise, and took no further action. He still praised USS *Saginaw* as "an admirable dispatch vessel, and well calculated to do good service on this station."[37]

Years later, officers who had served on *Saginaw* in China gave testimony concerning the incident. This was part of fairly routine questioning as part of their regular examinations for promotion. Paymaster Henry R. Day described Westcott's association with Lieutenant Barnett, the executive officer of USS *John Adams*, and how Westcott had attempted to pressure him into condemning Commander Schenck. Day would not do this, and in turn described Westcott as so often drunk as to be unfit to conduct his own business. Furthermore, Lieutenant John Hall from *John Adams*, who then replaced Westcott as executive officer on *Saginaw*, was also a "great inebriate . . . drunk often on duty."[38] The difficult conditions of service in China drove the men to drink, and they suffered from the effects of alcohol abuse in a number of different ways.

Following a somewhat cheerless Christmas in Hong Kong, *Saginaw* again was sent in pursuit of local insurgents. This time, a report had come in from Dr. George Whitefield Fish, the U.S. consul at Ningpo to the north, that an American trading lorcha (the name for a hybrid Western hull–Chinese sailing rig design) had been captured by pirates. Schenck and his crew were to locate the lorcha, recapture it, and return the vessel to her rightful owners, and then turn the pirates over to the Chinese authorities. If there was no immediate sign of the ship, *Saginaw* would cruise in the vicinity for a few days and then make her way to Shanghai to take on coal. From there it was back to Ningpo, or perhaps on to Fuzhou—port-hopping again.[39] This antipiracy patrol was not an easy assignment, for even the British and French, with much larger navies in East Asia, continuously failed to adequately suppress piracy. Navy vessels were often conspicuous on the coast, able to sneak up on no one, capturing no one unawares. Pirates and other insurgents operating on their own grounds had a much better chance of merging with the local population and quickly vanishing before the arrival of any authorities. The poor weather during January didn't help matters. *Saginaw* was both battered and unsuccessful.

Meanwhile, plans were being laid for a larger mission on the horizon. Commercial access to specific ports on the Yangzi River had been conceded by China to the West by the Treaty of Tianjin in 1858. Finally, Western merchants stood to gain China's vast interior markets and resources, a long-desired prize almost within their grasp, spurring competition between steam lines on the river. But the situation with the Taiping rebels made navigation on the river potentially hazardous.

In February, British Admiral Hope and eight ships left Shanghai for the Yangzi. A 90-foot gunboat was stationed at Nanjing to protect British interests. The Chinese cannon within the fortifications above the ship were permanently trained on the tiny gunboat. That same month, the American steamer *Yangtze* departed Shanghai upriver. The steamer was owned by the newly organized Shanghai Steam Navigation Company (a subsidiary of the American trading outfit Russell and Company), first vessel off the mark. The company soon boasted a fleet of five river and three coastal steam vessels. These vessels were issued passes by the U.S. consul in Shanghai, describing in both English and Chinese the ship, the master's name, the crew, all arms and ammunition carried on board, and notes recommending the bearer to the good graces of the insurgent chiefs where they had control of the countryside. Flag Officer Stribling naturally felt that "it is important that our flag should be shown that the inhabitants along the banks of the river should see that we have a naval force for the protection of our ships and countrymen."[40] USS *Saginaw*, built for this type of work, would come to hold the record for the longest passage upriver.

Ascent of the Yangzi River

In April, *Saginaw* was once more in Hong Kong, the crew hard at work coaling the ship and bringing on board provisions for the river passage. Steaming to Shanghai, *Saginaw* then fell in with the flag ship *Hartford*, her crew likewise bringing on board coal, coating themselves in the black, oily dust cloud that stained the decks, rigging, and once-white canvas. They were soon joined by USS *Dacotah*, a 1,369-ton steam bark, one of the eight vessels authorized by Congress in June 1858. *Dacotah*'s sailing master, recently arrived on June 12, had his first look at the small side-wheel steamer alongside. Though unknown to him at the time, in ten years Montgomery Sicard would be serving as the commander of *Saginaw* himself.

Stribling's small fleet would have to navigate the unseen shoals and snags of the famous Yangzi. But the greater unknown factor proved to be the future relationships with the Taiping rebels. The flag officer himself was not exactly certain where his country stood in this situation:

> They, the Insurgents, are quite willing and anxious to have free intercourse with foreigners; but can we with a proper regard to our Treaty obligations to the Imperial Government, hold intercourse with the rebel powers? . . . I propose about the first of May to leave Shanghai, to ascend the Yangtze, as far as possible, if up to Hangkow; and on the way up the river to have intercourse with the rebel powers to assure them that we have no hostile intentions against them. . . . Any effort to have *direct* trade with the Insurgents, would I think be just cause of complaint on the part of the Imperial Government. I shall discourage it all I can; but still, such is the eagerness of our countrymen, engaged in trade for profit, that we may expect some of them to endeavor to do business with the rebels; and if detected by the Imperial authorities difficulties may happen.[41]

Several sailors on board *Saginaw* took advantage of the increased shore traffic during the provisioning of the ship and elected not to accompany their vessel on this mission. They ran, and their timing was perfect. James Brown, William Robinson, and Andrew Jackson slipped off in the night and made their way through Shanghai's crowded streets, avoiding the British areas (the British were more adamant about policing their own territory), and past the many brothels and bars of the French and American concessions, the first place their pursuers might look. Morning inspection at quarters revealed them absent without leave, deserters, but it was too late to organize a search party. On the morning of May 1, the procession of *Hartford*, *Saginaw*, and *Dacotah* got under way.

By May 4, the three ships were at anchor off Nanjing, the rebel capital of hundreds of thousands of Taiping soldiers, known by then as Taiping Tianjing, or the Heavenly Capital of Perfect Peace. Cannon were still trained on the British gunboat, and along the banks near the city, *Saginaw*'s crew watched with foreboding as headless bodies were pushed into crude graves. Heavy clouds darkened the sky, hanging low over the city. The naval officers requested audience with the Taiping minister of state, but were (as expected) at first politely denied:

> Liang, Royal Chief of the Incipient Dynasty, with the Title of Lien-Tien-Ngan, Commissioner of Maritime Customs, and Chief Assistant General at the Imperial City with Nine Gates, of the Celestial Dynasty, addresses the following Communication to his Honorable Elder Brother the Great American Country's Admiral. . . . It is now many years since our Celestial King in propria persona, received the Holy Commands of the Supreme Ruler Our Heavenly Father, and of Christ Jesus, to rule the Tai-pings, and to destroy the warring customs of the Northern Barbarians; and raise the people out of the clay and ashes. I am deeply gratified to learn upon inquiry, that your Honorable Country's custom also is to reverently worship the Supreme Ruler Our Heavenly Father and Christ Jesus truly making but one family of all within the Four Seas with feelings toward each other of brotherly regard. How you are so kind and loving toward us as to come in your ships from afar; but I your younger brother am so stupid and weak and destitute of ability, that I am unable to receive and treat you according to reason and propriety; which grieves me inexpressibly. . . . Your younger brother has respectfully selected 9 o'clock tomorrow to visit your Honorable vessel to receive Your Great Instruction. If I am so favored as that you do not decline (my offer) to listen to your words will be truly the (most) fortunate event of my three states of existence.[42]

Refusing to be brushed off by this first denial of access, communications continued between ship and shore until permission was finally gained for a small party to enter the walls and come to a more formal agreement as to the protection of American trade on the river. Ornate passports and a contingent of military guides were furnished, seemingly sufficient to guarantee their safety. Stribling, in the absence of Minister Ward, took the role of acting minister, the chargé d'affaires. Yet even then he could not participate for the flag officer was of too high a rank to attend the meeting personally; indeed, he could not unless being met by an equivalent of his own standing. The landing party consisted of only five: Captain Lowndes, Dr. McCarter (missionary and acting interpreter), Lieutenant Law, Paymaster Gibson, and Captain Gibson (U.S. Marines).

Shoving off in the ship's gig, Lowndes and his party made their way up the adjacent creek to the walled city's moat, landing near the western main gate, where they found four saddled horses and a green sedan chair with bearers. The gate itself was long and dark, like a railway tunnel, and before passing through they were thoroughly searched and their papers examined. Inside, the city streets were deserted and desolate, with much of the area in ruins and only a few houses still standing. For miles, nothing could be seen but charred bricks and weeds. Following its capture years earlier, trade had never returned to Nanjing. They dismounted near the palace, at a gate ablaze with crimson and gold and dazzling color, and were led through a maze of passages to an interior chamber. Offerings of rice and meat had been laid before sacrificial fires among the empty rooms. Tsan Wang, the twenty-four-year-old son of the Taiping minister of state, met them and escorted them to a council of seven or eight officials already in session, with tea and betel nut being handed round. Hong Xiuquan, the Taiping leader, was of course not present. At this stage of the Taiping movement, only a very few chosen persons such as family members and female attendants were allowed personal audience. Foreign consuls and applicants often sat in concealed frustration before an empty throne, listening to the repetitious chants and booming of gongs, amidst the incense and charcoal braziers.[43]

The American naval contingent was lucky. They had been brought to what was the bureaucratic equivalent of a small working group. There was not really much question that the Taipings would have to allow Western navigation on the river; the missionaries and merchants were to get their access. At the palace, negotiations confirmed that, as with the British, the Taiping would allow American ships, once cleared by the Heavenly Customs House, to conduct trade upriver: "As regards Your Honorable Nation navigating the Yangtze River for the purpose of trade, what obstacle could be raised?" With minor alterations, the American demands were agreed to by the Taiping. No one, though, could be allowed to come ashore near Nanjing, and trade at that city was forbidden. (This would have been a commercial desecration of a holy place.) And no trade in opium would be tolerated. Furthermore, soldiers were not to amuse themselves in the camps surrounding the city's walls. Finally, a carefully worded warning: the Taiping acknowledged that "there are many places which we have not yet been able to obtain possession," and if Americans have goods or property there when the Heavenly Soldiers finally arrived, "it would be difficult to discriminate under the circumstances."[44] Despite official capitulation, rank-and-file Taiping soldiers no longer looked with favor on foreigners, particularly following the failed attack and perceived treachery at Shanghai the previous year.

A slow dinner followed an even longer blessing, and no wine or liquor was served. The apprehension earlier in the day gave way to impatience and indigestion. All in all, the Taiping chiefs struck the naval officers as something of a group of village worthies, neither exceedingly literate nor possessing much by the way of dignity or capability.[45] If Admiral Hope and the British were willing to recognize the rebels as the de facto power in the region, though, the Americans would do the same.

The following day, "younger brother" Liang and other officials from the palace made their visit on board USS *Hartford*. Later, Stribling, staging *Hartford* at a strategic point along the river, shifted his pennant to *Saginaw*, and on May 7, the reduced fleet was again under way upriver. The vessels, belching smoke, slowly headed west up the longest river in Asia (third-longest in the world), moving between a swath of ruined landscape. Rainy, disagreeable weather persisted, making the pilot's job avoiding shoals, banks, and snags and constantly judging the river's currents a difficult one. The trading towns of Kieukang and Nieuchang, like Nanjing, seemed empty and forlorn. The countryside between Shanghai and Hankou farther upstream had been devastated by rebel gangs. Commercial and religious representatives who had accompanied the earlier British expedition had a negative assessment: "The Rebels don't want us. We can do nothing for them until after peace is restored, except pay visits, preach to a few dignitaries and give them books."[46]

If Nanjing appeared depressed, the surrounding area was worse. For years, homeless refugees had roamed the banks of the river, caught between the regular and irregular armies of Taiping soldiers, bandits, pirates, local militia, Qing imperial troops, Western-led units commanded by Frederick Townsend Ward, and the British expeditionary forces. Whole villages were burned or stripped of all wood for fuel or makeshift supports for temporary bridges across the numerous canals and creeks.[47] These were the all-too-common effects of war on the countryside. Even the hardened British troops, veterans of many scenes of devastation, were affected by these conditions. Garnet Wolseley, quartermaster general on the British expeditionary force, wrote:

> In all such places as we had an opportunity of visiting, the distress and misery of the inhabitants were beyond description. Large families were crowded together into low, small, tent-shaped wigwams, constructed of reeds, through the thin sides of which the cold wind whistled at every blast from the biting north. The denizens were clothed in rags of the most loathsome kind, and huddled together for the sake of warmth. The old looked cast down and unable to work from weakness, whilst that eager expression peculiar to starvation, never to be forgotten by those who have once witnessed it, was visible upon the emaciated features of the little children.[48]

This was a dismal passage through a destroyed country for *Saginaw* and *Dacotah* while *Hartford* waited on station farther downstream. The cold east wind and overcast skies added to the crew's despondent gloom.

On May 12, the two vessels dropped anchor at Hankou, the important port city of Hubei Province. There Stribling appointed D. Williams as the first U.S. consul (acting) at the port. This location, where the Han River merges with the Yangzi, was busier, but still had not recovered enough to provide profitable voyages for merchants seeking silks and teas in the China trade. John Heard III, an American entrepreneur who had arrived in Hong Kong in March with the steamer *Fire Dart*, had made an exploratory passage on the Yangzi earlier, in the wake of the Shanghai Steam Navigation Company's *Yangtze*, the first foreign vessel to actually reach Hankou. The *Fire Dart* carried about twenty thousand dollars' worth of cargo, including three chests of opium. She had no arms or ammunition, though, items that were in the highest demand. Heard found trade difficult, if not impossible, on the river. The crops of tea and mulberry leaves (which fed the silkworms) had been razed. Only one cargo could support the business, the exodus of Chinese passengers from the ruined river ports to Shanghai fleeing the interior areas.

Leaving *Dacotah* at Hankou, Stribling continued upriver on *Saginaw* alone. His mission was to show the flag, not search for profits. After working the ship off a mud bank by shifting all the chains, guns, and boats to the port side, and then blowing out the starboard boiler, *Saginaw* passed out of the Yangzi River and into Tung Ting Lake, the largest lake in central China, coming to anchor off Yohchow City, where Commander Schenck "allowed about a thousand Chinamen to visit the ship."[49] There, about

700 miles from Shanghai, tiny *Saginaw* gained the record for the West's longest passage upstream. For this the ship received a seven-gun salute from USS *Dacotah* upon her return to Hankou. Bringing on board fresh stores (meaning live fowl, sheep, and pigs) and once again coaling the ship, *Saginaw* was prepared for the uneventful downriver passage. The fleet made additional progress by steaming at night, using colored lanterns as signal lights, though anchoring in the dark was tricky. By May 27, all three ships were swinging at anchor once again at Shanghai. Stribling's assessment of the Yangzi River was oddly positive: "singularly exempt from difficulties."[50] Sailors of the future American Yangzi River Patrol would disagree with him.

USS *Saginaw* had done what no other naval vessel had accomplished up to that time—and this despite her engineer being out of commission the entire time, a victim of seasoning on the China coast. James Sheridan had first suffered from bilious colic in June 1860. Then he spent half the month of January on the sick list for syphilis. Secondary and tertiary symptoms continued to plague him in March and April, and he exhibited confusion, nervous excitement, pale skin, and insomnia. Doses of quinine led to temporary deafness. At times, during the ship's ascent of the river, Sheridan lay on the verge of collapse, appearing moribund and able only to suck a little water from a damp rag. The motion of the ship distressed him greatly. It was not until June 10 that he finally recovered and returned to duty, after seventy-two days straight on the sick list.[51]

Other consuls still had to be transported to their newly opened ports and the flag shown and trade initiated. But following the Yangzi River passage, *Saginaw* returned to her usual mixed bag of port-hopping, mail delivery, and the pursuit of pirates. Seaman Henry Peters went absent without leave. Then Seaman James Romer followed. Then James Turner. Finding deserters ashore was a tricky business. American consuls, faced with the need to detain and punish civilian criminals but without jail facilities, could only attempt to impose a fine, a silly thing to try on poor sailors. Consul Smith, when faced with such a situation, often simply dropped the case altogether. Naval personnel who ran from their ships represented a more serious category. There were, however, hundreds of foreign sailors ashore, many unemployed, acting as mercenaries, or deserters from merchantmen. And ships were searching for crews all the time. Finding a particular sailor in Shanghai was as difficult as finding a particular pirate on the China coast—there were too many of them. The crewmen who did stay continued in their daily routine despite the sickness and chaos around them. Landing parties continued to drill at small arms training, and *Saginaw* still broke out the "great guns" at target practice. Others re-provisioned the ship, and brought on board the coal, once again.

While *Saginaw* was on the Yangzi River and unknown to them at the time, Secretary of the Navy Gideon Welles had ordered Captain Frederick Engle to proceed to Hong Kong in order to relieve Flag Officer Stribling of command of the East India Squadron. Welles had decided to recall all of the vessels on the China Station via the Cape of Good Hope, "with all practical dispatch." The Union garrison at Fort Sumter in Charleston Harbor had refused to surrender to Confederate forces, and on April 12, as USS *Saginaw* was standing through the channel near Ningpo, on her way toward Nanjing and upriver, the first shots of the American Civil War had been fired. They only now received the news, and this crisis would change the rest of their time in China. *Saginaw*'s first task, however, was to steam to Swatow in order to assist the aging USS *John Adams* out and on her way—tow her out if necessary, preparatory to her return to the United States. The ship would sail carrying yet more of the sick and invalid from the squadron.

Pirates and Privateers

While the rest of the squadron prepared for departure, normal patrol duties continued, and *Saginaw*, no doubt with impatience and frustration, was sent in pursuit of another reported missing vessel. On June 26, 1861, the ship was ordered to Cochin China (Southern Vietnam) in search of the bark *Myrtle* and her shipwrecked crew, lost a year earlier on that coast. Captain Bradford had been temporarily held captive in that distant area, and upon his return reported the missing ship, as well as the incident at Qui Nhon, a coastal farming and fishing village. The bark had wrecked and the crew took to the ship's boats, making shore separately in territory then unfamiliar to the Americans. The island of Pulo Cambin near the village was the starting point for the search. Stribling's orders were to make inquiries for the missing boat and crew, to communicate with the authorities and impress upon them the necessity of treating shipwrecked sailors with kindness, etc.[52] He doubted if they had been murdered, for the French were in the country. He felt it likely that they had been drowned in rough seas.

Steaming down the coast, *Saginaw* arrived at the harbor in four days, and Commander Schenck, with a very old French chart in one hand and the pilot instructions from Hasting's *East India Directory* in the other, ran straight in and dropped anchor in four fathoms of water, satisfied that the place matched Bradford's description.[53] Cochin China did not share the same treaty agreements with the United States as did China, and had been at war with France for an extended period of time. The area had been conquered and colonized in the mid-nineteenth century by the French empire, though administrative control was nominal and a nationalist movement against the foreigners (later to be led by Ho Chi Minh) had been born. As a precaution, Schenck ran up a white flag on the fore truck, and the American flag flew prominently at the peak. Steam pressure was kept up in the boilers, ready for orders. The vessel swung to about 600 yards from a fort mounting a hill. He planned to wait about an hour, and then attempt a shore visit to begin his investigation.

Instead, after only ten minutes, a well-directed shot was fired from the fort, splashing into the harbor very close to the ship. A second well-placed shot soon followed, passing close enough overhead that the sailors could hear it whistling through the air. Schenck promptly ordered the anchor weighed and the ship began to move slowly, but not before a third shot struck the water just forward of the starboard bow. By then he was ready. Lieutenant Marshall C. Campbell took command of the 32-pounder rifled pivot gun and its nine-man crew (including the "powder monkey," or ship's boy, running the explosive charges up to the deck from the magazine below). Taking time for deliberate aim, *Saginaw*'s crew wanted to make every shot count. And in Commander Schenck's eyes, they did "admirable execution." The first shell exploded immediately above the fort, after which they heard a dull heavy report, likely a bursting gun or the muffled explosion of a magazine. The fort was silenced from this point on. The crew continued a deliberate fire at intervals of about five minutes for half an hour, giving far better than they received. Without the numbers on board sufficient for a landing party, Schenck ended the engagement and returned to Hong Kong. The French admiral at Saigon would attempt to make future inquiries. The action may have temporarily relieved tension on board the ship.

The conflict in America had already begun to change attitudes on overseas stations, and suspicions and increased tensions greeted *Saginaw*'s crew on their return. On board, reasons for resenting service abroad, for putting up with the cramped quarters, for seeking out a fight, were ratcheted upward. And it was no secret which side some of their allies on the China Station, many among the British, favored. USS *Hartford*, *Dacotah*, and *Saginaw* swung at anchor together at Hong Kong, surrounded by

English ships, who were no longer compatriots abroad but now potential enemies. American commanders were instructed to convey a general order throughout the squadron:

> The Commander in Chief feels called upon at this time to address those under his command, upon the condition of our country. By the last mail we have authentic accounts of the commencement of Civil War in the United States by the attack and capture of Fort Sumter by the forces of the Confederate States. It is not my purpose to discuss the merits of the cause or causes which has resulted in plunging our country into all the horrors of a Civil War. But to remind those under my command of their obligations now, to a faithful and zealous performance of every duty. Coming as we do from the various sections of the country, unanimity of opinion on this subject cannot be expected, and I would urge upon all, the necessity of abstaining from all angry and inflammatory language upon the causes of the present state of things in the United States, and to recollect that here we have nothing to do, but to perform the duty of our respective stations and to obey the orders of our superiors in authority. To this we are bound by the solemn obligations of our oath. I charge all commanders and other officers to show in themselves a good example of virtue, honor, patriotism, and subordination, and be vigilant in inspecting the conduct of all such as are placed under their command. In honor of the nation, of the flag under which many of us have served from boyhood, our own honor and good name, require us, now if ever, that we suffer no blot upon the character of our country, while the flag of the union is in our keeping.[54]

The Fourth of July celebration, limited to just the American vessels and residents in China, was marked by the martial 21-gun salute from *Hartford* at meridian (noon). Ships were dressed and ensigns snapped in the breeze. Crews spliced the main brace (extra rations of grog, meaning rye whiskey, for the Americans), and wondered about home. Despite his own thoughts about his native South Carolina, Flag Officer Stribling was a loyal officer of the United States Navy and was determined to carry out his assignment to the end, whenever that would be. Stribling waited until officially relieved before leaving his post. His friends in Hong Kong sent him off with a letter dated July 25, 1861:

> Dear Sir: Understanding that you are about to leave this station and proceed to the United States, your countrymen in China are anxious

to express their regret at your departure, their high esteem for your personal character, and their appreciation of the manner in which the responsible duties devolving upon you in this part of the world have been discharged. In no instance, as far as we are aware, have American interests failed to receive the most prompt and assiduous attention at your hands. . . . [B]efore closing we cannot abstain from referring to the enlarged and patriotic views that you have taken of your duty in the present critical condition of American affairs . . . we cannot doubt that this will be fully appreciated by the Government of the United States.[55]

It was a letter of recommendation for the South Carolinian to the Union.

Captain Frederick Engle arrived in China on July 23, and as Stribling hauled down his flag, Engle hoisted his own pennant. The new flag officer was a Yankee from Pennsylvania. Like many of his generation, he had seen action in the war with Mexico. He was sixty-two years old, and had been sent to China not to run the squadron but to gather it home. Stribling headed for home via the overland route as dictated in his orders, and was placed on the retired list soon thereafter. Called to active service once again, he would take command of the naval yard at Philadelphia, and later command the East Gulf Blockading Squadron.

This was a period when many officers of the U.S. Navy had to choose between the states of their births and their loyalty to federal service. The Confederacy may not have begun the war with much by way of ships, but there was a core of experienced and professional officers who resigned their federal commissions and returned to their native states, a resource sometimes more important than vessels. There was necessity on foreign stations like China to maintain some kind of unity in the face of difficult circumstances, but perhaps the best that could be hoped for were mixed feelings and a number of resignations by southern naval officers as soon as current duties allowed. In December, Lieutenant James Iredall Waddell of North Carolina, who had served well enough if somewhat unremarkably on *Saginaw*, quit the U.S. Navy. He mailed his resignation to the Department from St. Helena, during his homeward-bound passage on USS *John Adams*. Dismissed in January, by March he was appointed a lieutenant in the Confederate States Navy. Waddell would see duty in the Pacific again, as captain of the infamous Confederate raider CSS *Shenandoah*.

USS *Saginaw* took Engle to Hong Kong, where the American merchants and residents had been organizing their argument to present to the flag officer. They were well aware that the squadron was being sent home, but could not help making a final plea for at least one vessel to be left on station. Admittedly, they were not in any immediate danger, but China had proven to be a difficult and often unpredictable experience.

> The coast of China offers a rich field for the enterprise of the holders of a Letter of Marque from the "Southern Confederacy"—and the ports of China, Macao and others, afford means, and opportunities for arming, manning, and equipping a privateer, as well as the market for disposing of captured property without references to the tedious process of adjudication by a Court of Admiralty established in Montgomery. A single vessel here would probably seem to check this option of privateering enterprise until the disappearance of the Government of the Confederate States. . . . With this chief expression of our wants, we ask that you would leave upon this station one of the vessels under your command. . . . We would take this opportunity to express our sincere wishes for your pleasant homeward cruise.[56]

Two days later, Engle made his rationalization to the secretary of the navy:

> I find it necessary to permit Commander Schenck to remain for following reasons. The S.W. Monsoon we shall have to contend with as far as Batavia, this vessel will use steam alone. Her sailing qualities can scarcely be noticed, she will use at least 800 tons of coal to take her to New York. That at 20 dollars per ton will be 16,000 dollars. She was built I am told of green timbers. Commander Schenck agrees with me that this season of headwinds, typhoons, and hurricanes is unsuited for a vessel of her capacity, build, and I therefore have concluded to permit her to remain. . . . Captain Schenck is an excellent steam officer, and knows how to humour a ticklish vessel. If any can take her home he can do it. The foregoing I trust you will consider sufficient for the vessel not returning with me.[57]

There seemed to be uncertainty on how to get the small steamer back. The following day, USS *Hartford* and USS *Dacotah* got under way for the United States. *Saginaw* steamed downriver as well, with Consul Smith on board, to investigate reported troubles on the American ship *Judge Shaw*. All would have much rather continued the passage out of the Hong Kong roads and been bound for the United States, but the weather was deteriorating, and Commander Schenck may not have felt the ship was even capable of making the voyage. He simply did not want to be the one to sail her home. In a letter to the secretary of the navy, Schenck continued to draw the distinction between himself and his ship.

> By this mail you will have heard that Flag Officer Engle has decided to leave this vessel upon the station . . . the present state of affairs at home have made my position a very awkward one, and in justice to myself, I feel bound to state why I acquiesced in the arrangement when it was posed to me. . . . [I]n the first place I am satisfied that the vessel is weak and built of unseasoned timber which is unsound, and she is not fit to encounter the weather as she would probably meet with. . . . I would have proposed to Flag Officer Engle to have the vessel in command of a Lieutenant, to which class of officer she properly belongs, but unfortunately the Senior Lieutenant of the Squadron, Mr. Parker, is strongly suspected of disaffection [Confederate sympathies], besides my unwillingness to abandon the officers and crew who have served with me faithfully for two years . . . they hope to be relieved from duty which under the existing circumstances is onerous.[58]

Schenck begged leave to request orders from the Department, on behalf of himself, his officers, and his crew, for a return to the United States. He had served his full two-year term under the most difficult conditions. In June, there had been yet another death on board the ship. Thirty-two-year-old seaman Edwin Merrill, from Maine, had been stricken with cholera and become cathartic. Indeed, he had been "debilitated for a long time, mental powers much impaired."[59] Despite opium pills and opium water injections, he grew progressively weaker, his pulse small and frequent, and his skin hot and dry. He died on June 25, 1861. *Saginaw* had only twenty-eight of her original crew of fifty who had signed on in California. Commander Schenk's argument for relief, though, was somewhat undermined when he added, as a postscript, that a privateer had been reported fitting out at Shanghai. *Saginaw* immediately went north in pursuit.

The French had called it "guerre de course," the tactic of preying on the commerce of the enemy. It had been a common theme in American naval history, indeed, in almost any circumstance where two navies of unequal abilities met on the high seas. Commissioned naval vessels had, of course, the right to capture enemy merchant ships, but the concept was made much more effective with the aid of private individuals and ships. Privateers, or non-naval vessels fitted out for war and granted authority to prey on commercial ships and goods by their letter of marque, greatly strengthened this tactic. This official letter of marque drew the line between recognized privateers and outright pirates, considered enemies of all nations. America had licensed privateers to take British ships in both the Revolutionary War and the War of 1812. Damaging the economy and trade of the enemy was the tactic of the weak against the strong. And the Confederacy had gone into the Civil War with almost no navy at all. Suddenly the protection of the vast Union commerce in China, which extended beyond the effective protection of the U.S. Navy in a careful if unstable state of neutrality, was threatened by any vessel carrying Confederate sympathizers and whatever weapons could be found on short notice.

On the western Pacific coast, the small handful of Union navy ships began looking into the many bays and harbors of Lower California and the Mexican coastline. Suddenly the activities of suspected steamers throughout the region, as well as the movements of Confederate officers and sympathizers in all the ports and harbors, became information critical to the national security. The president of the Confederacy, Jefferson Davis, had invited applications for letters of marque only four days after the surrender of Fort Sumter, five days after the beginning of the war. Privateer crews stood to benefit directly from the distribution of the prize, money from the captured vessel, or cargo. The international practice of privateering had actually been abolished by the 1856 Treaty of Paris, which had brought to an end the Crimean War. The United States, with its second- or third-rate navy, had declined to sign the annex that abolished guerre de course.

Back in China, the suspect vessel *Neva* turned out to be legitimate. USS *Saginaw* had caught up to *Neva* just outside Shanghai, beating out the Wusong River and showing no colors. *Saginaw* brought the topsail schooner to with a warning shot across the bow, immediately upon which the American flag appeared at her peak. Officers boarded and examined the ship's papers, but *Neva* had been properly cleared for passage to Kanagawa and then San Francisco. The rumors, it was found, had centered on the owner of the vessel, a man named Judge Cleary, the former naval stores keeper at Shanghai. Cleary's Confederate sympathies and boastful nature had excited suspicion that had caught on like wildfire among the local merchants.[60]

With Flag Officer Engle's departure on *Hartford*, Commander Schenck became the senior naval officer on the station, and as such assumed responsibility for upholding a broad range of naval duties. In September 1861, *Saginaw* returned to Japan, showing the flag and meeting with the

American consul and Japanese officials at Nagasaki. By midmonth, the ship was steaming through the inland sea again, and despite charges against Commander Schenck regarding his behavior in Japan during his last visit, which were technically still pending, *Saginaw* came to anchor off Yokohama once again, and the crew were employed in "breaking out the spirit room." By October, the ship was once more at the harbor of Kanagawa, officers paying visits to the consul there and to the American minister still not officially in residence at Yedo. The presence of an American ship of war, "even though insignificant," appeared to give a certain amount of confidence to U.S. citizens residing abroad.[61]

The return to China was sobering. Rebel movements in Zhejiang Province to the south of the Yangzi delta had forced the British to issue warnings to the Taiping army not to come close to Ningpo, the major treaty port there. Taking on naval stores at Shanghai, *Saginaw* arrived at Ningpo on October 24, anticipating a general attack. Once again, foreign residents were for the moment more alarmed than actually threatened, and *Saginaw* returned to the British colony of Hong Kong by the end of November. In December, the Taiping would capture Ningpo and hold the town for six months, this time boldly plundering the foreign dwellings.

To a certain extent, American residents in China, merchants and missionaries, had been able to rely on protection if needed from the British forces, for in the famous words of Josiah Tattnall: "Blood is thicker than water.... I will not stand by and watch white men murdered." Flag Officer Tattnall had actually acted in violation of the carefully crafted American position of neutrality when he took his ships into the fight at the Taku Forts to rescue British gunboats that had come under devastating fire during the Second Opium War. However, the American Civil War and an incident in the Atlantic would challenge this inherent support in China. On November 8, an armed party from USS *San Jacinto* (Captain Charles Wilkes) had boarded an Atlantic steamer and removed two Confederate commissioners, James Mason and John Slidell, against her captain's protests. The ship was the British steamer *Trent*. The commissioners were en route from Havana to Paris on a third country-neutral ship. USS *San Jacinto* landed its prisoners at Boston to Union acclaim, some much-needed good news amidst a string of initial defeats. The British, on the other hand, were outraged by what they saw as a national insult and violation of international maritime law. Plans were quickly made for convoying fifty thousand British troops to Canada, which had meanwhile doubled their own armed militia to one hundred thousand men. France (initially) agreed to side with the British in the event of a new war against the Americans. Fortunately, President Lincoln and Secretary of State Seward managed to defuse the *Trent* incident by releasing the commissioners. For the moment, USS *Saginaw*, the lone American naval vessel in China, swung at anchor in Hong Kong surrounded by merchantmen and ships of the British navy, unaware of the recent turn of events. News of the *Trent* affair would reach China in January, and then feelings toward the Yanks would really change.

It is hard to imagine just what *Saginaw* alone could really accomplish in Ningpo in the face of the city's occupation by rebel forces had she even been in shape to continue operating on the coast. Still stuck in China during the last months of 1861, Schenck and his officers grew increasingly frustrated with their situation. The Department of the Navy had not issued the hoped-for orders to return home. They had to get off that ship. Claiming that *Saginaw* was completely inoperable was perhaps their effort of last recourse. On December 13, *Saginaw*'s commander wrote Gideon Welles:

> Having discovered that she had lost some sheets of copper and required caulking badly, on the 2nd instant I took her to Whampoa and put her in dock. While repairing the copper and caulking the outside seams, it was discovered that the timbers were rotten. I extended my examination until I became satisfied that the ship was in a dreadfully unsound state, then suspended all work upon her, got her out of dock, where she had only been twenty four hours, returned to this place and ordered a survey upon her. . . . So far as my own opinion goes, I feel it safe to say I have never seen any vessel in so bad a condition. She has evidently been held together by her planking decking only, and even these, where they have been brought in contact with the laurel, are a good deal decayed. In my late cruise to Japan I escaped three violent Typhoons by prudently skipping in and out of port, avoiding them, and had we encountered either of them, the ship must have inevitably foundered. Had the original order to send her to the U.S. been carried out, it is my firm belief that she would never have reached there. . . . I deem it my duty to lay up the vessel.[62]

Schenck was well aware that he was proposing to disobey direct orders to remain on the China Station, and included in his letter the signatures of local witnesses who backed up his estimate. The American merchants in Hong Kong were glad to provide evidence that would keep any naval ship or officer in China. On December 31, following this bold assessment and not waiting for a reply, Schenck informed the secretary of the navy that he was proceeding to San Francisco with seven officers and forty-two crewmen on board the American ship *Swordfish*. For protection during the passage, they shipped one of *Saginaw*'s 24-pounder boat howitzers, 12 rifled muskets, 11 Colt navy revolvers, and assorted shot and ammunition. All other naval property was to be left on board *Saginaw*, in the charge of Lieutenant Charles J. McDougal, who was also given authority to employ a skeleton crew of local Chinese laborers. With McDougal on station were Third Assistant Engineer T. H. Bordley, one quartermaster, two seamen, one fireman, one officer's cook, and one officer's steward. The skeleton crew was to simply remain in Hong Kong pending any further orders, holding on to the three thousand dollars issued McDougal by the paymaster. USS *Saginaw* was decommissioned in Hong Kong on January 3, 1862, reportedly entirely rotten and condemned as unseaworthy. The *New York Times* carried a report on the affairs at Hong Kong to the American public:

> The exposed position of our commerce can be understood from the fact that not a single United States vessel-of-war is east of the Cape of Good Hope and nearer to us than the coast of California. The gunboat Saginaw cannot be counted, as she lays dismantled and utterly rotten off the office of the United States Naval Store Keeper in this harbor, awaiting her doom of condemnation. . . . Our noble fleet of merchant vessels is thus left utterly unprotected.[63]

The situation abroad had not gone unnoticed in Virginia, where the Confederate Secretary of the Navy, Stephen R. Mallory, wrote to James D. Bulloch, the South's chief foreign agent in England: "The enemy's force in the China Seas is very small, the little steamer *Saginaw*, of 400 tons, being the only ship, as I learn, left there . . . you will regard yourself as invested with the largest discretion as to your cruising."[64] Bulloch, however, felt the time was not yet ripe, and replied: "I see but little for a cruising ship to do at this time. There are no Federal ships abroad except those now watching the Sumter, who keep well together, and the little *Saginaw*, far away in the East Indies. The feeling everywhere in Europe is strongly against the simple destruction of private property at sea, which can not always be identified as that of your enemy."[65] His hesitation would soon change.

To the sudden surprise of the Mare Island commandant, William H. Gardner, Schenck and his crew arrived at the naval yard on February 12.

The sailors slung their hammocks at last in their old station ship USS *Independence* after an absence of almost two years. They were home again among the coastal hills and familiar towns of San Francisco Bay. Foggy, temperate mornings swept over them, offering a cool sense of relief that the typhoons, pirates, and cholera had been left far behind. No more monsoon rains, no more uncharted lee shores, no more merchants demanding *Saginaw* be in three places at once. Above all, the sheer weight of the oppressive situation in China—the hostile rebels and devastated countryside and never-ending throngs of starving refugees—began to fade into memory.

With some trepidation, Schenck immediately telegrammed the Navy Department, "Officers and crew of *Saginaw* have arrived for orders." Gideon Welles in Washington, D.C., immediately sent back: "Where is the *Saginaw*? Your telegram is not intelligible."[66] Schenck sent a brief preview of his letter from Hong Kong, the original was still in transit to the secretary of the navy, but he must have felt apprehension at the writing on the wall. Welles instructed the commandant to discharge those of the *Saginaw*'s crew whose times were expired, and to transfer the remainder to various other ships and locations in the Pacific Squadron as needed. Manning the expanding Union navy had quickly become an immense challenge. The officers were ordered to report to New York.[67] Welles waited, however, a cool six weeks before admonishing the captain.

> Sir, Your letter of December 31st and its enclosure have been fully considered, but in the opinion of the Department furnish no excuse for your conduct in abandoning the Saginaw without waiting for the necessary instructions and authority. The Department has accepted a proposition tendered by Captain J. L. Watkins of the Pacific Mail Steamship Company to bring the Saginaw from China to San Francisco at a moderate expense, and he has proceeded to Hong Kong for that purpose.[68]

Apparently the navy had not accepted the claim of *Saginaw*'s poor condition as being sufficient cause for abandoning her overseas, and felt the ship could be brought back with little difficulty. The Department ordered the commander to appear before a special board assembled by the secretary of the navy. Schenck was both bold and defensive about his dressing down: "I must confess I am greatly surprised at the tone of your communication. Instead of censure I expected commendation for my prompt action in this matter. . . . I will obey the summons and trust the board will afford me an opportunity of proving the propriety and rectitude of my conduct."[69]

Ultimately, only the wartime needs of the Union would prove to be James Findlay Schenck's saving grace. He languished for a short time, but by the end of April 1862, he was ordered from his home to Hampton Roads, Virginia, to take command of USS *St. Lawrence*, an aged naval supply ship. At least that was preferable to waiting for orders in Dayton, Ohio.

James Schenck did, of course, move beyond this minor censure following his service in China. After USS *St. Lawrence*, the old sailor took command of USS *Powhatan* as commodore on his flagship in the West Gulf blockading squadron. In July 1863, Schenck directed the third division of Admiral Porter's squadron in both attacks on Fort Fisher. His last command was the naval station at Mound City, Illinois. By the end of his career, he achieved the rank of rear admiral. Schenck died in Dayton, Ohio, on December 21, 1882. The destroyer DD-159 would later be named in his honor.

The citizens of San Francisco were not surprised by news that a senior captain of the Pacific Mail Steamship Company, Captain J. L. Watkins, was being sent to retrieve *Saginaw*, for they had their own ideas as to why she hadn't made the passage home yet. Rumor traveled fast in the maritime community: "Secretary Welles has sent a dispatch to Commodore Watkins of this city, authorizing him to proceed to Hong Kong. . . . The probable reason for this is that the condemnation is believed not to have been made in good faith, which theory is strengthened by the fact that some of the officers lately on board the *Saginaw* have been furnished with lodgings at Alcatraz Island, on account of refusing to take the oath of allegiance."[70]

In Hong Kong, Lieutenant McDougal had been idle for months. News of the *Trent* affair had reached East Asia, and former goodwill amongst the British community had vanished. If England had decided to come out officially on the side of the Confederacy, all U.S. personnel and property in China would have been immediately seized, but no such official position had been stated. However, on April 5, the harbormaster at Hong Kong paid a call to McDougal with an official proclamation from the British governor of the colony, instructing him to remove USS *Saginaw* from the harbor. This was a definite break with precedent and protocol. Regarding *Saginaw*, observers later wrote, "No one of her officers will forget to his dying day the savage manner in which the rules forbidding her hospitality were enforced."[71] The British took unfortunate delight in the dismal fortunes of the Union. McDougal had little choice: "There being no other course for me to pursue than that of complying with the requirements made, on the 10th instant I got underway and steamed over to this place [Macao]."[72]

This minor incident involving the last U.S. naval vessel stationed abroad touched off a diplomatic scuffle between Lincoln's irascible Secretary of State William Seward and the secretary's British counterparts. Seward chided the British in regard to their tacit support of the South and their concession of belligerent naval rights to "a seditious party in the United States which has never had control of a single port or harbor in its own country." He questioned the desire of the British government to allow "occasional irritations to ripen into fruits of animosity between them."[73] The Admiralty's Lord Russell defended the expulsion of *Saginaw* from Hong Kong. While the CSS *Sumter* had been allowed to stay at Gibraltar, the vessel had already been in port when belligerent rights were awarded. *Saginaw*, however, came into Hong Kong after the decision had been made. This excuse, though, did not sit well with the Yanks. Seward was surprised at the hesitation by the British: "The Chinese are engaged in civil war, which threatens the safety of not only all western commerce but of the foreign residents, of whatever country, in China. Practically, and by force of circumstances, we are allied with the British in protecting that commerce. . . . The exclusion of our vessels, therefore, seems unnecessary upon any ground."[74] McDougal's treatment in Hong Kong furnished diplomatic fodder for Seward's tireless efforts, but ultimately could not help the small gunboat. The United States had no naval yard in China.

Captain James L. Watkins departed San Francisco on March 7 on board the ship *Florence*. Once in China, he found the navy steamer at Macao, but was the ship completely rotten and unseaworthy? Upon his arrival, Watkins and Engineer Winship made an inspection of the vessel's frames and planking, and while Watkins did find some wood to be rotten abaft her mainmast (indeed, many of the upper frames or futtocks were completely gone), there was "sufficient sound wood to enable me to put her in condition for the safe performance of the voyage to San Francisco, and at a very small expense, for her repairs of every nature are less than $500. Most of the timber that is rotten is the laurel, but there is a great deal of it perfectly sound, and I am confident if the wood is cut with proper care, say between the months of November and March, and docked, that it will prove to be as fine ship timber as any in the United States."[75] *Saginaw*'s timbers had been cut at the wrong time of the year, and only a portion of them properly seasoned or aged.

Watkins, known to many simply as "the Commodore," was a senior captain of the Pacific Mail Steamship line, and something of a seasoned and aged legend himself. He was what people called a "rare old sea dog," so popular with steamship passengers that it was considered a special privilege to make a voyage with him, and businessmen would arrange their affairs in order to go on board vessels under his command.[76] For years he had plied the waters between San Francisco and Panama. He had first distinguished himself in China back in 1849, when he was the commander of USS *Antelope*. While cruising in search of the missing vessel *Coquette* (on board the borrowed Pacific steamship *Canton*), he crossed paths with a fleet of Chinese pirate junks. Taking the British brig HMS *Columbine* under tow, they proceeded to either kill or take prisoner 1,800 pirates (so the story goes). Watkins himself volunteered for the heated boat action, on hand at the capture of the largest of the pirate junks, when several of *Columbine*'s men were killed and more wounded in its explosion. Commander Hays could not say too much "in praise of Capt. Watkins's liberality in lending us the *Canton*, and of his conspicuous gallantry throughout."[77] It was said that the commodore personally dispatched a dozen pirates, hauling one by the "tail" (queue or braid) into captivity. His reputation for seamanship, bravery, and valor was well known.

Commodore Watkins, Lieutenant McDougal, and the small crew arrived with the side-wheel steamer at San Francisco on July 4, 1862, after a rough but uneventful passage of fifty-three days. The ship's time on the China Station was over. The local Californians recalled what some had thought initially of the vessel's construction, but had to take the proof of the recent successful passage (of a reportedly "unseaworthy" ship) as a better sign: "The Government finally concluded that the *Saginaw* was not entirely the worm-eaten, worthless thing these officers would have it believe, although, the public impression always was that the green timber of which she was constructed would not last many years. . . . [O]ur little California Government steamer must be quite a staunch vessel yet, to weather such storms."[78]

Gideon Welles expressed his appreciation to the commodore: "Your prompt offer to bring the *Saginaw* to San Francisco after she had been surveyed, pronounced unseaworthy and left on a foreign shore by her commander, is not less admired than the able and successful manner in which you have executed the task under hazardous and trying circumstances."[79] Commander Schenck was lucky that, when he and several of his other officers departed on the PMSS steamer *Golden Age* from San Francisco for

Panama, and then to the east coast, Commodore Watkins (prior captain of *Golden Age*) had by then turned the helm of the steamer over to Captain F. R. Baby.

Recovering *Saginaw* was yet another feather in Watkins's cap. Unfortunately, the commodore died suddenly only a few years later while on board the company steamer *Costa Rica* at Nagasaki, after a fall through an open cargo hatch of the main saloon on board. At first the accident did not seem serious, but convulsions and unconsciousness quickly followed, indicating apoplexy, a stroke. "No one can describe the deep melancholy which settled over the ship when this fact became known. All sound of mirth was hushed, and the passengers gathered in knots about the deck, their voices subdued with sad emotion."[80] On January 23, Commodore John R. Goldsborough assembled all of the American officers and visitors then at Yokohama and presided over the memorial service.

On the Edge of an Empire

The ship's tour of duty in China and East Asia was a surprisingly difficult and chaotic experience. There had been much sickness on board and a significant number of deaths. Seasoning had taken its painful toll. *Saginaw* was a small steamer in a small squadron on the edge of a giant and ancient empire, and that empire was in the process of falling apart. The Manchu officials of the Qing government were to be the last ruling dynasty of China's long history. And for the entire nineteenth century, the country was wracked by foreign economic and military pressure, internal warlords, rebels, natural disasters, and famine. The Chinese empire faced a maritime crisis. It had never been truly threatened from the sea before. For the imperial bureaucrats in Beijing, the South China coast was a distant region, beyond steep mountain ranges. Pirates and uprisings, and even the unwholesome contacts with overseas merchants and "foreign devils" were matters usually handled at the provincial level. But the sea was a highway that had brought the powerful ships of the new foreign devils to the China coast. The successful naval campaign of French and British warships cutting off the flow of food to the northern capital had turned the empire upside down.

During this time, the Western powers had begun to carve areas of treaty ports and hinterlands into spheres of foreign influence. The social and psychological consequences of this, along with the disruption of war and economic failure, are today quite difficult to imagine. Those were the conditions the crew and officers of *Saginaw* witnessed during their service. This was a formative stage in the United States' long and at times ambivalent relationship with China, one in which America rode the coattails of other nations that, at that time, were much more invested in the China effort than the United States.

During *Saginaw*'s service in China, the United States was careful to maintain what was usually called balanced neutrality. Squadron commanders used the display of force to protect American citizens, but did not (very often, anyway) speak out loud about taking sides in the war or rebellion. Americans might not have been the direct cause of social problems in China, but neither were they completely innocent. Through it all, the United States, while never technically at war, sought commercial gain by benefiting from British and French intervention. The treaties negotiated at the end of their cannon applied to the United States and other foreign noncombatants. The ports they forced open were available to American merchants as well. Is it really accurate to call that a carefully balanced neutrality? Measuring status on the world stage simply by whether the nation actively engaged or not in a war ignores the reality of the consequences of social and economic disruption brought about by its larger influence.

One aspect that must have mystified the Chinese, Manchu, and Taiping alike, was the clear commercial interest of the U.S. Navy. Trade was the reason Americans were in China, to the exclusion of almost all else. USS *Saginaw* sailed in the service of U.S. commercial interests, protecting American lives (merchants) and property (trade goods) abroad. That the United States did not have larger political or military objectives in China is supported by the willingness to enter into agreements with rebels, and also by the very small size of the East India Squadron. But in East Asia, the social disparity between the Confucian bureaucrats and the merchants, considered socially beneath even the class of farmers, was enormous. Chinese generals did not make agreements to protect Chinese businessmen.

Given U.S. neutrality and the commercial focus, and the enormous scope of events and disruption in China, USS *Saginaw* did her best to fulfill those tasks assigned to her. *Saginaw* successfully represented the United States and flew the flag to the farthest reaches into the interior to date, as well as making her presence known actively along the coast. As for actually projecting power and effectively protecting citizens and property, *Saginaw* played more of a peripheral and symbolic role. Even the limited riverine and coastal patrol against an irregular piratical force was too much to expect for any single vessel. This was not due to any flaw on *Saginaw*'s part. Piracy was a far larger challenge than can be handled by any small colonial patrol force, and China was a far larger empire than any colony overseas. The scant naval resources of the United States were stretched thin, and just enough had been committed to China in order to play the role of a full treaty power in all good conscience, but not much more than that. Flag Officer Stribling knew this when he pleaded for a minimum of six vessels and received only three. Commander Schenck knew this when he complained of the inappropriately small and insignificant nature of his command. Juxtaposing the importance of the China trade and the size of the East India Squadron, the U.S. Navy was simply overextended, involved in a region where events played out beyond its grasp, ending up too reliant on the broader coalition of Western powers in a distant land.

Few men-of-war from the United States visited China during the dark days of the American internal crisis. Another squadron, this time renamed the Asiatic Squadron, did not arrive in China until 1866, when the threat from the Taipings had been quelled, and the American commissioner could finally reside in Beijing.

3

The Civil War on the Pacific Coast

Shenandoah making depredations in the Pacific. Department
relies upon you to effect her capture. . . . Being an erratic ship,
without a country or destination, no definite instructions can
be given you.

Gideon Welles to Pacific Squadron, 1865

By any measure, the Civil War had an immense and devastating impact
on the United States. The issues of slavery and emancipation, the right
of secession and the nature of the union, and the violence and horren-
dous loss of life and destruction of property combined to literally tear
the country apart. Major actions were generally limited to battlefields on
land. At sea more than anywhere else, the two sides of the North and the
South were simply so unmatched as to never meet in any sort of decisive
engagement. The North began the war with approximately ninety vessels
outfitted to go to sea. By the war's end, Union naval forces had grown to
over 650 ships. The South started the war with ten ships, the core of the
Confederate Navy.

The Union's aptly named Anaconda Plan featured a naval blockade of
more than 3,000 miles of coastline along the Atlantic and the Gulf of Mexico, denying the Confederacy trade, military supplies, and access to the
sea. Like the Mexican-American War in 1846–48, which had served as a
training experience for many of the officers of the U.S. Navy, the maritime
Civil War featured blockade and shallow water environments. Offensive
operations on the Mississippi River completed the encirclement of the
war's western theater. Blockade, a well-established tactic recognized and
condoned by international agreement, was essentially a passive affair, involving weeks and months and sometimes years of painfully mundane
duty on board ships, inspecting merchantmen and battling weather and
tedium more often than the enemy.

The fact that the blockade was successful but not completely impermeable is not a contradiction, but a characteristic of all naval blockades. Some ships get through. Vessels from other countries such as England were purchased by the Confederacy and outfitted as blockade runners and also as commissioned raiders on the high seas. Fast steamships ran the gauntlet under the cover of darkness and through the close line of Union vessels stationed off the ports of the South, desperately trading cotton and tobacco for much-needed war supplies at third-country ports like Bermuda (British) and Havana (Spanish). And the South purchased foreign-built ships for operations abroad. For these fourteen Confederate vessels, the world was their theater as they sought to damage the commerce of the North. Sleek raiders like the CSS *Alabama*, the CSS *Florida*, and the CSS *Shenandoah* sought their commercial prey in places as distant as the South Atlantic, northern European waters, and the far Pacific.

The Mexican-American War may have served as a training ground for naval operations during America's internal conflict, but another nineteenth-century event, the Crimean War in 1854–56, more directly set the stage for technological innovations in ordnance and armor, initiating radical changes in war at sea. The Crimean War was fought between Russia and the one-time alliance of Great Britain, France, the Kingdom of Sardinia, and the Ottoman Empire, basically over an issue of religious and national authority in the Holy Land of Jerusalem, though operations were centered on the Sevastopol Peninsula on the Crimean Sea. The combination of armored ships and platforms, powerful cannon firing exploding shells instead of just solid shot, and steam propulsion were of critical note to observers, combatants and noncombatants alike. The naval battlefield provided a testing ground for armor, ordnance, and marine steam technologies. These tools were changing the nature of naval engagements, and that is the reason that even relatively minor encounters during the American Civil War can be seen as pivotal, despite the fact that there were relatively few major engagements during the essentially static coastal blockade campaign.

Most of the important naval events during the Civil War, like Hampton Roads and the Battle of Mobile Bay, were not Pacific events. The majority of the Union's naval efforts during the Civil War were naturally focused on the Atlantic and Gulf states, leaving the Pacific as, frankly, something of a backwater. But there were some real threats in the Pacific, greatly exacerbated by the reality of an unmanageably large area assigned to the responsibility of an exceedingly small squadron. A series of coastal forts had been constructed for the protection of entrances to critical ports in California, such as Drum Barracks at San Pedro Bay (Los Angeles), and Fort Point, Fort Baker, Fort McDowell, and Fort Alcatraz (San Francisco). But the Pacific Squadron was obligated to protect much more than just the Californian coastline. The issue was not blockade as with the Anaconda Plan, but the continuing protection of commerce, and the important lines of maritime communication stretching from San Francisco to the Isthmus of Panama. The gold shipments flowing from the foothills of the Sierra Nevada to San Francisco, and from there onto steamers and south to Panama, played an important role in stabilizing the economy of the North. The perceived threat lay in the potential for Confederate raiders and privateers being secretly prepared along more than 6,500 miles of coastline, bringing the guerre de course, or war on commerce, to the Pacific. The Civil War story of USS *Saginaw* is a window into just how pervasive wartime activity was on the national and even global stage.

While *Saginaw* was still on the China Station, the outbreak of war had sent the eastern Pacific into alert status. Navy vessels stepped up their visits, focusing on strategic ports such as Victoria, San Francisco, San Diego, Honolulu, Valparaiso, Callao, and Panama, stretched thin but covering an astoundingly large area of more than 8 million square miles of ocean. Forces in the Pacific had yet to be divided into separate northern and southern elements, so Rear Admiral Charles Bell, upon relieving Commodore John B. Montgomery as commander of the Pacific Squadron, was then responsible for the entire region. Bell, sixty-four years old, had entered the U.S. Navy in New York, and had served in Commodore Chauncey's squadron on Lake Erie during the War of 1812. He later served with Commodore Decatur on USS *Macedonian* in the war with Algiers. Most notably, though, when in command of the sloop-of-war USS *Yorktown*, Bell had captured two slavers off the coast of Africa in 1846, the *Pons* and the *Panther*. They arrived as prizes at Charleston, and Commander Bell's report furnished one of "the most shocking cases of outraged humanity which has ever appeared."[1] The American bark *Pons* of Philadelphia (with a mixed crew of Spanish, Portuguese, and Brazilians) had on board 896 African slaves at the time of her capture. Conditions were deplorable, and the stench was unbearable. There were no berth decks below, and 850 male captives were trapped beneath locked hatches piled on one another like bulk cargo. Forty or fifty female captives were locked in a roundhouse on deck, apart from the males and closer to the ship's officers.[2] Bell showed the nation an image of itself in 1846, of the Middle Passage, and the nation did not like what it saw. Fifteen years later, Rear Admiral Bell was sent from the Mediterranean to the Pacific Squadron following the *Trent* affair in November 1861, in anticipation of armed hostilities with the British.

Panama was a critical link in communication, but Bell's Pacific forces had been stripped by the needs of the eastern naval blockade, and consisted at the time of only six sloops-of-war: USS *Lancaster, Saranac, Wyoming, Narragansett, St. Mary's* and *Cyane*. Rumors were already in the air concerning bands of rebel traitors. In December, reports were forwarded regarding "movement thought to be on foot, by parties interested in the rebel cause, to fit a privateer in some port on the Pacific Coast to prey upon our commerce upon that ocean."[3] A few months later, rebel spies were reported at Valparaiso on the South American coast, commissioned agents intent on fitting out to "plunder, burn, and destroy as many as they could upon the coast . . . until the pursuit became too hot for them, run their vessel on shore and escape . . . there to enjoy the satisfaction derived from the discharge of . . . the policies of the leaders of this unholy rebellion."[4] The Pacific Mail Steamship Company (PMSS), from their headquarters at Benicia (nearby sister city to Mare Island's Vallejo), requested and received naval cannon to mount on board their commercial steamers. In some ways, the obstacles faced in the West directly mirrored those in China—too many harbors and bays, not enough ships and sailors. *Saginaw*'s former crew, assigned to other ships and quickly scattered, provided a brief but needed surplus of men. By necessity, the squadron's ships operated as individual units, unable to function as a combined force, and only rarely crossed paths with each other.

Mare Island had continued to evolve and support the Pacific fleet despite losing men and materials to the east. Captain William H. Gardner had replaced Cunningham as the yard's commandant. And the outbreak of the Civil War had brought its own troubles to the North Bay area, as questions of divided loyalty struck yard workers and townsmen alike. Complaints had been lodged, the word finally reaching the Department of the Navy, about employees at the yard who were "disloyal in sentiment." Secretary Welles pointed out to Gardner himself that "there are representations that some allied to you, and associated with you, are unfaithful to the Union."[5] This was a reflection of certain rebel sympathies among the civilian residents of Sonoma County and other areas in the vicinity of San Francisco. Was the commandant himself doing enough about the problem? Gardner was soon replaced at Mare Island by Captain Thomas O. Selfridge Sr., who had been badly wounded in the capture of Guaymas during the Mexican-

American War in 1847. Some Yankees moved in, and other Confederates moved out. Colonel Albert Sidney Johnston from Kentucky, commander of the U.S. Army's Department of the Pacific headquartered in Benicia, resigned his commission three days prior to the start of the Civil War. After refusing an ardent invitation to join southern sympathizers in Oregon and California and form a rebel Pacific Republic, Johnston left for the East. One of the Confederacy's great generals, he was killed at the Battle of Shiloh a year later. California may have been a Yankee state in name, but the region had a large number of residents and farmers originally from the Southeast, many of whom were sympathetic to the Confederate cause.

USS *Saginaw*, after hard service in East Asia, was at first in no shape to be a part of any of this. Her officers and crew dispersed, she was due for intensive repairs in the yard, out of the water, and in the floating dry dock. The ship's rig was overhauled (changing from a brig to a topsail schooner), all damaged frames and deck beams and hull planks replaced (avoiding the use of local laurel wood?), boilers scaled and brass tubes replaced, copper sheathing repaired, and hundreds of other items attended to that had been worn and broken from months of use and abuse in China. At this time, the layout of the ship's guns was enhanced by replacing the 32-pounder pivot gun on the foredeck with a 50-pounder Dahlgren rifle pivot gun, and moving the 32-pounder aft. *Saginaw* was five months in repair, not ready for relaunching until December 3, 1862. Once back in the water, *Saginaw* stood guard duty at San Francisco, with springs on her cables and prepared for action, while earthworks were built at Yerba Buena Island and batteries of cannon moved to Rincon Point to further defend against privateers and raiders that might slip into the bay under cover of darkness and fog, beyond the range of the guns of Fort Alcatraz.[6] Engineers continued work on "The Rock," though, and by 1864, Alcatraz possessed more than one hundred pieces of heavy artillery.

Later in December, Rear Admiral Bell recommended to Secretary Welles that Paul Shirley, then executive officer of the aging ship USS *St. Mary's*, be appointed the next commander of *Saginaw*. Welles, however, had already ordered Lieutenant William Evelyn Hopkins to Mare Island via the New York steamer to Aspinwall. Hopkins, loyal to the Union though born a Virginian, had been appointed midshipman in the navy in 1839, and had served on board the sloop USS *Potomac*, *Vandalia*, frigate *Cumberland*, and schooner *Falcon* while attached to the Home Squadron. In the 1850s, Hopkins was off the coast of Africa on the sloop *Marion* engaged in antislavery patrol, and just prior to his Pacific Squadron assignment he served as lieutenant in the Mediterranean on USS *Macedonian* and USS *Preble*. William Hopkins was promoted to lieutenant commander on July 16, 1862, a strict no-nonsense leader and well-known as a disciplinarian.[7] USS *Saginaw*'s new commander had more than twenty years of sea duty. He would prove to be a hard and bitter taskmaster on board the ship.

While many locations within the thousands of miles from Vancouver to Valparaiso had the potential of hosting rebel activities, the navy had three very good reasons to focus patrol efforts on Mexico and Central America. First of all, steamers passing between San Francisco and Panama carried not just the mineral wealth of California's gold country, but all the mails and communications between the east and west coasts. This line of communication connected Washington, D.C., with an entire Pacific hemisphere, and these ships touched by necessity at a series of regular Pacific ports such as Santa Barbara, San Pedro, San Diego, La Paz, Mazatlan, Manzanillo, Guaymas, and Acapulco. This line had to be protected. Welles's instructions earlier to Flag Officer John B. Montgomery were specific:

> Apprehensions having been expressed that attempts may be made by privateers or lawless persons to seize one of the Calif. steamers, your particular attention will be directed to that subject. The ports of San Francisco, Acapulco, and Panama, are points of special danger, and you will, in this crisis, concentrate your force on the route from Panama to San Francisco, unless there should be a demand for you in other quarters, of which the Department is not advised. You must exercise your judgment in discharging the responsible duties that devolve upon you.[8]

Secondly, whether as filibusters or "adventurers" engaging in private military action; as diplomatic agents seeking recognition of the Confederacy on the international scene; or as commissioned officers taking the war to the Yankees via third-country locations, there were an unknown but potentially large number of active southern sympathizers in Mexico. And finally, unrest in both Mexico and in America opened the door of opportunity for the overseas imperial ambitions of France's Emperor Napoleon III. During the American Civil War, when any real enforcement of the Monroe Doctrine—which declared protection for North and South America from European colonization and interference—was out of the question, France attempted to establish and support a monarchy in Mexico, led by an archduke of the royal house of Austria, Maximilian I. For Napoleon, the Monroe Doctrine was nothing more than a double standard that allowed the United States to monopolize the conquest of its neighbor to the south, while all others were prohibited from any benefit or territorial gain. And the French were already interested in the strategic potential of a sea-level canal at the Isthmus of Panama. Ultimately, though, De Lesseps's early attempt at a canal proved too costly in terms of both money and lives, and would fail. It would fall to the Americans to complete the project in 1903, benefiting sea-borne commerce and providing an endless source of revenue.

The French intervention during America's Civil War would not have been possible had Mexico not been already disrupted by internal strife. The country, a vast and underdeveloped land rich with mineral wealth and other natural resources, had been left demoralized and in shambles following the Mexican-American War and the loss of 50 percent of the national territory—all of its northern holdings—to the United States. Roving bandits, rebellious uprisings, and a war with Mayan Indians on the Yucatan Peninsula hampered efforts to strengthen the nation by the elected republican government. However, there was hope. President Benito Juarez's administration was a progressive and liberal movement, challenging the entrenched power of the Catholic Church and distributing confiscated properties to the lower classes, a true step forward. The years between 1858 and 1861 in Mexico are known as the War of the Reform period. But once Juarez's government had successfully established itself in the capital city, it faced the immediate international crisis of foreign intervention by Europe. The United States sided with the Juarez government. Such support during the American Civil War was an attempt to prevent Confederate filibustering expeditions and to allay fears of a Confederate attack on Lower California and Sonora. Such things had been tried there in the past. But support of the Juarez government was mainly diplomatic and symbolic. The United States was in no position to render real assistance in any way, as long as its own internal war continued.

War with America and economic ruin had left Mexico in serious debt to Spain, Great Britain, and France. By December 1861, when it became clear that Mexico could not and would not continue payment on these debts, the three European powers landed troops at Veracruz and seized the customshouse and all trade revenue. Spain and Great Britain eventually withdrew, but France used the incident as a springboard for broader plans. Warships gathered at Veracruz, and generals massed expeditionary troops to begin the march to Mexico City. Years of warfare and occupation would ensue. Ultimately, the effort would fail. In May 1864, when Austrian Duke Maximilian I was assuming the throne in Mexico City, Napoleon III was already making plans for the removal of his French troops. France could only support the expense of the costly occupation for so long, and Maximilian would have to be able to stand on his own. But he would not be ready. The French-backed puppet regime had never been more than an occupation force, holding certain cities and supporting limited movements in the field, while ceding the northern and southern countryside to Juarez's Mexican army and his generals, who, despite their often nonstandard appearances, fought a capable and effective guerrilla war. Basically the French had failed to appreciate the magnitude of the task before them and the true nature of the war they had precipitated.[9] They were not welcomed as conquerors, but despised as hated occupiers, for identity runs deep, and Austrian mercenaries in Mexico were forever unwelcome. Maximilian was captured in the northern town of Queretaro in May 1867. President Juarez had no mercy for this European interloper, and he was summarily executed by firing squad.

But in 1863, the final demise of Maximilian was still in the future. During the American Civil War, the puppet emperor's reign; Austrian, Belgian and French troops; and the French Foreign Legion dominated events in Mexico. In the Pacific on January 10, 1863, as refit worked continued on USS *Saginaw* at Mare Island, a small squadron of French warships, two steamers and two sailing vessels, entered the bay at Acapulco and was fired upon by the fortifications ashore. The ships returned fire, silencing the forts and destroying buildings in the town, and landed shore parties to spike the guns. USS *Saranac* remained, silent and neutral, near the Pacific Mail Company depot, while shells exploded nearby. *Saranac*'s presence may have displayed symbolic opposition to the French squadron, but she was effectively impotent, protecting only the lives and property of U.S. citizens.[10] The French then moved north to Mazatlan to enlarge their blockade of the Pacific ports. While the Civil War raged, U.S. Secretary of State Seward could do little more than politely rattle the sword against French aggression in defense of Mexican sovereignty. America could not challenge the French in the Pacific. According to Seward: "[T]he policy of this government toward Mexico as hitherto made known by the president remains unchanged. It rests with France to decide whether this is satisfactory. If we have war with her, it must be a war of her own making either against our ships or upon our territory. We shall defend ourselves if assailed upon our own ground. We shall attack nobody elsewhere."[11]

The Uncivil Civil War Crew

On March 23, 1863, a fine, clear spring day, Commander Hopkins gathered *Saginaw's* officers (Executive Officer Charles Smith, Paymaster Pelham W. Ames, Surgeon Francis Greene, Ensigns Cornelius Bartlett and Joseph B. Switt, Engineer G. Charles Seymour, Master's Mate James H. Brockway, and others) and to the ceremonial signals and commands, recommissioned USS *Saginaw* into the Pacific Squadron.[12] Enlisted men from USS *Independence* and the converted storeship USS *Farallones* (former screw steamer USS *Massachusetts*) began moving their hammocks onto the paddle wheeler and provisioning the ship. To their great and everlasting dismay, this no longer included liquor for the crew. Grog, the traditional rum and water mix, had been a fixture of the British Royal Navy for hundreds of years. For American naval vessels, the rye whiskey mixture (sometimes called "Bob Smith" after Secretary of the Navy Robert Smith) had likewise been doled out twice daily, once at noon and once at the end of the day in the traditional half-pint servings. In July 1862, though, all squadron and yard commanders had received the general order from the Department of the Navy "promulgating the recent act of Congress abolishing the spirit ration and prohibiting the admission of distilled spirituous liquors on board of vessels of war from and after the 1st day of September next. You will be careful to have several copies of this order distributed to each vessel in your squadron." The war was on, and discipline among the thousands of green hands and landlubbers had to somehow be maintained. Sailors had a habit of saving their rations, and then consuming the quantity all at once, going on a spree until incapacitated. But the navy had begun to go dry. The spirit room on board *Saginaw* had vanished during the ship's refit. The additional five cents per day for each sailor in compensation for this lost piece of nautical tradition did little to fill the void. It should be noted, though, that the alcohol continued to flow in the officers' wardroom and the captain's mess; in 1862, only the enlisted men made the sacrifice.

Whereas officers in the U.S. Navy were all American citizens, the enlisted men for *Saginaw's* Pacific cruise were often quite varied in origin. Foreign enlistments filled out the forecastle berths of the Civil War navy, and officers frequently found it useful to give orders in several different languages to be understood at all. An officer candidate's ability to speak several different languages was critical to his promotion. Diversity, of course, proved to be a challenge to the command, and such conditions

continued after the war as well. In the view of maritime historian Robert
Erwin Johnston:

> Such men could not be expected to feel a strong attachment for the flag
> under which they served, and must have been a very uncertain factor
> in time of emergency. They were even more susceptible to desertion
> than were their predecessors, and rare indeed was the small boat which
> returned its full crew to a ship. Desertion became so prevalent in the
> Pacific Squadron that the Department ordered all warships to stay away
> from San Francisco unless it became absolutely necessary to touch there.
> This did not cure the evil, and desertion plagued the Pacific Squadron
> throughout the period of naval decline. When the conditions of service
> and the pay and food are considered, it is very difficult to condemn the
> enlisted men for seeking to better themselves by flight.[13]

Forming an effective and unified crew was a priority, and a challenge, for
every commander.

After months of drills and target practice, attempts to shape the new
crew and officers into a single working unit on board the tiny steamer,
Hopkins received orders from Commandant Selfridge to proceed to the
remote volcanic island of Guadalupe, 150 miles offshore of Lower California (Baja Mexico), where reports suggested that, amid the high and barren
cliffs, Confederate agents had deposited a stash of munitions for outfit-
ting privateers. Apparently, earlier in March, a plot had been hatching
in the San Francisco area. A letter of marque had been procured in Richmond, Virginia, from President Jefferson Davis. Alfred Rubery, a British
subject, had arranged the purchase of the small, swift, 90-ton schooner
J. M. Chapman, and guns and ammunition and uniforms had been purchased and packed in cases marked "oil," "merchandise," "machinery," and
"quick silver." Ostensibly the ship's cargo was destined to an American
mining enterprise operating out of Manzanillo. Captain William C. Law,
who had been quickly relieved of command of the ship Storm Cloud as its
owners felt he might be planning to steal the vessel, signed on a crew of
sixteen men, yet recorded only one captain, one mate, and four seamen
on the ship's documents. The others stowed away deep in the hold. Guadalupe would be their base of operations, a remote island where they could
land and transform the schooner into a privateer. Their ultimate plans
included capturing a Pacific Mail steamer, and also salvaging some of the
$1.4 million worth of gold that had sunk when the SS Golden Gate, one of

the fastest passenger steamers on the west coast, burned outside Manzanillo in 1862. From there they would continue on to the China Sea. Word had inadvertently gotten out about this project, however, when Captain Law carelessly bragged about the plot in a local tavern.[14] Officers from USS *Cyane* (Commander Paul Shirley) put the *Chapman* under surveillance. On March 15, when the schooner left the dock, two boatloads of armed seamen boarded *J. M. Chapman*, and the ship was captured without resistance.[15] The prisoners were interrogated at Fort Alcatraz.

As in China, these missions in foreign waters demanded caution. International law recognized the right of each state to intervene on behalf of its own citizens abroad and to take such measures as may be necessary to safeguard their rights while overseas, even to the extent of the use of force.[16] But did these rights extend to capturing one's own enemies, former citizens, within a third-party neutral country (Mexico), itself in the process of being invaded by a fourth party outside power (France)? Conditions on the ground proved more complicated than legal distinctions in documents. Selfridge ordered *Saginaw* to search for the *Chapman*'s potential base at Isla Guadalupe, and reminded Hopkins in purposefully vague terms, "if you find such a depot you will take such measures in the premises as circumstances will justify without an infringement of the neutrality law."[17] Before the invention of the wireless, the captain on the scene was the interpreter of the law. *Saginaw* was also instructed to touch at the ports of San Quentin and Cedros Island to see if privateers were fitting out, and to call at the Channel Islands off of Santa Barbara, California, for the same purposes. Before Hopkins could get his ship out to sea, though, rumors much closer to home, of hostile military actions in the San Francisco Bay area, cancelled his departure.

Suddenly a much more immediate threat was at hand. The sheriff of Napa County reported the existence of a rebel plot to attack Mare Island Naval Shipyard itself, and this information was corroborated by two other independent sources. Commandant Selfridge immediately disposed his forces for defense as best he could. Two seventy-man companies of volunteers from Vallejo, mainly naval yard employees, took up arms.[18] *Saginaw* was immediately recalled from San Francisco, where she had been swinging at anchor preparing for sea. Pausing only briefly to retrieve the deserter Richard Jones, who was chained in double irons, the ship weighed anchor at 1:30 p.m. and went to general quarters two hours later, firing off shot and shell from her cannon in case there were any questions that a warship was indeed on station at Mare Island. Small arms were passed out and port and starboard watches stood by their posts, leaning on their cannon, primed for action. That night, and the following several nights, though, saw no sign of the enemy.[19] Had the plot been foiled? Had a force really been assembled that could conceivably attack a guarded naval yard across an open and windswept peninsula?

The Mexico cruise remained postponed. Alarms continued to sound along the coast, this time farther north. Commandant Selfridge next received an urgent communication from the U.S. consul at Victoria, British Columbia. Reportedly, Confederate agents, supported by the British, had clear plans for fitting out a privateer. *Saginaw* was dispatched immediately to Port Angeles and Port Townsend in the Washington Territory (which did not become a state until 1889), and from there to Victoria on Vancouver Island in the British possessions, and to "such places in the vicinity as may be necessary for the purpose of obtaining information."[20] If the report proved true, Commander Hopkins was to take action to prevent the enemy's escape, or lure the privateer outside British waters, where the enemy could be legally captured. *Saginaw* topped off her coal bunkers, piled on additional bags of potatoes, and departed San Francisco on April 24, but not before placing the captain's cook, William Thatcher, and Seaman John Robinson in the brig shackled in double irons for desertion and drunkenness, again.

The truth behind the various reported threats along the coast is difficult to ascertain now, but the general alarm, even though possibly a symptom of some hysteria, was real. News of the schooner *J. M. Chapman*'s capture had spread like wildfire, and was a hot topic of fervent conversation among merchants and shipowners, in the bars and on the docks, up and down the coast. Consul Allen Francis in Victoria did confirm to Commander Hopkins, upon *Saginaw*'s arrival, that a verified attempt had been made to seize the U.S. revenue cutter *Shubrick*. Fortunately, the plot had failed due to a lack of strong leadership. Some of the parties involved in the plot had reportedly left the area for the gold mines of British Columbia, and also for San Francisco, but others remained. The British-registered steamer *Fusi Yama* was the subject of more recent rumors. The 700-ton steamer, a "fast sailer," reportedly carried a large quantity of munitions on board and was due in to Victoria harbor soon, no doubt for privateering purposes.[21] Francis did his best, given his limited abilities to do so, to keep certain parties under close watch, but more than that from the U.S. consul was impossible. The British authorities made no secret of their displeasure at the arrival of USS *Saginaw*, and were ready to warn the ship off as soon as the allotted twenty-four hours of port time expired. Commander Hopkins departed the British port without having to be escorted.

Saginaw arrived at Port Townsend on May 8 and proceeded to form boarding parties and examine the papers of steamers on Puget Sound. The mere presence of the ship was an important statement, and as Consul Francis put it, Hopkins's "visit to this city was truly gratifying to the loyal citizens of the United States residing here; particularly was this the case to those acquainted with the efforts made by the secessionists and Confederate sympathizers during the last few months."[22] For *Saginaw*'s crew, the visit simply meant the usual rounds of holystoning the decks, painting the ironwork, airing the hammocks, and bringing on board provisions, wood, water, and coal, but the scenery was beautiful with longer summer days on the sound. The bays and channels and islands, lined with verdant greenery, echoed as the crew practiced by division at small arms, and loaded shot and shell into the pivot guns and howitzers for firing at floating muslin targets, putting on an auditory display for the British. The American merchants could hear the sound of their nation's support, at least for the three weeks of *Saginaw*'s visit.

No foreign plots to launch and outfit privateers were discovered, but *Saginaw* was not without her own internal problems at the hands of her crew. The cruise to Puget Sound revealed a surprising amount of dissatisfaction on board and highlights the importance of discipline in President Lincoln's Civil War navy. *Saginaw* had a total of five smaller boats with which to conduct varied tasks away from the ship: a first cutter, second cutter, third cutter, captain's gig, and ship's dinghy. If sailors were planning on deserting, getting chosen for boat duty on any of these various shore chores was the first step. Desertion, the most common court-martial offense in the nineteenth century, had usually been awarded twenty-five lashes with the cat-of-nine-tails. But flogging had been banned in the U.S. Navy in 1850 as a cruel and inhumane punishment. Upon the ship's arrival in the area, three sailors, Brady, Price, and Johnson, deserted from the first cutter while sent to shore for wood. After coaling at Bellingham Bay, John Moran skipped out from the same boat. Seaman Richard Jones was caught before he could run, and placed in double irons for intending to desert. Meanwhile, William Thacker was shackled for disobedience, and Joseph Casey placed in double irons for mutinous language. The list goes on: Charles Chase and Henry Tencil deserted from the third cutter at night; William Nelson ran from the gig; Richard Jones, upon being released from double irons after two days confinement, deserted from the third cutter. John and Nash Sullivan ran from the dinghy while on shore.[23]

Sometimes the men returned more willingly than not; perhaps those who had simply seen an opportunity for a little extra liberty felt that the difference between confinement and normal duty on board a navy ship was not truly that great. Sometimes they were returned by force. Peter Shannon, John Price, and John Conroy were brought back by authorities in Washington Territory, bounty hunters in a sense, and placed on board in irons. Hopkins paid twenty dollars for Shannon and ten dollars for Price. One of the main functions of consuls overseas, besides collecting dues from shipping, returning the bodies of Americans who had died to their home country, and processing immigration forms, was to see to the quick return of sailors who ran from their ships in foreign port towns. Sometimes this was fairly easy, for some sailors simply ran to the nearest tavern. Others, though, had no intention of being caught. On Puget Sound, was it the proximity of southern sympathizers on British soil? Or the lure of the gold strikes on the Fraser Canyon? On May 25, prior to heading south, *Saginaw* received a much-needed replenishment of thirteen enlisted men from USS *Cyane*, recently arrived from the South. The following day the crew housed the guns, made all secure, weighed the anchor, and steamed down the sound for home, auctioning off the possessions of the deserters among themselves as they went. It had been a surprisingly difficult cruise, such a high number of desertions for so simple a mission.

Hopkins brought *Saginaw* across the Bay to Mare Island on June 1, a Sunday. Before coming to his mooring, he went to general quarters and read his crew the Articles of War, in case they had forgotten. His report to Commandant Selfridge concluded that there was no substantial evidence of any scheme to outfit a privateer that might still be in effect in the Puget Sound area. At the yard, *Saginaw*'s officers sought to substitute insubordinate crewmen with replacements from the yard's station ship, or from any other ship of the Pacific fleet then in port. This was not an easy task, given the problems of manning the Civil War navy. Ship's commanders were protective of their men, holding on to the good ones as long as they could.

Squadron commanders were also protective of their vessels, for both men and ships were in short supply. In May, Rear Admiral Bell, then on board his flagship USS *Lancaster* at Panama, petitioned to get *Saginaw* into the Pacific Squadron. *Saginaw* had been commissioned, but had been quickly sent on her mission to Washington Territory by order of Mare Island's Commandant Selfridge, and not by Bell, the commander of Pacific Forces. These things mattered. Bell's squadron of aging ships, constantly deployed to distant locations, was wearing thin. He wrote to Welles: "I was in hopes that the *Saginaw* would have been added to my squadron, as we require a vessel of that class to cruise between Panama and the southern coast of Mexico. There are a number of small harbors in Central America where a steam privateer could be prepared, make a dash at one of our mail and treasure ships, and, if successful, breakup our communications between San Francisco and Panama for weeks before I could hear of it."[24] The argument was unnecessary. The secretary of the navy had already written to Bell four days earlier that *Saginaw* was to be considered part of the Pacific Squadron. Letters crossed the oceans at the speed of steam. Though in agreement, each would remain ignorant of the other's intentions for weeks.

Meanwhile, at Mare Island, wood, provisions, and coal were being stowed on *Saginaw*. And whether it was the lure of the nearby city (the ship had been moved to the harbor at San Francisco to make room at Mare Island for USS *Farallones*), an unwillingness to sail with a certain commander, or a general cantankerous nature, the ship's crew continued to cause trouble. On June 24, the third cutter was sent ashore for *Saginaw*'s dinghy, which had gone missing. The boat was found deserted, and a shore party then sent into the city in search of the sailors. The next day, Quartermaster John Dehlefts and Captain of the Hold George E. Hopkins were brought on board in chains by city police. They joined Peter Ingraham, the wardroom boy confined for disrespect, and Walter Ennis, the ship's cook chained for mutinous language, in the ship's two tiny brigs. These consisted of two small dimly lit cells on the port and starboard side of the main deck, above the fore hold. A summary court-martial was held for Ennis, Hopkins, and Dehlefts. Ennis was sentenced to double irons, hands and feet shackled, for ten days and placed on bread and water, and no shore leave for four months. The other two were likewise deprived of liberty for four months. In the meantime, John Price was brought on board in chains, a third-time deserter. Next, three more sailors, Firemen Joseph Robinson and James Buhler and Seaman J. L. Bolden, escaped from the first cutter while ashore. They were brought back by a search party and placed in double irons for drunkenness.[25] And so it went.

This state of affairs was not atypical. The insolence, drunkenness, disobedience, mutinous language, desertion, neglect of duty, and scandalous or ungentlemanly conduct faced by Commander Hopkins represented behaviors all too familiar to the officers, particularly on poorly run ships. These violations resulted in punishments proscribed by the Articles of War, the disciplinary code better known to the sailors as the "Rocks and Shoals." The sailors knew they could expect confinement, shackles, and reduced rations—but they could not be flogged. Hopkins did have a number of alternative punitive methods from which to choose, though: branding, bucking and gagging, tricing sailors up into the rigging or to raised deck gratings by their wrists, lashing thumbs together behind their backs, sweatboxes, and the like.[26] In the Pacific Squadron, long confinement in irons, often with both hands and legs shackled and with only bread and water for rations, was common.

While convening a general court-martial required between five and thirteen officers, the captain's mast (or simply "mast") on board a ship was a more frequent proceeding. The mast was a nonjudicial disciplinary hearing applying to enlisted men. With the mast, the captain was the sole arbiter of justice with no chance for appeal. Evidence was heard, sentence passed, and punishment carried out immediately. If a commander was not careful, the social dynamic between the commissioned officers and the landsmen and rough sailors could quickly degenerate into a prisoner-versus-guard mentality. Often the only time when the ship was not at risk of losing sailors to desertion was at sea. During the Civil War, some ships from Mare Island preferred the anchorage near Fort Alcatraz when readying for sea, rather than mooring too near San Francisco itself.

La Union, Salvador

Saginaw, now as part of Rear Admiral Bell's squadron, had orders for Panama and departed on July 10. On the passage, Commander Hopkins had armed boat crews board and inspect all vessels encountered, constantly on the lookout for privateers in disguise among the small ports. At Acapulco, *Saginaw* crossed paths with USS *Narragansett*, monitoring the tensions between French and Mexican forces in the area. A court-martial convened while underway sentenced deserter John Price to thirty days in double irons, on bread and water, and loss of three months' pay (seamen made twenty dollars per month at the time). Commander Hopkins was required to give the prisoner one-half normal rations once a week. By August 26, Price had been released, but within a few days was once again in irons and confined for insolence and refusing duty.

That same day, *Saginaw* arrived at La Union, where troubles in the form of armed incursions had been brewing with neighboring Nicaragua. El Salvador, like other provinces in the region, had revolted against Spanish domination in 1821. For a brief period, Salvador had joined Guatemala, Honduras, Nicaragua, and Costa Rica in the United Provinces of Central America. Liberal forces had high hopes for the establishment of a modern democratic nation, but this dissolved by 1840 under various revolutions and civil wars. The area was unstable as attempts at some kind of reunification came and went.

The port city of La Union, nestled at the foot of the Conchagua volcano on the Gulf of Fonseca, handled the maritime trade flowing from the eastern section of Salvador. Nicaraguan troops had invaded nearby Tiger Island, threatening American residents with "forced contributions" and other "excesses." U.S. Consul Noel L. Wilson in La Union, the lone American official in an office without even a flag or any consulate stationary, had been updating the secretary of state on the deteriorating conditions and state of confusion that gripped eastern Salvador. American consuls served a variety of functions, and yet contact and support from the United States was sporadic at best. Wilson's own health had been declining under the "continuous high heat" (La Union was at 13 degrees north latitude). He begged to be allowed to return to the United States, or "seek restoration in some other locality in Central America."[27] The consul would be dead from disease in two months.

For the military serving overseas, the farther into the tropics they went, the shorter their average life expectancies grew. "Marsh fever," the name for malaria, believed at that time to be caused by the miasma and bad air of swamplands, prevailed on the Pacific coast. The germ theory of disease and the discovery of a protozoan parasite that causes malaria were still in the future. Cholera, the infectious disease of the gastrointestinal tract, spread in tainted food and water. Following cramps, nausea, diarrhea, and vomiting, death usually resulted from dehydration. Yellow fever, called "yellow jack" or "American plague," was an acute viral disease causing jaundice, aches, fever, and even hemorrhaging from the digestive tract (bloody vomit). Liver failure, delirium, seizures, and coma could result in six to seven days from the onset of symptoms. Typhoid fever, dengue fever, and hepatitis also were present on the Mexican coast. Nineteenth-century treatments for these diseases inevitably involved doses of lead or mercury or copper or other noxious metals. Opiates in pills or laudanum were popular, of course. Surgeons still possessed devices known as "scarificators," for blood-letting, though this practice was beginning to disappear. In many instances, sailors bravely attempted self-healing by way of a number of folk remedies, rather than report to the sick list and submit to the surgeon's questionable potions. *Saginaw* was again subject to seasoning on station, this time in Central America. And her provisions were being spoiled by the heat. Inspection of the barrels of salted meat, bread, butter, etc., took place frequently, and hundreds of pounds of condemned food had to be tossed over the side. The storeships USS *Farallones* and USS *Warren*, making the rounds at Acapulco and Panama, could not always keep up with these losses.

Heat and disease, and the constant tension due to the precarious political and military situation, unsettled the crew. At 3:30 a.m. on August 31, two armed boats approached *Saginaw* from shore. Hopkins quickly brought the ship to quarters and hailed the boats. Receiving no answer, the howitzers were run out, convincing the unidentified parties to waive off. Later that same day, court-martial proceedings in the case of Marine Corps Private Franklin P. Hamerty got under way. The crew were jumpy. At La Union, illness struck the ship, claiming Albert C. Smith, the second assistant engineer, on September 1. Leaving a portion of the crew on board, officers and enlisted men went ashore for the funeral services. The science of embalming had made a number of advancements during the Civil War, for families desired the return of their loved ones, but discoveries such as formaldehyde were still in the future. *Saginaw* had no such facilities anyway, and her dead were to be left where they fell.

Upon the return of the shore party, Thomas Castigan joined other prisoners in the brig, shackled for refusing duty and insolence; likewise Thomas M. Groves, officer's steward.[28] The small prison spaces on *Saginaw*'s main deck were proving insufficient for holding so many men. Commander Hopkins had the carpenter construct a squat wooden sweatbox on the foredeck, a low, cramped, dark, and airless chamber that literally baked in the tropical sun. Presumably the box would put the damper on his unruly crew. Summary court-martial proceedings were begun for Groves, Price, and James William.

From La Union, *Saginaw* departed for Port Realejo in Nicaragua, Punta Arenas, and a stay at Panama for provisions and coal. There some of the sailors and officers could tour the town and walk among the historic four-story homes, but this didn't help conditions on board. The irons and the sweatbox were in almost constant use under the merciless heat and the breezeless doldrums prevalent on the bay. Even one of the ship's youth, second-class boy John Scott, spent three hours in the box. Sometimes the ship's ensigns had to take turns filling out the deck log so that they, too, could rotate themselves into the cramped contrivance. Sailors often went from irons and the brig directly to the sweatbox, and then back into irons and confinement below again. And at Panama, like elsewhere, drunkenness was added to the round of the usual charges of insolence and refusing duty.

Though the seamen were without their usual allowance of grog, contact with the shore meant numerous chances for smuggling alcohol on board the ship. Bottles were concealed in a variety of ingenious places: lashed beneath the gunwale, sunk on lines in the water. Some crews, while filling water casks ashore, contrived a method of filling animal "skins" (intestinal linings) with whiskey, and slipping these unseen into the wooden tubes that ran from the spring down into the barrels on the beach. Beneath the watchful eyes of their lieutenants, these barrels were given a secret mark, and later tapped again in the fore hold. Sailors were even known to inject a floating layer of whiskey between turpentine and paint in a single barrel. Inspection of the top revealed the lighter turpentine, and probing the bottom revealed the paint. But a straw carefully lowered into the barrel's midlevel could access the liquor, a dangerous technique known as "sucking the monkey." Given the restrictions in their daily lives, finding an escape was an important part of existence on board ship.

Hopkins returned to La Union on November 8, assisting the U.S. minister and the new consul, J. R. Livingston. Life on board the ship continued to be a constant round of disobedience, trials, and punishments. The deck log for September 29, 1863 (a typical entry), revealed: "Coal lighter alongside, discharging. George A. Hern in sweatbox. John Jones OS and Thomas Castigan Lnds double irons, drunk on duty. At 9:00 removed Hern from sweatbox and placed him in double irons. Placed Jones in sweatbox. Removed him, placed him in double irons. Placed Castigans in sweatbox. Finished coaling ship."[29]

Though there is little mention of specific events at La Union or Port Realejo in the ship's log or Hopkins's own correspondence, the commander had received specific instructions to cooperate with the consul and the U.S. minister in residence, Mr. Partridge, who later praised *Saginaw*'s efforts and expressed his opinion that "the presence of a man-of-war is indispensable for the protection of the lives and property of citizens."[30] The Nicaraguan minister of foreign affairs, however, felt differently, charging Commander Hopkins with violating the laws of neutrality. In his protection of American property, Hopkins had apparently used *Saginaw* to ship a significant amount of arms belonging to Dr. Segar, the agent of General Barrios in the United States, and even a number of officers, effectively using his ship as a vessel of the now-defeated forces. The Department of the Navy never received any report from the commander and therefore simply could not confirm any of these allegations.[31]

The *Golden Gate* and the Beach of Gold

The wreck of the large, 2,072-ton steamer *Golden Gate* provided *Saginaw* with a different sort of duty. The three-masted, 270-foot side-wheel steamship, owned by the Pacific Mail Steamship Company, was one of the fastest on the west coast, and held the record for passage between San Francisco and Panama—eleven days (an average of twelve knots). On July 27, 1862, while passengers sat down to dinner, a fire broke out between the engine room and the ship's galley. The ship was turned toward the shoreline, and frantic efforts were made to contain the blaze. Unfortunately, the flames spread, and smoke billowed out of the engine room hatches. Some of the ship's boats were launched several miles from the shore, rowing for the port of Manzanillo, during *Golden Gate*'s run to land. As flames began to appear above the deck, passengers started to jump into the ocean with or without life preservers or any other floating material. At 5:30 p.m., the SS *Golden Gate* was run aground in the surf zone about 300 yards offshore of the beach now called Playa de Oro (Beach of Gold), 15 miles northwest of Manzanillo. The fire and the surf broke the ship apart overnight, spilling the heavy cargo and some $1.4 million in gold specie onto the shallow sandy sea floor, and scattering the lighter baggage along the coastline, while the survivors struggled to pull the exhausted and the drowned from the ocean. Many had attempted to leave the ship with heavy money belts of silver and gold coins tied around their waists, quickly cutting these away once in the water or being pulled to the bottom. Out of the 338 passengers and crew, 213 lives were lost in the wreck. Only a quarter of the steerage passengers survived. Some of the castaways struggled for several days before arriving at Manzanillo. Others, once making the shore, were resuscitated by kegs of ale that had been dispersed along the beach. The dead that were recovered were later buried under the sands.

Manzanillo, with its fine natural harbor and abundance of local hardwoods, had provided the Spanish with their first Pacific shipyard in Latin America in 1531. The bay had sheltered the famous Naos de la China, the

Spanish Manila galleons bearing the wealth of Asia, and therefore proved attractive to Portuguese, French, and English pirates. The festival atmosphere of the town, though, had long vanished due to the series of wars in Mexico, and the port had become a squalid hamlet. Still, it was the entry point for the interior town of Colima. The mountain range, some 60 miles inland, loomed distantly above Manzanillo, with the great peaks of Agua and Fuego (Water and Fire), at more than 13,000 feet, capped with snow.

Initial attempts at the commercial salvage of the *Golden Gate* were foiled by the heavy surf and shifting sands, for the heavier artifacts and the gold lay under 12 feet of water in the breaking waves. Despite a number of salvage expeditions originating in San Francisco, it wasn't until February 1863—with the arrival of the clipper schooner *William Irelan* and commercial nineteenth-century dredging and diving equipment—that the bulk of the gold could be recovered.[32] The stout diving barge was run directly into the surf zone and secured, and heavy bronze-helmeted divers excavated many of the gold boxes with dredge hoses in the murky and turbulent waters, rigging them by feel for the lift to the surface while tumbling in the surge. Other efforts after this continued to produce treasure, and as far as Commander Hopkins was concerned, the site was American property, more specifically PMSS property, and a potential source of revenue for Confederate spies. *Saginaw*, ordered to the wreck, anchored near the site in December and January and stood watch over the controlled activity, while the ship's own crew eyed the parties combing the beaches and took liberty ashore in Manzanillo. When treasure is involved, almost no good can ever come of it.

While onsite, Deputy Consul Frederick A. Mann came on board to communicate with Hopkins. Two expeditions had actually been approved for the work, one directed by Mr. Irelan and the other by Mr. Smiley. Mann had been instructed by U.S. Consul William H. Blake to take charge of the salvaged treasure, putting it onto any American man-of-war. Boxes from the wreck, though, had been left in the care of Thomas Smiley, and these had mysteriously vanished. And then the situation became more complicated. Unfortunately, this treasure hunting proved too much of a temptation for four of *Saginaw*'s own crew, who stole one of the ship's cutters and escaped to the shore. Consul Blake and the port's authorities captured the deserters, who were placed in confinement. But, while the consul was transferring his prisoners, "while engaged in moving them for greater security and in defense of my life, I fired upon him [James Mulhean] and death ensued."[33] The details of the event remain unclear. It seemed that the four, once captured, appealed to the consul to change their plea. Three complied with the consul and willingly sat down to be put into the stocks. The fourth took the opportunity to attempt an escape, attacked Blake, and was killed.

On January 4, two armed boats were sent to pick up the three remaining deserters, Coxswain Peter Gough, Seaman Thomas Whelan, and Landsman Samuel O'Neil. Blake had been arrested for murder, but with the arrival of Hopkins and his officers, the guard that had been placed on him was removed. The Mexican judge of the district conceded to *Saginaw*'s commander that the consul would not be rearrested or prevented from attending to his duties, though the people on shore were "much exasperated against him."[34] Consuls in remote locations were sometimes entrusted with local funds for the fulfillment of their responsibilities, and the position was also susceptible to a substantial amount of bribery and corruption. Blake had become involved in a dispute with some of the parties at work on the *Golden Gate* wreck site. In his view, "there is a Secession element here, as well as an officer in charge of the Custom House [Labisteda, captain of the port] whose enmity I had gained by refusing to assist him in extortioning off the wrecking parties, as he had done without right, and he and the Mexicans are doing everything they can against me."[35] But the Mexican courts had no jurisdiction over the American diplomatic officer. *Saginaw* left the area on January 11, for Acapulco. Later Blake's killing of the deserter was ruled as justified, and the case against him seen as influenced by those bent on plundering the site of the *Golden Gate* and trying to have the consul removed.[36]

Harsh judgments were in store for the captured runaways, for desertion was a serious crime and an example had to be made. They had left their station in time of war, an act punishable by death. The court-martial was convened on board USS *Farallones* on January 25, 1864. Coxswain Peter Gough pled guilty and appealed to the mercy of the court. He had been enlisted less than four months, and this was his first offense, and he asserted that he had no intention of leaving the ship permanently. Gough was given a dishonorable discharge from the service and sentenced to five years at hard labor in a military penitentiary. He lost all pay during his imprisonment, of course. Likewise, Seaman Thomas Whelan attempted to defend himself: "When I left the *Saginaw* January 2nd 1864, it was with the intention of returning again. I had no intention of deserting the service and I can only appeal to the mercy of the court to mitigate the punishment of this, my first offense."[37] He was discharged like Gough and sentenced to three years at hard labor in the penitentiary. The landsman Samuel O'Neil, only a boy, was luckier. Sentenced to three years, the court recommended mercy on account of his youth and inexperience, finding more fault with the "influences and enticements of those about him to do wrong."[38] O'Neil's sentence was reduced to solitary confinement in double irons and with bread and water for three months. He lost his pay for one year. On completion of his term of enlistment, he was dishonorably discharged from the service.

Acapulco

The small port of Acapulco had been the historic transshipment point of Asian silks and spices brought across the Pacific by the famed Manila galleons of Spain for more than two hundred years. Despite the wealth that passed through its streets, though, the town itself remained poor. It consisted of only a handful of buildings, as well as Fort San Diego, a hospital, and a chapel. The old fort had been considerably damaged in an earthquake in 1776. Beginning with the gold rush in California, the port grew into an important way station for the California steamers, providing the vessels with docks and warehouses and coal on their passage to Panama. It was therefore a critical communication point in the mail route to the east coast. In addition to conducting his usual duties of tracking the shipments of plantation machinery, cotton, flour, and hides in and out of his port, U.S. Consul Lewis S. Ely also updated the secretary of state on ramifications of the French intervention. The merchants of the port were increasingly disturbed by recent reports of troop movements from Mexico City. Trade was beginning to fall off. The consul railed against the brazen French interference on Mexico. Furthermore, Ely was not shy with his own opinions on the possibility of American expansion southward and the untapped potential of the country. The states of Sinaloa and Sonora, he felt, were ripe for independence, with a view of joining the United States: "I am animated by the hope that the wisdom of acquiring this country shall surround this administration like a halo of glory."[39] Acapulco, during the recent disruptions, had become a hot and empty town, filled with dilapidated hovels and earthquake-broken adobe walls.

Saginaw arrived at Acapulco from Panama on January 13, 1864, where she could reprovision from USS *Farallones*, transfer four sick sailors to ships bound for the hospital at Mare Island (including the ship's executive officer Charles Smith and Ensign J. B. Switt), forward the results of numerous summary court-martial proceedings to the Navy Department, attempt to recruit replacements, and hold the (aforementioned) court-martial of Gough, Whelan, and O'Neil. The hills about the harbor were covered in luxuriant vegetation, and the palms waved in the sea breezes. Dark cactus clung to the rocky cliffs. Bulk quantities of salt pork, salt beef, rice, flour, butter, molasses, beans, pickles, coffee, clothing, shoes, handkerchiefs, soap, brushes, and the like replenished *Saginaw*'s stores. Hopkins reported directly to Rear Admiral Bell on board his flag ship USS *Lancaster*, also in port.

At the time, Seaman John Price was again in irons for mutinous and insolent language, refusing to keep silent and resisting orders to be confined. He was sent on board USS *Lancaster* along with *Saginaw*'s carpenter Timothy Curran for "safekeeping," awaiting their own general court-martial. The company of other U.S. ships, particularly their officers, made the necessary but distracting duty of court-martial that much more convenient. Curran was accused of insolent, abusive, and insubordinate language against the acting master's mate, violently and brutally assaulting Quartermaster John Dethfts, and violently resisting lawful authority when ordered to be confined. Price was sentenced to six years hard labor, and Curran was reduced to rank of landsman and received five years hard labor (with ball and chain) under confinement at Marine Barracks Mare Island.[40] Commander Hopkins was getting rid of some of the troublemakers; he was cleaning ship. The crew had given him more than enough opportunity. Acting Ensign Charles S. Coy went on board *Saginaw* from *Lancaster*, but not without some trepidation. *Saginaw* still remained short two engineers.

Rumors abounded regarding a French squadron approaching the coast, and imperial armies of occupation were approaching San Blas. Guns and earthworks were reestablished at the old Fort San Diego above Acapulco harbor by republican forces. The majority of these, though, pointed inland in anticipation of the land attack. On January 28, Consul Blake reported the arrival of the French steam frigate *D'Assas* and steam corvette *Cordelliere* at the port of Manzanillo to the north. Two hundred imperial marines landed and took control of the customshouse, and the port fell under full blockade.[41] This applied to the American steamers calling at the port, and armed boarding parties conducted shipboard inspections of papers and cargoes. The American schooner *Golden State* touched at Manzanillo with a cargo of flour, was boarded, and three crates marked "merchandize" but containing firearms bound for the Mexican republican forces were removed.[42] Later, Consul Ely would be implicated in a scheme to smuggle cargo ashore in the *Golden State* incident. The ship's manifest showed irregularities to the amount of $1,600, yet when proof was sought by the captain of USS *Lancaster* and Admiral Bell, these papers mysteriously vanished from the consul's office. Consul Ely would give no explanation as to why the schooner apparently sailed without its papers, nor would he allow any examination of his offices.[43] The admiral was outspoken about the "imbecility" of the American consul, who continued to issue approval to merchants to trade, and "did not seem to understand the meaning of a blockade. . . . Scarcely an American vessel enters this port without some grave difficulties occurring, arising generally from the incompetency of this officer."[44]

The following day, Mr. Van Brundt, the agent for the Pacific Mail Steamship Company at Acapulco, received a note from the commander of the French frigate *D'Assas*, stating that if the authorities did not take the necessary steps to submit to the regency of the empire, the French would enter the port with a squadron of warships and one thousand troops, and "could not be responsible for the consequences."[45] The commander of the frigate actually seemed to be negotiating the fate of Acapulco with both the Mexican forces and the (neutral) military presence of the United States, via the steamship company agent. It was, in a sense, a warning. On February 2, the frigate came into port, and both USS *Saginaw* and USS *Lancaster*, moored on springs near the steamship docks, cleared for action. Crews went to quarters and guns were run out, but *D'Assas* fired only an 18-gun salute (which was returned by *Lancaster*) and then turned to leave. The frigate anchored outside the port, later to be joined by the ship *Pallas* and corvette *Le Diamant*. The blockade was on, and so long as it abided by the laws of nations, it was to be respected by all American ships. Rear Admiral Bell, as the senior officer on the scene, was able to negotiate a modification to the blockade at Acapulco, exemptions allowing U.S. mail steamers to touch at the port for coal and supplies only. After all, the mails from San Francisco and Panama benefited the French as well as the Americans.

For *Saginaw*, the immediate threat at Acapulco was over for the moment, and following the ship's recent duties in La Union and Panama to the south, Hopkins was allowed to cruise northward into more temperate climates, to the ports of Mazatlan, Guaymas, and La Paz, "in consequence of the state of health of your crew requiring a change of latitude." Accurate or not, reports also suggested a large number of Americans in that area

were watching for any opportunity to seize any vessels suitable for privateers. Bell warned Hopkins to "be extremely careful, particularly when at
anchor, that no boats approach without being ready to repel any attempt
which may be made to take you by surprise. A sufficient watch on deck,
at night, with arms at hand, and the men drilled to rush on deck without
waiting to dress, is absolutely indispensable in a low deck vessel like the
Saginaw."[46] The armed, shallow-draft side-wheeler would have made an
ideal privateer herself. Except for discovering a dozen deserters (one a
lieutenant) from Texas, all else was quiet for the moment.

Mazatlan, more so than other locations, most represented a European-
style city located on the Mexican coast. The town was founded in the 1820s
by German immigrants who developed the port in order to bring in agricultural equipment. The architecture of the town, therefore, reflected a
mixture of German, Spanish, and French influences. Mazatlan had been
blockaded and occupied by the U.S. Navy during the Mexican-American
War, and some of *Saginaw*'s own crew recalled fondly the many shops,
restaurants, markets, gardens, and dark-eyed local women. Even while the
navy ships stood offshore in 1847, sailors and officers mixed with Mazatlan society at dances and gala events. Importantly, the Pacific port lay at
the end of its own trans-Mexican route from Corpus Christi on the Gulf.
California gold seekers crossed the land and waited for the steamers coming north from Panama and touching at Mazatlan. Times, though, had
changed, and recreational activities at the port and fishing village were
now a mere shadow of their former existence. *Saginaw* returned to Acapulco on March 29.

In April 1864, the U.S. House and Senate forwarded a unanimous reso-
lution to the government of France, via the American minister, strongly
opposing the recognition of any type of monarchy in Mexico. Despite initial setbacks to the Union's military campaign, many observers now felt
that the ultimate successful outcome of the Civil War was in sight. And
a northern victory meant bolstering American support for Benito Juarez
and his liberal forces. Nonetheless, the establishment of Maximilian as
emperor in Mexico proceeded as scheduled. On April 10, the Treaty of
Miramar was signed by Napoleon III, stipulating the scheduled reduction
and ultimate removal of all French troops in Mexico (perhaps a face-saving
strategy or a phased troop withdrawal). Maximilian's empire would now,
theoretically, stand on its own two feet, and to do that, it needed more
money, and badly. Blockading the Pacific ports damaged the trade revenue available to the Juarez forces, but occupying the Pacific ports would

make that revenue available to the regime. And the French fleet of Admiral Bouet remained in Pacific waters. The defenses at the port of Mazatlan, where American companies had busily been pursuing agricultural and mining developments, had been shelled by the corvette *Cordelliere*, and the vice consul, B. R. Carman, reported a distinct change in attitude among the local officials. The blockade or siege of the town was expected daily. "I trust you will forward to me instructions," he wrote to Thomas Corwin, the American minister in Mexico.[47]

At Acapulco, *Saginaw* had been standing by, fighting drunkenness among the crew and conducting the usual series of masts and court proceedings and punishments. But conditions were changing; tensions were on the rise among the merchant community. This time, the French wanted more than just blockade, and it was clear that the Mexican forces would evacuate Fort San Diego rather than face annihilation, falling back to Pueblo Nueva and the rancheros inland from the port. The three thousand republican troops were unpaid, underfed, and ill-supplied, and they thoroughly abandoned the town following a simple message from the squadron outside the harbor, sent ashore under a flag of truce. The greatest threat then came from the potential for bandits and other bodies of irregular forces taking advantage of the power vacuum and looting the customshouse and merchants' residences. Acapulco was a port town, and the surrounding countryside, ravished by republican and imperial military forces, possessed no shortage of armed desperate and starving men.

At 8:35 a.m. on June 3, at the request of Consul Ely, Commander Hopkins passed out the swords, Colt navy revolvers, and Sharps breach-loading carbines; divided the majority of his crew into two parties; and led them ashore. One party took charge of the American consulate; the other set up defensive positions around the offices of the Pacific Mail Steamship Company. As in China, once again *Saginaw* men went ashore to protect their own citizens from the ravages of someone else's war. Many of the American businessmen armed themselves as best they could with an odd variety of weaponry and occupied the town square. Then, from the surrounding hills, small parties of Mexican irregulars, some troops once under the command of General Moreno, began running for the buildings and probing entrances into the port, but most were shot down by the shore parties and the defenders of the town. At 10:45 a.m., the French ships *Pallas*, *Victoire*, *D'Assas*, *Le Diamant*, and the storeship *De Rhin* steamed into the harbor and came to anchor in line of battle opposite the town and fort, gun ports open, cannon protruding. That afternoon the squadron commenced landing 250 cavalry and 500 marines and soldiers, who quickly dispersed the remaining groups of plunderers. The French imperial troops then accepted the unconditional surrender from the town, and raised the French flag over the fort. At 4:15 p.m., *Saginaw*'s landing parties returned to the ship.[48] The following day, Admiral Bouet came on board USS *Saginaw*, paying a courteous but strictly official visit to Commander Hopkins. Two days later, Mexican forces at Pueblo Nueva were routed, and the occupation of Acapulco was complete. As the United States refused to recognize Maximilian's forces or France's presence in the Western Hemisphere, Consul Ely lost whatever diplomatic authority he had maintained to that point. In fact, American captains at Mazatlan and Manzanillo as well could no longer count on any assistance in capturing deserters or criminals on the run. Consuls in occupied ports were to be regarded as mere commercial agents, unable to address any political issues.

Striking a Blow at the California Trade

The situation at Acapulco stabilized following the occupation. The French forces held the town by virtue of their fleet alone, while the outlying suburbs and surrounding fortified haciendas belonged to the Mexican nationals. The damage to trade meant considerably less port revenue than hoped for or truly expected. *Saginaw* remained at the port through July 1864, and then she was sent south to Guayaquil, Ecuador, a coastal city at the mouth of the Guayas River, in response to reports that an American steamer had been seized by Ecuadorian revolutionaries who were employing the vessel in active hostilities against the legitimate government. Ecuador had also declared independence from Spain in 1823, but since then stability in the country had been bought at the price of the authoritarian regime of General Garcia Moreno, and increasing revolutionary discontent.

Guayaquil, sometimes called the "Pacific Pearl," was the main port of tropical Ecuador and central to maritime commercial activities. Its market, Moorish-style clock tower, and naval yard stretched back into the early Spanish colonial days. Both the American minister and the consul in Guayaquil had become overinvolved in the politics of the situation and, in the view of the navy, could not be counted on as objective parties.[49] As it turned out, Hopkins was able to verify the sale of the steamer *Bolivar* to Ecuador, nullifying any protection by the American government and the right of the vessel to fly the American flag. Thus, *Saginaw* avoided any conflict with the Ecuadorian squadron, which outgunned the tiny steamer by ten to four. Incidentally, while in Guayaquil, *Saginaw*'s crew discovered a new trick for deserting. Seaman Neil Louis slipped overboard and swam toward the shore, then turned and cried for help. The call "man overboard!" automatically launched the ship's gig, from which John Niland and John Scots could then promptly disappear into the thick mangrove swamps.[50] *Saginaw* did not return to Panama from Guayaquil until November, when once again the ship rendezvoused with other vessels of the squadron and transferred her sick for treatment at Mare Island's naval hospital. Guayaquil had been ravaged many times in the past by epidemics of yellow fever.

The Thomas Hogg Incident

For years, reports had filtered in to the Department of the Navy about Confederate plans to capture one of the Pacific steamers. These were more than mere rumors, for various plans and documents had actually been discovered regarding the Union's steam traffic in both the Pacific and the Atlantic. The fact that *Saginaw* herself had yet to apprehend a privateer was not confirmation of the Confederacy's lack of interest. Late in the war, the South desperately needed money for military supplies of all kinds. On May 7, 1864, Steven R. Mallory, the Confederate secretary of the navy, set these exact plans into action. Writing from Richmond, Virginia, Mallory gave the following instructions to Confederate naval officer Thomas E. Hogg:

> Sir: You will proceed with men under your command from Wilmington by the shortest and safest route to the port of Panama. At that port you will take passage on board either the Guatamala or San Salvador, the two Federal screw steamers trading between Panama and Realejo. After reaching the high seas you will consider upon and devise a means to capture without fail. Your conduct toward the people of the captured vessel will be guided by that spirit of humanity which ever characterizes the conduct of our naval officers. Having secured the steamer, organized your crew, and hoisted the flag of the Confederate States, you will adopt prompt measures to arm your vessel and proceed to cruise against the enemy of the Pacific. If practicable, you will report or communicate with Captain R. Semmes, of the C.S.S. Alabama, and obey such orders as he may give you. The rights of neutrals must be strictly regarded. The importance of establishing and maintaining a wholesome naval discipline

is enjoined upon yourself and your officers. Should you seek neutral ports for supplies or otherwise, you will be careful to observe the usual naval courtesies and customs toward those in authority, and upon all proper occasions you will seek to place the character of the contest in which we are engaged and the principles involved in it in their proper light. Should you at any time hesitate in your course as a Confederate cruiser, your judgment may be governed by the consideration that you are to do the enemy, in accordance with the rules of civilized war, the greatest harm in the shortest time, and you will enjoin upon your officers and men the performance of their duty in that spirit of humanity which ever distinguishes a Confederate naval officer. You will endeavor to strike a blow at the California trade and whalemen in the Pacific, and should you capture bullion, it is suggested that, if no better means for shipping it to Europe offers, you place it in the hands of a British merchant of established character at Valparaiso. A French man-of-war might receive it on board in freight for France. P.S. You will ship your men regularly in the service of the Navy, in the usual manner.[51]

This would not technically be the cruise of a privateer, for some of these men were commissioned in the Confederate navy. This was a covert raid by combatants who were out of uniform, and the risk was great. The captured steamer would represent a converted raider flying the flag of the South, but they had to get on board first. Once sufficiently outfitted, the ship could be a threat to the many generally unarmed merchantmen, a shark among the minnows. Some Union mail steamers on the Pacific coast had been issued cannon for defensive purposes. The steamers *Salvador* and *Guatamala* each carried two guns, 12- and 24-pounders. The *Guatamala*, in particular, was known as a fast steamer, capable of eleven knots and of carrying coal for sixty days.

Separate parties of men converged on Havana to finalize their plans. One group of seven was led by a man named Bradford, who had been third mate on board the steamer *Columbus* on the Pacific, and thus was familiar with the schedules and coastline. The steamer *Columbus* had wrecked on the coast, and Bradford later worked as a diver on the site of the PMSS *Golden Gate*, reportedly robbing the wreck of a significant amount of gold. He had been living in Cuba since that time under the name of Johnson. Thomas Hogg and others successfully ran the blockade out of Wilmington, North Carolina. Acting Master Thomas Hogg, also known as Eylenzer Esson and as William Eason, was a native of Baltimore and subsequently a resident of New Orleans. Several of his men were also from New Orleans, including Master's Mate Edward Swain, a.k.a. P. Young; Paymaster William S. Black, a.k.a. J. S. Black; and Midshipman Thomas Reynolds. New Orleans may have been where the plans for breaking into the Pacific originated. The plot also included Sailing Master Robert B. Lyon; Paymaster's Clerk Joseph Higgins; Quartermaster Sullivan Stoddard; Chief Engineer John Hiddle, a.k.a. John Smith; and Assistant Engineer Thomas Mallory, a.k.a. Timothy Grady.[52] Hogg's group was the core portion of a larger party, totaling some sixteen to twenty men. At Havana they swore an oath to remain true to the enterprise:

> I do solemnly swear before Almighty God, and by all that I hold dear on Earth that I will bear true faith in the matter about to be laid before me, concerning injury to be inflicted upon the Merchant Marine of the United States. I, acting under orders of Acting Master T. E. Hogg, Confederate States Navy, [promise] that wherever I may be sent, strict security will be observed, and my actions so governed as to be free from suspicion. Should I willfully at any time or place, seek to damage the secrecy of the enterprise or divulge anything that would damage the person or liberty of any engaged in the enterprise, I hereby adjudge myself guilty of a flagrant breach of a trust, and a violator of my oath, and as such justly merit any punishment that my associates in this matter may adjudge, thus I do solemnly swear so help me God.[53]

From Havana the group boarded a British mail steamer for passage to Aspinwall via an interim stop at St. Thomas in the West Indies. They outfitted themselves with a veritable arsenal of small arms and equipment: charts, landing permits, uniforms, clothing, flags, medicine chests, Bowie knives, 50 revolvers and holsters, 25 Sharps rifles, 200 pairs of handcuffs, blasting powder, etc. Union agents were on the lookout for suspicious activities. Hogg traveled with a large and heavy trunk containing only innocuous items, and the plan stipulated that if he managed to get this on board the Pacific steamer without being searched, the others would follow with their more deadly baggage. At 200 miles from Panama, they would make their attempt to take the ship.

Despite their best efforts, the plot was detected early on in Havana. Paid informants described Hogg's plans for the steamer *Salvador* to Thomas Savage, the U.S. consul there, who quickly communicated with both consuls F. W. Rice in Aspinwall and Alexander R. McKee in Panama. Captain George Frederick Pearson, who had relieved Rear Admiral Bell of command of the Pacific Squadron on October 4, 1864, thus began his new position immediately facing this serious threat. Captain Pearson, a native of New Hampshire and now almost seventy years old, had served in the Mediterranean, West Indies, and East Indies squadrons, and was close to the end of his naval service career. Younger officers were needed elsewhere, but experience still counted. With this advance notice, Pearson made his plans to capture the group with Commander Davenport, USS *Lancaster*. The "scoundrels" arrived at Panama on November 5, where, in the words of Consul McKee to Secretary Seward, "You may be satisfied, that everything that can, will be done to seize them."[54]

With the cooperation of Captain Douglas of the steamer *Salvador*, Hogg's party was allowed to board the ship and stow their gear without any prior inspection. Pearson ordered Davenport and a sufficient number of men to board the steamer. The officers and marines launched four armed boats and made their way temporarily out of sight behind the PMSS Company ship *Sacramento*, where they awaited a prearranged signal from Captain Douglas. *Salvador*'s captain had called all passengers into the main saloon for an examination of their tickets, away from the railing and a view of the ocean. In less than a minute, the navy boats were alongside *Salvador*, and Davenport and five others quietly climbed onto the ship. While his men surreptitiously hid themselves away, Captain Davenport entered the saloon, claiming to be an off-duty police officer, simply on board to make sure nothing was wrong, and conversed freely with Hogg's men. Meanwhile, *Salvador* raised anchor and got under way. The following morning, some 12 miles outside Panama and beyond the territorial jurisdiction of the United States of Colombia (also called "New Grenada" at the time, or Venezuela, Colombia, and Ecuador), Davenport assembled the passengers and informed them that, by virtue of his commission and the fact that they were now under the protection of the American flag on the high seas, he "desired the pleasure of the company of several of them on board my ship."[55] Examination of their baggage revealed the guilty parties. Seven "pirates" were captured: Hogg, Swain, Black, Hiddle, Mallory, Higgins, and Lyon. The documents carried with their weapons and equipment revealed much of the larger plot. The silent prisoners were removed to USS *Lancaster*, and Captain Davenport returned to port and dropped anchor.

Plans to capture the second steamer, *Guatamala*, were foiled not by the navy but by the steamship's captain himself, John M. Dow. Bradshaw's group had attempted to board *Guatamala* in La Libertad, Salvador, but

Dow, in receipt of the news from Havana, let go the mooring buoy and left the group behind, shouting halloos from their shore boat. Bradshaw remained unsuspecting, though, blaming the delay and the missed embarkation on the pilot of the launch. The steamer next arrived at Acajutla to the northwest, where Dow learned of

> two men calling themselves Englishmen and engineers, who were going in the steamer to San Jose [*Salvador*]. Toward evening a launch came alongside from shore bringing the two intended passengers, their faces marked all over with villainy. . . . I directed the purser, as soon as they reached the deck, to ask them their names and for their passage money, which he did, but they already had taken time to cast their eyes about them to see their friends expected from La Libertad were not on board, and to the purser's question they replied that they would not give their names then, as they expected a friend to arrive at the port with their baggage, and if he did not come off on the next launch they would return to the shore and await the arrival of the next steamer. . . . Their actions and conduct while on board were so transparent that the meanest intellect could discover in them a deeper motive for their visit than they would be willing to allow.[56]

At Acajutla, Dow shared his suspicions with his company's agent on shore. The agent had actually been introduced to Bradshaw at the British consulate in Sonsonate, inshore from the harbor. Both of the passengers who had gone on board *Guatamala*, "Americans del Norte of the roughest type," were there as well, trying to make it appear that Bradshaw was a stranger to them. Bradshaw, though, was a familiar figure on the coast, having made more than one passage to and from Panama on board *Guatamala*, whose steward even recalled his remark that the steamer would make a capital privateer. Captain Dow's armament, only a half dozen rifles and one revolver, was not enough to equip even half of his officers. And the crew of *Guatamala* "are a motley set, waifs gathered from the beaches of Panama and Aspinwall, half of them would gladly join an enterprise where money is promised to be gained cheaply." Dow explained to company president David Hoadley that he would not attempt to trap Bradshaw on his vessel. Bradshaw was dangerous, and Dow simply did not have the resources to take him down: "I might tell you more about this man, but I think I have said enough to convince you that I now know enough about him to prevent his ever again walking my ship's deck as a free man . . . they will be arrested ashore."[57] They were not; Bradshaw's party disappeared. Later, naval officers were placed on board *Guatamala* temporarily to protect the ship from the threat of the remaining conspirators.

In the following months, the larger story emerged regarding the attempt on the steamships *Guatamala* and *Salvador*. Had *Guatamala* been taken, one of the fastest vessels on the coast, she would have intercepted and robbed a down-bound steamship from San Francisco with twenty-four other sympathizers on board (they dispersed when the plot was foiled). With the additional manpower, *Salvador* then planned to head for Callao and the Chincha Islands, destroying American shipping there. The three Chincha Islands, off the southwest coast of Peru near the town of Pisco, were guano islands, the source of fertilizer and nitrates for the booming Pacific plantations. Tall ships lined up to take on hundreds of tons of bagged cargo in this dirty but lucrative trade. The captured *Guatamala* would seek American whalers and all vessels bound for East Asia. Both would later rendezvous in China.[58]

Naval officials planned to bring Hogg and his men across the isthmus and then to New York for trial. But despite repeated pleas to the citizen president of Panama to allow the military guard and captives transport to Aspinwall on the company's railroad (over a neutral country), His Excellency Jose Leonardo Calancha remained adamant, protecting his nation's sovereignty. Pearson even learned of letters threatening to effect the escape of the prisoners by a large number of Confederate sympathizers, by means of breaking up the railroad tracks: "I am induced to believe that he [Calancha] is doing all in his power, and that surreptitiously, to prevent the rendition of these criminals to our Government, and that he does this not from animosity to the United States, but from his fears of the French, and his desire to pamper to the appetites of the people around him, many of whom are the associates of the piratical hordes now infesting the ports of Central America with the known intention of stealing our steamers."[59] Consul McKee in Panama felt that nine out of ten Americans sojourning in that port "entertain the same feeling, but more intensely; besides, the English and English passengers, as well as many English officers and men of other nationalities, not only sympathize with the South, but would give aid and comfort and assistance, if necessary, to Southern pirates."[60] And still more plots were brewing. Other informants, like William H. Allen, late colonel of the First and 145th New York Volunteers, reported two small iron steamers being shipped in pieces to St. Thomas, there to be assembled and sent around the Horn to prey on American shipping near Costa Rica. The Confederate officers and crew were headed to Havana, from there to cross Nicaragua and meet the vessels. Allen claimed to have firsthand knowledge of these plans, knowing many of the principals personally, having served with these men during the Mexican War.[61]

The Confederate prisoners would not be allowed to cross the isthmus, but fortunately, USS *Saginaw* arrived at Panama on November 19, and Pearson settled for sending the prisoners to Mare Island. *Saginaw* was small to begin with and not suited for the transportation of seven Confederate captives, but nonetheless, Hogg and his men were placed on board three weeks after their capture. Hopkins's nervous and inexperienced crew was suddenly expected to handle loaded muskets in confined quarters below decks and act as guards over actual prisoners of war. Two hours after getting under way from Panama on December 6, Gunner's Mate Robert Forman's weapon accidentally discharged, hitting Ensign J. H. Brockway in the left arm, crushing the bone and nearly severing the limb. *Saginaw* put about and returned to port, where Brockway's arm was amputated. The following day he died.[62] There was no time to bury the dead ashore. At 3:15 p.m., Commander Hopkins called all hands, and after the solemn and brief ceremony Brockway slid over the side of the ship, sewn in his own canvas hammock, two cannonballs dragging him down to the bottom of the sea, a sparse but moving nautical tradition. At 6:00 p.m., *Saginaw* departed Panama and headed up the coast.

By this time, the French controlled approximately 75 percent of the national territory of Mexico, and the suffering throughout the country had grown worse. The cruise north on board *Saginaw* was difficult. Disciplinary problems continued, requiring the usual punishments and another court-martial, this time sentencing Captain of the Hold John Hulnaps to be dis-rated, confined, and deprived of liberty for six months. Furthermore, the heat and moisture continued to spoil provisions, which had to be thrown over the side: 800 pounds of bread, 90 pounds of butter, 39 pounds of flour, 50 pounds of coffee, 100 pounds of sugar, 200 pounds of beef, and 200 pounds of pork.

The passage was marked by a rare display of the democratic process. In obedience to the general order for the fleet, a vote was held on board ship for the presidential election. Ten whites on board favored McClellan, and twenty blacks favored Lincoln.[63] The Civil War had eased, somewhat, the navy's self-imposed restrictions on the employment of African Americans, and more black sailors found the opportunity to serve in something other than the familiar cook and steward ratings. Additional manpower was desperately needed.

Farther along the coast, the French blockade of Mexican ports was still in effect. Warships were on the lookout for the Pacific Company steamer *John L. Stevens*, suspected by the French of carrying contraband from San Francisco, arms and ammunition for the Liberal forces in Mexico. Commander Poor, on USS *Saranac*, wrote: "if she violates her neutral character I can do nothing for her. The French, as belligerents, have rights as such, and know them, and have sufficient force here to enforce them."[64] *Stevens* had been caught once already running guns out of San Francisco in April 1864.[65] And the ship would be caught again by French forces, actually becoming Maximilian's steamship for a period before being retaken by Californian Francis Dana (residing in Mazatlan) and nine others in May 1866. Dana then took *Stevens* to La Paz and turned her over to the Juaristas.[66] Smuggling weapons and ammunition to the generals of Benito Juarez was a kind of cat-and-mouse game, but no one doubted that it was occurring.

The physical capture of Mazatlan by the French was expected soon, and following that, Guaymas and Manzanillo. These contests devolved into a three-way conflict between the French, the Mexicans, and the irregular forces surrounding the ports. Bandits plundered any who seemed vulnerable, and the citizens in the countryside often feared the demoralized national troops more than they did the French, for the unpaid Mexican forces had to survive off what they could take from the land. Some of the foreign residents were arming themselves and fleeing for the hills.[67]

Saginaw, though, left these places and problems in her wake, and arrived with the prisoners under the cool, rainy winter climate at Mare Island on December 31, 1864. The ship's crew hadn't been home to Vallejo for more than seventeen months, almost a year and a half. Captain David Stockton McDougal had replaced Selfridge as Mare Island's commandant. McDougal had just returned from the China Station, where, as commander of USS *Wyoming*, he had engaged six shore batteries and three Japanese warships (which had been purchased from the West) in a fight near the Straits of Shimonoseki, sinking one and heavily damaging the other two. Violence still plagued the situation in Japan. At Mare Island, McDougal had no satisfactory facility or situation for the Confederate prisoners. Hogg and his men soon found themselves confined at Fort Alcatraz.

Boiler mechanics and carpenters employed themselves to good purpose on *Saginaw*, work that would continue for several months. But some damage cannot be repaired so easily. On March 9, 1865, Commander Hopkins was condemned by the medical board examination and sent back east, where he took up residence in Philadelphia, later to return to his native

Virginia. He had actually requested transfer from command of *Saginaw* several days prior to the medical examination, being physically and mentally exhausted with the often frustrating service on the Mexican coast. It was grueling duty in a remote tropical climate. At times, the commander seemed to be more at odds with his own crew than with any enemy. Hopkins was relieved by Commander Charles H. Baldwin, a temporary replacement by the yard's own ordnance officer. Baldwin would remain on board *Saginaw* less than two months, basically serving to attend to the sick, stand by the defense of San Francisco, and see to the final repairs on the ship's boilers. Embarrassingly, the ship's hard-worn engines broke down while on light duty at Angel Island, stranding *Saginaw* in the bay.

On April 6, 1865, *Saginaw* fired salutes and was dressed in flags in honor of the taking of Richmond, Virginia. On April 9, General Lee surrendered at Appomattox, and the Civil War was over. These hard-won celebrations, however, were immediately cut short when, only five days later, President Abraham Lincoln was assassinated. The following day, guns at Mare Island as well as from all the navy ships at the yard were fired every half hour from sunrise to sunset, flags flown at half mast, and officers dressed in crepe. Yards were cock-billed and rigging slacked to show an uncommon slovenly and unseamanlike appearance, the naval ship's version of expressing grief.

This was the most solemn experience of *Saginaw*'s service career. San Francisco, California, and the whole nation were cast into mourning on Saturday, April 15, as the news of the assassination spread, devastating the exhausted and damaged country. A vicious strike against Secretary of State William Henry Seward had been attempted as well. French ships then at Mare Island for repairs, taking a reprieve from their blockade duties in Mexico, fired 21-gun salutes. The reaction of mob violence was of immediate concern to the navy, fanned by rumors in the press of Negro soldiers killing rebels in Richmond, and public hangings of notable secessionists in New York, Philadelphia, and Boston. "Assassination," the *San Fransisco Daily Dramatic Chronicle* proclaimed, "is the legitimate offspring of Treason and Rebellion."[68] Baldwin was quickly occupied on *Saginaw* transporting troops between Angel Island, Fort Alcatraz, and the city, where campfires among the groups of bivouacked soldiers lit the night up and down Montgomery Street. Impromptu meetings were held throughout San Francisco, where thousands pledged their allegiance to their country. That was no honorable way to end the bloodiest conflict in America's history.

The Greatest Threat Never Seen

Ironically, the greatest single threat to Union shipping in the Pacific continued to operate beyond the end of the war, and yet was never once encountered on the west coast. That was fortunate for USS *Saginaw*, for the speed
and firepower of the Confederate raider CSS *Shenandoah* were far beyond
the small paddle wheeler's ability to handle. *Shenandoah* had begun life as
the British troop transport *Sea King*, built on the Clyde River in Glasgow,
Scotland, for service in East Asia. Through a series of secret machinations,
Sea King was purchased by Confederate agents. Sailing from London in
October 1864, ostensibly on a trading voyage to Bombay, the ship rendezvoused at Madeira, where she took on the Confederate core of her crew,
ordnance, and ship's stores from the British steamer *Laurel*, and began
her transformation into a warship. James Waddell, former lieutenant on
board USS *Saginaw* and a veteran of twenty years service in the U.S. Navy,
stepped on board as her commander. The CSS *Shenandoah* was a sleek,
230-foot-long, three-masted screw steamer, featuring a lifting device that
hoisted the propeller out of the water when not in use, improving the
ship's sailing qualities. On deck, *Shenandoah* boasted four 8-inch smooth-
bore cannon, two 32-pounder rifled guns, and two 12-pounder boat howitzers, a formidable enough broadside once the raider had signed on enough
volunteers from the crews of her captured prizes to operate them.

Like her Confederate raider sister ships, *Shenandoah* sought to avoid
contact with federal cruisers, but once among merchantmen prey, acted
like a wolf among the sheep. Sailing down the Atlantic and across the Indian Ocean, the ship's first port of call was Melbourne, a sympathetic town
where the crew was warmly welcomed. Upon *Shenandoah*'s departure from
the neutral country, a close inspection somehow "failed" to reveal the forty
or so stowaways on board, who immediately signed on as crewmen once in
international waters. Fully operational at last, the whaling grounds in the
South Pacific proved frustratingly empty of targets, so Waddell turned his
ship northward. Most of the *Shenandoah*'s thirty-eight prizes were whalers captured and burned near the Aleutian Islands in late June.

At the heart of the *Shenandoah* story is the matter of timing. Commanders on the Pacific had been warned by reports of enemy raiders being
fitted out for distant cruising, but they first became aware specifically of
Shenandoah's Pacific operations in early August 1865, four months after the
official end of the Civil War, when news of the depredations of the whaling fleet reached the coast. Secretary Welles wrote to Captain Pearson,

commander of the Pacific Squadron: "*Shenandoah* making depredations in the Pacific. Department relies upon you to effect her capture." A tall order, indeed, and one not followed by the offer of any assistance. "Being an erratic ship, without a country or destination, no definite instructions can be given you."[69] The ship was, by that time, a pirate, a nationless predator, though not by intention. At Mare Island, USS *Suwanee* and USS *Saranac* were immediately set upon the hunt. *Saginaw*, initially chosen to escort the Pacific Mail Company steamship *Colorado* as far south as Santa Barbara, was clearly too small to risk an encounter with the raider, and given the weakened condition of the ship's boilers, too slow to keep up with her charge, and the mission was cancelled. Instead, the commercial steamer *Colorado* herself was modified by the addition of ordnance and joined in the pursuit. They would not find the raider, though ships would not stop looking until confirmation of her whereabouts was reported in November, some three months later.

On August 2, just one day prior to Welles telling Pearson to "effect her capture," Waddell and *Shenandoah* spoke at sea with the British bark *Baracouta* thirteen days out of San Francisco and bound for Liverpool. News from the British bark confirmed what the Yankee whaling captains had been unsuccessfully trying to communicate to Waddell. But one could really not trust their enemy, could they? In the words of *Shenandoah*'s executive officer, the British bark "brought us our death knell, a knell worse than death. Our dear country has been overrun; our President captured; our armies and navy surrendered; our people subjugated. Oh! God aid us to stand up to this, thy visitation."[70] The large majority of *Shenandoah*'s prizes had been taken after hostilities had officially ended between North and South. The ship was already on her way out of the Pacific when Pearson's squadron started their search. The last southern raider made an impressive nonstop voyage back to London round the Horn, becoming the first and only Confederate vessel to circumnavigate the globe. On November 6, 1865, *Shenandoah* was surrendered by Commander Waddell to Captain J. C. Paynter, Royal Navy, on board the British guard ship HMS *Donegal*. The CSS *Shenandoah* had destroyed hundreds of thousands of dollars' worth of northern shipping, yet despite planning an attack on San Francisco (which Waddell believed to be lightly defended), she had never come close to threatening the treasure steamers and the lines of coastal communication guarded by the Pacific Squadron.

Following the Hogg affair at Panama, and while *Shenandoah* searched for her prey in the northern Pacific, reliable reports continued to reach the squadron regarding other parties of Confederates assembling in Havana with the common goal of taking a Pacific steamer. The U.S. consul general in Havana even furnished a complete description of the men involved. They had been cleared to sail in March 1865 on the schooner *Transit* for Honduras: "Prince is about 50 years of age, 5 feet 10 inches high; grey hair and beard dyed; beard covering chin only. Austin is about 40 years of age, 5 feet 10 inches high; dark hair and dark reddish beard, covering nearly the whole face and chin."[71] In hindsight, it seems surprising that more of these kinds of efforts weren't either attempted or carried out. Given the number of vessels in the Pacific Squadron and the area assigned them, a small group of dedicated men could very well have disrupted the thin line of steamships maintaining the connection between the two coasts. Except for a handful of instances, the threat of privateers fitting out in remote bays and harbors remained simply that—a threat. But it could not be ignored.

Service on the coast from Vancouver to Salvador for a small 155-foot paddle wheeler was difficult, and took its toll on the ship's equipment and the ship's crew. Time away from the navy yard meant only limited access to repair facilities. Boiler tubes and replacement parts could be sent via storeships to Acapulco or Panama, but many of the movements of the vessels of the Pacific Squadron reflected last-minute changes in rotation to cover posts as the older ships returned, one by one, to the floating dock at Mare Island. By the end of the war, *Saginaw*'s boilers were in sad shape. The ship's engines had been strained to the point of not even being able to steam across the San Francisco Bay; she required an extensive lay-up. For the crew of *Saginaw*, service in Mexico and Central America can be summed up as seventeen months of never-ending heat, humidity, and drills, punctuated here and there by spoiled food, discipline and punishment, disease, and smuggled booze. Duty in the more temperate climate of the northern ports like Guaymas and Mazatlan, and liberty ashore, made some of this easier, but these port villages had little to offer sailors during the chaos in Mexico.

The American Civil War was over, but the conflict south of the border would continue for two more years. In Mexico, as in China, *Saginaw* seemed to stand on the periphery of someone else's conflict. This was a strange situation for a young America still in the stages of working out its own Pacific mandate. We had invaded our neighbor to the south in 1844 under the pretext of a minor border issue, and proceeded to lay quick claim to California, Arizona, New Mexico, Texas, and parts of Colorado, Nevada,

Oklahoma, Utah, Oregon, and Wyoming.[72] The Mexican-American War had shattered the economy of Mexico and opened the door to the French intervention. Many of the commanders of the U.S. Pacific Squadron had blockaded, bombarded, and occupied the very ports they later warily watched the French ships blockade, bombard, and occupy. Hundreds of thousands of people had died in Mexico during the nineteenth century. Once again, *Saginaw* had found herself amidst a landscape of ruined villages, deserted villas, and destroyed farmlands. Was it just bad luck or a sign of the times—symptoms of disorder all around the Pacific in the mid-nineteenth century?

4

Hard Times on Coastal Patrol

The French can win no laurels in a war of this character, and are said to confess themselves heartily sick of it. They treat Americans with courtesy, and salute our vessels with punctilious ceremony; but there is a marked diminution of the old cordiality of feeling.

San Francisco Daily Evening Bulletin, 1866

On May 9, 1865, Commander Charles Baldwin was relieved of his temporary duty on *Saginaw* and returned to the naval yard as ordnance officer. Lieutenant Commander Charles J. McDougal replaced him as commander, but like Baldwin, his term on *Saginaw* would be short. Still, command of a vessel in active service was better than watching over one that had been decommissioned and condemned, for Charles McDougal had last served on *Saginaw* in Hong Kong as she lay abandoned, waiting to be brought home across the Pacific. Charles McDougal, son of Mare Island's Commandant David Stockton McDougal, would eventually find his niche in service ashore as inspector of the Twelfth Lighthouse District. Tragically, though, he would die while attempting to land a small boat in the surf off Cape Mendocino. Weighted down by the payroll he was carrying to the station, McDougal was dragged under the breakers and drowned. He was well liked in the service, and friends of the lighthouse inspector made sure his wife, Kate, and their four young children were looked after; Kate McDougal continued as keeper of the lighthouse at Mare Island until 1916.[1]

Long before that, though, McDougal made a good living in the service, and for a very brief period USS *Saginaw* provided him with the experience of his own seagoing command. Two weeks of McDougal's month-long temporary posting were spent on a short cruise to Monterey, San Pedro, Santa Barbara, and the California Channel Islands. This was not tedious duty at war-torn ports in the tropics; this was virtually a pleasure cruise, conducted by a young connected lieutenant ultimately destined for other things. In fact, during this cruise, the ship had been officially removed from naval service and placed under the responsibility of the collector for the port of San Francisco. Her commander left behind the articles of war, the "rocks and shoals," along with their mandated disciplines and punishments. This was a revenue run, as well as a chance to test some of the repairs to the ship's machinery, and a welcome chance for rest and relaxation for the crew. It was an easy and domestic task for the small *Saginaw*, as the rest of the once-large Civil War navy was being laid up, and many more unfortunate officers put on leave.

The region of Santa Barbara and the central California coastal range was dominated by horses, cattle ranches, and agriculture and was little changed from its Spanish mission days. This was the setting of the tallow and hide trade in the olden days, familiar to Richard Henry Dana (author of *Two Years before the Mast*), an oasis of rolling hills and oak trees, rancheros and vineyards. In the post–Civil War years, though, the community was growing, reflecting a mixture of French, Italian, Spanish, Irish, and Yankee culture. Grand Victorian houses were making their stately appearance. There were towns and plazas where the officers and crew could go ashore and enjoy their liberty in tranquil surroundings. The islands of Santa Cruz and Santa Rosa, the original maritime homes of the coastal Chumash Tribe, were surrounded by blue water, and their rich kelp forests were filled with the call of seabirds. Boat landings at Smuggler's Cove, Pelican Bay, and the other small anchorages were allowed, and as long as sailors left the sheep and cattle on the ranches alone, all was fine. Pig hunting was the sport of the islands. All agreed that the short two-week cruise ended far too soon.

A break from hard service was long overdue for *Saginaw*, but the end of the Civil War did not alleviate the duties of the Pacific Squadron in Mexico. In fact, with the reports of thousands of ex-Confederate soldiers crossing the border and taking refuge (some joining the French Foreign Legion for three-year terms), and the increased federal support now available for Benito Juarez and his forces, the situation on the Pacific coast took on greater importance. In 1865, attitudes toward controlling the gunrunning from San Francisco were changing. In June, the American schooner *William L. Richardson* had been seized and detained at La Paz with a cargo of gunpowder.[2] The American steamer *Ajax* carried a shipment of arms south in August, while reports indicated that federal troops were openly sheltering Juarist partisans.[3] In October, with the discovery of yet another ship transporting arms and ammunition, an investigation was opened into three armament and supply depots maintained on the Pacific coast. In December, the American ship *Enterprise* was caught with ammunition, the cargo being unloaded under the supervision of American officers.[4] This all culminated in March 1866, when officials in San Francisco relaxed their own prohibitions against the Pacific coast arms trade. Customs inspectors were instructed to set up no obstacles in the way of the arms shipments to either of the belligerents (as if the United States were actually going to sell arms to France).[5] Along the interior border with Mexico, hundreds of tons of newly surplus military equipment were transferred to Juarist forces, and more than three thousand discharged veterans of the Union army joined the cause.[6] The end of the American Civil War intensified the fighting in Mexico.

At Mare Island on June 13, 1865, Lieutenant Commander Robert Wainright Scott took command of *Saginaw*, with orders from Rear Admiral Pearson for an extended cruise back to the Gulf of California and the northern ports of Mazatlan, La Paz, and Guaymas, where active fighting between national and imperial soldiers was again endangering foreigners. The thirty-eight-year-old Scott, originally from Old Point Comfort, had already served twenty-four years in the U.S. Navy. A Virginian by birth like William Hopkins, Scott was, however, very different in demeanor. During the Civil War, he spent most of his service on board USS *Powhatan* in the South Atlantic Blockading Squadron. In 1863, though, he had been returned to shore too ill to even pen his own request for transfer to the naval hospital. Restored to active service, Scott reported to the New York navy yard for brief command of the fourth-rate steamer USS *Nyack*, a vessel similar in size to *Saginaw*. He was regarded by many as one of the most gallant and accomplished officers in the service.[7]

Once at sea, *Saginaw* began her usual rounds at Mazatlan, but soon suffered another engine breakdown. Surprisingly, the French admiral sent his own mechanics on board the American steamer for emergency repairs. (A peacemaking gesture?) Furthermore, at Guaymas, where the expected supply of coal proved unavailable owing to the unsettled state of the region, French supplies were made available by the same admiral—40 tons of coal for USS *Saginaw* at no charge. In August, Juarez's national forces were pushed to their most northern extent by the imperial troops, resulting in an implied threat to the border of the United States. This was apparently the appropriate time for the French navy to smooth over any possible friction with the Americans. Commandant McDougal at Mare Island offered payment in kind by transferring 40 tons of coal to the French steamer *D'Assas* then at the navy yard, but this was politely declined. Perhaps the favor could be returned at some other point in the future?

Saginaw was forced to return to Mare Island for the completion of yet more repairs begun while under way, but soon enough Commander Scott again prepared to head south, the small steamer needed on station in lieu of the larger sloops-of-war then in pursuit of the CSS *Shenandoah*. Additional bayonets and cutlasses and other armaments were brought on board in anticipation of more frequent assignments ashore.[8] An assortment of all the other usual material came on board as well: rope, chain, pitch kettles, sperm whale oil for the lanterns, etc. On August 22, the repairs to her machinery were complete, and Scott took the ship to San Francisco in preparation for sea, departing from there a week later. Rear Admiral Pearson needed *Saginaw* at Acapulco, where she arrived on September 6. General Alvarez and his national troops were evacuating the town, falling back to the outskirts, once again leaving a power vacuum and exposing the American merchants to unacceptable risks. Scott formed a guard on shore, placing his armed marines at the offices of the Pacific Mail Steamship Company. The company had a large amount of property and funds warehoused at Acapulco, as well as a spare steamer standing by ready to transport passengers in case of an accident on any other company ship, a continuing attraction to piratical types even after the Civil War.[9]

Burying the Captain

By this time, Maximilian's regime was in desperate need of money in order to continue paying the contracted European mercenaries so critical to the occupation. Meager customshouse returns for an empire that was still generally unrecognized by the world were simply not enough, so the French navy was forcefully reoccupying ports like Acapulco and levying stiff fines for any and all infractions of the imperial rules. On September 11, the French ships *Victorie* and *Lucifer* arrived. Two days later, they landed 400 infantry of the line (Mexican mercenaries), taking possession once again of the port and the town without firing a shot.[10] For Emperor Maximilian, though, it had finally become clear that the ill-planned occupation was not going to work. It was time for a change in strategy, time for the gloves to come off. Repeated attempts at leniency and amnesty for the national forces had failed. On October 3, the infamous "Black Flag Decree" was officially promulgated, branding all Juarist forces as bandits, as outlaws, eliminating all established international rights or protections.

This was based on the (false) assumption that the war was finally at an end, and therefore the Mexican enemy was actually made up of nationless insurgents, terrorists by definition who, if taken in battle or captured with arms, would be summarily shot within twenty-four hours.[11] The decree was brutal and savage, and would backfire by alienating the entire class of more moderate Mexicans and further uniting opposition into more fervent action.

Quiet conditions returned only briefly to Acapulco, for French ships regularly landed troops ashore and conducted drills, noisily demonstrating their limited control of the town and immediate vicinity. Despite the maritime connection, General Alvarez's Juarist troops, encamped among the surrounding hills, continuously threatened counterattack, firing over the town at the enemy ships. The French garrison at Acapulco was isolated and in desperate straits. Between September 1865 and February 1866, the French landed 900 men and 230 women for the occupation effort, but the mortality rate proved alarming. Imperial numbers were quickly reduced by two-thirds through death and desertion.[12] Sporadic fighting also continued throughout the other coastal Pacific ports as imperial troops were sent from the interior to Mazatlan, and French engineers were at work at Guaymas establishing defensive positions.[13]

Saginaw was a participant in these events. At 9:00 a.m., *D'Assas* at Acapulco came under fire from republican artillery and returned fire at the enemy shore batteries, though the shells fell short of their mark. To the delight of the crew, the "saucy little *Saginaw*," while avoiding directly engaging the French ships, gave a practical demonstration of the superiority of American gunnery by throwing a few of her own shells much farther than the French guns—prudently, though, in the opposite direction.[14] Commander Scott then quickly landed his armed marine contingent to protect the familiar steamship company offices, after which armed parties of *Saginaw* crewmen were continuously kept ashore for more than a month. For the rest on board, the regular schedule of inspections, drills, practice with small arms, pikes, and swords, and occasionally running out the ship's guns, continued. Long in-harbor duty and contact with the shore, living in the cramped quarters of the ship in the tropics during the wet months, meant that the sailors increasingly took ill, suffering from intermittent fevers and chills. There was no way to isolate *Saginaw* from disease while on station.

In November, Napoleon III decided that enough was enough. French intellectuals and opposition members in the chamber of deputies protested against the massive expense and continuing loss of lives in the seemingly endless and unwinnable war against guerrilla forces defending their own territory. The growing support from the United States for the Juaristas was clear; the window of opportunity for empire in the Western Hemisphere had closed. The whole affair, according to observers in California, deserved no praise at all:

> The French can win no laurels in a war of this character, and are said to confess themselves heartily sick of it. They treat Americans with courtesy, and salute our vessels with punctilious ceremony; but there is a marked diminution of the old cordiality of feeling, for their sometimes offensive enforcement of the revenue measures, and their conviction that the refusal of the United States to recognize Maximilian inspires the Mexicans to continue resistance.[15]

The emperor ended Maximilian's line of credit and, in January 1866, announced the timetable of retreat, the three-phase staged removal of all French troops. Urgent pleas from Maximilian produced no results in Paris. In July, Empress Carlota left her husband's side and traveled to France to beg for support. She would see neither Mexico nor her beloved emperor again. Tragically, the empress became mentally unbalanced and spent the rest of her life in guarded seclusion, mistakenly believing her husband was alive and soon to return to her and the throne. She died in 1927.

For the United States, events were turning for the better. November brought more good news for the U.S. Navy in the Pacific when word reached the coast of the CSS *Shenandoah*'s surrender at Liverpool. A relieved McDougal wrote, "so there is an end to her depredations."[16] Furthermore, a special service squadron under the command of Commodore John Rodgers, including USS *Vanderbilt*, *Powhatan*, and *Tuscarora*, had been formed at Hampton Roads and set out to join the Pacific Squadron, albeit with all proceeding around Cape Horn at the crawling pace of the slowest vessel, the twin-turreted monitor USS *Monadnock*, a powerful but unseaworthy ship designed only for coastal defense. Additions to the west coast were finally on the way. Secretary Welles in Washington, D.C., could legitimately entertain expanded duties for the squadron, such as detailing a steamer to the Russian territory of Alaska in order to assist with soundings for a Western Union Telegraph Company submarine cable between Asia and America, but only if the unstable situation in Mexico would allow it.[17]

Submarine telegraph cables were a boon to worldwide communications. The first attempt to connect Europe and America across the Atlantic had already begun in July 1865. The only ship capable of carrying the necessary 2,300 nautical miles of cable proved to be Isambard Kingdom Brunel's gigantic 692-foot steamship *Great Eastern*. Brunel's leviathan, the size of a World War II aircraft carrier, launched in the era of paddle wheels and sail, was simply too big for any other conceivable mission. Unfortunately, the initial Atlantic effort ended in disaster when the cable snapped after two weeks into the slow crossing. Other regions, though, such as Russia, Alaska, and the Bering Sea, joined the competition.

Welles was supportive of this progress, but for now *Saginaw*'s duties lay toward the south. The decisions of the emperor in France aside, fighting continued on the Pacific coast. Executions of insurgents by the French in the port towns became a frequent and gory spectacle. In January, the American consul in La Paz reported: "a great deal of insecurity exists and nearly all business is suspended . . . robberies are frequent and nobody is punished. I beg to say that an American man-of-war is imperatively needed here. I feel that there is no security for future protection. All influences here at this time are more personal than political."[18] It is frequently the case that past vengeance from a variety of causes finds ample opportunity during war. Meanwhile, on board *Saginaw*, multiple terms of enlistments were expiring, the men being shipped back to San Francisco alongside their sick crewmates bound for the hospital at Mare Island. The regular steamers to Acapulco swapped medical supplies for invalids. Seasoning was again taking its toll.

Idling, *Saginaw*'s complement grew thin; the vessel was not in shape to stand in for other ports like La Paz and assist American citizens there. As if to emphasize this fact, from mid-December through the first week in January, *Saginaw*'s commander himself suffered from *calentura,* the local term for a virulent fever accompanied by diarrhea. He grew steadily worse, and was then moved to Mr. Bowman's house, the Pacific Mail Company agent at the port. Scott was placed under the constant care of both Dr. Marsh, the surgeon on board *Saginaw*, and Dr. Crook, from the steamer *Colorado*. For several weeks, the commander complained of a "gathering" in his head, sporadically enduring paroxysms of delirium.[19] The plasters and pills had little effect. On January 5, after almost seven months with *Saginaw*, Scott passed away. This shocked the crew, for Commander Scott had been a competent and well-liked leader, particularly when compared to Hopkins. He had experience on fourth-rate steamers, and there had been significantly fewer instances of trials and punishments, and no reappearance on deck of the much-hated sweatbox. The funeral procession at

9:00 a.m. the following day provided an honorable pause in the fighting. As the ship's company carried him to the grave they had dug, the only sounds heard were *Saginaw*'s own guns being fired at regular ten-minute intervals. The belligerents ceased fire; it was a different time, and it had its own rules. The company marched past the consulate in reverse order, enlisted men first and officers last, in a tradition that dated back to ancient Rome. Flags all along the route, as well as on the American and French ships in the harbor, flew at half mast. Three volleys were fired, and the bugle sounded taps. Robert Scott's effects were shipped back to Benicia on board the steamer *Colorado*, and Lieutenant Charles S. Coy took temporary acting command of *Saginaw*.[20]

While some lieutenants might have viewed command under any circumstances as a favorable event, Charles Coy had already served in the Pacific Squadron for over four years, in both China and Mexico. For Coy, it may have seemed simply a matter of time before he fell prey to some unhealthful threat, and he requested that the Navy Department allow him to be detached from the Pacific and transferred back to New York. He had had enough. A shipmate of Scott's from his days as a young lieutenant on USS *United States*, Lieutenant Commander Samuel Rhoades Franklin, received orders to join *Saginaw* at Acapulco and relieve Mr. Coy. Franklin came by steamer to Aspinwall, and by railroad to Panama. From there, he caught the company ship *Golden City* to Acapulco. The liner was commanded by Commodore James Watkins, who of course gladly spoke to Franklin about his new command *Saginaw*, the little vessel Watkins had brought to Mare Island from China several years earlier.

A veteran of the old sailing navy, Samuel Franklin brought not only a wealth of experience, but also an amazing capacity for making the most of his naval service on *Saginaw*. Born in York, Pennsylvania, Franklin was appointed midshipman in 1841 at the age of fifteen. His first cruise was on the frigate USS *United States*, flagship of the Pacific Squadron under the command of Commodore Thomas ap Catesby Jones. Franklin had been fully engaged with the "army" of occupation and the abortive capture of Monterey in October 1842. Jones, operating on faulty information from the U.S. consul in Mazatlan and convinced that the French and British fleets in the Pacific had immediate aims on California, took his squadron into port and negotiated the surrender of the Mexican district of Monterey. Midshipman Franklin, in the landing party, marched ashore and raised the Stars and Stripes over the deserted Mexican fort, only to lower them the following day and pack the tents and equipment back to the ship. Local papers eventually convinced Jones that the war had, in fact, not started after all. Commodore Jones had acted prematurely in anticipation of the coming Mexican-American conflict, which would not begin for four more years. He was relieved of command, but only temporarily. Franklin and his shipmates then spent a very pleasurable winter dining ashore on fine food and drink and attending Spanish dances. He was still in the squadron, and coincidentally at Monterey again, when the war finally did break out in 1846.

Following this turn on the coast, the "*States* frigate" cruised in the South Pacific, where Franklin had a chance to sail with Herman Melville, a castaway picked up on the island of Tahiti. Melville, of course, would in his later years write the epic *Moby Dick*, using much of his firsthand knowledge of whaling in the Pacific. The author's experiences on the *United States* would also compel him to write *White Jacket*, a strong condemnation of American naval discipline as it was practiced in the early nineteenth century. In the span of a few short years, the book would almost single-handedly bring about the prohibition of the practice of flogging, its extreme use seen by some as a type of torture. But, as all captains knew, other barely acceptable alternatives were still necessary and available.

Franklin then served on the Mediterranean Station and off the coast of Brazil on USS *Independence*, *Falmouth*, *Macedonian*, and off the Atlantic coast on the steam sloop USS *Dacotah*. In the days of the old steam navy, squadrons were not that large. Franklin personally knew and had served with Frederick Stribling, Robert Scott, and James Schenck during his days as a midshipman. Then, during the Civil War, he served as a volunteer on USS *Roanoke* in the engagement with the Confederate ironclad *Merrimac* in March 1862. *Roanoke* was intentionally grounded and escaped destruction. As lieutenant commander, Franklin took charge of USS *Aroostook* in the James River Flotilla and in the West Gulf Blockading Squadron. At Mobile Bay in the spring of 1865, Franklin was on the staff of Rear Admiral Thatcher, and in fact was the naval representative in the demand for the surrender of the city of Mobile.[21] And through it all he somehow found ample time to enjoy some of the rare pleasures of command: fine wine in the wardroom, the officers' mess, social calls ashore, and the sporadic but treasured old navy privileges that made up for the months at sea. Naval command in the nineteenth century was a world unto itself. Commander Samuel Franklin was a large man, well liked and competent, but as noted by others during his various examinations for promotion, somewhat prone to indolence.[22] He made the best of his navy career.

Arriving in Acapulco, Franklin wasted no time and took command of USS *Saginaw* at once. The small ship, though, was obviously not up to the standards of comfort to which he was accustomed, so Franklin immediately accepted the not-unexpected invitation offered by Mr. Bowman to live ashore at the agent's house. And there, despite the disturbed conditions and sounds of fighting between French and Mexican forces, the two men carved out a comfortable niche of their own tropical paradise, breakfasting and dining "in the open air in a little embowered nook just outside the house, enjoying all the freedom of tropical life in our loose summer attire."[23] This was not to last very long, for the Navy Department had received a second request from the Western Union Telegraph Company for a naval vessel, and orders came in February from Rear Admiral Pearson to bring *Saginaw* home. While Commander Franklin relaxed, the crew brought on wood and water from the barge alongside and coaled ship, pausing only on February 22 in observation of Washington's Birthday.

Putting to sea in early March, *Saginaw* beat into the prevailing wind and waves for ten days on the rough passage north. Coming in through the Gate on April 15, 1866, Franklin scarcely recognized San Francisco, a port he had last seen in the 1840s, when the small village was known as Yerba Buena. The sailors were among their friends again after only seven months, though they had lost their previous captain on the cruise. The ship was due for a considerable stay at the navy yard, for in the eyes of her current commander, *Saginaw* was very much out of shape. A survey of the vessel recommended hoisting the boilers out for yet more repairs, work requiring sixty days for completion.[24] Commandant McDougal at Mare Island wrote to Rear Admiral Pearson, "I don't think I have ever seen boilers in the condition of hers."[25] They were indeed a sorry sight, a hodgepodge of patches, scale, wear, and rust. *Saginaw* might be ready for sea by mid-June.

For ship captains, navy yards could be dull places, and Mare Island on remote San Pablo Bay was no exception. One had to make do as best one could. Franklin messed (joined for meals) with his fellow commanders Davenport and Parker (USS *Lancaster* and USS *Independence*, respectively), and the three spent many an evening being entertained in the comfort of various officers' homes on Mare Island, lovely houses built on the hill overlooking the straits. While the yard's carpenters, boilermakers, painters, and riggers were at work on both *Saginaw* and *Lancaster*, the trio of commanders had time for occasional visits to the Union Club in San Francisco, and some of the other legendary establishments on Montgomery

Street, such as the Flood, the O'Brien, and the Poodle Dog, the city's most renowned French restaurant: "Many a thirsty soul was refreshed at these famous houses of entertainment."[26] Taking several weeks leave, Franklin even made time for a recreational excursion to the Valley of the Yosemite, traveling by steamer to Stockton and from there into the Sierra Nevada Mountains on horseback, through the gold country to the uninhabited wilderness. Meanwhile, on the ship at the navy yard, the usual 72.5 pounds of meat and 72.5 pounds of vegetables came on board with numbing regularity for the crew. At least the stay in port meant fresher food, steak and onions and fruit and fresh-baked bread, instead of reconstituted salt beef and salt pork and pickles and maggoty hardtack. And it meant familiar liberty for the sailors, and welcome profits for the taverns in Vallejo.

Dinner at Esquimalt

In May 1866, the expanded forces in the Pacific were split by the Department into southern and northern squadrons. Gideon Welles appointed Rear Admiral Henry Knox Thatcher to command the North Pacific Squadron, which at that time consisted of USS *Vanderbilt*, *Comanche*, *Saranac*, *Saginaw*, *St. Mary's*, and the storeship *Jamestown*. They were soon to be joined by the *Pensacola*, *Mohican*, *Resaca*, and the side-wheel gunboats *Suwanee* and *Mohongo*. USS *Lackawanna* was being prepared to join the group, that ship to be stationed in the Sandwich Islands. With increasing U.S. commercial and political interests in Hawai'i, at least one lucky vessel of the squadron could normally be found at Honolulu. The rest of the squadron would embrace the coast of North and Central America, with Panama being the common location shared with the South Pacific Squadron as well.[27] Thatcher, sixty years old at the time, had years of experience in the Pacific. He had served for four years on board the frigate *United States* in the 1820s, and also commanded the sloop *Decatur* in the Pacific from 1857 to 1859. Additionally, he had extensive service in the West Indies, the Mediterranean, off Africa and South America, and had directed the successful efforts to capture Mobile, Alabama, in the weeks prior to the end of the Civil War. (Franklin, with *Saginaw*, came under Thatcher's command again.) The reorganization of forces reflected the navy's renewed ability to focus on the Pacific, and the recognition that the French fleet on that coast had outmatched the American fleet there for quite some time.

On board *Saginaw*, the thinned ranks of officers and enlisted men were again filling out. Mate J. H. Wing and Second Assistant Engineer John King, fully recovered at the hospital, returned to duty. The ship's cook, Joseph Robinson, having been confined for smuggling liquor, was released. Acting Ensigns Fagan and Chesley reported to Commander Franklin. Three seamen from the monitor USS *Monadnock* and seventeen from the station ship *Independence* transferred over.[28] Additionally, the armament on deck was replaced. *Saginaw* now carried two 30-pounder Parrott rifled cannon fore and aft on pivot carriages, and four 24-pounder broadside Dahlgren howitzers.[29] The rifled guns, developed by Robert Parker Parrott at the beginning of the Civil War, were very common army and navy ordnance at the time. With their reinforced wrought-iron bands at the breech, the 30-pounder naval version had a maximum range of 6,700 yards, though its accuracy at that distance (particularly fired from a rolling deck) was questionable.

In early July, the afternoon onshore winds brought the fog bank across the bright summer skies of Mare Island. The crew was engaged in bringing provisions on board: pork, beans, beef, pickles, molasses, butter, flour, sugar, rice, dried apples, coffee, saltwater soap, tobacco, cotton, shaving soap, clothing, boots, candles, etc. On July 13, Franklin moved his ship to San Francisco in preparation for departure. *Saginaw* was ordered to report to Colonel Charles Bulkley, the former superintendent of military telegraphs and chief engineer in charge of the Russian and American Telegraphic Expedition, and to assist in laying the cable across the Bering Strait. Agents from the Western Union Telegraph Company came on board at San Francisco, and on July 18, the ship put to sea. The clear skies had darkened, though, with the arrival of an off-season Pacific storm.

Perhaps Franklin can be partially forgiven for setting out into the storm, for the ship had been delayed in its mission by its many repairs, and he was eager to get away. Early the next morning off the northern California coastline, *Saginaw* was forced to lay-to under reduced sail and batten down the hatches. Heavy weather punished the vessel, the rig, and the ship's crew. At 7:00 a.m., sheets of copper sheathing were torn from the hull by the seas. Beating into the prevailing swells, the ship's martingale, the rigging that holds the jib boom down against the upward pull of the foretopmast stay, was broken apart. Later that night, the jib boom itself was carried away. The ship was pitching so heavily that the crew could not get the split damaged spars and rigging onto the deck, and they had to be roughly secured alongside. Multiple leaks were discovered near the rudder, the source of four inches of water in the magazine passageway at the stern. At 11:00 p.m., Franklin wore ship and raised steam.[30] Heading into this weather had been a foolhardy endeavor, and now getting back to the protective bay would be difficult. Running south to the estimated vicinity of the rocky Farallon Islands, which lay twenty-seven miles outside the entrance, the commander put the ship into the wind and seas and began casting the lead, searching for and eventually finding 45 fathoms depth and shell bottom. Changing course, he then sighted the Farallons nine miles to the southeast. His position thus confirmed, the ship stood in carefully toward Fort Point Light, past the swells breaking on the shallow bar and through the dangerous Gate shrouded in heavy fog. After ten more days at Mare Island for another round of repairs, the ship was once again making passage up the coast.

The cable project across the Bering Strait, the plans and surveys and logistical preparations, had been years in the making, a massive project in global competition with the as-yet-unsuccessful efforts to span the Atlantic. Officially named the Russian American Telegraph Expedition, this was Western Union's attempt to capture its share of the very lucrative transoceanic telegraph business. The proposed line ran from New Westminster in British Columbia up through the Yukon, across the Bering Strait, and to the coastal cities of Gizhiga, Okhotsk, and Nicolayevsk.[31] From there, it was 7,000 terrestrial miles to St. Petersburg. The total route was much longer than the transatlantic path, but the portion underwater was significantly shorter, and therefore significantly cheaper. One of the most important results of the western project was an increased awareness of the role of Alaska in the future of the Pacific region. Secretary of State William Seward would soon purchase Alaska from the Russian empire in March 1867 for a little over $7 million.

On August 7, Franklin and *Saginaw* arrived at the tranquil wooded British harbor of Esquimalt, only a mile upriver from Victoria on the southern tip of Vancouver Island. Esquimalt, from the native Indian expression "es-whoy-malth," meaning "gradually shoaling water," had first served the Royal Navy as early as 1837, and the naval port was christened there in 1848. During the Civil War and the tensions with the United States, the harbor had been fortified by the British with sixteen 68-pounder and 32-pounder cannon, placed on the headlands commanding the narrow entrance. These actions seemed well justified when reports reached British Columbia describing the turreted ironclad monitors then arriving on the Pacific coast, such as USS *Comanche* at San Francisco. British Rear Admiral Sir Thomas Maitland saw such vessels as intended "for no other purpose than to act against us."[32] The sporadic visits of USS *Saginaw* and USS *Narragansett* and other ships in search of Confederate privateers at Esquimalt and Victoria further strained relations between the two countries. The admiralty's forty-eight-hour restriction for belligerent ships at Vancouver Island was strictly enforced. But that conflict had ended, and relations were finally on the mend.

For Franklin, surprising news waited at Esquimalt. On July 27, just ten days prior to *Saginaw*'s arrival at Vancouver Island, Brunel's leviathan steamship *Great Eastern* had completed the second, and this time successful, attempt to lay the Atlantic cable. Europe and America had been joined in modern telegraphic communication, and celebrations spanned the ocean. The Bering Strait project had suddenly become redundant overnight, and Western Union Telegraph Company wasted little time in cancelling its ambitious and expensive plans. Commander Franklin requested instructions from Rear Admiral Thatcher, but those instructions would not arrive for more than four months. Communications were delayed. For some reason, the squadron commander, attending to other duties in the Hawaiian Islands at that time, still considered the ship to be "on special service."[33] *Saginaw* would swing at anchor in the cove, temporarily forgotten, riding the ebb and flood tides well into the Pacific Northwest rainy season, only occasionally moving past the entrance to the roads for target practice and beating to quarters. The enlisted men endured long months of gloomy monotony and rain.

The nearby town of Victoria had boomed with the early gold strikes on the Fraser River and at Caribou, but these were not long-lived, and with the decline in mining returns, the town of Victoria dwindled, offering little by way of diversion for captains waiting for orders. Fortunately, while his crew warmed themselves around the galley and attempted to dry their sodden clothes and bedding, Commander Franklin consorted with Admiral Joseph Denman on board the British flag ship *Sutlej*, dining with the admiral and his wife frequently at their house on the shore, only a stone's throw from where *Saginaw* lay at anchor. Franklin also became intimate with Commander Porcher, captain of the flag ship's tender *Sparrowhawk*, the two dining together nearly every day, alternating between *Sparrowhawk* and *Saginaw* and hiking the countryside beyond the bay regardless of the weather. Despite these few amusements, though, Esquimalt proved "an exceedingly dull place . . . life very monotonous."[34]

In search of diversion, Franklin left *Saginaw* and joined a group of friends for a trip to Port Townsend, Seattle, and Steilacoom, "insignificant and unimportant places" in those days, according to Franklin. Washington Territory was not thought to amount to very much as an agricultural country because of the shallowness of its topsoil.[35] From there, he caught an American steamer up the Fraser River, the boilers of the stern-wheeler glowing red-hot as the boat fought against the whitewater. The scenery was grand, with snow-clad Mount Baker almost always in sight. At New Westminster, Franklin dined with the governor of British Columbia, Arthur Kennedy, and with the head of the Hudson's Bay Company, Sir James Douglas. The navy officer made the best of any situation and spent his years in the service literally roaming the world.

Finally, in mid-December, orders came to return to Mare Island, and the crew cleaned ship and prepared to get under way. Like the passage northward, the ride home would prove harrowing, with violent gales all the way down the coast. Commander Franklin had never really considered Saginaw a completely safe craft in a storm, "although somehow she managed to keep on top of the seas that were sufficiently high, had we been caught in their trough, to have engulfed us."[36] The crew were soaked in their damp forecastle, tossed in their hammocks and often thrown weightless in the pitching bow of the ship. By December 27, the weather was still squally and dark when the ship moored at San Francisco and Franklin reported to Rear Admiral Thatcher on board USS Vanderbilt. The following day, Saginaw moved to Mare Island, where Samuel Franklin was promoted to full commander. A survey of the ship generated another long list of repairs, and Saginaw would not be fully ready for sea again until October of the following year. As Mare Island remained the only U.S. Navy yard in the Pacific, the expansion of the squadrons meant a line of vessels waiting for attention. And the maintenance and repair of the larger ships usually took precedence over the fourth-rate gunboat.

While Saginaw was at Esquimalt, Rear Admiral Thomas Tingey Craven had relieved David McDougal as commandant of Mare Island. Craven, born in Washington, D.C., in 1808, came from a long line of illustrious naval officers. His father, Tunis Craven, had been a navy purser and storekeeper, and his maternal grandfather, Commodore Thomas Tingey, had long commanded the Washington navy yard. Craven's brother, Commander Tunis Augustus Macdonough Craven, had gone down with his ship in 1864 while commanding the iron-hulled monitor USS Tecumseh at the Battle of Mobile Bay, gallantly uttering his famous words at the base of the ladder, "After you, pilot . . . ," as the heavy iron ship sank under him. In the final days of the war, Commodore Thomas Tingey Craven, with

USS *Sacramento* and USS *Niagara*, had blockaded the ironclad ram CSS *Stonewall* at El Ferrol, Spain. But when the rebel *Stonewall* made a run from the port expecting a fight to the death, Craven refused to pursue, not wanting to pit his wooden ships against the armored ironclad vessel despite his own substantially greater firepower. This inaction may have been unwise. He was court-martialed in December 1865 and sentenced to two years suspension of duty.[37] The light verdict was then overruled by the secretary of the navy, and Craven was sent to Mare Island a short year later and promoted to rear admiral. Commander Franklin, returned from Esquimalt, was soon fast friends with Craven and his family, spending the nights playing cards and the days on the small yard schooner *Joe Smith*, shooting waterfowl on the marshes and in the tule swamps of San Pablo Bay.

Meanwhile, *Saginaw*'s men were secured on board *Independence*, and the carpenters, boilermakers, and engineers were again hard at work on their never-ending project in the crisp clear mornings of the northern California winter. The rest of the squadron continued to stand by at ports to the south. In Panama, the storeship *Jamestown* was suffering an outbreak of yellow fever. In Mexico, the French were continuing their phased withdrawal, expanding the transportation of troops to include the transportation of all French citizens and all Austrian and Belgian auxiliaries out of the country.[38] Guaymas had been handed over to the Juaristas, and Manzanillo and Mazatlan were soon to follow. Then, on May 15, Emperor Maximilian and what was left of his forces were captured at Queretaro in northern Mexico. France's imperial ambitions were at an end, and nothing at all had been gained by the costly occupation. The French empire never really recovered from this monumental blunder. In 1870, following a war with Prussia, Napoleon's reign collapsed, heralding the new age of the French Republic.

The Thieving Whalers of Baja

On July 15, with repairs on the boilers still under way, Lieutenant Commander John Gardner Mitchell relieved Franklin of command of *Saginaw*. Franklin would go on to command the European Squadron from 1873 to 1876, and then serve as the commandant of the Norfolk navy yard in Virginia. He retired in 1887 at the rank of rear admiral and happily commenced writing his memoirs. John Mitchell, a merchant's son from the whaling port of Nantucket (with "salt water in his blood"), joined the navy out of high school and graduated from the Naval Academy in 1856. He served for over three years with the Pacific Squadron on USS *Cyane* and *Lancaster*, and then during the Civil War with the Mississippi River Squadron on the frigate *Santee*. He had also taken a turn as an instructor in mathematics and navigation at the Academy, a post he much preferred over tedious blockade duty. In August, Commandant Craven started putting together a new crew for Mitchell and *Saginaw*. Officers and enlisted men transferred from USS *Mohongo*, *Mohican*, and *Independence*. On September 16, in recognition of Mexico's Day of Independence, ships at Mare Island were dressed with the green, white, and red ensign at the fore. Mitchell's first cruise on board would take him to the ports on that coast. Following Maximilian's reign, peace was slow in coming to the states of Mexico. *Saginaw* was ordered on its familiar police rounds to the south.

Even though the demand for sailors had eased with the end of the Civil War and the decommissioning of much of the Union fleet, finding a crew for the postwar Pacific Squadron still proved to be a difficult task. *Saginaw* had too few men to fill her own holds with provisions, and so "volunteers" from USS *Independence* and yard employees at Mare Island chipped in to complete the task, bringing on provisions, coaling the ship, and striking the ammunition below.[39]

For several hundred years during the so-called heyday of sail, nations like England depended solely on their navy for their very survival. This wooden wall of ships protecting the country had to be manned at all costs, legitimizing the practice of literally kidnapping men from coastal towns, sometimes directly from merchant vessels bound for home. British officers led armed press gangs ashore, forcibly recruiting sailors and landsmen alike. This harsh reality no doubt played a role in the number of rather infamous mutinies that later shook the British fleet. The United States had broken away from many European conventions during its own revolution, and though much of the structure and tradition of the British admiralty carried over to the new country, Americans did not legitimize or adopt the hated press gang. Indeed, the nation had fought the British in the War of 1812 over this very issue of the illegal impressment of American sailors from vessels at sea. So finding enough sailors for the navy was difficult. But there were other ways to fill out the local ranks.

For sailors, San Francisco in the late 1860s was a city exceedingly fraught with pleasure and danger. The California boomtown featured a steaming district of boardinghouses, gambling joints, dance halls, seedy dives, bars, and bordellos usually referred to as the Barbary Coast, a crowded waterfront area where even the toughest police on the beat feared to tread. City police went into the Barbary Coast armed with nightsticks, pistols, and often a large knife upward of a foot in length, and they never went alone.

In addition to the usual hazards and corruptions to be found, sailors were threatened by an illegal but open trade in their services. This was, after all, the place where the term "Shanghaied" may have first been used. Finding sailors for commercial ships in the long-haul trades (which in the Pacific often included Shanghai) was the most difficult, for these vessels were setting out on voyages lasting many months, if not years, in duration. "Shanghaied" came to mean being stolen away for any long-distance voyage. Kidnapping laborers for these ships became a lucrative trade in San Francisco.

Officials often turn a blind eye to illegal activities if they prove critical to the commerce of their city. Such was the case with the trade in sailors. Incoming ships were met by "runners," men who worked for the boardinghouses, enticing sailors to their own particular establishments with smooth promises of women and cheap liquor. Runners were armed with brass knuckles, knives, pistols, and (drugged) booze, and were paid for each sailor they managed to get into their shore boat and hustled off to the "crimp," their boardinghouse master. Once there, the crimp's job was to fleece the sailor of all his pay and keep him as drunk as possible, making it that much easier to force him to sign ship's articles when he was "sold" to an outbound captain. Vessels coming into port did little to protect sailors from this vicious cycle, for it was often in the shipowner's interest to run off his crew and allow them to desert. By doing so, leaving the vessel early, they forfeited their pay. Vessels leaving port often had no choice but to purchase their crews, being unable to recruit in any other manner. When the trade was high, runners could earn more than five hundred dollars a week, while crimps stood to make over fifty thousand dollars a year, but no one will really ever know the total number of Shanghaied sailors who came and went through the Barbary Coast. As early as 1852, there were twenty-three gangs engaged in this nefarious trade in men.[40]

As an officer in the navy, Commander Mitchell could not take advantage of the illegal mechanisms in place to fill ships, but he did know where to find the sailors. Officially the Bureau of Navigation at that time handled recruitment efforts for enlistment, but in a last-minute pinch, officers had to rely on their own resources for filling out their muster rolls. On October 16, 1867, Mitchell moved the ship over to the harbor at San Francisco to recruit for his voyage. It would be three weeks before the ship had sufficient hands to sail for La Paz.

Baja is a 600-mile-long narrow finger of barren desert that stretches to the southeast from Lower California. The protection of American citizens at La Paz, due to its isolated position at the end of the Baja peninsula, was an even more challenging task for Consul F. B. Elmer. In fact, La Paz had been a difficult location during the Spanish colonial period, owing to frequent Indian revolts, disease, and the harsh, dry setting. Permanent settlement wasn't even achieved until 1811. Later, beginning in the mid-nineteenth century, companies were engaged in mining operations in the hills of the Baja interior, and oyster beds and the pearl industry took hold in the stillness of Pichilingue Bay adjacent to the deep inlet off the Sea of Cortez. These businesses sustained the city all the way through the 1930s. During the French intervention, the out-of-the-way harbor served as a transshipment point for illegal arms from San Francisco. The French fleet, of course, took particular notice of this, and by July 1866, Consul Elmer reported to Secretary Seward that La Paz was no longer open to foreign commerce. The mining companies had suspended all work.[41]

Saginaw arrived at La Paz on November 23, 1867. The ship's track for the next two months kept her roving between La Paz and Cerralvo Island, just to the south of the entrance to Pichilingue Bay, and the fishing villages of Altala (Altata) and Topolocampo (Topolobampo) and Jiacampo (Agiabampo), picturesque ports on the coast of Sinaloa and Sonora across the narrow, placid Sea of Cortez. *Saginaw* also appeared once more at Mazatlan and Guaymas, where conditions were only beginning to return to normal following the evacuation of the occupation troops. Benito Juarez had been elected to a third term as president in October, but that did not automatically solve Mexico's problems. These were familiar rounds for the ship, showing the flag, calling at the isolated consulates, and maintaining discipline on board the steamer during the tropical rainy season. Men lined up for inspection at quarters, practiced by division at the great guns, small arms drills, and "single sticks." Liberty parties went ashore, and intoxicated sailors were locked in irons and confined. These repetitive and seemingly timeless familiar events forever made up the world of the post–Civil War sailor on the Pacific coast.

One new task had been added to the ship's regular duties—hydrographic survey. In 1866, by order of the Department of the Navy, all vessels started carrying survey tools for confirming soundings, charting bays, and generally adding to the navy's collection of hydrographic information.

Mitchell was instructed to search for a reported submerged rock obstruction in the vicinity of Cerralvo Island. Such hidden hazards could spell doom for regular ship traffic. In early January, during a stretch of clear weather, the ship riding easily beneath a full moon, *Saginaw* tracked back and forth on parallel courses, towing the patent log and sounding with the ship's lead. The next day the bottom shoaled suddenly from 90 fathoms to 6 fathoms. Engines were stopped, and the cutters sent away to chart the reef. The unseen rock was found in only nine feet of water.[42] The passage to La Paz would be a bit safer for the regular steamers, and the whalers who lingered on the coast (particularly between October and April), provisioning at Mexican ports and continually searching for their elusive prey.

The American whaling industry achieved its zenith during the several decades of the midcentury, and as recorded by Herman Melville himself, the masters of this hunt were the austere Yankee whaling captains from New England. Vessels shipped from the ports of New Bedford and Fairhaven for voyages of no less than three or four years to the distant Pacific, where the prize of the hunt, the pelagic sperm whales, yielded the most sought-after oil. As whaling grounds around the world were depleted over time, the fleet was forced to move farther north. By the 1860s, Alaska and the waters of the Bering Sea were the focus of activities, but only during the warmer summer months. Whalers tracked south during the winter, reprovisioning in Hawai`i and cruising warmer waters from there, waiting for the ice to recede from the Arctic coastline. Many whalers tended to avoid San Francisco and the possibility of losing their crews to the temptation of the gold fields or other enticements.

The gray whales of the eastern Pacific are magnificent creatures, some of which exceed 50 feet in length and 36 tons mass. Grays migrate annually close along the western coastline from their feeding grounds in the Bering Sea to the warm water lagoons of Baja and back, a round trip of more than 12,000 miles, a global record for marine mammals. There, in the secluded and protected southern bays, the whales mate, and the pregnant females calve. Indigenous groups such as the Makah Tribe in Washington traditionally hunted the gray whales with dugout canoes and copperheaded harpoons. Once the hunters had secured a kill, they slipped into the waves and sewed the mouth of the whale shut while still at sea. The gases of decomposition then kept the catch afloat as it was towed slowly back to shore. Though western whalers hunted many types of whales in the Pacific (humpback, right, blue, sperm, minke, etc.), the gray whale had not been initially targeted due to its nasty habit of turning and putting up a violent fight, smashing the whaleboats into pieces and endangering the lives of the boatmen. Grays had earned the moniker "devilfish" for this very reason. They were not hunted, that is, until Charles Melville Scammon made his profitable voyage to Laguna Ojo de Liebre in Baja, a spot later called Scammon's Lagoon.

In 1858, Scammon was the first whaler to take his boats right through the narrow and treacherous channel at the southern end of Bahia de Sebastian Vizcaino, Vizcaino Bay. There he found himself surrounded by hundreds of grays, trapped among the shallows of the lagoon. His first efforts, though, were discouraging. The currents and tides swept the fragile whaleboats aside. The wary whales used the channels and shoals to their advantage, and females with calves were particularly prone to attack the hunters. At that point, the crews broke out a new weapon, the whaler's bomb lance. This was a 21-inch-long explosive missile with a time-delay fuse, fired into a whale with devastating effect. Scammon's men positioned themselves on the shoals, in the shallows where the grays could not make a charge, and fired into the herd passing by in the deeper channel entrances. The explosion often killed the whales outright. Stripped carcasses drifted later onto the beach and the dunes, where local inhabitants rendered the last of the oil from the whale's internal organs, and sold this back to the whalers along with their provisions and locally brewed mescal.[43] This was the new and brutally efficient method that opened the whale fishery in Baja, and brought the majestic gray whales to the edge of extinction in a matter of a few years. (Fortunately, several calving grounds in Baja are now protected whale sanctuaries.)

One by one the whaling grounds of the world's oceans were exhausted in the global pursuit of nineteenth-century energy, of whale oil, and Baja was no exception. The following season at Scammon's Lagoon the rest of the whaling fleet arrived, some using bomb lances and some continuing the traditional battle with line and harpoon. San Ignacio Lagoon and Magdalena Bay to the south were also discovered and quickly emptied of whales. By 1868, only a few ships were wintering in these places, the great herds of gray whales were gone. The other vessels from the Pacific fleet spread out along the coast. But the whalermen were opportunistic, and sought to turn a profit during these hard times in any available manner. At Cerralvo Island, *Saginaw* crossed paths with the American whaling bark *Harrison* and became involved in the case of the Topolocampo copper treasure.

In early January, the bark *Harrison*, commanded by Captain P. M. Cooly, was cruising for whales in the vicinity of Topolocampo on the eastern shore of the Sea of Cortez. A cargo was spotted in the sandy shoreline while the boats were out pursuing a herd. Open to taking advantage of any opportunity, the sailors landed and inspected the site. A pile of large copper ingots, ninety-seven "planchas" each marked with the initials "PV," were there on the beach, seemingly abandoned in the judicial opinion of the whalers. The ownership of these being "unclear," the sailors practiced restraint, each boat only taking one heavy ingot apiece. Captain Cooly questioned the boat crews: Had they seen anyone on shore? Had anyone seen them? The next day, the boats were back, and they laboriously hauled away the rest, the weight of the heavy ingots limiting each boat to nine planchas per trip. This time the ownership issue was not so ambiguous. Several men had appeared on horseback, firing pistols as the boats pulled away with the last of their booty. The optimistic suggestion that "they were chasing us away from the beach," that the men on horseback were unconcerned with the treasure, did not sit well on the captain's mind.[44] Over the next several days, the mates on board the whaler *Harrison* managed to convince him that the copper was indeed stolen. But what to do now? No one wanted to take it ashore, where armed men and campfires could now be seen. They landed it several days later at a spot seven miles away.

Weeks after the theft, an official inquiry decided the final disposition of the copper ingots on board USS *Mohican*, then at La Paz. *Saginaw* took on board a whaleboat and some of *Harrison*'s crew, and returned to Topolocampo to supervise the final movement of the planchas. No hostilities were encountered, and *Saginaw* stood offshore and monitored the whalers obligingly returning the stolen copper to its original location, all ninety-seven ingots. The first mate was sent under orders to notify the locals of the copper's return, but he reported no one at the site. As if in retribution for *Harrison*'s actions, the whaler struck the submerged rock that had been so recently charted at the entrance to La Paz, pounding her keel on the pinnacle as the swells worked the vessel across the reef. Divers were sent over the side in Pichilingue Bay to assess the damage, and reported the keel all gone and bottom injured badly.[45] It was not turning out to be a lucky "greasy" cruise for the bark *Harrison*. The depletion of the whaling stocks in the Pacific, the commercial extraction of petroleum in Pennsylvania providing a viable replacement for whale oil, and the depredations of the CSS *Shenandoah* all heralded the decline of the American whaling industry. Whalers were now apparently scavenging cargo from beaches in Mexico. Unfortunately, *Saginaw* herself was next to run aground, this time on a shoal outside the port of Jiacampo. Sounding around the ship revealed 3 fathoms off the port side, and 1½ fathoms on the starboard.[46] Reversing engines brought the ship off the shoal, and Mitchell proceeded on to Guaymas, and from there back to La Paz.

Exercising the great guns proved popular with Commander Mitchell, who trained his gun crews hard and at the same time provided a tangible sign of American support in Mexico. *Saginaw*'s crew, however, found themselves under the strict discipline of a "driver," a hard master, once again, and the sweatbox made its ominous reappearance on *Saginaw*'s deck. Whereas William Hopkins had restricted his use of the box to the stipulated limitations (and Robert Scott had done away with it altogether), for some reason Mitchell did not feel bound by those same rules. On one occasion, the captain's cook, Joseph Roberts, was confined in the box for twenty-four hours. This provoked a reprimand: "The Department calls on you for an explanation, and desires to know by what authority you inflict or allow to be inflicted such punishment on board USS *Saginaw*."[47] Mitchell had no satisfactory answer, but the sweatbox remained. How bad could twelve lashes have been?

In March, *Saginaw* was back in Mazatlan, swinging at anchor off the broad beach. Fresh paymaster stores arrived with the mail steamer *Montana*: bread, sugar, dried fruit, pork, coffee, butter, flannel, sheeting, shoes, soap, blackening, brushes, brooms, buttons, eagle buttons, beeswax, candles, pepper, preserved meats, mess kettles, etc.[48] The crew were employed stowing provisions below. It had been a regular cruise, with no unexpected circumstances, but the ship suffered several desertions nonetheless. At Mazatlan, Seamen Thomas McCarty and Peter Blacall disappeared from the third cutter while ashore. Fortunately, Mitchell signed on two others for terms of one year each, Hawaiian sailors John Mohee and John Kanaka. The ship was lucky to get them, for Hawaiians were renowned for their seamanship and water skills. Following Captain Cook's famous Pacific voyages and Western contact in 1778, Hawaiians signed on board sailing ships in great numbers. At times, up to one-fifth of the American whaling fleet in the Pacific was made up of Hawaiians—so many, in fact, that King Kamehameha issued legislation requiring bonds be set to assure the return of young Hawaiian men going abroad. Communities of "kanakas," the foreigner's nineteenth-century term for Pacific Islanders, had existed on the west coast, at Astoria and Puget Sound and Santa Barbara, for decades. Certain hazardous jobs, such as the lifesaving service at the mouth of the Columbia River, required strong swimming skills, something that Western sailors simply didn't have compared to the islanders. With the arrival of USS *Resaca* on March 15, Mitchell took his ship to sea, stopping one last time at La Paz, and then rounding the peninsula and moving up the coast of Baja for San Francisco.

Sailing in the Wake of Commerce

To date, the actual protection of the whaling fleet, for which Secretary of State William Seward had made such an impassioned plea to Congress years earlier, had existed only as an abstract concept for *Saginaw*. For Americans, who had long since turned away from shore and coastal whaling in favor of the pelagic, or deep-sea, hunt, the "subjugation of the monster of the seas to the uses of man" took place far beyond the effective range of the small Pacific Squadron, a fact that the CSS *Shenandoah* had amply demonstrated. The U.S. Navy sailed in the protection of important commerce by establishing a limited colonial-style police force in foreign ports, and it was only there they crossed paths with the deep-sea sailors. The nation did not really have a blue-water navy in the Pacific for anything more than that; the size of the ocean made a greater role for the small squadron impossible. Support for the American whaling industry consisted, instead, of much larger objectives, such as the opening of Japan to American ships, the purchase of Alaska, and the annexation of the Hawaiian Islands. But the whalers sailed alone.

The withdrawal of the French fleet from the Pacific was a welcome event, as was the increase of forces for the Pacific Squadron. Nonetheless, the post–Civil War period marked a significant decline in support for the navy. In 1864, the U.S. fleet stood at almost 700 vessels and mounted almost 5,000 cannon. By 1870, this had shrunk to 200 vessels capable of mounting only around 1,300 guns.[49] The navy, which had become the largest and possibly the most powerful in the world by the end of the Civil War, again became a third-rate power at best.[50] Most of the ships in the Pacific Squadron were aging wooden vessels, castaways relegated to spend the rest of their days under repair at Mare Island or on overseas stations. Development of the navy went into a retrograde phase, for America was not truly committed to maintaining a presence on the world stage much more than occasional vessels showing the flag at foreign ports. Steamships like USS *Saginaw* and others had proven their utility in all coastal and riverine functions, yet after the war the navy made an effort to revert to sail technology. Many officers saw steam propulsion as perhaps suited for these limited roles, the "brown water" coastal roles, but still unable to challenge the self-sufficiency of sail for distant blue-water assignments.

This emphasis on sail power was not simply a response to the reduced naval budget in the post–Civil War years. There were social factors for the return to the more familiar white canvas navy as well. Engineers were a new class of navy professional, unfamiliar entities to the traditional ranks of the line officers, those who had achieved their status through command at sea. The question "Are engine-drivers sailors?" summarized the growing tension faced by the service during the formative stages of the new steam navy in the 1880s and 1890s. The creation of equivalent ranks in the engineering corps was a threat to the singular nature of sea command. And it was not just the engineers; there existed a larger contest for authority between line officers and staff officers, those who commanded offices and navy bureaus ashore. But for the most part, it was simply a question of technology. The lack of affordable and dependable sources of coal overseas meant that maintaining a steam navy was an expensive commitment, one that the country was not yet prepared to make. Affordable technology had simply not yet progressed to the point where the efficiency of steam engines made distant cruising under power worth the cost involved. Technological progress is a slow affair.

In 1869, a general order stipulated that all navy vessels must be outfitted with full sail power, whether they carried engines or not. Navy regulations in 1870 prohibited the use of steam power unless absolutely necessary.[51] Commander Franklin on board USS *Saginaw* felt the effects of this movement to restrict steam as early as 1866, when he was ordered to return the ship to Mare Island under sail. All steamers, without regard to class or rig, were to proceed while at sea under sail alone. Franklin referred to the economizing orders as "ironclad instructions," impractical for many circumstances. The relatively poor sailing qualities of *Saginaw*, the small amount of canvas she carried, and the lack of wind in the Bay of Panama made this an almost impossible proposition. The navy ship would have drifted about aimlessly at the mercy of the currents and tides. In consultation with Commander Scott on USS *Saranac*, Franklin simply ignored these orders and steamed to the north.[52]

The limitations on coal and steam power aside, other factors were reshaping the navy's role in the post–Civil War era. For instance, the handful of Confederate raiders had an effect on Union commerce far beyond just the numbers of ships they captured and sank. The CSS *Shenandoah* took 38 ships, the CSS *Florida* took 21, and the more successful *Alabama* took some 69 prizes by the end of her wartime career. In all, perhaps some 5 percent of the North's merchant fleet was captured. But for every prize taken by the South, eight other vessels voluntarily changed their flag of registry, many switching to British rolls for the protection granted by neutral status. It was simply too dangerous to make a profit at sea in the face of the increased threat of the Confederate raiders. And by law, once enrolled in a foreign registry, these ships could not return to the U.S. flag. In 1857, 120 U.S. vessels were active in the foreign trades. By 1865, there were seven. Ships fled the country registration out of necessity, for self-preservation, due to the fact that the U.S. Navy was in no position to either convoy or protect trade at sea during times of war. This was the long-term result of America's refusal to sign the 1856 Treaty of Paris that ended the Crimean War, and more importantly prohibited guerre de course, or privateering and the conduct of legalized war on commerce. In the face of international competition for commercial cargos, America's merchant marine would never recover from the blow of the Civil War. These were the vessels the U.S. Navy had sought to protect in foreign ports, and they were vanishing. *Saginaw* would be lucky to continue serving in any role under these circumstances.

5

Exploring Seward's Icebox

And again, you are cut off for the greater part of the time from the world, and are, in fact, as much exiles as you would be in Siberia.

Robert Mitchell, 1868

Fortunately, a new role did emerge for the little ship. Following years of service in sweltering tropical climates, *Saginaw* and her crew were finally in for a drastic change to a beautiful, cold, and mostly unknown region. The ship's move north was prompted by one of the most cost-efficient yet highly ridiculed territorial acquisitions in American history. Many Americans called Secretary of State Seward's 1867 purchase of the Alaskan territory "Seward's folly," "Seward's icebox," or even "Andrew Johnson's polar bear garden." Acquiring 600,000 square miles for around $7.2 million worked out to about two cents per acre, but unless gold had been discovered up there, why on earth do it? (The Klondike gold strike would provide the answer to that question in 1896.) Why extend the borders of the United States to include a high-latitude noncontiguous block of ice? The country had neither the population nor the capacity to settle this northern land. After all, it had the entire western frontier, which came with its own challenges. The *New York Tribune* captured the general public opinion at the time:

> The Indians within the present boundaries of the republic strained our power to govern aboriginal peoples. Could it be that we would now, with open eyes, seek to add to our difficulties by increasing the number of such peoples under our national care? The purchase price was large; the annual charges for administration, civil and military, would be yet greater, and continuing. The territory . . . contained nothing of value but fur bearing animals, and these had been hunted until they were nearly extinct. Except for the Aleutian Islands and a narrow strip

of land extending along the southern coast the country would not be worth taking as a gift.[1]

None of these arguments held water with William Seward. Both Seward and Senator Charles Sumner were dedicated and loyal expansionists, and there was little question that they were going to accept the opportunity offered by the czar. Russia had held onto her distant colony since 1741, and the Russian American Company had grown wealthy by supporting the few trading posts there and removing a bounty in fur seals and sea otters from the productive waters. These rich pelts lined the robes and the boots of the Russian and Chinese officials in the Manchurian north. But with the growing British presence in the Pacific, it looked better to sell to the Americans and get something back for the land than lose it for nothing to the British. (The Russians and the British had fought their own remote and minor Pacific war in the 1850s.) And frontiersmen from both Britain and America were pushing northward into the southern borders. Furthermore, the fur-bearing animals from Alaskan waters had been essentially wiped out, and the cash-strapped Russian government needed the gold. The negotiation, arranged with Baron Edouard de Stoeckl, the Russian minister to the United States, was concluded in the dead of night on March 30, 1867. It would be more than a year, however, before Congress finalized the appropriation and the sale was complete for this unpopular purchase. And so the country moved with only half a will toward making its presence known in the new territory.

For Seward and Sumner, the acquisition played a strategic role in limiting British involvement in the Americas. Napoleon III had left Mexico, Spain was clearly no longer a contender in South and Central America, and that left only the British, so recently antagonistic during the American Civil War despite their proclaimed neutrality, challenging the Monroe Doctrine in British Columbia. With Alaska, the United States would now surround this British foreign presence on both borders. This flanking move on Canada was openly acknowledged in the press. The goal, as summarized by Sumner, "can be nothing less than the North American continent with the gates on all the surrounding seas." The purchase of Alaska would "dismiss one more monarch from this continent."[2] The mineral and timber resources, and fur and fishing and whaling grounds in Alaska simply made the deal that much more attractive.

Even before the actual sale was completed in July 1868, the U.S. Army had begun sending soldiers to garrison the abandoned Russian forts. The initial governance of Alaska, spearheaded by an administration that soon found itself entangled in impeachment proceedings for a variety of other reasons, thus fell solely to the military. President Johnson and the Congress, having purchased the territory, failed to establish a civil administration there. It was up to first the army, then the Treasury Department, and finally the navy to make the best of the situation and act as de facto colonial agencies until 1884. The administration of America's first colony of her westward oceanic empire was without clear legal authority or adequate funds, and without precedence.[3] In that sense, during the initial military governance of Alaska, the territory really was just "Seward's icebox."

On October 10, 1867, two army companies sailed for Sitka on the Pacific mail steamer *John L. Stevens* (recaptured from Maximilian at La Paz the previous year). On October 18, General Jefferson C. Davis established himself in the governor's house at Sitka, and the first of his soldiers moved into the log barracks. The transfer ceremony happened that day. Russian and American troops formed up in front of the former company headquarters, and the Russian colors were lowered. Ironically, the ensign halyard stuck on the pole, and a Russian soldier was sent aloft in a boatswain's chair, throwing it (shamefully) down onto the troops below. The hoisting of the Stars and Stripes elicited a few cheers from the attending Americans, but such display was discouraged as possibly offensive to the former occupants.[4] The majority of Russian citizens returned home, leaving only a few traders and Eastern Orthodox priests who chose to remain.

Sitka, or New Archangel, as it had been known, was the territory's capital and former center of the sea otter trade; it consisted of about 116 log buildings and 968 "civilized" (white and creole, those of mixed Russian and Indian parentage) residents. There were perhaps 500 whites in the entire region of Alaska. As the center of the Russian American Company operations for years, the town featured a flour mill, hospital, governor's house, shipyard, and wharf. Dry goods shops and liquor stores sprouted up following the arrival of adventurers and entrepreneurs from the lower states, though business at Sitka initially plummeted after the departure of the Russian American Company traders. St. Paul on Kodiak Island, where vessels had once congregated for fur seal pelts, had 100 cabins and about 283 residents. The much larger native population that existed outside the stockades of these settlements always proved more difficult to estimate. Sitka was surrounded by (or perhaps more correctly, the foreign settlement at Sitka intruded into) some 1,500–2,000 Tlingit Indians, living in solid split-plank cedar houses of the local village. The American acquisition had brought approximately 26,000 Alaskan natives under the flag of the United States.[5] Inuit groups inhabited the coastline north to the Arctic Sea. Aleuts inhabited western Alaska and the chain of islands known as the Aleutian Archipelago. Tlingit and Haida Indians were spread throughout the maritime passages of the southeast. Tensions were high between the new settlements and the tribes in the territory.

Some of the obstacles to the army's early administration of Alaska, besides the absence of official direction or authority or adequate funding, were a lack of information about the geography of the area, and a lack of basic maritime transportation among the islands and passageways of Alaska's long coastline. General Davis simply had no way of moving his small groups of soldiers in response to any events; he had no ability to even survey the region he was responsible for, and relied on chartered steamers and navy ships when and where they were available. And with the steamers came the search for local sources of coal, something the Russian American Company's sailing vessels had not previously pursued. For these tasks, the shallow-draft side-wheel steamer USS *Saginaw* was, in Gideon Welles's opinion, aptly suited, and he ordered Rear Admiral Thatcher to send the ship north. On Mitchell's return from La Paz, the preparations commenced.

Greenhorns Go North

Saginaw arrived at San Francisco on April 7, where she would outfit and recruit for Alaska, skipping the longer call at Mare Island across the bay. Commander Mitchell was back among the seedy dives in the Barbary Coast again and having the same trouble locating a crew to replace those sailors whose times were expired, and those who ran. Third Class Apothecary Edgar Hogan failed to return from liberty, and was replaced by Assistant Surgeon Robert A. Whedon. Then Seaman A. J. McDonald disappeared, followed by John Wilson, Isaac Hideman, A. S. Thomas, and L. Cami. Were sailors voting with their feet, registering their discontent with being sent to the cold and rainy north, or maybe their discontent with Mitchell? Ensign Parker transferred to USS *Independence* by order of the admiral.[6] It was hard to hold onto a full crew while swinging at anchor in the harbor of San Francisco. Meanwhile, carpenters were sent to the city and put on board, repairing the starboard paddle box and rigging a new swinging boom. The watch not on liberty coaled the ship, loading 60 tons of anthracite rock into the dusty bunkers.

Early on the morning of April 18, the tug *Monterey* came alongside with final stores for *Saginaw*, including tea, bread, molasses, beans, vinegar, and sugar. Despite the illegal and violent trade in nearby boardinghouses, Commander Mitchell and the ship's officers managed to sign on seven men and two ship's boys from the streets of the city. As usual, the ship's roster featured a dynamic and ever-changing list, the navy constantly seeking sailors from almost any location or career. Some enlisted just hours before the ship sailed. Mitchell sailed at 10:00 a.m. with forty-eight enlisted crewmen, eight of whom were landsmen, greenhorns with little or no experience at sea. The crew were a mixed bag. Enlisted men on the Alaskan voyage came from Prussia, the West Indies, Ireland, England, Germany, Italy, Scotland, and other nations, as well as Boston, New York, Pennsylvania, Vermont, California, and other states. Rear Admiral Thatcher's orders charged Mitchell with "making explorations and surveys and of determining the most suitable harbors and anchorages on the coast and in the adjacent islands."[7] As in China and Mexico, *Saginaw* would of course serve in a number of other roles once on station.

After six days' passage north, the first major port of call was the British naval base at Esquimalt, where the ship again coaled and reprovisioned, with some of the men granted liberty ashore in the woods and nearby Victoria. From San Francisco to Vancouver Island, ships transited at sea along the exposed coasts of Oregon and Washington Territory. But once at Esquimalt, after coming into the southeastern panhandle of Alaska, the route to Sitka weaved its way through the inside passage, between islands and through sounds and narrow straits. *Saginaw* was the first naval vessel to work inside. The waters were calm and protected from gales and storms, but fogs, strong currents, and hidden rocks and reefs made safe navigation a most difficult business. In Victoria, Mitchell obtained the services of Mr. Robert Hicks for $150 per month. Hicks was an experienced north-coast pilot who had worked for both the American and British navies and also for the British Hudson Bay Company on vessels making trading voyages between British Columbia and Alaska.[8] He knew the local waters like the back of his hand, and took the ship through the trickiest of passages, running the copper-clad steamer aground only once in the Wrangell Narrows near the Russian settlement of Petersburg. Today the inside passage is known as the Alaskan Marine Highway, a popular cruising destination featuring the forested banks and glacier-capped mountains. The territory abounded with brown bears, black bears, black-tailed deer, wolves, and mountain goats. Farther inland, beaver, mink, marten, wolverine, and river otter were common, and along the waterways, porpoises, whales, sea lions, and seals were in evidence. Alaska was far different from either China or Mexico.

Assistant Surgeon Whedon noted that, with the change in climate, the men suffered a noticeably different set of symptoms from what they experienced in the tropical stations. Bronchitis, chest pains, and severe coughs would be active concerns on this cruise. Rheumatism became a frequently repeated diagnosis. And the fact that the crowded berth deck was often tightly closed due to inclement weather made the rounds of fever and chills among the men that much more contagious. In his own medical journal, Whedon began to note the lowering temperature (low 30s Fahrenheit) and weather on a daily basis. He made connections between exposure to cold and elements of the Northwest and disease, as the ship moved into the realm of fog, rain, hail, and dark skies.

Climate and environment during the nineteenth century were interpreted as playing a much larger role in human health than they are granted today. A more thorough understanding of the microscopic and biological origins of disease remained for the future. On *Saginaw*, it was thought that sailors like Ensign Abraham Vail took on alternating chills and fever simply due to the change in climate, by "coming north from Mexico."[9] Acting Master James B. Wood, exposed to the night air on April 22, was "taken by a chill." Temperature alone carried with it the ability to infect. At times it was not uncommon for more than a tenth of the ship's crew to be on the sick list, subject to Surgeon Whedon's quinine, pills, plasters, and poultices—and to his general and continuing efforts to improve the conditions for the men. Hygiene was a difficult issue. Philip Campbell, a twenty-two-year-old sailor from the West Indies who had been on board the cramped ship almost a year, "was very filthy and dirty in habits, and was ordered to have thorough scrub and wash . . . and change of clothing." Campbell, whom many considered "very offensive in his person," had to eventually be removed from the berth deck during his convalescence.[10] Whedon believed that Campbell's poor hygiene had contributed to his severe bronchitis. Treatment in this case (and in others) was beyond the capabilities of the assistant surgeon. At Sitka, Campbell would be transferred ashore and placed under the care of the army hospital.

Saginaw departed Esquimalt on April 26, going east and then up the Strait of Georgia and through Discovery Passage to Queen Charlotte Sound. Once north of Vancouver Island, the ship called at Bella Bella, the location of a Hudson's Bay Company trading post just upriver, and at

another Company post called Fort Simpson on Hecate Strait. Passing Fort
Wrangell, newly established by General Davis on the site of the former
Hudson's Bay Company outpost known as "Redoubt Saint Dionysius," the
ship navigated carefully through the Wrangell Narrows, sounding with
two leads all the way. Mitchell then rounded Admiralty Island and proceeded, on the advice of Pilot Hicks, to conduct a thorough hydrographic
survey of what the pilot called Kake Bay after the local native tribe, assessing its suitability as a harbor. The ship's boats spent two days sounding
the depths, and evidently Mitchell found it satisfactory, for the following month the commander would give the cove its modern name, "Saginaw Bay." By May 7, *Saginaw* made Sitka harbor, where the storeship USS
Jamestown had arrived the previous September, her exhausted crew seeking relief from yellow fever and the heat and humidity of Panama. Mitchell
worked his own men, coaling the ship and cutting wood and bringing on
board fifty brass boiler tubes and jackets, pants, blankets, shirts, mat-
tresses, etc. from *Jamestown*. And then the sailors had their first taste of
life at New Archangel.

The area of *Saginaw*'s operations lay at the end of a very long line of
logistical supply. This practically guaranteed that naval service in Alaska
would be both expensive and difficult. For instance, Mitchell had been
promised specie in San Francisco, but had received only paper greenbacks.
But he was now beyond the range where paper money meant much. His
description of Sitka to Rear Admiral Thomas T. Craven—promoted from
commandant of Mare Island Naval Shipyard to commander of the North
Pacific Squadron (thereby replacing Thatcher) in September 1868—focused on the issue of resupply:

> In the first place, there is only one town or corporation, which pretends
> to have any civil government; and that is Sitka, the inhabitants of which
> exclusive of the military and the few Russians about leaving, are a few
> speculators, and Jews, and the Sutlers Dept.
>
> Outside the town are the Indians, the tribe of Sitkas, about 1000
> (one thousand) in number, living in all the filth and stench imagin-
> able. . . . The balance of the inhabitants of the territory are Indians, and
> some of them not particularly tame.
>
> From these last, we, the officers at least, are obliged to purchase the
> greater part of our mess supplies, viz: vegetables, meats, fish etc. The
> Indians do not know what paper money is. They say, on looking at it,
> that they can get similar papers from cans of preserve fruit, vegetables,

oysters, any can, in fact. . . . For the time being, let Sitka be considered as being Alaska and Alaska American soil, and then let the question be put: why should those of our Squadron there receive their full pay in Greenbacks while other vessels have their expenses in coin?

The answer can only be: you have a Sutlers store there, and the privilege of paying more than double price for the necessities of life: or additionally; you have the further privilege of being rained or snowed on for ten months out of the year, and have to purchase at advanced prices many mere articles of dry and warm clothing.

And again, you are cut off for the greater part of the time from the world, and are, in fact, as much exiles as you would be in Siberia.[11]

Enlisted men were fed from ship's stores, but if the officers could at all afford it, the wardroom existed on a higher standard of living.

Of course, the definition of a "standard of living" was a relative term in Alaska in the nineteenth century. What most may now see as deplorable conditions on board a ship or at a garrison may have been considered pretty well off then, particularly when compared to what the Western inhabitants perceived as the state of the natives who lodged in their own village outside the garrison walls. However, the impressions of soldiers, often tainted with common bias, should not obscure the complexity of the established cultures of the region. The Tlingit Nation was the most socially and economically advanced group in the area. This group was divided into thirteen different tribes, or "kon," each having its own permanent village and hunting and fishing grounds. Their lifestyle was adapted to the rich abundance of marine resources in the area, allowing the accumulation of goods and skills and the development of an extensive trading network among their own kon and other tribes in the interior. The formal ceremony known as the potlatch, as well as traditional feasts, allowed the regulated sharing of the tribe's wealth. Natives who chose to live in close proximity to military camps and Western trading posts benefited from the proximity to trade goods, but also often suffered the social and physical consequences of that increased contact: disease and alcoholism. The Americans looked down on the native occupants, describing them as filthy, thieving heathens. In general, the hundreds of Tlingit residents at Sitka, or Sitka-kon, managed to live in peace with the outsiders, but not without a good deal of suspicion and contempt between the two groups. General Davis felt the tribe had "the reputation of being very hostile and insolent. . . . Notwithstanding they evidently fear us, they frequently boast they can and will whip us one day."[12] In this they shared their reputation with the Yakutat-kon to the northwest.

For their own part, the Western merchants and adventurers at Sitka were not the selected shining paragons of humanity. One measure of this is the rather large number of soldiers needing to be regularly confined. At the end of January 1868, out of a garrison of 270 enlisted men, 46 were locked in the guardhouse. The daily average was around 26, about 10 percent of the army complement at Sitka.[13] Like the navy, the army suffered an extremely high incidence of alcohol abuse. General Davis attempted to control the problem by limiting the troops to only beer and ale, and limiting the purchase of those products between certain hours of the day. However, Sitka's civilian population had no such constraints, and the thriving black market and the employment of runners meant that alcohol was available to troops who sought it. During the late nineteenth century, one out of every twenty-five army men was being treated for serious manifestations of alcoholism. Many more remained more or less in control of their drinking.[14]

Shipwrecks, Coal, and Whiskey

General Davis's administration of the territory included establishing posts throughout the coastal region to protect the two major trading areas at Sitka and Kodiak. The two posts farthest to the southeast were Fort Wrangell near the mouth of the Stikine River, and Fort Tongass on a tiny islet near the Portland Canal. Both were unfinished and under construction in 1868. Wrangell was located at the former site of a British trading post, and Tongass, the first "customshouse" encountered upon entering the new territory from the south, consisted only of a tent encampment for fifty enlisted men and ten officers. After gathering up her dissipated crew from Sitka, *Saginaw* was soon steaming through the straits and sounds to Wrangell Island with a load of army supplies, pausing at anchor there for four days. On the way there, Mitchell had touched at Saginaw Bay and taken on board a chief of the Kake tribe, a Tlingit Kake-kon, as an interpreter. While at Sitka he had heard rumors regarding the loss of the merchant ship *Growler* and the murder of the entire ship's crew. And, as *Saginaw* had done in China, the commander took on the investigation for the protection of American trade, after first off-loading the army's quartermaster stores.

The vessel *Growler*, a small, well-built schooner launched at Whidbey Island in Puget Sound in 1858, was a familiar sight on the trade routes between San Francisco and Vancouver. And with the purchase of Seward's Icebox, *Growler* had been sent north. On January 21, 1868, the ship set out from Sitka southbound for San Francisco with a heavy load of copper and lead sheathing material (18 tons), cordage (14 tons), zinc (1 ton), tin (3 tons), iron (1 box), calf skins and hides (5 tons), five brass cannon (2.5 tons), and eight brass bells (2.5 tons).[15] This was just a part of the ship stores left behind by the departing Russian American Company. On her return passage from Victoria to Sitka in March, carrying 20 tons of salt and other items, the ship was wrecked at what is now called Cape Chacon among the Queen Charlotte Islands.

> The schooner Growler, Captain Horace Coffin, which sailed from Victoria on March 19 for Sitka, was lost with all hands near the entrance to Clarence Strait. Word was brought down by the Otter, which arrived at Victoria on April 19. The Otter was at Masset harbor on April 9 and received word from the Indians who had returned from where evidence of the wreck was found, which was at Cape Murray [Chacon], some 40 miles distant. The bodies of three men and a woman were found and a boat, some boxes of apples and two small kegs of liquor. . . . The supposition is she was struck by a squall during the night, shifted cargo and either sank or drifted on the reef and broke up. . . . The Captain was well and favorably known as Tom Coffin. He had been a long time in these waters and was the pilot for the Telegraph Company and also for our own men-of-war after the acquisition of the territory of Alaska. . . . The other 11 people on board were George H. Nicol, Abraham Jackson, Thomas Riley, A. Steward, C. A. Timson, John Shephard, Samuel Thompson, a young man from San Francisco, name unknown, and two half-breed Natives, male and female.[16]

Additional articles reported that the crew had been slain by Haida Indians. Leaving Fort Wrangell, Mitchell proceeded directly to Cape Chacon, overtaking a canoe and bringing on board three Indians as pilots on the way. One of the three, Ka-oun, had lived in Victoria and assisted in interpreting between the local groups. Mitchell was able to determine that the Kou tribe had not been the first to the scene of the wreck, and soon departed for the village of the Masset tribe. Two kedge anchors and chains were recovered from the scene prior to departure and carried on board

Saginaw. A third anchor and more chain were recovered from a village near Gardner Harbor.[17]

The chief of the Masset tribe was not much help to Mitchell, admitting only to "having taken a considerable quantity of articles from the wreck, the principal part of which was Whiskey and other liquors, which had already been drank."[18] At the Masset village, Mitchell's officers discovered more pieces of the puzzle: a quadrant (navigation tool), part of a clock, a "magazine," and a ring.[19] Two natives were detained on board the ship, taken on board as "passengers." Mitchell continued to steam throughout the area, touching at villages and seeking information. No other traces of the lost *Growler* were discovered, though the commander claimed two more "passengers."

Saginaw returned to Sitka with four prisoners, each telling a different version of events, and there was no satisfactory conclusion. In port, Mitchell learned from an informant via a local Indian woman who was "kept" by an American garrisoned there that a party of thirty or more of the Hoonah tribe, along with their chief, Steen-yah, had been the first to reach the wreck site and had committed the brutal murders. But the informant refused to confirm this before Commander Mitchell, who then had him locked on board the ship. The Hoonah-kon inhabited the Cross Sound area to the north of Sitka and Chichagof Island. In fact, a large party of Hoonah-kon dressed in Western clothing had passed through Sitka the day Mitchell and *Saginaw* had arrived, whereas previously "they scarcely had a blanket apiece." Alerted to *Saginaw*'s activities, no further proof was forthcoming.

Left with only a handful of prisoners, all telling contradictory and unconfirmed tales, the investigation ground to a halt. Mitchell would continue searching sporadically while engaged in other missions among the islands, but nothing would come of it. Material from the wreck had been scattered throughout the Tlingit homeland, stolen and/or salvaged and traded among tribes, but the trail had been lost. *Saginaw* returned to the tasks of shuttling bricks for construction and transporting army personnel between Fort Wrangell and Fort Tongass. The consensus of opinion sided with the Sitka woman's account, although she was drunk at the time she reported it. According to her, the schooner had run aground during a violent storm. The crew had tried to reach shore in the ship's boats but were driven back by gunfire from the Hoonah party. Most drowned in the rough surf, though the few that succeeded in getting onto firm ground were killed outright.[20] But this story came from the Sitka-kon, not the Hoonah. Others believed that the mutilated condition of the bodies found at the site was a result of the sharp rocks on the beach, not intentional murder.[21]

Continually operating the steam engines on *Saginaw*, necessary for transiting the narrow straits and the strong and unpredictable currents, demanded coal. The navy had established contracts in Nanaimo, British Columbia, for shipping coal supplies northward, but commanders were constantly on the lookout for new sources of fuel while making their rounds in Alaska. At times, this meant turning sailors into coal miners. In June and July, Commander Mitchell pursued rumors of coal seams on Kupreanof Island and Admiralty Island. After transferring expensive imported Nanaimo coal from the British schooner *Black Diamond*, Mitchell headed south. Kupreanof was Kake-kon territory. A good deal of friction had existed between the Russians and the Kake Indians, confrontations that more than once led to Kake villages being burned in retribution for unspecified transgressions. Mitchell anchored at Kalahoo Bay, which he renamed Hamilton Bay in honor of George Hamilton, who had been hired to build the customshouse at Fort Wrangell and had tipped Mitchell to the possible coal seams. The newness of the territory offered the commanders of *Saginaw* opportunities to name or rename natural features in Alaska, to impose a new and more familiar template on the wilderness, and they took advantage of the fact. The sailors spent three long, hard days digging and blasting at the 18-inch narrow crevice of black rock, working out about 3 tons and ferrying it down to the cobble beach.

Saginaw had neither chemist nor lab on board, so the test for the new source of coal was carried out in the boilers themselves. Mitchell noted to Rear Admiral Thatcher that the Hamilton coal raised steam in approximately the same amount of time as the Navarino coal from British Columbia—an hour for the former compared to fifty-five minutes for the latter. He gave the hot-burning Hamilton coal high marks, the ship making 9½ knots during a five-hour run with only four of the six furnaces stoked.[22] Coal back in the nineteenth century was what oil is now, the single most important resource at the heart of industrialization and transportation. So even as the post–Civil War navy downsized and reemphasized the primacy of sail, Alaska opened the door on potential strategic sources of fuel and reports from commanders in the field were read and forwarded with critical interest.

On the eastern shore of Admiralty Island, Mitchell explored the Kootz-nahoo Inlet, in search of outcropping seams indicated by specimens brought to him by the local Indians. Here the Killisnoo-kon lived in relative peace with the European settlers, and a number of tribesmen were willing to be employed at collecting coal for the promise of future wages. Mitchell found poor holding ground near the village, and so moved *Saginaw* farther into the deep inlet, finding a secure cove now known as Mitchell's Bay. The sailors spent four days digging into the rock, only leaving Kootznahoo for Sitka for more supplies to expand the mining operation. There, from the supply steamer *George S. Wright*, the sailors-turned-miners acquired lumber and tools, blasting powder and pickaxes. And from the American ship *Winged Arrow*, *Saginaw* added ten head of cattle, abundant and fresh beefsteak for the enlisted men at last.[23]

Saginaw focused on these new potential sources of coal, but could not ignore her other duties. The subsequent weeks were spent running errands among the islands, touching at Saginaw Bay and Cape Grindall, Fort Tongass and Fort Wrangell. Supplies, equipment, and army passengers spread throughout the islands, and the continuing inquiry into the case of the lost *Growler* was never far behind. Like Minister Ward in China, General Davis used the navy steamer to tour his domain, finally able to make personal contact with the scattered chiefs and gain firsthand knowledge of the region he theoretically managed.[24] At Tongass Island to the south, *Saginaw* rendezvoused with the survey steamer HMS *Beaver*, and from there paid a diplomatic visit across the border to the British outpost at Fort Simpson. Then, turning north again and stopping at Kootznahoo for more coal, Mitchell took his ship through "Saginaw Channel" and into Lynn Canal, a long fjord of brilliant blue water bordered by majestic glacial mountains. *Saginaw* explored as far north as the Taiya Inlet (in the vicinity of modern-day Haines and Skagway), the country of the Chilcat-kon, the most powerful of the Tlingit tribes and one held in high esteem by neighboring groups. The Lynn Canal passage was a salvage run. A report of a missing vessel had reached Sitka. Alaska has always been a maritime region of extreme navigational hazards. (Today there are more than four thousand wrecks recorded along the state's rocky and ice-choked coastline.)

In Lynn Canal, the schooner *Louisa Downs*, a 45-foot trading vessel captained by Michael Sullivan, had grounded onto the cobble beach, stranding five crewmen along with her cargo and equipment on "Sullivan's Island."

The vessel, on a trading and prospecting cruise, carried a variety of cloth, flour, tobacco, jewelry, pipes, gunpowder, shot, and whiskey. Mitchell anchored near the island and recovered the castaways, along with the cargo and anchors, chain, sails, and rigging from the wreck. The ship was later refloated from the rocks and brought to Sitka for repairs, only to be lost to shipwreck again some months later.[25]

The schooner carried liquor by special permission of General Davis, for military regulations sought to strictly control the trade in these items, severely limiting their sale to the troops and prohibiting all sale to the local Indians. In truth, there was no real expectation that dealing in contraband or the continuation of the covert British trade could actually be checked among the hundreds of miles and hundreds of islands and coves of the territory in the southeast panhandle. The restrictions imposed at specific points along the route simply created higher prices for the thriving British and American whiskey smugglers. In fact, prior to the loss of his ship and his life, Captain Coffin on board *Growler* had been in the business of distributing "villainously bad alcohol" and manufacturing "a drink which would veritably take a man's scalp off at forty rods!" Naval commanders in Alaska knew what they were up against:

> The natives themselves give aid and comfort to the whiskey-smuggler by timely warning of approaching danger, by false information to the officers of the law, and by secreting the small vessels of these smugglers when searched fur [sic]. The myriads of islands and harbors along this coast, which resembles Norway in the character of its fjords; the thick, foggy weather, and the innumerable channels and straits, many of which are not even marked on the charts, give an advantage to the whiskey-trader he is not slow to avail himself of.[26]

Alongside his other duties, the commander found the tour of the new territory fascinating, and pursued additional interests more suited to his academic inclinations. Mitchell collected a wealth of information for his lexicon of the Chinook language, the dialect common among most of the Tlingit tribes. In fact, he compiled all sorts of information on the tribes, anything that could be seen as possibly useful to the Department. The men also regularly drilled at target practice and running out the great guns, for in Mitchell's view, friendly contact as well as the demonstration of military presence would go far in "reforming" the tribes: "I have made it a point to stop at every place where there was even a village however small on my passages to and from different points in our possessions

North. . . . Until the military have some means of transportation, the *Saginaw* will have to do the principal part of the work of disciplining the Indians. Thus far our presence in, and among those we have visited has been very salutary, as has been shown at Wrangle [Wrangell] Island, Kessen, Kau Island, Koutznow [Kootznahoo] and at the mouth of the Tchillcat [Chilcat] River."[27]

Relations between the U.S. Navy and the natives were "salutary" only in the existing context of overall tensions, for the balance of power was clearly one-sided. For instance, the commander's clerk, Mate John Ponte, left the ship at Kootznahoo to oversee the mining operation. (*Saginaw* depended more and more on this local source of coal given the irregularity of supply at Sitka.) Ponte had lumber for the construction of a shelter and a Sharps carbine for protection.[28] The Killisnoo-kon had been cooperative in cutting wood and mining coal for Commander Mitchell, but wanted silver or trade goods, not paper greenbacks, in payment. When *Saginaw* touched at the Kootznahoo Inlet again in early August 1868, three natives were placed in irons and taken on board, ostensibly for "creating troubles on shore," but in all likelihood they were hostages, ensuring the safety of Mate John Ponte at the mine.[29] *Saginaw* could never escape its role of a colonial policeman, an instrument of gunboat diplomacy, this time at a domestic or territorial level.

By mid-August, *Saginaw* had been in Alaska for three and a half months, steaming constantly in the straits. Much of the time, the ship burned local fuel, and the effects were beginning to show. The Kootznahoo coal was too volatile, containing too much resin and too many impurities, and it burned extremely hot. This warped the boilers, burned away the insulation, and heated the lower portions of the smokestack to glowing red. Also, the Kootznahoo fuel in the bunkers was more liable to spontaneous combustion.[30] Without the supplies and facilities necessary for the boiler repairs, Mitchell took the ship south to Victoria, arriving there on August 13 and remaining in port for almost a month. The abduction of the Killisnoo hostages, thus carried to British Columbia, caused a great deal of anxiety among the tribe, and consequently some degree of consternation for General Davis at Sitka. The Tlingit tribes operated under a reciprocal system of justice, an eye for an eye, a hostage for a hostage. Davis sought to avoid any recriminatory actions.

Not much is directly revealed in the records regarding Commander Mitchell's control of his crew, and no doubt Alaska was not a suitable location for the employment of the sweatbox, but the irons and the brig had been neglected. Mitchell was not a hard taskmaster in the mold of William Hopkins, but his crew were for the most part fresh recruits from the roughest walks of life serving in the unrestrained region of Alaska. Over the summer there were several minor confrontations at Sitka. The Sitka-kon resisted the increasing encroachment upon more and more of their land, and even forcibly disarmed a military surveying party. In another incident, several hundred natives marched to the garrison walls, demanding the return of an Indian youth who, intended as a sacrifice at a chief's funeral, had escaped to the sanctuary of the military post. The Americans refused to surrender the boy and, with the assistance of *Saginaw*, Davis prohibited all canoe movement by water until conditions settled and the Sitka-kon requested a return to the status quo.[31]

Whether cruising in the straits, delivering army men and supplies, or lying at anchor at Sitka, life on board the small steamer was difficult at best. Dysentery, fevers, chills, and coughs had preceded apace, nothing unusual beyond what Surgeon Whedon might have expected. At times officers clearly engaged in alcohol abuse, Ensign Vail, for example, once having participated in an extended bout of drinking for several days ashore.[32] Enlisted men knew better than to allow their imbibing to be so plainly obvious as the consequences for them could be more severe. And prostitution, along with other types of relations ashore, brought a host of other problems. Symptoms of syphilis and gonorrhea among the sailors seemed to coincide with the visits to Sitka. These were usually presented to the surgeon in an advanced stage, after the men had failed at long and sometimes painful self-treatment. Then in June, while *Saginaw* lay off Kake, William Fowler, a young Scottish yeoman (boy) newly shipped at San Francisco prior to the voyage, began to show unusual signs of mental derangement. Fowler initially exhibited typical symptoms of dysentery, but with intense pain and apprehension accompanying his movements; "Frequent passages . . . much straining," as the surgeon put it.[33] This soon transitioned into a marked nervousness and weakness, though the pain diminished and the fever and headaches improved. By July 9, poor Fowler was exhibiting "marked symptoms of derangement of mind, symptoms of insanity, roaming around the ship, ongoing agitation and fear."[34] Fowler absolutely refused to remain on the berth deck. Whedon postulated that this unusual behavior was due to the fact that, a few days prior to the outbreak, the young boy had been involved in an accident. Explosive shells for the Parrott rifled pivot guns had broken loose within the magazine, crashing down on the yeoman and trapping him for an extended period until his shipmates could dig him out. The surgeon believed this had literally scared Fowler temporarily out of his mind.

How much did all the other realities of the voyage contribute to his odd behavior? The cramped and dirty conditions, the exposure to drunken garrison life at Sitka, the tense contacts with the Tlingit, the unfamiliar and difficult surroundings? Fowler remained fearful and constantly on the move, unable to feel safe in any one location, unable to be left alone. After a week of nervousness, he finally began to show signs of improvement, yet he had no memory of his derangement. Whedon placed him on stimulants, meaning regular small doses of alcohol, and recommended to the commanding officer that Fowler be removed from the magazine as his duty station during quarters.

Delayed for repairs to the boiler at Victoria, the ship was struck by multiple desertions. It was an opportunity for the sailors to run at the British port rather than return to the moldy life in the ship's forecastle and the constant rain at Sitka. Following repairs, a telegram arrived by dispatch boat as the ship was leaving the harbor. Much to the commander's surprise, for Mitchell had planned the in-port at Victoria as a repair stop only, *Saginaw* was ordered to return to Mare Island. The ship continued south, not north.

Unfortunate Yeoman William Fowler, having recovered from his temporary mental state, relapsed on the passage to San Francisco: "After having suffered once before from a derangement of the mind, and having been acting well for some weeks, was taken again last evening with mental derangement . . . imagining a great variety of things, his mind taking a moral turn, more than anything else. Imagining he is to be shot, and so is constantly praying, and at times tries to jump overboard."[35] Surgeon Whedon placed the boy under suicide watch and prescribed regular doses of opium, which seemed to calm his nerves.

Mitchell arrived at San Francisco on September 15, and the ship spent almost two months at the navy yard undergoing a more thorough refit. Captain James Alden, who had relieved Rear Admiral Craven as commandant of the yard, called for an inspection of the ship on report of its unprecedented uncleanliness, and sent on his survey of *Saginaw* to the Department.[36] The holds of the ship were emptied, scrubbed, and painted, but not all of the funk could be removed.

The Kake War

While *Saginaw* was at the navy yard, a most unfortunate and tragic event occurred that necessitated another change in command. Commander John Mitchell had once again returned to San Francisco to recruit for new enlistments. Between 7:00 and 8:00 on the evening of October 21, two men accosted the officer on the Sutter Street waterfront, one fracturing his head with a strong blow. William O. Smith and his accomplice, Thomas Savage, then robbed the body and fled into the Barbary Coast, only to be caught by police a short while later. Smith claimed the murder was done in a moment of passion, on account of an offensive remark. Yet the body had been dragged into the street and across the rail tracks in an effort to fake an accident scene. Mitchell had left Mare Island that morning for the city, informing Commandant Alden that he would be recruiting to fill the multiple vacancies in *Saginaw*'s crew, and he carried a large sum of money in a pocketbook. Alden wrote to the Department that "this may account in some measure for the kind of company he was found in at that time, and by which he lost his life." A witness described the two men bending over the body and removing a package, though his watch and a small sum of cash were left.[37]

The news of the very public murder came as a shock to the navy yard: "Such an outrage perpetuated upon one of the principal thoroughfares of our city, at an hour too when the streets were thronged with people, seems quite incredible, and bears with it strong evidence of being unpremeditated, and almost accidental."[38] *Saginaw*, scheduled to be ready to sail for Alaska by October 27, was necessarily detained pending arrival of yet another captain. Lieutenant Commander Lester A. Beardslee took temporary command while the commandant communicated with the secretary of the navy. The remains of John Mitchell were buried with military honors at the Mare Island Naval Shipyard cemetery.

Richard Worsam Meade Jr., born into a tradition of naval service, was the next commanding officer selected. Meade Jr. was an independent and outspoken man of action. His father, Richard Meade Sr., was the same. As a young lieutenant on the brig USS *Washington* in 1839, Meade Sr. had taken part in the famous boarding of a Spanish vessel off the coast of New York. Fifty African captives had been en route to Cuba when they overpowered their captors and took control of the ship. The case of the brig *Amistad*, and the involvement of abolitionists and of President John Adams's son, John Quincy Adams, raised troubling issues for a young nation.

The fate of the Africans, initially referred to in the subsequent trial in the U.S. court system as cargo, galvanized the slavery issue in pre–Civil War America.

By 1868, Lieutenant Commander Richard W. Meade Jr. had blazed through an active and volatile service career of his own. Entering the Naval Academy in 1850 at age thirteen, Meade served as a midshipman on USS *San Jacinto* and USS *Merrimack* in the Mediterranean, and as lieutenant on USS *Cumberland* off the coast of Africa. In September 1859, Meade was on board USS *Saranac*, cruising off Panama and the coast of Central America, but his service on board was contentious. In March 1860, he was tried by court-martial for his strong denunciation of and personal attack on Marine Lieutenant Thomas Y. Field. The charges were upheld by the court, and Meade received a solid reprimand. He was detached from *Saranac* a few weeks later, transferring to *Cyane*, and then going ashore at La Paz for the protection of American property and lives during the Wars of Reform in Mexico. In 1861, Meade's request to return to the Atlantic coast was granted when he was sent to New York to recover from yellow fever he had contracted at Acapulco.[39]

During the Civil War, Meade served as a commissioned lieutenant commander in charge of the ironclad steamer USS *Louisville*, actively engaged on the Mississippi River dispersing rebel guerrilla forces. Ultimately, Meade took command of four ironclads and two wooden steamers on the river, landing his troops and engaging the enemy alongside the army led by Major General William S. Sherman. This led to commendations from Admiral Porter. Unfortunately, owing to "contusion and debility consequent upon fever," Meade was again transferred to the Atlantic seaboard, serving as ordnance instructor ashore at the naval yards in Boston and New York. On July 13, 1863, riots broke out in New York, and Meade, in command of a naval battalion (100 marines and 250 seamen), took control of the entire lower portion of the city. The role of command under pressure was a natural one for Meade. At sea again in 1864 and 1865, he captured a number of blockade runners and vessels sailing with contraband while in command of USS *Marblehead* and later USS *Chocura*.[40]

Meade had proved to be an active and zealous, if somewhat hot-headed, officer—a temperament that, from the navy's perspective, had its uses. In recognition of his talents, after the Civil War he was appointed head of the Department of Seamanship and Naval Tactics at the U.S. Naval Academy, in part to instill that aggressive nature into the officer candidates. But Meade, naturally enough, lobbied for an active command, a return to the deck of a ship. Rear Admiral Samuel L. Breese, defending Meade in his pursuit of active service at an earlier point in his career, stated, "I am certainly ignorant of . . . any want of zeal in the performance of your [Meade's] duties; on the latter quality, on the contrary, its over exercise would be more the rule than the exception, and the result of a naturally very impulsive temperament."[41] Years later, Admiral Seaton Schroeder, who had served under Meade on *Saginaw* as a midshipman, described him as a "daring and skillful seaman but disconcertingly frank in both look and spoken expression whenever anyone incurred his displeasure or failed to meet his professional expectations."[42] In October 1868, Richard Meade transferred from Annapolis to San Francisco, where *Saginaw* was being prepared for sea. It is possible that some of the naval establishment considered Richard Meade the right type of commander for disciplining the natives in Alaska, a stern hand in dealing with what was sometimes called in the nineteenth century the "Indian problem."

Commander Meade arrived in San Francisco and took firm charge of the ship on November 20, just as the executive officer was getting the final provisions on board, and the inevitable deserters were returning from one last fling at the bars in the city. Like Samuel Franklin, Meade felt less than enthralled with the galley and mess situation on *Saginaw*. The one small wood-burning stove, located in the forecastle's berthing deck, had to serve the entire crew, officers and men alike. Typically, Meade stocked his own pantry, and messed ashore in surroundings more suitable to his rank until the last possible moment.

Repairs to the engine and boilers took up the rest of the time at the harbor, but by November 30 the ship departed San Francisco. *Saginaw* attempted to push through the large surf on the bar at the Gate, only to encounter a breaking wave that swept the decks, and the ship was forced to turn back until the following day. The enlisted crew took advantage of the momentary delay. Peveril Meigs, Meade's cousin, sailed as the captain's clerk on the cruise, and recorded: "whiskey has got on board somehow although the men were searched whenever they came from shore; several of them were put in double irons. Three men deserted this morning before daylight."[43] Two more were lost at the last moment. Landsman William Taylor, a young Englishman who has signed on board the ship at Victoria, and Captain of the Hold Joseph Remicilli, a sailor from Italy, were both transferred to Mare Island Naval Hospital before sailing, for treatment of advanced syphilis.[44]

Meade tried the departure again on October 1. The small ship found herself beating into the wind and waves on a very rough passage, the officers and crew and particularly the greenhorns turning seasick from the horrible rolling, and the berth deck was doused with seas. This necessitated burning a considerable amount of coal, and Meade chose to pay for resupply in Victoria, which he could procure there for ten dollars per ton rather than the eighteen dollars per ton the navy had procured on contract with Hutchinson and Company in Alaska. Meade, with a constant eye to "economy" (reminiscent of Captain Bligh's legacy in the Pacific of an earlier age), wrote Admiral Craven that he would just as soon charter a schooner, load her with coal for thirteen dollars per ton at Navarino, and tow her to Sitka, rather than allow Hutchinson to continue "bleeding the government to the fullest extent."[45] He made Victoria on December 7, planning to continue with even more repairs to the engines and bunkers as well, which he felt were overlooked in San Francisco.

Formal relations with the Royal Navy had improved a great deal since the Civil War, but the men remembered those days well. Six days in the British port gave Meade and Saginaw's officers enough time to answer an official invitation to the governor's house for lunch, where they were received rather coldly, fleeced of twenty-five-dollar contributions "for the orphans," and left to walk back to the port and their ship in the rain, muddying their shoes and uniforms. Few things were more important to officers in the nineteenth century than the meticulous care of their uniforms. Clerk Meigs felt the humiliating experience proved the British to be "a darn blarsted dirty set of blarsted asses."[46]

The passage to Sitka touched at the familiar ports of Bella Bella, Fort Tongass, and, finally, Kootznahoo Inlet, where cast-ashore shipmate Ponte had succeeded in overseeing the removal of 60 tons of the resinous and volatile coal, though it was unclear if the natives had really been paid for their efforts. Saginaw also landed Captain Mitchell's Indians at Kootznahoo village, returning the hostages/passengers who had sailed south with the commander. About their impressions of the voyage we know nothing.[47] On December 22, Saginaw was again swinging at anchor in Sitka harbor, protected by the small islands of the southeast coastline and the thick beds of kelp rolling beneath the fog. Meade communicated with the general, and finding things quiet among the garrison and local Tlingit, immediately fell sick. Surgeon Whedon diagnosed "cholera morbus," and Saginaw's commander spent a long and uncomfortable night purging.

The next day, with some effort, he returned to duty, seeking to determine what exactly constituted his instructions, for all had proceeded in great haste. No specific orders awaited Meade at Sitka, and he wrote to Craven, "I find no instructions among my predecessor's papers, and shall therefore act according to my judgment and the circumstances of the moment until I hear from you."[48] Meade had, in fact, been instructed by the admiral to "render such assistance as may be necessary in the protection of the military forces while building their fortifications."[49] But the lack of communication was not an uncommon trait for Admiral Thomas Tingey Craven. He had been censured more than once by Gideon Welles as to navy regulations 298 and 299, the Navy Department having received only one telegram and some random dispatches from the admiral in the months since he took command of the squadron.[50]

Meade's temperament suited him for running a tight ship and finding more ways to save the navy money. At Sitka, he immediately laid off the local coast pilot, Robert Hicks, who had been employed by Mitchell for $150 per month. Meade found the civilian Hicks to be a good pilot and a handy interpreter, but in personality too independent-minded to submit to what Meade thought of as the proper naval discipline, in short: "spoiled for service in a man-of-war . . . allowed too much latitude. In mid journey he refused to take the vessel to Sitka, and I was obliged to deal in a summary manner with him."[51] Meade, the former Civil War officer, had no love for the British Hicks. As for paying the natives for their labors at the coal mines, Meade had no intention of doing so until it was clearly proven to him that they had not already been compensated.

Saginaw's crew, meanwhile, welcomed themselves back to Sitka in their old and familiar ways, and Landsman Edward Bell was soon confined in double irons for smuggling liquor on board. But all was not as quiet as had initially been perceived. At 6:15 p.m. on New Year's Day, the ship was ordered to general quarters, and the pivot guns loaded with explosive shell, the broadside howitzers loaded with antipersonnel shrapnel. During the disorganized revelries at the Sitka garrison, a confrontation between the Chilcat-kon and the garrison guard had occurred, and one soldier and two locals lay critically wounded. General Davis instructed Meade to raise the alarm, and *Saginaw*'s third cutter was quickly armed and dispatched under Midshipman Pillsbury's command to prevent the escape of a local chief from a nearby village. Pillsbury repulsed the heated attack of six armed war canoes at the village, while the ship (forced to stand off from the rocky shores) fired one round of shrapnel from its 24-pounder. But the ship could not get in close to the cutter in order to assist directly. Meade sounded the retreat recalling the armed party, and the other cutters were launched as picket boats for the night. The following day the chief associated with the attack was taken into custody and placed in the guardhouse, increasing the tension between the parties. The incident led Meade to recognize that in dealing with hostile populations in southeast Alaska, smaller was better. The villages "are remote from the sea, and man-of-war cannot get near enough to shell them. The tribes are the most numerous and warlike in this region, and their chief is a person of great influence over them. I think vessels cruizing in these waters should have a steam launch."[52]

This would prove to be the minor prelude to a larger confrontation to come. Observers later reported that between one and three locals had been killed (a Kake, as well as Sitka and Chilkat natives) during Pillsbury's attack on the canoe. A subsequent request for payment and restitution from a subchief of the Kake tribe (the brother of the murdered native) to the garrison commander went unfulfilled. That was a mistake. At that point, understandably, the Kake-kon took the next step.

Saginaw stayed in Sitka for two more weeks in the rain and winter gales before returning to the coal mining operations at the Kootznahoo Inlet and Mitchell's Bay. Then the ship conducted a northern cruise of exploration along the passages of southeast Alaska. Maneuvering through strong tides and currents, Meade took his ship to "Sauloy Bay in Peril Strait, Koteasok harbor on Admiralty Island, Mitchell's Bay in Kootznahoo Archipelago, Freshwater Bay on Tchitchagoff Island, William Henry Bay in Lynn Channel and Pyramid Island harbor at the mouth of the Tchillcat River." During the cruise, Meade himself named Koteasok harbor, Mitchell's Bay, and Pyramid Island harbor.[53] Meade also finally addressed the debts to the native laborers at Mitchell's Bay: "They had commenced to feel angry and dis-satisfied at not being paid for their labor. Very naturally—as they had heard nothing from any Govt. Officers since last September. Instead of paying them in money I caused the Paymaster to purchase, at this place [Sitka], some coarse articles of clothing, leaf tobacco and calico, which they took more readily than money, which they don't understand or appreciate the value of."[54] During the tour, *Saginaw* made her way from Kootznahoo to the Chilkat River, the most northern point of her Alaska service, beyond 59 degrees latitude. Rather than mentioning the beauty of the spectacular mountains and glaciers of Alaska's Lynn Canal, the commander remained focused on his bottom line—economy ruled. Meade found that, by using a combination of the cheaper but volatile Kootznahoo coal, and alternately burning green wood (hemlock), he could cruise at an average of eight knots for a grand total of $32.56 per day. Compared to the existing contract, this was a rather large daily savings of $173.60, the precise amounts being carefully calculated by the commanding officer himself.[55]

Tragedy almost struck when the ship balanced briefly on the precipice of disaster on January 31 in aptly named Peril Straits. After *Saginaw* navigated past the first rapids successfully, the tides and current near the second grabbed hold of the vessel. With the paddle wheels churning away, and the pressure in the boilers reaching 23 pounds per square inch (usually never more than 10 or 15), and the foresail and foretopsail set, the struggling *Saginaw* fought being dragged into the whitewater. The ship remained at a dead standstill for twenty minutes or more: "The tide was rushing furiously over the rocks astern of us, making the water one mass of foam, and we were drawing nearer and nearer to it every moment. . . . All the officers were on deck and all said she was lost and expected every minute to see her go furiously into the breakers."[56] Meade finally committed to throwing the hot-burning Kootznahoo coal into the fires, risking bursting his boilers but desperately needing more steam. It wasn't enough. Only a fortuitous shift in wind eventually pushed the ship out of danger.

Surgeon Whedon faced his same enemies as during the last Alaskan cruise, and tended to his feverish and catarrhal crew by dispensing quinine and arsenic. He looked after their usual sufferings of chills and rheumatism and bronchitis, lacerated limbs and sprained joints as best he could. Despite the galley fires being up constantly, it proved impossible to keep the berth deck dry, and the crew were constantly exposed to the cold and the wet. Most would survive, but not all. Ordinary Seaman Alex Leslie was the most difficult of Whedon's charges. The Scottish sailor had contracted gonorrhea during the ship's last tour in Alaska, but now reported excruciating pain in his left abdomen. Whedon placed him on morphine, and then shifted to frequent doses of whiskey, with mustard poultices applied to the stomach. Not much did any good; the pain increased and Leslie lay prone and sinking. By the end of the month, he was constantly vomiting a watery dark matter, unable to move, eat or speak. Intravenous fluids were unknown; Whedon was obliged to attempt nourishment by introducing a beef broth enema.[57] By the time the ship had returned to Sitka, the patient seemed somewhat better. At least, Leslie was well enough to be placed on a diet of beef, ale, and whiskey, and transferred to the care of the army hospital on shore. There, General Davis and an armed party of soldiers awaited *Saginaw*, as well as rumors of a treacherous murder to the south.

At 6:30 a.m. on February 11, 1869, all hands were called to weigh anchor and get under way. On board were fifteen privates from the Sitka garrison, two noncommissioned U.S. Army officers, four natives as guides, General Davis, army Captains Kennique and McIntyre, and Captain Bryant of the U.S. Coast Survey. According to the report from Sitka, two white traders, Ludwig Maager and William Walker, had procured a large, open boat and left there in December in the company of two friendly local natives, in order to buy pelts. On the night of January 13, camping at a small cove on the south end of Admiralty Island, they were fired upon by Kake Indians. Walker was killed and Maager wounded, only to be finished off later with a knife. The pelts and the two Sitka natives remained untouched. According to the Kake attackers themselves, the justifiable retribution had been provoked by the killing of a Kake-kon at Sitka on New Year's Eve by a U.S. soldier.[58] *Saginaw*'s Midshipman Pillsbury had precipitated this incident. This was eye-for-an-eye justice, revenge, the familiar practice in the region.

Meade believed his role in this case was to end the cycle of retribution and killing by carrying an overwhelming force against the Kake, thereby extinguishing fire with fire. He was to assist the general in punishing the alleged murderers. With the army party, as well as sufficient weapons and ammunition and provisions for one week, *Saginaw* headed south, pitching through blustery snow squalls and rain. Two survivors of the attack, the Sitka natives, were also on board. No sooner had they set out than they were forced to pause. At 9:15 a.m., the ship ran easily aground in the Whitestone Narrows of Neviski Straits, not an uncommon occurrence in Alaska. By 9:35 a.m., the ship was kedged off the gravelly shoal, and soon entered the first rapids of the Narrows.

At noon on the first day out, the ship encountered a canoe and a party of natives, paddlers bringing the remains of the murdered traders to Sitka. Upon inspection, Meade and Davis confirmed their identity, the "remains of which were in shocking condition. Though they had been interred by the Sitkas, the wolves and the crows had eaten the flesh from the bones, leaving but a foot and a leg and some shreds of clothing. The leg was identified as Maager's and the terrible gash in the calf sufficiently verified the truth of the report as to the manner in which he had been finished."[59] The remains were returned to the canoe and sent on to Sitka, but the soldiers and *Saginaw*'s crew had now seen the evidence of the attack for themselves.

Over the next two days, the crew drilled at going to quarters in the drizzling rain, the soldiers cleaned and readied their weapons, and the ship made its usual call at Mitchell's Bay for coal. On February 14, the vessel hove in sight of a small Kake settlement near Saginaw Bay on the northern coast of Kuiu Island. The ship's crew beat to quarters, howitzers were cast loose, and pivot guns loaded. There was no sign of active resistance, or anyone for that matter, on the wooded shore. Midshipmen J. E. Pillsbury and E. W. Bridge were ordered to ready their cutters for landing. Before the landings, the ship opened fire on the villages with explosive shells from the Parrott rifled pivot guns, the sounds echoing across the water, and then sent the armed crews in to finish the job. For the next couple of days, the midshipmen took charge on shore, as *Saginaw* stood off in Saginaw and Security Bay at the ready.

The position of midshipman had originally evolved from the traditional practice of sending the sons of nobility and gentry to sea, where early experience was necessary to maintain a corps of professional experienced naval officers. Later the evolution of midshipmen included specific schooling, followed by tutelage and then service on board an active vessel, and finally an exam marking the rite of passage to the rank of lieutenant. Midshipmen were young, and their job in the navy was to learn something of everything, and the Kake settlements on Kuiu offered them an opportunity to experience some of that firsthand.

Pillsbury's action report to his commanding officer demonstrated that, despite the fact that they failed to encounter any natives, he'd done his best to carry out his orders and exact some form of immediate punishment:

I landed near the villages on Saginaw Bay about 8:30 AM with seven men from the ship's company and seven soldiers from the garrison at Sitka, and carrying the necessary combustibles. After making a proper disposition of the soldiers as pickets, I proceeded to destroy whatever property I could find. I burned four houses with their contents and destroyed six canoes, leaving one house, one open shed and one canoe belonging to a friendly Indian woman. Upon our approach, two or three men retreated into the woods, and with this exception none were seen. At 10:00 AM I returned to the ship with all the men. At 12:30 I landed at Kiku village with seven seamen and sixteen soldiers. I destroyed there fifteen houses and one canoe. No Indians were seen and the village had every appearance of having been abandoned for several days. At 2:30 I returned to the ship. On the 16th inst., at 11:00 AM, I landed at Tom's ranch on Kou Island with seven seamen and sixteen soldiers, and found it deserted as the last. I destroyed ten houses and one canoe, and returned to the ship at 11:50 AM. At Kiku and at Tom's ranch I found iron-work and chains which evidently belonged, originally, to some vessel.[60]

The woman's name was Sheksham, and she had on past occasions proven helpful to the Westerners, such as giving them information on the fate of the crew of the vessel *Royal Charlie*, who had been killed by Kake Indians in 1865. The investigation into that case, like others, had never been satisfactorily completed, and Pillsbury pointed out the possible artifacts at the settlement perhaps related to that event. Likewise, E. W. Bridge reported to the commanding officer:

In obedience to your orders to proceed to the head of Security Bay, and make search for, and destroy if possible an Indian village said to be located there, I left the ship at 1:30 PM. Of this date with an armed force in two boats, consisting of 17 seamen and 15 soldiers, the latter a detachment from the troops at Sitka. I found two stockade forts and one fishing ranch at the head of the Bay, a distance of about 5 miles from our anchorage. The forts were about 100 feet square, from 15 to 17 feet high and built of logs from 9 to 15 inches thick. These with the ranch I completely destroyed. They had apparently been deserted for some time. I found a good channel to within a mile of the forts, the water varying from 4½ to 9 fms in depth. I returned to the ship at 4:30 p.m.[61]

This was probably not the manner in which General Davis and Commander Meade had foreseen the action playing out. The enemy had vanished, leaving property damage as the only option, the fires being set only with difficulty in the constant Alaskan rain. Without the Kake's own point of view, it was hard to estimate the long-run effect of the destruction of these dwellings and forts, but the perception of abandonment did not mean the sites were not still in regular seasonal use. Shackrain, one of the Sitka survivors on board, confirmed that the Kake had fled the area, some probably into British territory.[62] No chiefs had been taken hostage, but the punishment was enough for now. *Saginaw's* men were disgusted that the Kakes had not given them a fight.[63] Meade called a halt to the action and set sail for Kootznahoo (always sparing his bunkers), returning to mining coal and collecting wood. He later highlighted the details of the expedition in a letter to Rear Admiral Craven: "Their houses cannot be replaced without great labor and time, some of those destroyed were rated at 300 blankets. They cannot rebuild the houses under a year, even if we suffer them to do so . . . no peace should be allowed them until they sue for it by sending in the murderers. . . . [T]he Kekous or Kakes have long been notorious on this coast as being a bad tribe and the murder[s] of Mr. Ebey U.S. Collector and that of the crew of the *Royal Charlie* schooner [have] . . . never been avenged."[64] The unpleasant weather added to the crew's gloom when, upon their arrival back at Sitka, they learned that their shipmate Alexander Leslie had died. The final diagnosis was an aneurysm of the abdominal aorta, a weakening of the main blood vessel in the lower torso. There was nothing they could have done.

Some may have seen this kind of punishment as simply another turning of the cycle of revenge, more of the same. Weeks after the expedition, Adolph E. Borie had a chance to review the reports. In March 1869, Borie had succeeded the venerable Gideon Welles as secretary of the navy. Borie had been an established businessman in Philadelphia, and had become a close friend of General Grant during the Civil War. (He had been a very liberal supporter of the troops during the conflict.) His appointment as secretary was a surprise to some. While Borie was glad that Commander Meade had assisted the army in Alaska, it was hard for him to see how any good could come from this continuing retribution. These actions did not bode well for the future. Borie wrote that the Department "regrets . . . to learn of the difficulties which seem to have sprung up between the Indians and our forces. The Russians held that country many years and it does not appear that there has been any serious trouble between their military authorities and the Indians, and it is to be hoped the United States can hold the possessions with like results. In the opinion of the Department such results can be secured with greater certainty and more satisfactorily and humanely by mild measures rather than harsh ones. The Indians ought to be treated with kindness, which would in the majority of instances prevent difficulties."[65] Commander Meade was perhaps not the man for this type of kinder and gentler approach.

Headed Home

The crew continued to suffer from the cold and rain into March 1869. One-fifth of the ship's complement could be found on the sick list at any given time. Ailments ranged from pneumonia to rheumatism to bronchitis to tonsillitis. Surgeon Whedon was kept busy administering to his patients with various effective and ineffective cures. Rumors circulated about attempts to the south to unite several of the tribes in a unified attack on Fort Wrangell. Meanwhile, at Sitka, General Davis grew suspicious of the schooner *Louisa Downs*'s repeated absences (the vessel had grounded months earlier in Lynn Canal). Once again the schooner was missing, and the general suspected the ship was off on a smuggling operation. That was a revenue issue, according to Meade, and his own orders prioritized the protection of Fort Wrangell from any potential threat. Heavy northern gales swept over the coast, however, delaying preparations. *Saginaw* dragged anchors and then parted the hawsers, and had to ride out the worst of the blow under increased steam. The storm passed, and on March 16 the ship departed southward for the fort, still stopping the occasional canoe in search of the guilty Kake Indians.

Unknown at the time to *Saginaw* and her commander in Alaska, the Navy Department had, at that very moment, already decided the fate of the gunboat. Having recently united again the separate North and South Pacific Squadrons into one single Pacific Station, and also facing the continuing downsizing budget of the peacetime post–Civil War navy, Secretary of the Navy Borie had sent Rear Admiral Craven instructions to lay up *Saginaw* and discharge her crew. The ship's senior officers were to be ordered home, with junior officers filling their vacancies.[66]

Thomas Tingey Craven responded to this suggestion from the Department, as well as Borie's instructions to lay up USS *Mohongo*, in classic Craven fashion. Wanting to increase rather than decrease his forces, as any squadron commander would, Craven waited a full week after receiving the Department's telegram, then informed Borie that *Mohongo* had just sailed so it would be impossible to lay her up until she returned. For *Saginaw*, Craven went on the defensive:

> In reference to the Saginaw I would respectfully state that on the 14th instant I received a letter from the Hon. Secretary of the Navy enclosing a copy of letters received from the Hon. Secretary of the Treasury, stating that it was absolutely necessary for the interests of the Government that a United States war vessel should be in the Alaskan waters for some time yet. The Saginaw, which is now there, is peculiarly adapted for this service by reasons of her small size and light draft (8 feet), coupled with good speed and economy of fuel, also her complement of officers and

men is quite small, say about sixty (60) all told. The Saginaw is in good order in every respect, hull, boilers, and engines. Under these circumstances I would respectfully suggest that the Saginaw be kept in commission for some time yet.[67]

In the years following the Civil War, the U.S. Navy underwent massive and immediate downsizing. Shore facilities were closed, ships laid up, and officers put on leave. The nation simply did not envision a role for a powerful overseas fleet, nor did it have much of a merchant marine left to protect in foreign ports as it had prior to hostilities. Between December 1864 and December 1870, the list of navy vessels was reduced from almost 700 to less than 200. And many of those left were truly worn out or otherwise unfit for sea duty.[68] That was what Craven strove against in defense of the tiny *Saginaw*. It might not have been exactly true that the aging sidewheeler's engines and boilers were in such exceptional shape, but it was hard for Craven to envision a more suitable vessel for the treacherous waters of Alaska's many channels, narrows, and rapids. No answer from the Department was sent to their irascible west coast admiral.

The rumors having proven unsubstantiated at Fort Wrangell, Meade continued southward, passing the Casaan fishery, stopping briefly at Fort Simpson, and rounding to Victoria by the end of the month. By April 5, Meade had learned, via the mails on board the steamer *Active*, that *Saginaw* had been ordered home, bound to be put out of commission. The news was not good. Eighteen sixty-nine was not the time for a naval commander to be losing his vessel. In all likelihood, Meade would be put ashore on reduced pay. By April 12, the ship was moored once again off the familiar quays at San Francisco. No liberty was granted her crew, though, for they were to be discharged soon and were needed for preparing the vessel to be decommissioned. Someone had to be on board and sufficiently sober in order to move the ship across the bay.

At 8:45 a.m. the following day, all hands were called to weigh anchor, and *Saginaw* stood out for Mare Island. By 12:20 p.m., the ship was secured at the naval yard, and the lighter was alongside for discharging her provisions: paymaster stores, engineering and navigation stores, rigging stores, and ammunition—all came off. The crew were soon engaged in unbending sails and unreeving the running rigging. The ship's cutters were hauled ashore, and during the passing squalls of April 17, with rain blowing through her bare sticks and empty deck, *Saginaw* was placed out of commission.

After his term on USS *Saginaw*, Richard Meade continued to rise in the ranks. In 1872, Commodore Meade surveyed the islands of what is now American Samoa, noting the possibilities for a naval station and coal depot there. His expertise in naval ordnance developed, and Meade co-authored *Ordnance Instructions for the United States Navy* with Montgomery Sicard. Meade eventually achieved the position of commander of the North Atlantic Fleet, the capstone of a successful and active career. He came, after all, from a line of military commanders. Unfortunately, their own service careers had not always ended well. In 1868, Meade's father, Rear Admiral Richard Meade Sr., lost his mind. Meade Jr. was forced to place his father in the Bloomingdale Asylum, as a danger to himself and others. For months past, Meade Sr. had been making threatening statements against a variety of relatives and officers, including Secretary of the Navy Gideon Welles. He carried several revolvers on his person, and four more in his valise, supposedly for self-defense against a gang of "roughs" bent on attacking him. The problem had been developing for years.[69]

Richard Meade Jr. retired from active duty at the rank of rear admiral in 1895, following forty-five years of service to the navy. Yet despite his impressive service career, his retirement was not voluntary. By 1895, his outspoken statements on the ineptitude of the current administration had raised the possibility of a court-martial for *Saginaw*'s former commander. He criticized "the un-American policy of an Administration that is [in Meade's estimation] saturated with anglo-maniacism."[70] Meade was an officer of the Civil War, and harbored no great love for the British, or for administrations that pandered to them. He stated publicly: "I am an American and a Union man. Those are two things that this administration cannot stand."[71] Meade welcomed the opportunity of a court-martial, stating to some of his friends that if he were brought before a court, "there would be some developments which would make the administration regret its action."[72] President Cleveland, perhaps wisely, chose not to allow the rear admiral his day on the stand, and forcibly retired him, stating in a harsh rebuke that he "regrets exceedingly that the long active service of this officer, so brilliant in its early stages and so often marked by honorable incidents, should at its close be tarnished by conduct at variance with his commendable career and inconsistent with the example which an officer of his high rank should furnish of submission to restraints and of a wholesome discipline and manifest propriety."[73] He'd had enough of Meade, who remained hotheaded to the end. Many in Congress and in the nation sided with the old sailor.

The forests, glaciers, waterfalls, and wildlife of the Far North made *Saginaw*'s experience in Alaska a study in extremes, long months of confined service in the cold and the rain set among a pristine wilderness of staggering beauty. For the narrow straits and unpredictable winds and currents, the small shallow-draft paddle wheeler was the answer, capable of running on and off gravel bars, setting sail and economizing fuel usage, operating off a variety of green wood and local coal of indeterminate quality. But in terms of fulfilling her military role, even *Saginaw*'s shallow draft was too deep to get into range of the hidden villages in the Northwest. Commander Meade's suggestion of a steam launch was endorsed by others. At this stage in the colonization of "Seward's purchase," confrontation was still a matter for small bands of armed men and close action. America had purchased Alaska, but as to administering it, the job was raw and unfinished.

Those actions that the ship did undertake were, in fact, regrettable from the viewpoint of the secretary of the navy. In Borie's eyes, Commander Meade's vigor and Civil War experience were not the best suited to a situation that called for more diplomacy and more sensitivity. Meade, like Mitchell, had close contact with the natives at the coal deposits and elsewhere, but the actions taken during the Kake War were unfortunate. Americans knew very little about Alaska, and, as was the case so often in other parts of the nineteenth-century world, generals and naval commanders were sometimes not the best of cultural ambassadors. Nonetheless, America's commitment to Alaska would continue, in fits and spurts. The minimal military administration of the territory, without adequate legal or fiscal support, would continue for years. It would be many decades before the resources and true wealth of the region began to be realized. USS *Saginaw* was the first naval vessel to make the inside passage to Alaska, charting the narrows and future harbors. But the ship would not be returning to the North.

6

Hawai`i and the End of the Archipelago

The United States . . . are more interested in the fate of these
Islands and in their government, than any other nation can be.

Daniel Webster, 1842

Lieutenant Commander Montgomery Sicard, looking down on USS *Saginaw* as she was decommissioned at Mare Island from the nearby deck of USS *Pensacola*, may have recognized the little side-wheeler from his days on the China Station, when he had served as sailing master on USS *Dacotah* in East Asia. Following in the wake of Commanders Schenck, Hopkins, McDougal, Scott, Franklin, Mitchell, and Meade, Sicard was to be *Saginaw*'s next commander. In some ways, he would be the ship's best commander, but assuredly he would be her last.

Sicard was born in 1836 in New York City, the son of Lydia Hunt (sister of Supreme Court Justice Ward Hunt) and Steven Sicard, a merchant. In 1840, following his father's death, the family moved upstate to Utica, Lydia's former home. Prior to the Civil War, he served as a young midshipman on both USS *Potomac* and USS *Wabash* in the Home Squadron. At twenty-four years of age, he was promoted to the rank of ship's master and sent to the East India Squadron. During the Civil War, Sicard served in the West Gulf Blockading Squadron on USS *Oneida*, participating as an executive officer in the capture of New Orleans in April 1862 and the passage of the Vicksburg batteries several months later. Rank moved quickly during the conflict, and Sicard was promoted to lieutenant commander that same year. He was a promising and talented officer, and a rising prospect, as long as he survived the war. During temporary leave ashore in 1863, he married Elizabeth Floyd, a descendant of William Floyd, a signer of the Declaration of Independence. The

Left: FIGURE 9. Lieutenant Commander Montgomery Sicard, *Saginaw*'s last commander, ca. 1870. From Read, *Last Cruise of the* Saginaw.

Right: FIGURE 10. Rear Admiral Montgomery Sicard during the 1890s, briefly in command of the North Atlantic Squadron during the Spanish-American War. Courtesy of Library of Congress.

couple would have three children. At sea again, Sicard took command of the steam gunboat USS *Seneca* during the hard-fought assaults at Fort Fisher in December 1864 and January 1865. After the war, he returned to New York and then Washington, D.C., and took up shore-side ordnance duties, serving as chief of the Bureau of Ordnance from 1881 to 1890 (see figs. 9–10). But before any of that occurred, Sicard was a thirty-four-year-old lieutenant commander, looking at his new peacetime command, a small vessel out of commission at Mare Island Naval Shipyard.

Craven had initially defended *Saginaw*'s role in Alaska, but to no avail. He had obediently laid the vessel up. But plans had inexplicably changed back East, and again there seemed to be the usual difficulty in communicating with the recalcitrant rear admiral. Had Craven's overly optimistic report on the condition of the ship had an effect? Sicard's own inspection of the ship, ordered by Craven while *Saginaw*'s crew was busily removing their provisions and equipment, revealed that though the vessel was generally in good condition, she could not be considered ready for sea duty:

the "engine frames are loose, two holding down bolts corroded and broken off. Possible defective state of inside keelsons."[1] Was another mission being planned? Only a week after the final stores had been removed from the ship, Borie wrote to Craven, again admonishing him that the Department had received but few acknowledgments of their communications: "The Department has telegraphed you today not to put the *Saginaw* out of commission but to order Lieut. Comd'r M. Sicard to command her."[2] Such crossed signals could be more the general rule than the exception. The telegraph system, though a great advancement in communications, had not, after all, made information instantaneous. Craven had already laid up the vessel and sent all her officers east. Sicard would have to start with a brand-new group, many lacking in experience on small gunboats. Nonetheless, Craven assured Borie that the ship would be ready for sea in two weeks. Actually, it would be more than two months.

At first, it seemed that *Saginaw* would again be headed north, for the Department did finally realize the usefulness of a vessel like the side-wheeler in Alaska and supported the continuing efforts to establish a military administration. The pelts of the remaining fur seals, the subject of several acts of Congress, were still acknowledged as important resources. But the availability of coal, a necessity for navigating the channels, was a problem. It was even more scarce among the sealing archipelago of the Aleutian Island chain than it was at Sitka and the inside passages. Commander Meade's economy with fuel sources during *Saginaw*'s last cruise was no anomaly. The entire navy faced the issue of limiting coal use. And naturally, it was an issue of money, meaning lack thereof, in the post–Civil War period. Commanders were required to carefully note in the deck log the specific amounts of coal burned by each vessel. And if their superior officers deemed that use to be anything other than absolute necessity, they could be liable for the costs themselves, out of their own pockets. Rear Admiral Thomas Turner, who had replaced Craven as commander of the newly reunified Pacific Station in June 1869, received explicit instructions: "Such of your vessels of your squadron as have not been ordered to the Atlantic Fleet, will be supplied with full sail power as soon as you can send them to the Navy Yard at San Francisco. They can be ordered there in turn—as soon as one has been altered and resumes duty on the station, another can go to the yard for that purpose."[3] *Saginaw* was not a great sailer. Typically, the ship did best with the wind abeam or aft, being able to make very little headway into the wind without the assistance of the engines.

This was a peacetime navy, manned by officers experienced in the coastal blockade, naval engagements, and amphibious actions of the recent war. Some of the new conditions and tasks must have seemed somewhat mild to them. Hydrographic survey claimed a new priority. Nonetheless, as part of his preparations for Alaska, Sicard still carried on board 15 revolvers, 15 pistols, 25 cutlasses, 40 carbines, two 30-pounder Parrott rifled cannon on the fore and aft pivots, and four 24-pounder broadside howitzers, along with the dinghy and gig and cutters, and all the sails and running rigging and ship's stores necessary for long duty at sea.[4] USS *Saginaw* was a war vessel and would not be going to sea unarmed no matter the nature of the mission.

Rear Admiral Thomas Turner had long experience in the region, having been in charge of the South Pacific Squadron before the squadrons were rejoined. Born in 1808 in Washington, D.C., he had been part of Pacific exploring expeditions in 1838 on USS *Macedonian*. He had served early on in the East India Squadron, on the flagship USS *Columbia* from 1838 to 1841, during which time he participated in the destruction of the Malay pirate towns of Quallah Battoo and Mucke on Sumatra. During the Civil War, he commanded the ship *New Ironsides* in the South Atlantic Squadron, and was highly commended for his skills and abilities displayed during the attack on Fort Charleston in April 1863. He formally assumed command of the Pacific Station on June 28, 1869, and reported to the secretary of the navy that he would have USS *Saginaw* ready to be dispatched to Alaska in three days.

Meanwhile Commander Sicard, in his own careful manner, had been computing the logistics for the passage north. At maximum capacity, *Saginaw* could take on 115 tons of coal. Figuring on an average sea performance of 7½ knots or 11 tons of coal per day, this meant that the ship would arrive at the sealing islands of St. George and St. Paul with a scant 9 tons left on which to cruise for several months and then return to the navy yard. And even that was assuming sufficient coal remained at Nanaimo in the British Territory. The delays and the distances being proposed for this new mission to the sealing islands caused Turner to reconsider. His scribbled notes in the margins of the correspondence read: "nearest point to receive coal 1750 [from Nanaimo to sealing islands], 9 tons coal left. *Saginaw* not suited for the location. Besides, the time has passed as I said . . . ice doubles by the 1st April, after which access to the island is interfered with. Consider it would be useless and perilous now to send a small vessel to that distant sea. . . . It was my intention to have dispatched her tomorrow, but upon further reflection and in a more mature consideration of the subject . . . my duty is not to send her until I hear from the Department."[5] Alaska was out; Sicard was on standby. Fortunately, this gave him more time to assemble and train his officers and crew with the usual rounds of gunnery and infantry practice, and perhaps make yet more repairs on the aging vessel. Ten years was a long time for a small wooden ship.

And there was time for a shakedown cruise in less taxing waters. As with all cruises, the commander drew his men from wherever he could find them. Five sailors, including Seaman William Halford, were transferred from the receiving ship *Independence*. Others came from USS *Ossippee* and USS *Cyane* and USS *Pensacola*, and USS *Dacotah*. The rumor that they were no longer bound for months of cruising on the Bering Sea may have helped. Sicard "swung the ship" (calibrated the compass on board), using Mt. Diablo across the bay as his reference for due north. Slowly the roster of stewards and cooks and coal heavers and firemen and petty officers filled out. And as the newly transferred men were slowly accumulated (what ship ever desires to see its prime members sent away?), *Saginaw's* brig went back into action. An assortment of men were placed in detention for the usual reasons—insubordination, taking leave without permission, drunkenness, striking the master at arms, overstaying leave, etc. The men had little more to do than stand by, making signals to the other ships moored at Mare Island. But where were they bound? The first mission would be to familiar waters. On July 28, Sicard and his men departed San Francisco for Mexico.

As all expected, drills at quarters and division exercises in reefing and infantry tactics were scheduled at a steady and regular pace once underway, the work serving to hone the sharp edges off the mixed groups and form them into a single team. In the heat of tropical August, the ship provisioned at La Paz and the Bay of Pichilingue once more. Several sailors ran at Mazatlan, but were shortly captured and placed again in the brig. Landsman James Kelly, in particular, provoked authority on board, often facing back-to-back periods under confinement.

Sharp lightning and bright moonlit skies alternating with gales greeted the ship off San Blas, where the surveying gear was put to use searching for the reported Richmond Rock, a navigational hazard of some concern to the Panama steamers, somewhere off Cape Corrintes. Surveying meant the ship moving in parallel transects, the engines stopping and starting, the patent log heaved over the stern, and the sounding lead in constant use. Bearings and angles were taken at the extremities of the transects, when clear landmarks could be made out at all. This was a nasty and tedious business in the rough seas and foul weather of August and September, the ship rolling deeply day and night. There was little chance for men to go ashore during survey. There was some chance, however, of shaping them into something resembling a unified crew.

Unfortunately, the success of the cruise was marred by mechanical breakdown and disease. The piston rod on one of the trunnioned cylinders had broken, and the ship made painfully slow passage up the coast under sail alone. The ship was more than thirty days in transit from Mexico to San Francisco, and yellow fever struck the men down at Manzanillo at the start of the long return leg. The "coast fever," as it was called, had ravaged the town, and the ship, touching at that port, was not immune. More than two dozen sailors were completely incapacitated, and the ship's surgeon administered to them as best he could until he, too, fell ill. Apothecary Randolph William died at sea in the line of duty on October 27, 1869. Ironically, the doctor was the only fatality of the outbreak. By November 8, when Sicard and Saginaw finally returned to the North, once more reaching the clear and cool weather of San Francisco Bay, only a half day's provisions remained in the ship's galley. It had been a difficult cruise, and a number of men were immediately transferred to the hospital at Mare Island.

The Sandwich Islands: An Indispensable Waypoint

While the ship conducted surveys in Mexico, plans for a different Pacific mission were again being laid. This time, Saginaw would leave her former roles of piracy patrol and colonial policeman far behind. The Hawaiian Islands (called the Sandwich Islands by the British following Cook's encounter in 1778) would provide a completely new mission.

Today it is very clear that there has been and is no other location as important to the U.S. Navy's position in the Pacific than the Hawaiian Islands. And the Pacific, as defined by the U.S. Navy, is a wide-ranging area of responsibility that today includes the Indian Ocean and the Arabian Sea. Some might say that there is no other single location as strategically and logistically important to the nation as a whole than the Hawaiian Islands. Nevertheless, this current status was not inevitable in 1870. The United States had actually gotten off to a slow start. The U.S. Pacific Squadron had a presence in Honolulu, but they were visitors, with no permanent facilities. Actually it had been the British, not the Americans, who were the first to conduct hydrographic surveys of the Pearl River estuary, and to name the "lochs" there in the 1820s. (The first surveys were carried out by a Scottish engineer, Lieutenant Charles R. Malden.)[6] In their wake, Commander John Downes, arriving on USS *Potomac* in July 1832, merely made official note of Hawai`i's possible wartime significance: "During a war, what interest would not these islands hold out to us, as sources of refreshment for our men-o'-war, while protecting our commerce and other interests in these seas?"[7]

American dominance in Hawai`i might not have been inevitable, but by 1870 it was becoming more likely. U.S. Navy ships called at Hawai`i to reprovision, and to lend support for the activities of American merchants abroad. They sailed in the wake of Yankee merchants, who had pioneered the transpacific routes in the late eighteenth century. John Jacob Astor's sandalwood trade ships were in the islands by the 1790s. Vessels from New England sought far-flung profits by rounding Cape Horn and trading for seal furs on the rugged northwest coast. From there they crossed to Asia, stopping at Hawai`i for necessary provisions and secondary trade. Reaching Canton in southern China, they then began their passage home to New England across the Indian Ocean and around the globe. Many of the sealing vessels in the early nineteenth century wintered in the islands rather than remain in the Northwest. American whalers began operating in the mid-Pacific early in the century, carrying another unruly lot of sailors to paradise. More than once the whalers came into direct conflict with Boston missionaries in Lahaina and Honolulu. By the 1840s, the American whaling fleet consisted of more than 700 ships, hundreds of them in the Pacific at any one time, many moored together at Honolulu and Lahaina. The flag naturally followed American commerce into Honolulu harbor.

The strategic location of the islands did not escape any of the early naval commanders in the Pacific. Early in the century, both Britain and America offered informal advice to the Kingdom, each navy keeping a careful eye on the influence wielded by the other. The French were also wary of their allies and/or adversaries in the Pacific. But by the midpoint of the century, with the increasing number of American whalers and American merchant ships anchoring at Honolulu, Lihue, and Lahaina, a clearer picture of future trends began to emerge. In 1841, an editorial in the *Polynesian*, a journal for foreign residents in the Hawaiian Kingdom, supported the construction of a naval base in the islands to protect the interests of Americans, particularly those in the whaling industry.[8] British observers were quick to take this as further evidence of America's rush for annexation of the Kingdom, despite official denials by the U.S. government. On December 14, 1842, American Secretary of State Daniel Webster made clear the United States' position (at that time) regarding other countries who sought to influence Hawai`i:

> The United States have regarded the existing authorities of the Sandwich Islands as a government suited to the condition of the people, and resting on their own choice, and the President is of the opinion that the interests of all nations require that the Government should not be interfered with by foreign powers. Of the vessels, which visit the Islands, it is known that a great majority belong to the United States. The United States, therefore, are more interested in the fate of these Islands and in their government, than any other nation can be: this consideration induces the President to be quite willing to declare, as the sense of the Government of the United States, that the Government of the Sandwich Islands as a conquest, or for the purpose of colonization, that no power ought to seek any undue control over the existing government, or any exclusive privileges of preference in matters of commerce.[9]

It was, indeed, a fine political line to walk, between respect for a sovereign government and the clearly developing American interests. Despite this stance, in February 1843 Lord George Paulet on board HMS *Garysfort* sailed into the harbor, dispensing with the normal salutes to the Kingdom. Ostensibly addressing some typical grievances stemming from a commercial lawsuit, Paulet threatened violent retribution in an attempt to annex the islands for Britain. Formal cessation (of a temporary nature) took place at the Honolulu Fort, set against the music of "God Save the Queen." USS *Boston* in the harbor stood by, and the subsequent pointed arrival of USS *Constitution* publicized the incident and signaled America's opposition to this overly bold move. Authorities in London later disavowed Paulet's brash actions, and the British flag was soon lowered from the palace. Then, when France agitated for special concessions from the Hawaiian government in the 1850s, American advisors suggested to the Hawaiian king that he draw up a deed of cessation to the United States.[10] Like the British incident earlier, this too came to naught, but the Navy Department transmitted specific orders to maintain the naval armament in the Pacific in order to guarantee the safety of the Hawaiian government. Furthermore, "special commercial privileges were granted to Hawai`i in exchange for the exclusive material and military privileges secured to the

United States."[11] In the 1860s, American army and navy engineers began seriously considering the physical features of Pearl Harbor and the potential for a Pacific "Gibraltar."

The Hawaiian Kingdom was of course a neutral power during the American Civil War, but the period in general served to strengthen the economic ties between the islands and the American mainland. During the conflict, the collapse of the South's agricultural exports initiated the plantation boom in distant locations, such as islands in the Pacific. The California gold rush of 1848 itself had already created new demands for foodstuffs (cattle and potatoes) from Hawai'i. In fact, San Francisco had been such a sleepy little town that laundry was often sent by ship to the Chinese shops in Honolulu. These linkages had been developing between the islands and the mainland for decades. Finally, the Confederate cruiser CSS *Shenandoah*, claiming some thirty-eight Yankee prizes to her name, proved to the Pacific Squadron that even the distant ocean came with its own security concerns. The ties that drew America closer to domination in Hawai'i grew over time, though the cautious tendency of Kamehameha IV and other Hawaiian leaders leaned toward a pro-British and anti-American outlook in foreign policy.

In Hawai'i, the 1860s were a continuing extension of a period of enormous change. Contact with the West had started as an interisland trade in provisions, gathering supplies to the ports of Lahaina and Honolulu for sale to the infrequent visitors. There was obviously advantage to be gained in the new exchange with foreigners, and a heavy price to be paid. The hundreds of whalers in the Pacific, from the 1820s through the Civil War and beyond, turned the provisioning activities into a full-blown industry. And then, in a handful of decades this had transformed into a business of plantation-style exports as the original control and conservation of resources was broken and Western entrepreneurs began to purchase Hawaiian land. Missionaries and foreign commercial interests grew to critical influence within the royal government. And throughout the whole time, the diseases brought by the foreigners took a terrible and devastating toll. It would be hard to overestimate the amount of social change initiated in the islands, as well as the damage done to the islands' host culture, and perhaps the only ones who can in any way understand are those who have been subjected to this same devastating impact. Familiar social structures had been broken, a belief system shattered, and the ways of land and sea reshaped.

Amidst these changes, the presence of U.S. Navy ships provided a clear reminder of the growing influence of the colonizing power. Navy officers were a direct line of communication to the government of the United States, and as such were included in the formalities of national diplomacy. At times, the navy provided a balance against the competing interests of other foreign powers, and at other times, those foreign powers provided a balance against the United States. But that balance was clearly shifting. In 1860, when USS *Saginaw* had first cruised to Honolulu during her passage to China, His Majesty King Alexander Liholiho (Kamehameha IV) was beginning to worry that the United States was growing too dominant over the Kingdom of Hawai`i, and he sought then to limit the islands' dependence on American commerce. That proved to be a difficult task, indeed.

In 1866, the screw sloop USS *Lackawanna*, a veteran of the Civil War, was recommissioned and transited the Straits of Magellan, arriving in Honolulu in February. *Lackawanna* cruised off and on in the Hawaiian Islands for the next nineteen years, surveying the reefs and islands of the northwestern archipelago and operating among "a locality of great and increasing interest and importance."[12] Middle Brook Island—more specifically the circular atoll and islands that are now known as Midway—was claimed as a possession of the United States by Commander William Reynolds in 1867. The navy later renamed the atoll due to its geographic location at the center of the North Pacific.

Midway, or Middle Brook: "Vastly Superior"

First sighted in 1839 by Captain Daggett of the ship *Oscar*, Brooks Island was officially "found" when Captain Charles Wolcott Brooks of the American bark *Gambia* landed on the sandy shoal twenty years later on July 5, 1859. Brooks claimed possession under the awkwardly named Guano Act of 1856, an act that enabled companies to stake out uninhabited islands for the purpose of mining phosphates. And Brooks Island certainly appeared to be uninhabited. No guano was ever mined, but steamship companies in the Pacific took an immediate interest, and the U.S. Navy soon sent USS *Lackawanna* to complete a hydrographic survey. The captain's report spoke glowingly of the potential for a critical coal depot located midway between San Francisco and Yokohama:

Within is an excellent harbor, easily entered at all seasons from the west, with a mouth three quarters of a mile wide, bounded on either side by a compact coral wall, with banks well defined. This main channel, the only one suitable for large square-rigged ships, has a generally uniform depth of four to five fathoms, excepting a narrow bar which extends about three hundred feet. . . . The bar is well within the entrance, and has no swell upon it during the prevalence of trade winds. . . . There appears to be enough true soil of sufficient depth to raise large quantities of vegetables; and with little trouble, and with skillful Chinese gardeners, who are thorough economists in gardening, and are easily obtainable, the extent of area suitable for crops may be considerably increased. . . . We predict that some persons now living will witness steamers leaving our West Coast daily for ports in the Orient, and this harbor will benefit the nation which holds it, in time of war as well as in peace.[13]

In August 1867, Captain William Reynolds took formal possession for the United States, making Midway the first land annexed outside the continental U.S. borders. Reynolds took six boatloads of men and officers ashore, fired a salute, raised the Stars and Stripes, caught a bunch of fish, and immediately had a barbeque for his crew. The harbor was (strangely) described as "very much like Honolulu, as rather more roomy and safe, but with not quite as much depth of water on its bar. . . . [T]he soil will produce a good many kinds of vegetables." In the age of paddle-wheel oceanic steam, the United States needed transpacific coaling stations. The islands at Midway were the first fruits of Secretary of State William Seward's expansionist policies. The harbor was names Welles Harbor, and the roadstead there Seward Roads, after the secretary of the navy and the secretary of state.

Midway was, in all ways, a quintessential coral reef atoll, an exposed oceanic place for only the wind, the birds, and the flotsam of the sea. During Captain Brooks's cruise to the remote archipelago, he noted some fourteen shipwrecks, but no traces of human life remained.

On the east or lagoon side of this island are the remains of two Japanese junks, their lower masts stranded high up on the beach. The northeast shore is lined with driftwood, among which are many redwood logs of formidable size. . . . Driftwood from Columbia River and Puget Sound distributes itself throughout the North Pacific. . . . On the northeast beach lies a broken lower mast of some wrecked ship. It is a fished mast, two feet and a half in diameter, strengthened with iron bands, with the step and head wanting.[14]

William Reynolds, from Lancaster, Pennsylvania, was another officer who had served under Commander Wilkes on the U.S. Exploring Expedition in 1838–42 in the Pacific. Reynolds, as a young midshipman under Lieutenant Joseph Underwood on the whaleboat *Greyhound*, circumnavigated Tutuila in the Navigator Islands (now American Samoa), charting the coastlines and harbors. Spending the night in Leone with the Samoans, he found the people among the most kind and generous he had ever met. A dedicated officer, yet one troubled frequently by illness, Reynolds had been forced to retire early from the service, only to be brought back into command in 1851. While assigned to the Pacific Station at Hawai'i as the U.S. naval storekeeper, Reynolds fell in love with the islands. He found his duties very much to his and his wife's liking, and they spent eleven years living on Kaua'i, where they had a 100-acre farm. He was among those instrumental in forging early commercial ties of reciprocity between the Kingdom and the United States.

For anyone who has had the luck to visit both Honolulu and Midway, though, Brooks's and Reynolds's easy comparisons between the two locations are enough to stop one dead in their tracks. Midway is, in short, almost completely unlike Honolulu in every way. Midway is a low-lying coral atoll with nothing but sandy soils, the ancient geological remnant of what once had been, thirty-some millions of years ago, a high basalt island, borne of a submarine volcano from the depths of the sea. As the tectonic Pacific plate slid slowly toward the northwest over the magma hot spot in the ocean, the eruptive island-building processes cooled, and the unstoppable forces of erosion reduced the island until it vanished far beneath the waves.

Today the level of the remaining igneous basalt at the atoll lies 500 feet below the surface of the sea. But the living coral, which originally formed as a fringing barrier around the young mountainous island of Midway, continued to build itself into the sunlight, and remains now as a circle of surf-washed reef enclosing an interior shallow lagoon, some six miles in diameter. These tiny coral polyps encased in their calcium carbonate shells, their millions of clones forming a living reef, are the basis of entire ecosystems in the world's warm tropical waters. In the mid-nineteenth century, the life processes of these "marine insects," and the geologic question of how the atolls had come to exist in the middle of the wide and deep ocean, gave rise to a number of different theories. Scientists with the Wilkes expedition in 1838 had begun to suspect that atolls had volcanic origins, but still spoke of the origins of the reefs as "the mysterious operations of the zoophytes."[15] The public found the subject equally fascinating:

> The more accurate maps by no means convey a correct idea of the innumerable islands, reefs, rocks, and shoals which dot the surface of this peaceful ocean. Most of them are of volcanic origin; while others seem to be wholly the work of those wonderful coral insects, which, while constructing for their tiny homes, dwellings of exquisite delicacy and variegated hue, of white, purple, yellow and the richest crimson coral, are at the same time the diligent co-workers of the all-wise Architect— in constructing new abodes for discontented and restless man. The natural history of these wonderful microscopic insects—their species, habitat, and modes of labor, still remain among the unsolved mysteries of Nature.[16]

Prevailing winds and currents from the northwest and recurring North Pacific storms have shaped the atoll over time. A shallow opening into the lagoon developed on the leeward western edge of the ring, and two low, barren sand islands—deposits of sand ground from the calcium carbonate reef—were pushed up by currents inside the southern rim.

Midway was a classic barren, deserted island, a place void of trees and shade, and initially void of all shrubs or grass. Low vegetation blazed its natural path there over time, though. It was a land made purely of weather, sun, and winds, an exposed place settled only by Hawaiian monk seals in search of a safe haven from the tiger sharks, and thousands of clacking, singing Laysan albatross, affectionately known as "gooney birds" for their amusingly simple and ungainly behavior. Midway was so exposed that USS *Saginaw*'s paymaster, following the ship's first visit, purchased goggles for the crew in Honolulu to protect their eyes from the blowing, stinging sands.[17]

Hundreds of years before Captain Cook made his landing in the main Hawaiian Islands a thousand miles to the southeast, Midway Atoll had already likely been visited by native Hawaiians, expert voyagers across the ocean, but of these possible visits no physical trace remained on the low, shifting sands. Midway was land, yes, but it was scarcely terrestrial. There was absolutely no trace of the mountains and waterfalls and palm trees and abundant fruit and provisions found in Honolulu. There was no shelter from the sun or the salt-laden wind. Equating the two locations is almost beyond the realm of imagination. Nonetheless the Department, foolishly, based its initial assessment on Commander Reynolds's single report.

> The charts of the survey represent . . . a perfectly secure harbor, accessible to vessels drawing less than twenty feet, and affording an abundant supply of pure, fresh water. These islands . . . on the track of the mail steamships, furnish the only known refuge for vessels passing directly between the two continents. . . . [T]he bar at the entrance of the harbor might be deepened at a very small expense, and a port vastly superior to Honolulu be thus opened to mariners, where a depot might be established for the supply of provisions, water, and fuel.[18]

How could the initial assessment have been so wrong?

USS *Saginaw*'s Last Role

The goal for improvements at Midway focused on developing a critical coal depot for commercial and naval purposes in the middle of the North Pacific, and the first objective of this large project was to clear a channel of sufficient width and depth into the protective lagoon, a passage for ships to find refuge from the weather and the open ocean.

At the end of the Civil War, the government contract for steamship service between the United States and China by way of Honolulu and Japan had been awarded by Congress to the Pacific Mail Steamship Company. For an annual subsidy not to exceed $500,000, the company was to operate round-trip monthly service for a period of ten years. Their first steamer crossed the Pacific in 1867, departing San Francisco on New Year's Day. The PMSS *Colorado*, though, did not touch at Honolulu. The company had earlier expressed its dislike concerning the mandated stop at Honolulu even before the contract had been finalized. The main Hawaiian Islands were to the south of the more efficient great circle route; Midway was closer. And, at that time, Honolulu lacked proper harbor facilities for the large steamers. With plans for exploiting the northern great circle route and thus saving on coal, the Pacific Mail Steamship Company had sent the schooner *Milton Badger* and Captain Henry W. Burditt of Boston as their agent to Brooks Island. Burditt had erected wooden buildings there, had established 600 tons of coal in a sandy pit, and dug three wells down into brackish water. When the steamer *Colorado* sailed from the west coast in 1867, she carried on board the original drawings of the atoll made by Captain Brooks. Brooks, ever the optimist regarding Midway (his "discovery"), had carried them in his valise for years.[19] After considerable discussion, Congress agreed to remove the obligatory Honolulu stop from the PMSS contract in March 1867.[20] Two months later, the secretary of the navy ordered Captain Reynolds to proceed to Brooks Island and conduct his survey. Five months later, Reynolds took possession of Midway for the United States. So went the commercial sale of the Midway project.

What was strategic for navy vessels was of logical benefit for commercial transportation as well. In 1869, Congress passed an act granting $50,000 for channel improvements at Midway, and senators wondered if even that much was needed. George M. Robeson, who had succeeded Adolph Borie as secretary of the navy in June 1869, took up the Pacific mission directly with Rear Admiral Turner:

> For the purpose of carrying out the intentions expressed in the act I have entered into a contract with Mr. Geo. W. Townsend of Boston, under date of the 13 ultimo, who agrees to perform the work required on the conditions therein named. Mt. Townsend has been highly recommended to the Department and it is hoped the work will be prosecuted diligently and successfully. You will see from the contract, one part of which is herewith enclosed, what aid is to be rendered by the Department to Mr. Townsend: also that the work is to be subject to the inspection and advice of such officer of the Navy as shall be ordered by the Secretary of the Navy to that duty. The general supervision of this work and the duty of seeing that it is executed properly and faithfully is committed to you, as the Commanding officer of the Pacific Station. You are authorized to detail any officer in your Fleet whom you may deem suitable, to have the immediate supervision of the work and will be regarded as the inspecting officer contemplated in the contract. You are authorized to use any vessel of your Fleet or any vessel at the Mare Island Navy Yard, that may be suitable for the purposes indicated in the contract. You will, on the receipt of this order, inform the Department by telegram, the earliest day on which a vessel can be ready for this duty on. You will procure the scow needed, also the blasting materials required. All payments for these purposes as well as those falling due under the contract, will be made by the purchasing Paymaster in San Francisco upon bills approved by you, to be charged to the appropriation

of "Naval Station, Midway Islands." Every facility contemplated by the contract will be extended to Mr. Townsend. Very Respectfully, Geo. M. Robeson, Secretary of the Navy.[21]

Proponents of the Midway project, and particularly Captain Brooks, applauded the decision, and extolled the benefits of what seemed to them, what they proclaimed to be, a perfect harbor:

> Congress fortunately took immediate action in regard to this island, and with far-seeing sagacity, authorized an appropriation of $50,000, to be expended in deepening the bar, and improving the harbor. . . . The Pacific Ocean will daily claim greater attention, affording unlimited opportunity for enterprise, requiring but capital and skill, well directed, to develop a future our anticipations can scarcely over-estimate. America is not wanting in either of these. . . . She now has this ocean to herself. . . . We may now welcome Brooks Island as a desirable annexation, remembering that a little stepping stone may often enable us to cross a stream, which would otherwise bar our progress. How much in this world depends on little things![22]

In October, the paddle-wheel steamer *Saginaw* was chosen by Turner to serve as the main support vessel for the work party of commercial divers from Boston, George Townsend's submarine engineers. The project, as many do, had multiple supervisors. Commodore William Rogers Taylor would officially take charge of the northern "squadron" of the Pacific Station in September 1870. When Rear Admiral Turner was called away to Hawai`i on USS *Mohican*, Taylor assumed direct charge of the Midway expedition. For the time being, Craven remained in charge at Mare Island and assisted with the preparations there as well.

Meanwhile *Saginaw*, now with a more efficient crew but nonetheless still an aging wooden gunboat that had seen duty throughout the wide Pacific for a long and hard decade, limped northwards on a damaged engine. Sicard was apprised of the Midway expedition upon his return from Mexico to the navy yard, and it was clear from the number of repairs needed on board the ship, particularly following a survey of the boilers and engines, that work had to begin immediately. Throughout the months of November, December, and then January 1870, the riggers, painters, carpenters, laborers, plumbers, boilermakers, and mechanics swarmed once again over the small *Saginaw*. It was sometimes cold work during the winter storms in northern California, but it kept the laborers of Vallejo employed, and the home fires burning.

In late November, a party of guests toured the shipyard and observed the preparations centered on USS *Saginaw*. These were Japanese commissioners, hosted by the navy and guided by Charles Walcott Brooks. This, coincidentally, was the second time a group of ambassadors from Japan on an overseas mission had crossed paths with *Saginaw*. In 1860, a Japanese embassy had been in Honolulu when *Saginaw* had first crossed the Pacific to the China Station, on her way to her first tour of duty. Now she was preparing for her last.

The list of necessary repairs, despite Craven's earlier optimistic assessment to the Department, was long indeed. The old main topmast was landed and a new one fashioned in its place. The rudder was removed and the hole for the rudder head modified to eliminate rubbing. One ship's boat was sent back to the boat shop for complete repairs. All of the lower standing rigging was removed from the ship and examined. The main bilge pumps were overhauled. Carpenters took on fixing the light work over the paddle boxes. Boilermakers cut out iron tubes from the starboard boiler and replaced them with copper composite tubes. Mechanics repaired the main bilge steam pumps, rebored the cylinders of the boiler hand pumps, and fitted a new piston to the after engine. And still, the mizzen mast and cap awaited attention, along with a growing list of other, more minor items.[23] The work continued for weeks.

By December 10, men were transferring on board, and the inevitable casks of vegetables and beef were making their way up the gangplank. Like the proverbial joke, updates forwarded to the Department regularly included the phrase "probable time required two weeks." Everything was said to only take two weeks. On December 18, the yard's large floating dock was flooded down, and *Saginaw* was warped into the wooden cradle. Fifteen inches were added to her keel aft, and twelve inches forward, in an attempt to reduce her roll and improve her sailing qualities. Men were inspected, trained, and rated. At 10:00 a.m. on January 1, 1870, Commodore John R. Goldsborough replaced Rear Admiral Thomas Tingey Craven as commandant of Mare Island Naval Shipyard. An 11-gun salute was fired from the yard's battery, and a 12-gun salute fired from *Saginaw* herself. And then the men went back to work. Goldsborough was another officer of the old school, having entered the navy in 1824 and distinguished himself in engagements with Greek pirates in the Mediterranean. At one point, he captured a pirate schooner of four guns with only a ship's boat and eighteen men.[24] Now he oversaw *Saginaw*'s refit.

Following sea trials, and yet more repairs to her engines (broken standards on the rocking shaft), Sicard began coaling his ship. Meanwhile, Rear Admiral Turner, returned to Mare Island, sent a singular request to the secretary of the navy for a $12,000 allocation to "Naval Station Midway Island."[25] Coaling was complete by February 8, and over the next week final provisions were brought on board. Additional fair-tackle and line were carried on for her specialized mission of surveying a distant entrance and bar, along with large amounts of extra chain. Fifteen gallons of sperm whale oil came on board for the navigation department, for lamps. Near the final loading process, the yard schooner fetched ammunition from the magazine for *Saginaw*, coming alongside to carefully load the powder and shells. The ship received on board: pistol and revolver cartridges; percussion caps; 2,000 rounds carbine ammunition; 23 saluting charges, in 50-pound tanks; 30 charges for pivot guns, in 100-pound tanks; 15 charges for the light brass 12-pounder; 10 charges shrapnel; 5 shell; and 15 charges for the 24-pounders.[26]

The crew were kept hopping, Sicard beat to quarters and conducted inspections, and intensified division practice at carbines and the great guns, the sound of *Saginaw*'s cannon carrying across the water as she fired at the floating wooden targets. On February 12, in the cold drizzle and fog, Sicard got up steam and brought his ship to San Francisco, the last mainland stop before setting out for the Hawaiian Islands.

What the sailors in San Francisco knew about Midway at that time is unclear, but there probably was sufficient rumor going around confirming the atoll's complete lack of grog shops and brothels. Landsmen Henry Brown, Daniel Donovan, John Kelly, Seaman William Higgins, and Fireman Thomas Jones therefore all jumped ship while still near Vallejo. Landsman William Yates waited until *Saginaw* moved across the bay before he deserted.[27]

The ship was to rendezvous with Mr. Townsend and the contractor's party in the city, and meet the supply schooner *Kate Piper*, which had been chartered to support the mission as well. Perhaps fortuitously, delays in the arrival of the contractors and the contractor's stores (eight more anchors, more chain, additional whaleboat and disassembled ironwork scow, 200 kegs of additional blasting powder, lumber for the construction of temporary dwellings on Midway Island, and the deep-sea diving rig including lead weights, umbilical, bronze helmet, and hand-cranked compressor) meant the chance of additional liberty for *Saginaw's* crew. Predictably enough, Seamen Jameson, Reynolds, Muir, Brennan, McGeach, Buchanan, and others began again to make their stolid rounds into confinement, shackled at the wrists and ankles in double irons and placed on bread and water for five days. The litany was the same: various charges of drunkenness, going absent without leave, overstaying leave, insubordination, etc. As many ship captains could testify, extended stays at San Francisco had a way of dissipating a finely honed crew.

The schooner *Kate Piper* took on board a strange contraption, a special invention patented in 1869 by George Townsend and John Foster known as a submarine rock-drilling machine (patent no. 93,610). The apparatus, drill, frame, and connecting linkages to the surface for operation were designed to drill into submerged rocks, allowing divers to place charges and, triggering the electric fuse, blast obstructions cleanly apart for clearing. Townsend's divers had used the device successfully in Boston, and similar work was also being carried on in San Francisco and elsewhere. As steam propulsion advanced, and iron-hull construction led to larger vessels, harbors and ports needed to be deepened to keep up with the growing maritime industry.

Diving at that time was still new and fascinating for the public, and there had been a number of public "submarine exhibitions" of "walking underwater, diving and torpedo experiments."[28] Hard-hat commercial divers in 1870 worked on dams, harbor wharves, and breakwaters; cleared obstructions to channels by blasting; salvaged equipment or raised sunken vessels; and performed a variety of other exotic and usually unheard-of tasks. Townsend, an engineer of some proven success in Boston, planned to demonstrate to the navy the efficiency of his new machine in a brand-new environment, a coral atoll in the Pacific. The drill was one of the reasons the Suffolk County businessman had won the government contract in the first place.

> Witnesseth: That said party of the first part [Townsend] will, at his own risk and expense, furnish all his materials (with the exception hereinafter mentioned) and do all the work of blasting at the entrance to Welles' Harbor in the Midway Islands of the North Pacific Ocean, and of moving off and depositing the debris arising therefrom, and superintending this work, for the purpose of suitably deepening the entrance to that harbor . . . it being understood that the party of the first part is to furnish and make use of his submarine drilling machine in this work,

together with the necessary engines, hoisting gear, diving apparatus, voltaic batteries, and blasting material, with the exception of blasting compound and powder hereinafter mentioned, at his own expense.[29]

Townsend's work would at all times be subject to inspection by an officer, Lieutenant Commander Sicard, appointed by the secretary of the navy. The government retained the option to terminate the work "whenever the appropriation especially made for it by Congress shall be insufficient for its further continuance, and whenever in the judgment of the U.S. Inspecting Officer it can no longer be persecuted with advantage, either from the lateness of the season, or from other unfavorable circumstances not now foreseen."[30] The Department, as well as Congress, expected the channel clearance to be accomplished in a single season. Townsend's monthly fee, minus the special compensation and naval allocation, could be stretched out for a maximum of eight months.

When all preparations were finally in place, Sicard's wayward and straggling crew were rounded up, and the ship once again readied for sea. At 9:00 a.m. on February 22, all hands were called to hoist the anchor, and in rough and rainy weather *Saginaw* departed San Francisco and pitched into the swells beyond the Golden Gate, the incessantly rolling blue seas marching in from the west. On board were George Townsend (who would supervise the beginning of the project for two weeks before returning to San Francisco and then Boston); seven divers and employees of his company, the "Yankee experts in submarine diving and blasting"; and an unconfirmed number of Chinese laborers, about whom very little is heard again.[31] (They may have left the atoll following the initial establishment of the work camp.)

Saginaw's Final Officers and Crew

Not all of the officers who served on the 1870 cruise left a record from which to understand a bit of their lives, but the handful who did allow a brief glimpse.[32] Twenty-two-year-old Ensign James Kelsey Cogswell, born in Milwaukee, Wisconsin, entered the Naval Academy in 1863. He had a bit of a difficult struggle, having failed at his midshipman's exams in 1866, only to persevere and graduate from the Academy two years later. In 1870, the Pacific was relatively new to Cogswell, who had been on his duty station for a little more than a year. Ultimately, though, Ensign Cogswell would have an extended navy career, specializing in ordnance and torpedo construction. But in 1870, he was just an ensign.

Twenty-one-year-old Ensign Perry Garst, from Dayton, Ohio, had entered the Naval Academy at age seventeen in 1863. During the Civil War, Garst had served on board USS *Marion*, and subsequently on the Pacific Station on board USS *Terror*, *Potomac*, and *Frolic*, and then on the China Station on board USS *Palos* and receiving ship *Franklin*. By 1870, young Garst had seen many of the former duty stations frequented by *Saginaw*. His ability to speak Spanish and translate French made him useful in the navy's multicultural setting.

Ensign Arthur H. Parsons was also on board the ship, perhaps more scholarly than the other young midshipmen. In 1869, Parsons was ordered to the academy for examining midshipmen in the languages of Spanish and French. Like Garst, Parsons was a multilingual officer useful in the nineteenth-century navy.

Twenty-nine-year-old Passed Assistant Engineer James Butterworth, originally born in Rochdale, England, was by Commander Sicard's account "a zealous, energetic and careful officer and perfectly reliable," and his experience and cheerful nature were a welcome addition to the small ship. He was generally known as a very Christian gentleman. Butterworth had previously served on board the navy steamer *Niagara* in Japan, and USS *Dacotah* in the South Pacific, having been in the service for more than eight years.

Twenty-four-year-old Second Assistant Engineer Herschel Main, from Illinois, had enlisted in the navy during the Civil War, spending much of the time at the naval engine workshops in New York. He was ordered to the Academy in 1866. Prior to his time on *Saginaw*, Main was assigned to USS *Pensacola*. In his later career, Main was quite active in the Bureau of Steam Engineering, becoming a chief engineer and retiring in 1895, having served more than thirty years.

Twenty-seven-year-old Passed Assistant Paymaster George Henry Read, from Philadelphia, had served on board USS *Pocahontas* at the beginning of the Civil War, taking part in the battle and capture of Port Royal, South Carolina, on November 7, 1861. Read then spent years on tedious blockade duty until the end of the war. Born in Philadelphia in 1843, he traced his ancestry on the maternal side back to the *Mayflower*, and was also a member of the Sons of the American Revolution. Read was "a fine type of gentleman, dignified, kindly, and polite."[33]

Lieutenant John Gunnel Talbot, appointed as executive officer on board *Saginaw* (probably the most demanding position among them all), was originally from Danville, Kentucky. Following his term at the Naval Academy, Talbot served as ensign on an impressive number of vessels—*Winnepec*, *Macedonian*, *Rhode Island*, *Susquehanna*, *Guirriere*, and *Kousac*. The multiple postings were not necessarily a positive mark of distinction. His commanders found that Talbot generally performed his duties well, but at times had a tendency to be forgetful; they moved him on. But then, in 1867, Commander Corbin on the flagship *Guirriere* saw a change in the young officer. Corbin found that, during the early part of the cruise, Talbot "did not perform his duties efficiently, his heart not being in his profession and he expecting to leave the service; since he has given up that hope, he has performed his duty better."[34] It wasn't necessarily a case of an officer exhibiting any habits that might disqualify him from promotion, but perhaps evidence of a reluctance, a certain indecisiveness regarding commitment to the service. Corbin wrote that Talbot showed a "habit of abstracting himself from thought in his duties, which I think, since the refusal of the Secretary of the Navy to accept his resignation, he may overcome."[35] More experience was necessary, hence the long list of training vessels for the conscientious but absent-minded midshipman. By 1870, Talbot had made the decision to dedicate himself to his chosen career. Lieutenant Talbot was not originally assigned to the Midway mission, but was sent out to the Hawaiian Islands later in order to replace Ensign John M. Logan, *Saginaw*'s initial executive officer in 1870.

In addition, the ship sailed to Hawai`i in February with Assistant Surgeon Adam Frank, Ensign Hamilton Perkins (Navigator), Second Assistant Engineers John J. Ryan, Jones Godfrey, and Cyrus S. Foss, Captain's Clerk Frederick E. Haskins, and Master's Mate Gustavus (George) H. Robinson. First Assistant Engineer Henry C. Blye also joined the ship. He was to be left ashore on Midway with the work party as Sicard's representative while the ship transited back and forth to Honolulu.

USS *Saginaw*'s officers in 1870, at least what is known of them, represent a particularly eminent sample of naval service. They would achieve much in their subsequent careers, but in 1870 that was all before these young men. All were young (Commander Sicard, at thirty-four, was ten years their senior), and all had been through the Civil War. For most, their experience on *Saginaw* would be only one formative part of their longer dedicated careers in the service. Most had entered the Naval Academy or graduated from there in the same class, and most already knew each other as friends and comrades. The service was still small. This final group of officers alone, including Montgomery Sicard, produced at least four rear admirals.

The ship's muster roll for January 1, 1870, paints a multicultural and multinational picture of *Saginaw*'s enlisted crew, and that was typical for the day. Frustratingly, only the briefest of descriptions exist for these men, for the regular sailors were transient marine experts transferred between vessels and navy yards with regularity. This was and is an established and time-honored mobility. The muster roll describes seamen, ordinary seamen, landsmen, firemen, and coal heavers representing eighteen different nations, including America, Peru, Greenland, France, Ireland, Jamaica, Scotland, England, Germany, Sweden, Barbados, Philippines, Belgium, Canada, Finland, Poland, Nicaragua, and Austria.[36] These were the quartermasters, the captains of the hold, the ship's cooks and wardroom cooks, the stewards and coxswains and carpenter's mates and boatswains and yeomen—a skilled and mobile population. Sixteen crewmen were described as Negro, mulatto, or a combination of dark, dusky complexion and dark eyes and hair, all indicators encompassing a wide category of African Americans in the nineteenth-century sailing trades.[37] And the ship had yet to recruit in the Kingdom of Hawai`i.

Most sailors had transferred on board from other naval vessels. Most had enlisted in the navy in 1869 for a term of two or three years. They were by trade the blue-collar experts, originally mariners and laborers and shoemakers; they were carpenters and rope makers and painters; they were butchers and clerks and bricklayers and mechanics and farmers. And most, as was common during the nineteenth century, were near or under five and half feet in height. On the cramped berth deck, shortness was an advantage, and the average height of all Americans 150 years ago was significantly less than what it is today. Such was the group that Commander Sicard and his officers had been attempting to forge into a unified crew. Of course, with last-minute transfers, enlistments, discharges, and desertions, the actual roll for any vessel was in a state of constant and dynamic change up to the point of departure, and sometimes even after that as well.

In addition to the officers and enlisted men of the navy, USS *Saginaw* carried on board a twelve-man contingent of armed marines. The marine guard, a tradition from the earliest days of the military services, provided sharpshooters to man the fighting tops in ship-to-ship engagements; trained shore parties for shore actions; and provided a conspicuous and effective measure of protection for the ship's officers from the enlisted men.

Once clear of the entrance, the course was set, canvas and spars were secured, and the ship filled away for Honolulu. Winds were light, and *Saginaw* rolled easily on its southwest course. The essence of sailing, like much of the essence of naval service, was monotonous routine. And routine at sea is a good thing, for its opposite can often consist of surprise and calamity. Sicard was meticulous. Inspection at quarters was routine; exercises in reefing, shortening, and furling sail were routine; division practice at gunnery was routine; and divine service every Sunday was absolutely routine. This was the opportunity to inculcate Episcopal values into the crew, and to read aloud, yet again, excerpts from the Articles of War.

Nothing eventful happened on the cruise, for which Sicard was grateful. On March 9, sixteen days from San Francisco, USS *Saginaw* came into Honolulu harbor and dropped anchor. Some of the spring fleet of Arctic whalers rode in port, hard-worn ships bound constantly for the Bering Sea, having chased their prey to the ends of the earth. The highpoint of American whaling had been reached decades earlier. But in 1869, the fifty-vessel Pacific whaling fleet had still brought in some 49,000 barrels of whale oil and 600,000 pounds of whale bone (baleen).[38] The American minister came on board *Saginaw* and cleared the vessel for landing. And then, following two days of coaling ship, the men were granted twenty-four-hour liberty ashore in alternating watches. Almost all of them came back, though Ordinary Seaman William Day decided apparently that O`ahu had more to offer him.[39]

Honolulu at this time was a town of some growing importance. The early center of power had actually been on the beach and among the coconut groves of Waikiki. Honolulu, a few miles to the west, had been a collection of huts closer to where the foreign ships came to moor. It was the development of the harbor that accounted for the growth of the commercial town, a protected port of sufficient depth and protected by a fringing coral reef. The harbor actually had natural origins. Close to shore, the freshwater runoff from Nu`uanu stream had prevented coral growth, and produced a round basin between 4 and 6 fathoms in depth, providing good holding ground. A narrow channel between the reefs led into the port. By 1860, the steam tug *Pele* replaced the native canoes and trackers man-hauling ships through the entrance, and steam dredges and wharf construction marked major improvements to what became the official capital of the Kingdom. That was the year that the United States first established a coaling station at Honolulu harbor, the location that eventually became Naval Station Hawai`i. The harbor provided a seemingly endless supply of good water, salt beef, pork, flour, potatoes, firewood, etc. Commerce from every point on the globe seemed to pour into Honolulu, and the harbor was the center of all business, industry, and transshipment of agricultural products.

For the liberty men ashore, Honolulu offered up an exotic and busy mix of island and foreign culture, and a civilizing exposure to international news in the Pacific. There was the sailor's home, established by the Honolulu Sailor's Home Society in 1855 adjacent to the Seaman's bethel. The charitable organization was dedicated to the great modernizing effort at temperance and providing a benevolent shelter for wayward mariners. Books and newspapers could be found there. Officers paid six dollars per week for table (board) and lodging, sailors paid five, with "showers and baths on premises." The news in town provided a stimulus for the sailors. In 1870, there was a lively ongoing debate regarding women's rights, a sometimes heated discussion of the emerging commercial reciprocity relationship between the Kingdom and the U.S. mainland, and a more pointed dialogue regarding sovereignty and the increasing presence of naval vessels at Honolulu. Otherwise, there were recitations of Shakespeare by Professor Walter Montgomery to relieve "the usual dearth of entertainments," and the more casual news of Mark Twain's recent marriage. Horseback riding was a popular pastime, particularly judging by the number of sailors arrested on charges of "drunkenness and fast riding."

> Sailors on horseback are not by any means as good navigators as they are on the rolling deep, nor yet when rolling along on foot on terra firma. But somehow a sailor, when he gets on shore, almost invariably wants to mount a horse and go careening along at breakneck speed,[40]

But there was good precedence for this. Hawaiian women themselves raced through the dirt streets of Honolulu at outrageous speeds with flowing colorful gowns and flower lei, a sport enjoyed by many locals. Sightseeing excursions to the sheer cliffs of Nu`uanu pali to take in the "Grand Panorama" were also common. The steep pali cliffs, over which King Kamehameha I had pushed the defeated army of O`ahu to its destruction in his bid to unify the Kingdom, were a continuing inspiration. And the ride up the valley was lined for miles with the handsome residences of foreigners and natives. "Many a sailor, as he has strolled up this valley and gazed at the neat dwellings surrounded by spacious yards, has been ready to 'sell his ship and buy a farm.'"[41] One could also relax at a beautiful and unspoiled spot called the Cocoanut Grove at Waikiki: "The Cocoanut Grove is one of the charms of Waikiki. We believe it is much the largest cluster of cocoanut trees on the Sandwich Islands. We never counted them, (although we once tried,) but suppose there are two or three thousand."[42]

There were many civil and social opportunities, such as frequent lavish dinners hosted ashore for the ship's officers at the growing number of elegant buildings, held under swaying palms and lamplight. This was the old Hawai`i as it existed for many American sailors in the post–Civil War years. And there were numerous grog shops and taverns, well frequented and prospering from the Pacific trade. There were opium dens as well, in Chinatown along River Street. Brothels were discouraged, frowned upon by the prominent missionaries so active in Honolulu society, but their reach frequently fell short of the waterfront and other haunts. Yet to label all the relationships between sailors and women "prostitution" is perhaps to do a certain disservice to many of the sailors, both American and British, and to the women themselves. Often sailors had regular arrangements with women ashore that went beyond sexual services. Some regarded such arrangements as types of informal "marriages"; indeed, it was the only type of marriage available to these transient mariners. And some women in Honolulu cooked and washed for their temporary men, perhaps in exchange for pay or goods, perhaps out of genuine affection, or both. For some it may have resembled a normal life, and a home, if only for a moment. Whatever the case for *Saginaw*'s men, all too quickly liberty ended. On March 15, the ship departed for Midway.

The local merchants and foreign whalermen in Honolulu were well aware of the ambitious task that the U.S. Congress had in store for the little side-wheel steamer. Some saw the Midway scheme as a potential benefit, which would indeed save them thousands of sea miles in their yearly roving. Merchants in Honolulu had, after all, had made their own effort in clearing the shallow bar outside of Honolulu harbor. The dredge worked best in protected waters, but the project had been foiled by the nature of the coral and sand deposits: "our experiment on the bar was a failure, for it was found impossible to operate successfully, as the firmness of the sand . . . the depth of the water, and more especially the swell of the sea, even in the calmest and most favorable times, conspired to defeat the attempt. . . . We now have an opportunity to see a coral reef attacked . . . and shall learn what can be done with it."[43] Others, more familiar with the realities of the remote Pacific atolls, questioned early on the logic behind these east coast navy plans of choosing Midway over developments at Honolulu:

> To those who are acquainted with the coral and sand formation at the mouth of the lagoons, it seems the acme of absurdity to ask an appropriation of $50,000, or even $100,000, for the purpose of dredging them to any required depth, and keep them so. Again, when the Senator urges the importance of the islands for "our whalemen, who are now whaling in the northern seas of the Pacific," who now "have to go to Honolulu every year to winter—but if this improvement is made they can winter at Midway Islands, where there is plenty of fresh water, and save some twenty-four hundred miles of somewhat dangerous navigation,"—we must smile. This is rich, and will make the whalemen who "have to go to Honolulu every year," laugh. . . . The Senator's ideas in regard to the outfit of a whaler do not seem to have got beyond "plenty of fresh water."[44]

The voyage to the Northwestern Hawaiian Islands was a beautiful passage, the ship running into the setting sun with the prevailing easterly winds and seas. The deep blue skies, and deeper marine blue of the seas, surrounded the tiny vessel. Under sail alone, with the banked fires in the boilers simply turning the engines over in order to condense freshwater, *Saginaw* rolled to the west-northwest. The same processes that produced Midway Atoll had borne a string of other atolls and islands, the older low reefs like Midway farther to the west, the younger and higher islands with their remaining rocky remnants, farther to the east. Headed west, *Saginaw* would pass these in stately procession, a trip going backward in geologic time. The rocky outcrops of Nihoa and Necker islands were the first sighted by the ship, marked by the upright stones of ancient Hawaiian temples, and the traces of terraces and habitation sites of the distant Polynesian past. Older then, with its single narrow rock known as La Perouse Pinnacle appearing like a frozen ship on the horizon (the white guano on its sides had been consistently mistaken for canvas sails in the moonlight by passing vessels), French Frigates Shoal extended its shallow reefs in a broad backward C open to the west. Numerous sandy islands provided seals and sea turtles perfect breeding grounds. Its predecessor in time and next neighbor to the west, the low rock of Gardner Pinnacles provided a difficult haul-out spot at best for the monk seals. But there, as everywhere in the archipelago, screeching seabirds whirled above their nesting grounds. Maro Reef was next, perhaps the most treacherous of all the navigational hazards. Its maze of submerged coral did not even break the surface, but served to toss the open swells into a confused mass

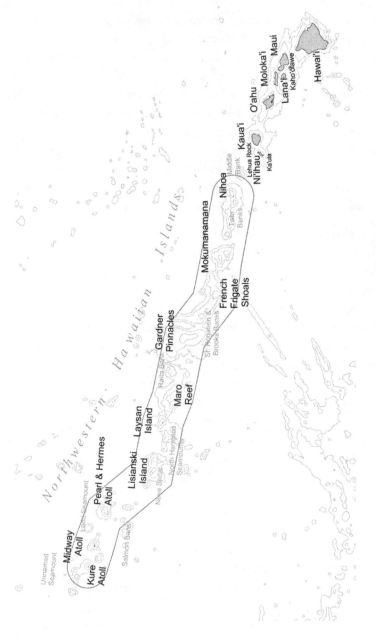

FIGURE 11. The Northwestern Hawaiian Island chain, stretching 1,200 miles west-northwest from the main Hawaiian Islands to Kure Atoll. Courtesy of Papahānaumokuākea Marine National Monument.

of rogue seas. And then came Laysan and Lisianski islands—flat, sandy, scrub-covered locations (but without the circular coral reef of a true atoll). Of more ancient age, Pearl and Hermes Atoll revealed the true circular shape of an oceanic atoll, with the scattered sandy islands on the southern and eastern lagoon edges. The atoll was named for the British whalers *Pearl* and *Hermes*, wrecked in 1822 while sailing in consort for the newly discovered Japan Grounds in search of sperm whale oil. And finally, almost 1,200 miles from Honolulu, lay their destination, windswept Midway itself (see fig. 11).

Bright moonlit nights accompanied the ship, and calm and pleasant days, with only brief passing showers and a couple of minor squalls. Staysails were set, and on the ninth day at sea, the navigator, Ensign John Logan, fetched up Midway Island. Ominously, the first real Pacific storm crossed paths with *Saginaw* upon her arrival, rendering the atoll's reef crest a circle of angry surf, lifting white spray into the air like a formation of spouting whales. With the arrival of the schooner *Kate Piper* and the rest of the contractor's gear, work commenced.

Naval Station Midway Island

Commander Sicard's role in the construction of the harbor and depot was not limited to just observing Townsend's work. He was to do everything he could to bring the project to a successful completion. This meant breaking out the surveying gear and carefully determining the best possible path across the western bar into the lagoon. Rear Admiral Turner placed considerable faith in Sicard:

> Your first object will be to examine the channel carefully for the purpose of determining the best direction for cutting through the obstructions. I can give you no definite orders upon this point; but I will say generally, that it will be best in my opinion to ascertain the shortest distance for a cut, and then to open a narrow passage entirely through. This can then be widened as far as the appropriation will allow, or as much as you may think advisable. In depth I should think it best not to attempt to go below the average of four fathoms, at low water, as that will afford an easy entrance to the large steamers employed in the China trade. If the direction of the channel can be made to favor the entrance of sailing vessels with prevailing winds, that will be an important object to consider. Much, if not everything, must be left to your intelligence and

discretion, upon which I confidently rely, for bringing this important work to a successful and satisfactory conclusion.[45]

The entrance into Welles Harbor was a wide but shallow break in the reef crest, studded with sharp submerged coral heads, each more than capable of tearing into a wooden ship's hull. When storms and swells rolled in from the west, the entrance could close out, angry breakers rising up across the whole side of the atoll. But under normal conditions with the prevailing easterlies, relatively small vessels could navigate into the lagoon—if they could avoid the coral heads, and if they were of shallow enough draft to clear the submerged bar. Once inside, ships found calm, turquoise waters even in the strongest blows, patches of loose coral sands in water 5 fathoms deep or more. The lagoon offered poor to fair holding grounds nearer to the island. Larger vessels dared not come close. Though the Pacific Mail Steamship Company touched regularly at Midway beginning in 1867, these deep-draft steamers had to heave to outside the reef and coal by lighter or small boat from their temporary sandy depot established on the island.

USS *Saginaw* was well supplied with extra boats, cables, anchors, buoys, and sounding leads. The task of determining the path into the lagoon involved establishing fixed stations or markers on the bar and taking the exact depths at multiple specific locations throughout the area. In short, it meant small boats doing slow and tedious work in the swells of the North Pacific, the surf nearby always breaking on the adjacent reef crests. It was not the most pleasant of undertakings, particularly for those with weak stomachs, but it was critical work. But before that could begin, the contracting party needed to be established on their new island home (see fig. 12).

Despite the continuing overcast and squalls, Sicard and Navigator Logan boarded the ship's first cutter and went directly out to the bar to orient themselves for the coming survey. They were quick to return. Meanwhile *Saginaw* set both port and starboard anchors in 4½ fathoms inside the harbor, and prepared to strike yards and topmasts due to what looked like a freshening gale. At the same time, work parties were sent ashore to assist in the transfer of stores, and to begin to knock together the disassembled boat. A Pacific Mail Steamship Company scow, buried in the sands, was located, recaulked, and put back into use. The next day, the gale came up in earnest, blowing from the northeast, and Sicard raised steam to relieve the strain on the anchors (now dragging through the loose coral sands) and struck the yards, riding and rolling out the gale in the lagoon's

FIGURE 12. The shacks at Midway Island in 1870, a windswept deserted sandy atoll setting. From Read, *Last Cruise of the* Saginaw.

small but steep chop.[46] The weather, it seemed, was quite capable of bringing all work to a halt.

Over the next month, *Saginaw* fell into her Midway rhythm. The skies cleared, becoming cool and bright, and the ship's crew were set to loading the lighter and moving back and forth to shore from the ship and the schooner *Kate Piper*. Those remaining on board took up polishing the brightwork, maintaining the rigging, and painting the vessel. Hammocks were turned and cleaned, clothing aired. Surveying parties were regularly sent out to the bar. The vessel was kept in motion resetting the anchors in the loose sand. Following quarters and inspection, the captain read divine service every Sunday, and admonished the crew. Officers condemned spoiled foodstuffs and heaved them over the side, and increasingly they had to punish the men.

The sailors grew used to the repetition of tasks, but Midway offered almost nothing by way of amusements and very little of almost everything else. There was no liquor to smuggle on board, and no liberty. For naturalists, the setting was truly beautiful, with the bright moon overhead, the turquoise waters of the lagoon surrounded by the deep blue sea beyond the circle of white surf, and the abundant dolphins, monk seals, fish, and seabirds of an unspoiled Pacific atoll. But the ship's crew were not naturalists. Tempers flared on the small ship, and fights broke out. Captain's

Cook Nolan Francis was placed in double irons and on bread and water on multiple occasions for disobedience to orders and negligence of duty. Seaman John Ellington was confined for fighting. Landsman Thomas Kearney was shackled for insolence to a superior officer. Landsman William Coombs was shackled for fighting. Seaman George Ellington was placed in double shackles and on bread and water for using disrespectful language toward the boatswain's mate. Upon his release several days later, on May 7, he was immediately placed in confinement again for insolence to the executive officer.[47] And so it went. The men were bored.

On Midway Island itself (today called Sand Island, one of the three islands on the southern edge of the lagoon), Townsend's men worked to build themselves a temporary home. They lifted a small house up against the wind, to secure their provisions from the weather and for cooking. And they built a separate magazine to keep the blasting powder dry (at a distance from the house of course). The Midway expedition party consisted of foreman George A. Bailey, J. Henry Russell, William G. Loring, Charles H. Mitchell, John C. Toumey, Joseph Battersby, Charles Collins, James Muir, John Brown, Frank Quigley, E. P. Judd, and Edward Cahill. They were engineers and divers from Boston, men who had never been on a barren coral atoll in their lives.[48] Clearing channels in New York or Boston is one thing, but working on a remote and barren desert atoll island in the middle of the Pacific quite another.

On April 2, Bailey made the first dive on Midway's western bar, and probably the first dive ever in the Northwestern Hawaiian Islands. *Saginaw*'s boat was initially used as the diving platform, the scow still being rigged with the coral hoisting apparatus. Bailey donned the cumbersome commercial suit and climbed heavily over the side into the warm, blue water. On the bottom, he found good visibility for the moment and was able to assess the topography and formations of coral heads and coralline substrate, but the surge and current were difficult to work in, threatening to sweep him off his feet. The ocean constantly caught his heavy umbilical and pulled it out of the lagoon into deeper water. At times the current could run from one to two knots, a speed that might seem slow only to those who have not experienced it underwater. Strong currents on the bottom also meant a fog of light sediment blowing in from the lagoon, meaning either that the diver's visibility was limited or that he was working blind. Nonetheless, Bailey believed the "rock" to be very favorable for blasting, with many overhanging ledges and deep crevices in which to place the charges.[49] He envisioned large pieces breaking cleanly away, to be hauled clear in chunks. An experimental blast of 50 pounds powder was put down on the reef on April 14, with what were reported as satisfactory results.[50] Regular blasting began on April 19.

Montgomery Sicard's first report on the deepening of Midway's channel, written to the secretary of the navy on April 4, 1870, acknowledged the influence of the weather, and the difficult working conditions on the bar, which Sicard found very troubling. In addition, it was already apparent that the contractor may have misjudged the difficulty of the work, given the wholly new environment: "I find that the contractor has sent but one suit of submarine armor with the expedition. I asked the agent, Mr. Bailey, why more had not come. He told me that they could only work one man at a time on the bar (underwater); and that if more were down they would be of no use."[51] Sicard had begun to question the possibility of success on his very first trip to Midway. The work being started, though, and the initial survey of the bar complete, Sicard prepared to return to Honolulu. Before weighing anchor, he detached First Assistant Engineer Henry C. Blye and five others (Charles Clark, Michael Jordan, Dennis Fitzgerald, Martin Doran, and Jose Adam Aguire), leaving them to assist on the island.[52] The hoisting scow was moved out to the site, and the first efforts to move the blasted coral began. On May 15, *Saginaw* raised her steam, hauled her sails, and began to beat into the ocean swells and prevailing trade winds, a bumpy "uphill" run eastward and back to Honolulu.

Working on a Desert Island

It was a peaceful existence on distant Midway Island, for the sounds of the wind and the seas were only broken by the mating songs of the ubiquitous albatross and the snoring of the monk seals and the divers. But for the men working on the bar, Midway meant pulling in the boat to the western pass, mooring and unmooring the diving scow, tending the divers over the side, and hauling coral debris in the hot sun. Between May and the end of September 1870, Commander Sicard and *Saginaw* made two more round-trip passages to the islands in support of the channel improvement, monitoring progress and provisioning the laborers on their barren home. These sailing passages were, for the most part, uneventful, except for the unfortunate death of Seaman William Reynolds (no relation to Commander Reynolds), lost to cholera. On June 18, Sicard called all hands to bury the dead, and after he read the funeral service, the body was taken ashore and placed under the sands of Midway with the usual naval honors.[53]

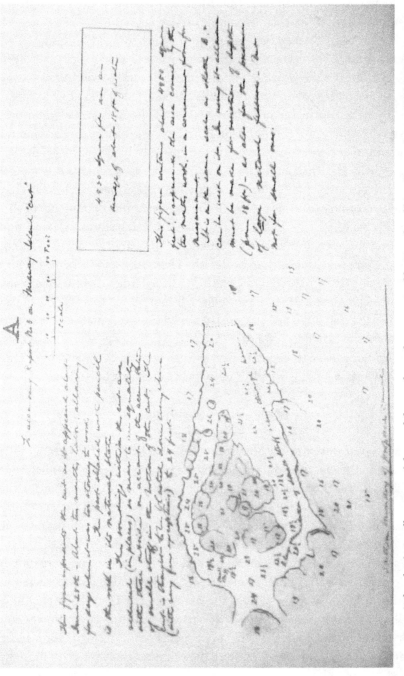

FIGURE 13. A sketch of a small portion of the much larger channel cut, surveyed by Sicard and his officers, along with detailed notes. Courtesy of National Archives and Records Administration, College Park, Maryland.

The survey work at the bar continued. The complex nature of the task became more clear as time went on, for the cut needed to run straight into the lagoon for the safety of the ships. Sicard and his navigator produced highly detailed charts of the entrance, down to the level of individual coral heads, but they were often forced off by wind and waves (see fig. 13). The open ocean swell necessitated the daily movement of the diving scow from its four-point mooring on the bar to a more sheltered location at night. Multiple buoys had been established across the cut and at mooring locations, marking out on the surface the submarine landscape below. And when the seas built and ran heavy, no work could be conducted at all. The sea possesses an unstoppable power in the face of any vessel or platform or person trying to maintain a fixed position. And the last thing the diver needed when carrying charges of blasting powder in the surge was to be yanked across the bottom of the ocean by his umbilical as the scow broke free from its anchors. They could not fight the uncooperative sea.

The much-anticipated submarine rock drill could not be effectively deployed in these conditions. It was simply too delicate a contraption in the face of the surge and swells (see fig. 14). Likewise, the canisters with the charges could be battered and leak, making the powder inert. Electrical leads to the fuse could be broken, and the divers' umbilical tangled on the sharp coral and cut. The atoll was a high-energy environment, unlike the protected harbors on the east coast. There was no way Townsend's team could have experienced anything like it until they had committed themselves to the job.

Though they were limited by having only one diving rig, in good weather the men could put down as many charges as they needed, the average size being about 30 pounds of powder. But it was the effort of hoisting and clearing the debris that slowed the work. The scow, with its donkey steam engine and winch, could lift between one and five tons at a time, but that meant the diver had to rig the larger pieces underwater or load the smaller material into the large tub. And, as Engineer Henry Blye put it, "the rock was breaking small." At first, large ledges and fractures had split nicely into sizable pieces that could be swung away from the cut by repositioning the scow. But the more the divers blasted, the more they became aware of the true nature of the substrate. The upper surfaces and edges were much harder than interior portions. The inner coral was "so soft that it will work in the hands like putty . . . the very softest portion is entirely disintegrated, and driven into the form of lime, which (like whitewash) discolors the water within a diameter of some 50 feet."[54] The explosions,

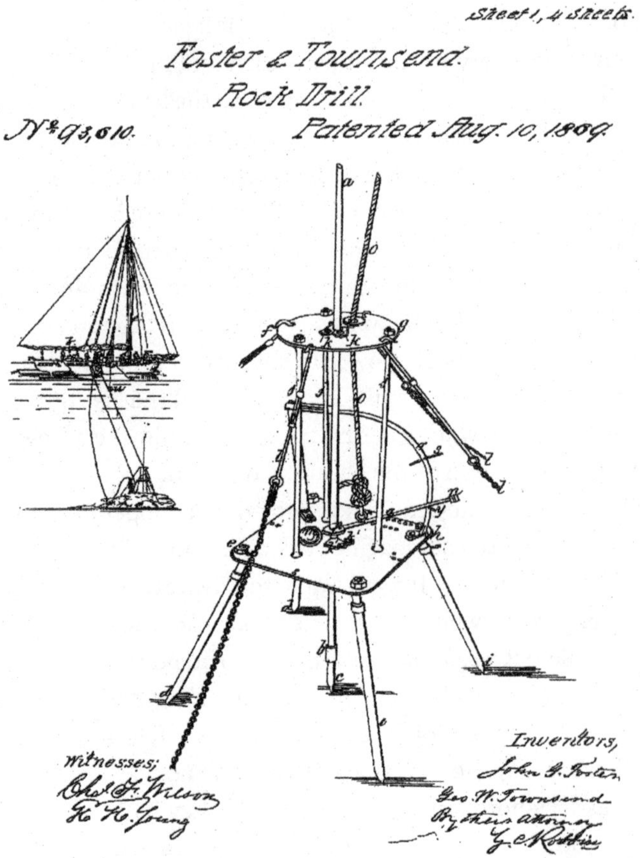

FIGURE 14. George W. Townsend's patented rock-drilling machine, 1869. The device proved completely ineffective in open-ocean conditions. Courtesy of National Archives and Records Administration, Washington, D.C.

rather than clearing anything, created an inrushing of water as the gases from the charge disappeared, pulling all of the small pulverized coral debris back against the wall of the cut, leaving it there in a massive mound, too heavy to wash away, too small to be cleared efficiently. The divers had to wait for the milky waters to clear before they went back down to survey the damage, begin to scoop up the loose debris by hand, and dig with picks to open the next hole for the charges, backbreaking work. This method was simply too slow, as Sicard noted in his third report to Rear Admiral Turner in July:

I have hoped that when communication is opened entirely through the bar, the sea may wash all the small stuff out of the bottom of the cut, but if it should not do so, I fear that the labor of removal will be very great, as the stuff will have to be brought up by dredge or tubs. This would entail so much expense and time that I have thought, perhaps if the sea does not remove the stuff in its present state, it would be well to try breaking it up very small by subsequent blasts, when perhaps (in its then lighter state), it will be carried off. In that case jets of water might be introduced among it (by nozzles). . . . But in any case in which the small stuff has to be acted on artificially, [this will add to] the great expense and the length of the operation.[55]

This was very discouraging news. It was also a reason to terminate the project, as laid out in the original contract. In Commander Sicard's careful estimate, blasting the necessary 170-foot-wide passage into the lagoon at Midway would require a minimum of thirty-eight months, far exceeding the appropriation from Congress. By his fourth report in September, Sicard estimated a minimum of fifty-two months and at least $214,000 dollars for the job.[56] And if the sea did not naturally clear the detritus once the cut had been thoroughly opened, Sicard estimated those costs could double. But beyond creating the passage, he had also grown skeptical of Midway's other assets:

Even with that cut finished, there would be times when a large ship would not like to attempt its passage. I cannot help thinking that the amount of time and work required to make this canal were never properly appreciated and I think it proper to say that to get the canal through in a creditable and useful manner is really a first class undertaking. Of course, it could not be known beforehand the difficulties of working and of removing the coral rock. I have tried to explain as clearly as possible the method of working and the results thus far, so that a judgment may be found of the probable duration of the work. The "Haven" after it is once entered, is a poor one for a large ship, a springs would probably be necessary to keep her head right for going out, or to turn her around (particularly a side wheel steamer)."[57]

What Congress and the navy had thought was a $50,000, six-month job seemed now more like a $250,000, five-year major undertaking. Somewhere in the whole planning process some rather large mistakes had been made. Both merchants and mariners in Honolulu, however, could not help but find amusement in the government's predicament. Locals, already familiar with conditions in the remote northwestern atolls, and having invested heavily in the prospects of Honolulu being the major stopping point in transpacific trade, were not shy about what they saw as another example of government mismanagement, an attempt to make a silk purse from a sow's ear. Washington, D.C., was some 5,000 miles away, and could at times exhibit its unfamiliarity with the realities of life in the Pacific region.

> Through the misrepresentations of interested parties, backed by the recommendations of a naval officer [William Reynolds] who was either incompetent to judge or who was influenced by unworthy feelings of prejudice and spite against the Government and the people of these islands, the North Pacific Mail Steamship Company was led to believe that, by the expenditure of a reasonable sum, a good harbor could be made at Midway Island, a barren sand-bank, enclosed in a coral reef. . . . It is very much to be doubted whether the United States Government will consent to the throwing away of any more money in the useless attempt to make an available harbor at Midway.[58]

In the short term, the merchants were correct in their assessment of the atoll's commercial viability, though Captain Brooks, one of their own, had been a great promoter of Midway. Honolulu was, to them, the most perfect harbor and depot that could be desired. But in hindsight, the local merchants fell short in their vision. The project was more than just a commercial venture. The naval effort to develop Midway was simply started before its time. The establishment of the transpacific submarine cable facility in 1903; the Pan American flying clipper service in 1935; the naval air facility and submarine base in 1939 and 1942, not to mention the pivotal events of the Battle of Midway in World War II (a watershed moment in history) bear witness to the critical role played on the world stage by the tiny coral atoll. The real value of Midway lay not in the nature of its harbor, but in its strategic location. But that was all to come later. In 1870, Midway was destined to remain a deserted island and be returned to the gooney birds, the seals, and the wind.

Later in his career, Secretary of the Navy George Robeson (a lawyer by training), who had signed the contract for Midway's improvements, was charged with various fraudulent transactions, this time in much greater amounts (millions). It seemed that the government's money had a tendency of being spent on projects for which "failure was inevitable . . . there are evidences of fraud in almost every direction. . . . [A]n immense sum of money, four millions of dollars, which was voted by Congress on the pretense of an impending war with Spain, has been squandered. . . . [T]here have been frauds on a large scale in the purchase of timber for new ships, and the repairing of old ones, in manipulating the pay of sailors."[59] Though not all proven, the series of apparent delinquencies and corruption within the Navy Department marred Robeson's legacy.

By September 1870, *Saginaw*'s fourth in-port at Honolulu, the crew had become enamored with all that the town and island had to offer. At times, groups of six or seven men would go absent without leave, but the marines usually had little difficulty rounding them up and returning them to the ship. With few exceptions, these were not serious attempts at desertion, but merely sailors exercising their right to choose. Several had taken on temporary wives. And, except for the boredom at Midway, the duty was a pleasant one, consisting of sailing under blue skies, trade winds, and liberty in Honolulu. Sicard had proven to be a strict but even-tempered and very fair commanding officer.

In late September, USS *Saranac* was in Honolulu, and officers and enlisted men were transferred back and forth (John Talbot and Perry Garst joining *Saginaw*). The marines busied themselves returning men overstaying their leave on shore. Some were transferred back to the hospital on board the steamer *Moses Taylor*. Their shipmates carried on board the usual stores—beef, pork, butter, molasses, apples, canned meat, flour, sugar, beans, pickles, limes, oars, rolls of canvas, turpentine, linseed oil, coal tar, manila rope, hemp rope, zinc, white lead, bread, rice, lumber, and 25 gallons of sperm whale oil for the navigator's department—while Sicard waited out the squally weather. These basic provisions were the tools of American expansion into the Pacific. As the crew coaled the ship, 250 kegs of blasting powder were off-loaded for transportation back to Mare Island.[60] It would not be needed after all. On October 1, *Saginaw* was away, arriving at Midway Island on October 12 after a rough and wet passage.

7

The Castaways of Ocean Island

It gives me very great pain to think that I should have lost the vessel but I feel that I exercised my usual vigilance and care in navigation, and that I am habitually vigilant and careful. I believe all those under whom, and over whom, I have served will testify. I regret very much to say that owing to the speedy destruction of the vessel, but little was saved.

Montgomery Sicard, 1870

USS *Saginaw* was sent to Midway to terminate the channel project and take the Boston divers home. To their credit, Townsend's men continued to work at blasting and hoisting on the bar, weather permitting, for a week following the ship's arrival. If the Navy Department wanted to find a reason for the failure of the Midway project, it wasn't going to be for lack of effort on their part. Sicard also pushed his own men to extremes, for it was late October and he was eager to get clear of the area before the storms that could trap them inside the atoll and put the ship onto the reef. The sailors commenced to laboriously dig a sand canal on the island, a trench into which the work scow could be hauled and safely secured. Surgeon Frank kept his concerns to himself in his journal, rather than confront the captain: "The men are all employed on shore, they are constantly wet and worked very hard, disease or injury may result."[1] The rough passage from Honolulu had bashed the men about. With assistance from the engineering department, Frank had fashioned a makeshift "retentive apparatus" in order to treat the pulled groin injury of seventeen-year-old Harry Edwards. (Edwards had shipped at Honolulu a few days prior to the ship's departure.) Six others remained on the sick list, suffering from sprained arms, inflamed eyes, old cases of malaria, rheumatism, and intermittent fevers. Frank busied himself with his plasters and his pills.

When the work parties were ready for bringing the scow on shore, operations at the bar finally ceased, and the men shifted to loading *Saginaw* with the government property from Midway, and all of the contractor's equipment. The final cut through the bar was 450 feet in length, but only 15 feet wide, rather than the planned 170-foot width needed for transpacific steamers and ships of any real size. Underwater, coral detritus was piled in mounds and gullies, slowly being spread out to seaward by the currents. With their departure, the reef could now begin to heal. On the island, the lonely wooden huts would remain, while the contractors and sailors gathered up the machinery, spare parts, rigging, tools, remaining blasting powder, diving rig, compressor, muskets, cooking pots, and extra food, etc. Space was running out on *Saginaw*, and items such as the drilling apparatus and the donkey boiler were moved aft on deck and lashed down. The desire to return to San Francisco after six months of grueling labor on a remote sandy atoll gave a last boost of energy to the weary men.

The ponderous wooden scow, now with the hoisting apparatus removed, was hauled onto rollers, brought ashore, and secured on heavy blocks, a fresh coat of yellow ochre being applied to protect it from the weather. Certain other items remained on shore as well, placed securely in the dwellings. Sicard left a chest of books, six charts, old ensigns and jacks, a side light and deck lanterns, and whale oil.[2] Hopefully, the survivors of any future shipwrecks at Midway could signal for aid or navigate their way home. In the meantime, they could read. By October 28, the equipment and the work party had been embarked, and the recent squally weather having abated, the ship weighed anchor from Welles Harbor and set out at 3:55 p.m. for home—but not directly.

Meanwhile, the secretary of the navy had already been planning *Saginaw*'s next mission. Earlier that month, Robeson had telegrammed Rear Admiral John A. Winslow to have the ship back at the yard at the earliest date possible, and to notify the Department upon her arrival. Winslow was the latest in the line of commanders of the Pacific Station, following Turner. Born in Wilmington, North Carolina, in 1811, he had entered the navy as a very young man in 1827 and later served during the Mexican-American War. Despite his southern roots, he was a loyal officer of the U.S. Navy. In July 1862, he was chosen to command USS *Kearsarge*, a screw sloop-of-war carrying eight guns. On June 19 of that year, off the coast of France, Winslow led the attack against the infamous Confederate raider CSS *Alabama*, sinking the enemy ship and securing for himself ever-lasting fame. The Pacific Station had a genuine Civil War celebrity, but not for long. The aging rear admiral was forced to resign his command due to illness and died at his Boston residence in 1872.

In response to Robeson's instructions, Winslow, on board USS *Saranac* at San Francisco, sent orders by steamer to Honolulu. He then informed Robeson that it was unlikely that *Saginaw* would be back to Mare Island before mid-December.[3] He also sent orders directly to Sicard at Midway, via the Pacific Company China steamer that departed San Francisco on October 1 and planned to touch at the atoll.[4] These orders directed Sicard to stop at Honolulu on his way to San Francisco, and transfer command of *Saginaw* to Lieutenant Commander Greene, the ship's next command-ing officer. (*Saginaw* never rendezvoused with the PMSS steamer.) The Department wanted to expedite the return of its side-wheeler in order to send the ship on a critical task to the Isthmus of Darien, Panama. There the ship was to cooperate with Commander Thomas Selfridge's expedi-tion, conducting surveys at the entrance to the Darien River, for there were no other vessels suitable for this coastal work on the Pacific side. The isthmus, of course, is where Ferdinand de Lesseps would start (but not complete) a Panama Canal project in 1880. The United States com-pleted the canal in 1914, a project central to commerce and the maritime defense of the nation. *Saginaw* was to have been a part of that great work, contributing at the very early stages. Robeson wrote to Goldsborough at Mare Island to have USS *Saginaw* ready for the survey in ten days after her arrival at the yard.[5]

Shipwrecks in the Northwestern Hawaiian Islands

The geologic processes that reduced the tall basaltic islands of Hawai`i to low coral atolls created remote but pristine ecosystems for marine spe-cies, and also created some of the most treacherous navigational hazards known to mariners. In oral tradition, Pele, the Hawaiian goddess of vol-canoes, had produced the islands herself, a mythology descriptive of the volcanic hot spot that had raised an island chain strewn along a course bearing to the northwest. These then eroded over time to a line of low and unmarked reefs and shoals lying across the transit routes of the North Pacific. The atolls of the northwestern archipelago had been straining the flotsam and jetsam of the Pacific like a watery sieve for hundreds of years.

And the more Western ships voyaged through the area, the more they ended up broken on the reefs.

The British whalers *Pearl* and *Hermes* were among the earliest of the reefs' known victims. On a dark August night in 1822, *Pearl* ran hard aground, and *Hermes* moved closer to help, only to ground herself on the uncharted atoll. More than fifty whalermen were stranded on the featureless sand spit. That same year, the New Bedford whaler *Two Brothers*, Captain George Pollard, was lost at French Frigate Shoals. Captain Pollard, having previously lost his ship *Essex* to a deliberate attack by a sperm whale in the middle of the South Pacific, decided at that point that lightning could, indeed, strike the same place (or same captain) twice, so to speak. He soon retired to Nantucket as a humble lamplighter and night watchman, never to go to sea again. Next came the British whaler *Gledstanes*, lost at Ocean Island at midnight, July 9, 1837. And then the American whaler *Parker* lost in 1842, smashed into the reef during a terrible storm, leaving the survivors with barely the shirts on their backs for the next seven months.

And then came the whalers *Daniel Wood*, *South Seaman*, *Konohasset*, and *Holder Borden*—all American whalers, all intrepid hunters from New England out to earn a profit on the wide Pacific. Quite a few mariners claim the dubious distinction of surviving on oily gooney birds and turtle meat, and the occasional gamey monk seal. (Some sailors survived five or more shipwrecks in the Pacific.) Whalers were some of the most far-flung voyagers on the world's oceans, and by 1870, at least ten whaling wrecks alone marked the Northwestern Hawaiian Islands as hazards to be avoided. In time, many more vessels in a variety of sailing trades ended their careers there. These little-known reefs were claiming so many ships, so many American whalermen in particular, with their expensive cargo, that the government made the scientific survey of the Pacific a priority for a number of separate naval expeditions.

These dangers shaped Commander Sicard's decision to augment the huts at Midway with at least the rudimentary elements of survival, a sensible and conscientious act of kindness. And more importantly, they influenced his decision, upon his departure and prior to returning to Honolulu and San Francisco, to set course for Ocean Island, a mere 50 or so nautical miles to the west of Midway. Ocean Island (now known as Kure Atoll) is the most distant point in the chain, literally the far edge of the Pacific archipelago world, and an "end" of the earth. Japan was the next port of call, half an ocean away. Sicard's officers were aware of the wrecks of the whalers *Gledstanes* and *Parker* at Ocean Island, and may have heard more recent rumors of others. USS *Saginaw* was in the vicinity, and the responsible action was to touch there briefly before turning to the east. Simply rounding the small atoll with spyglass in hand would be enough. The commander "thought it my duty to do this, as the place is quite out of the usual track of vessels; and as I was so near it, the detour would delay me but a few hours."[6] His one concern centered on the quantity of contractor's stores on deck, heavy iron equipment, and the potential effect it might have on the ship's compass.

The homeward-bound atmosphere of Midway Island had worn off, and the exhausted crew, work done and facing a slow passage under sail, were quick to take advantage of their hammocks as soon as they could. Or at least they tried to do so. The contractor's men had crowded into the already small berthing deck, and others slept where they could find an open space. Ninety-three souls fitted themselves as best they could into a ship designed for fifty-nine. The ship rolled easily into the western swell, the partial moon above obscured by passing clouds.

A Bright Lookout on a Dark Night

The tangible darkness of an overcast night far out at sea is a rare and striking experience in sensory deprivation, particularly when known hazards lie in the ship's path. The inky darkness at times was thick and complete, the ship moving forward in a negative void. Sicard and Ensign Cogswell, who was serving as the navigator on the return leg, shaped their course carefully, each aware of the inherent danger of departing Midway in the afternoon. The ship's westward progress would be carefully controlled during the night to assure that they didn't arrive in the vicinity of Ocean Island until well after daylight. Neither mentioned the fact they that were departing on a Friday, though there may have been some comment from the crew. Originally, Friday was a day sacred to Freya, the mythical Norse leader of the Valkyries. She was thought by early Christians to be a witch.[7] Many ships' crews carefully avoided beginning trips on a Friday when they could, whether aware of the origins of the Viking myth or not. The sea inspired many such superstitions, most or all of which were peremptorily ignored by the Department of the Navy, of course. Oddly though, Surgeon Adam Frank had a clear premonition of impending doom, which he communicated to Paymaster George Read as the two walked the beach at

Midway Island, the last to climb on board the boats. Read pooh-poohed his shipmate's premonition, dismissing Frank's concern out of hand.[8]

Appropriately, Sicard was careful to draft the night orders, his instructions to the officer of the deck, for maximum caution. During the 8:00 to 12:00 p.m. watch, the course was west by one-half point north, the engines slowed to making only five revolutions per minute, just enough to keep the buckets from dragging, and to continue condensing freshwater. The ship's speed was to be kept under four knots. The night orders consisted of both written and verbal instructions: A "bright lookout" was to be kept for rocks, shoals, discolored water, and for squalls, and to take sail in, in case of the latter; the officer of the deck was to stand his watch on the forward part of the hurricane or weather deck, and to keep a personal lookout for rocks, breakers, and shoals, and to "walk forward occasionally to see that the lookouts are vigilant, to be very particular about this, as this part of the ocean is imperfectly known."[9] Mate George Robinson had the deck from 8:00 to 12:00 p.m. Ensign Perry Garst relieved Robinson at midnight.

At 1:00 a.m., the topgallant sails were clewed up; by 2:00 a.m., they were furled. Commander Sicard was awakened, as he had ordered, and at 2:15 a.m., he came on deck to take his seat at the port paddle box, checking the speed of the ship—four knots. Garst informed the commander that, by the deck log, the ship had made 35 miles to the west since 5:00 p.m. on the previous day. Sicard instructed Garst to stop the engines, slowing the vessel further, and he moved his own seat to the starboard quarterdeck.

At least seven other crewmen remained on deck in the early quiet hours of October 29. Chief Quartermaster George Sellers could not sleep on the crowded berthing deck and had come up to take the air. Landsman William Coombs and Ordinary Seaman Michael Jordan were on deck but no longer on watch, tired but not inclined to go below given the sounds emanating from the foredeck companionway hatch. George Bailey, the diver and agent for the Midway party, was awake as well. Quartermaster Peter Francis was at the helm, his vision from the ship's wheel forward along the deck obscured. Seaman John Daley was stationed at the life buoy on the stern quarter, prepared to render assistance if needed. And Ordinary Seaman Dennis Fitzgerald was on the forecastle at the bow, the forward lookout. These nine pairs of eyes peered into the darkness, the quiet being broken only by the occasional "All's well" call of the watch, and the splash of the log astern, monitoring the ship's speed. Occasionally the moon emerged from behind the thick clouds, lighting the black surface of the ocean, the sails suddenly materializing into ghostly canvas shapes above. Then the moon swept behind clouds, and darkness again. The ship rolled silently forward over the heavy ocean swell into the thick of night. *Saginaw* was under sail, economizing the use of coal as per Navy Department orders.

Progressively the ship's pace slowed, for the unseen reef somewhere ahead of them began to weigh heavily on the commander's mind. *Saginaw* crawled forward at 2½ knots, which still seemed too fast for the situation in Sicard's estimation. And yet they were not on soundings (heaving the lead to sound the depths), the commander having no reason to suspect that they were in the immediate vicinity of Ocean Island. By their own meticulous calculations, they were still some 10 to 15 miles off. Nonetheless, at 3:00 a.m., Sicard ordered Garst to take in the mainsail and proceed under jib and topsails alone. The ship's speed dropped to little more than two knots, just making headway, just maintaining steerage. That task completed and logged, Ensign Garst went forward with binoculars in hand, for the third time on his watch, to check on the lookout, and to make sure Seaman Fitzgerald remained vigilant and "bright," as instructed by the captain.

It's hard to imagine a gentler pace; one could walk faster than the speed the ship was making, and yet none of these careful precautions mattered in the end. At 3:13 a.m., Garst "told the lookout to take a bright look and see if he could see anything; as I reached the rail, he, the lookout, asked me if those were not breakers ahead. I said yes, and immediately ran aft."[10] Garst shouted orders to Jones Godfrey, the engineer on watch, to stand by for backing engines. Sounding three bells, Garst called out for the captain, who immediately confirmed breakers ahead, less than 400 yards from the bow, and went into action. The quiet night was immediately broken.

The captain's orders rang out, urgent and clear. Topsails were clewed up and halyards let go; the engines were ordered back hard. The word was passed for "all hands." Given that the majority of the ship's crew were below and only moments before snoring in their hammocks, it was no easy task to muster the dazed men topsides and into the rigging. The men, taking the deck, appeared to be paralyzed with fear and only slowly and reluctantly moved to man the rig.[11]

In the handful of minutes between spotting the breakers and actual contact, in that odd span of time when the doomed ship still lived on the sea, there seemed only a few basic decisions to be made, and, in fact, there was only one. Dousing sail and backing the engines were practically automatic reactions and put into motion immediately, though neither would have much effect. The steam pressure was inadequate. And it was clear, even at the ship's slow pace, there would be no time to unrig the bower anchors and lower away, in an effort to keep from going on the reef. The only decision worthy of consideration was whether the ship could be brought about quickly enough to avoid impact. Could the old and heavily laden *Saginaw*, slow to maneuver under the best conditions and with barely any headway on, come about in time? By then, six ship lengths remained between the vessel and the rocks. Sicard instinctively knew the answer to this question. No orders were given to Peter Francis to change the helm. It was better to either back the ship away, or run onto the rocks bow-on, in hopes of preserving her hull from the broadside action of the waves—perhaps even touch on the unknown shoal and carry through to deeper water beyond. But the sound of the surf grew closer.

Sicard's orders to reduce sail awoke James Butterworth, the first assistant engineer, and he dressed as quickly as possible and made his way to his station in the engine room. There he found Godfrey "backing by hand" (operating the steam-valve bars by hand to reverse engines), as *Saginaw's* single eccentric was fastened securely to the paddle-wheel shaft. The engine valves were designed to work forward only.[12] Godfrey had already spread the two banked fires in the boilers and cut off the distilling pump, an attempt to quickly generate steam pressure. There was barely seven pounds per square inch, not nearly enough to stop her forward motion in time. The surf was now a deep, rolling sound, like low thunder. The ocean floor shoaled up quickly under the ship's keel.

Mate Robinson, asleep since going off watch, "was awakened by hearing the Captain say let go the maintopsail halliards, afterwards let go the maintopsail sheets and clew up the topsails. I jumped out of my berth and had reached the top step of the steerage ladder, when I felt the ship strike the rocks and a few minutes after the sea commenced to break over her."[13] The first impact, at approximately 3:22 a.m., was nothing more than a strong bump, but the pounding instantly grew worse. Each surging wave picked the ship up and drove her farther into the maze of sharp coral topography, now shaking the vessel with impacts from different quarters. *Saginaw* pressed her stem into the reef crest with the sound of breaking timbers and crashing coral (see fig. 15). Finally the hull fixed into a crevice, and commenced to slam the keel and stern repeatedly into a solid

FIGURE 15. Sicard's sketch from memory of USS *Saginaw* hard aground at Kure Atoll. Breakers are striking the starboard side and spraying into the air. From Read, *Last Cruise of the* Saginaw.

submarine pinnacle. The quaking and trembling beneath the men's feet was both frightening and unnatural, an aquatic living vessel in her death throes, in contact with solid earth.

Engineer Herschel Main felt the ship strike and bolted out of bed. Pulling on his pants, he made it to the fire room, his duty station at quarters, in time to see a large black rock "push itself right through into the fire room just on the starboard side of the keel, lifting up and pushing the fire room plates to one side and the water began to rush into the fire room from below." He reported to Butterworth the conditions in the fire room, that it was useless to continue trying to back the engines. Godfrey and Main then headed back to ready the pumps, but "had hardly gotten down into the fire room, when a great volume of smoke and gas came pouring through the furnaces. This was owing to the smokestack being carried away just at that moment; being perfectly suffocating, we were compelled to leave the fire room directly." The boiler and engine rooms were abandoned. On deck, "everything at this time seemed to be in perfect confusion, and the men seemed paralyzed. The waves were dashing over the ship, each wave driving her further on the rocks."[14]

Ensign Arthur Parsons also snapped awake at the first irregular motion of the ship's hull, and also to the sound of George Bailey singing out, "There she strikes!" and he hastily dressed. He heard Lieutenant Talbot give orders to prepare to lower the boats, and the captain sing out for all officers to man their stations. By the time Parsons made the deck, the ship was thumping heavily: "I heard the Captain then give the order for the men to lay aloft and furl the topsails, and he remarked at the same time, get the topsails furled and keep the engines backing and we may get her off yet."[15] Parsons did his best to get the stunned crew into the rigging. William Halford was one of the men chosen. Halford recalled later: "Nobody, naturally, wanted to go aloft. . . . You understand there was a heavy sea running, making it a very risky job to do anything aloft. We got the sail pretty well in hand several times, when a sudden squall would rip it out again. Finally, seeing that it was a hopeless job, the Captain ordered us down."[16]

At that moment, Engineer Butterworth reported to the captain the flooding in the engine room, "that he could get nothing more out of her. The Captain replied very well, and gave orders to get out provisions." Without hesitation, Commander Sicard realized that they could no longer hope to rescue the ship, but maybe they could rescue themselves. Eleven years, seven months, and twenty-six days after her keel had first touched water, *Saginaw*'s life on the ocean was finished.

At 3:33 a.m., a dark wave swept across the decks and took away the ship's launch, along with the iron boat davits and all the boat's tackle and line, smashing the launch to pieces before the men's eyes, sweeping the tangled mess into the darkness of the waters beyond the breakers. It had been lowered too early from the starboard quarter and taken by the sea, its stern hitting the water first while the bow was still up in the air. Lieutenant Talbot quickly took firm charge of the remaining boats. *Saginaw*'s 27-foot second cutter, on what was now the weather side of the ship, was laboriously swung inboard and moved to the port or lee side in preparation for launching. This alone was no small task, the bow of the cutter being damaged against the ship in the process. And then the main boom began to swing wildly, threatening to smash the ship's smaller gig to pieces, and was only secured with difficulty.[17]

After the initial impact, the ship had begun to grind painfully and pivot clockwise, slowly being pushed sideways to the waves, which then rose up with greater force along the hull to spray over the entire deck. The exposed broadside increased the massive power of the sea against the wooden frames and hull planks of the vessel, twisting the thick copper fasteners and breaking open the caulked seams, and water began to flow through the ship. *Saginaw*'s timbers emitted occasional cracking and tearing sound, terrifying to hear, and the ship's fastenings began to pull from the wood with sharp, screeching cries. The smokestack had gone by the boards. All efforts to clew up the sails had ceased, but in the chaos the officers and men focused on two important objectives: prepare the boats, and bring up the provisions. No land could be seen; no island was in sight. Only the whitewater swept close alongside, and the stars above between patches of cloud. The loosened rigging shook angrily overhead in the darkness. The men prepared themselves to be cast adrift in the middle of the Pacific.

Sicard ordered Robinson and Parsons to go to work on the provisions, though both main and fore holds were soon full of water, the seas coming in through the gaps in the broken hull. Flooding had the one positive effect of setting the ship down harder onto the reef, stabilizing it temporarily, reducing the pounding. Now the surf broke around the ship as if *Saginaw* were a permanent feature of the reef, though they could still feel the vessel shift under their feet. Teams were organized to clear the main hold, working in darkness and at times underwater. Provisions were brought up on deck and stored in the pilothouse until daylight, when the remaining ship's boats could be brought close alongside. Seven casks of beef, part of the contractor's stores from Midway, were stowed in the fore hold. Only four of these were hauled out before the ship shifted and the hold became too dangerous. Other critical items, such as charts, sextants, and chronometers, were also gathered. Water would prove the great difficulty. *Saginaw*, like many ships of that time, carried her water in large iron tanks, not the floating portable water casks of an older age.

Through it all, the efforts to save what could be saved were assisted by a most unlikely musical accompaniment. The wardroom steward, Joseph Ross, had been confined in double irons and placed on bread and water prior to departing Midway. The infraction was the usual disobedience to orders and showing disrespect toward a superior officer. Ross, an African American from New York, had originally been a waiter. He now sat, chained on the hatch of the hurricane deck and surrounded by the roaring surf, whistling "Way Down upon the Suwanee River" as the master at arms searched hastily for the keys to his manacles, without luck. The irons were soon severed by hammer and chisel, but for a while the tune had an oddly calming effect on the men.

A path needed to be found through the surf and the coral into the calm waters of the lagoon, but this was an impossible task without light. With the coming of dawn, around 5:30 a.m., Talbot ordered the ship's boats (all that had survived) lowered, and passed the call for volunteers to go onto the reef. Daylight revealed more than just access into a placid lagoon. A low, dark line, first confused with a cloud on the horizon, could be made out somewhat over a mile away to the southwest. The "cloud" soon changed in color to the emerging green scrub of Ocean Island. This considerably relieved the men, who now knew with certainty where they were, and at least had a bearing on an immediate and dry destination. And as the light increased, another dark spot on the horizon to the north also appeared. This was examined with growing urgency until someone cried out, "Ship ahoy!" But instant hope and cheers faded with the breaking dawn, for the smudge proved to be the aging timbers of the British whaler *Gledstanes*, lost on Kure Atoll in 1837, a portion of the hulk still emergent from the sea. The identification was sobering. In the flat world of the atolls, any object protruding above the water can be seen for miles. *Gledstanes'* bones provided an ominous welcome to her new neighbor on the reef.

Dawn had brought the hope of survival, but the danger was not over. In places, the coral provided tricky footing at best, washed with surf and strong currents, lacerating the men's feet and lower legs. Many of their shoes were now underwater in the fore hold, or somewhere on the berthing deck. The sun beat down mercilessly on the men, and reflected back up from the water's surface into their eyes and against their unprotected skin. The crew were organized into lines and passed provisions across the reef and through the surf to the boats operating in the shallow of the lagoon, an aquatic caravan stretching from the noisy open ocean and windward reef crest to the calm and sandy beach on Ocean Island's northern shore (see fig. 16).

And all the while the ocean continued its relentless attack on *Saginaw*. At 6:25 a.m., accompanied by the dry, cracking sounds of snapping bones, *Saginaw* broke in two just forward of the hurricane deck. The forward section, with its hold, extra anchors, and heavy chain locker, collapsed and broke up into deeper water, a hidden fissure in the reef. The stern, where the men remaining on deck had braced themselves against the inevitable destruction of their home, listed over steeply on its port side, but remained for the moment above the waves. In an attempt to relieve the growing stress on the aft section, Sicard ordered the mainmast cut away,

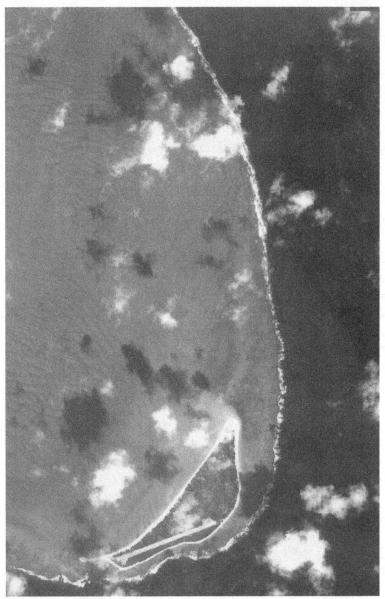

FIGURE 16. Satellite image of Kure Atoll, showing Green (Ocean) Island, the light color of the shallow lagoon waters, the eastern reef crest and surf line, and the darker deep waters to seaward. *Saginaw* was lost approximately halfway up the eastern atoll crest. Imagery data source courtesy of IKONOS.

and the deck crew broke out axes and hatchets and went to work on the starboard shrouds. In a few minutes, the mast went over the side, adding a makeshift stable bridge to the boats in the surf.

Working over the side of the listing ship was treacherous, a matter of timing between the sets of heavy swells still sweeping the deck. At 7:00 a.m., Private Thomas Wiseman, one of the marine guard, was swept off the slanting deck by a breaking wave, only to be whirled into an eddy near the ship and then fished out, with "hardly a square inch of skin intact," but at least alive, to the amazement of his shipmates.[18] (He was drunk.) Fireman Edward James was less lucky: having been swept onto the reef, he broke his clavicle on the substrate. Surgeon Adam Frank dressed him as best he could with supplies from the Midway contractor's chest, the majority of his own medical dispensary being broken and lost underwater in the forward hold. The difficult situation was complicated by some of the men who (as happened in numerous shipwrecks) "became utterly unable to work on account of drink. In clearing out the hold they had discovered the wine locker in the ward room, and had helped themselves, and although there was nothing in it stronger than ale and claret, on men who are debarred from all liquors, and who were fasting, the effect was soon apparent."[19]

The casks of provisions and all the tools and supplies the men could lay their hands on moved in a continuous stream out of the broken ship over the side and along the line of wearied men standing on the sharp coral. The boats pulled back and forth to the sandy shore. The crew toiled for twelve hours straight, standing waist deep in the water, caught between the ocean and the blazing sky. In time, though, the caravan of provisions took on some of the familiar nature of yet another routine drill, and jokes began to travel along the line, most regarding the culinary potential of some particular sodden or ruined item.[20] At 5:00 p.m., the order was finally passed to completely abandon the ship, and with hopes that the stern would remain relatively intact the next day, the boats picked up the exhausted sunburned wet men and brought them to their new home. The island welcomed them with the smell of guano, a strong, acrid, dry but not altogether unpleasant odor.

On shore, the boatswain's whistle piped the men to their supper, which consisted of a meager one-half cup of water, half a cake of hardtack, and a small piece of boiled pork, as well as a portion of the boiled mutton meant originally for the wardroom table that night. Commander Sicard then gathered the crew and, following a simple Episcopal prayer of thankfulness for their deliverance from the unhappy fate of their ship, remarked on the importance of economy of provisions, good nature, and discipline. The commander emphasized, as did all leaders faced with similar situations, that shipboard rule would be maintained, and the commanding officer remained responsible for the administration of all law and order. It was a message of hope, and a warning against anyone who might mistake their new circumstances as beyond the realm of the military justice they had been subject to on board. *Saginaw* had gone in search of castaways on Ocean Island, and indeed castaways had been found—they were the ship's own crew.

Home on Ocean Island

The first night on the island was not a pleasant one. Men were salty, wet, bloody, thirsty, exhausted, barefoot, and dressed in clothes that had been shredded by the coral reef. And what bedding had been saved was soaked. Nonetheless, the chaotic night on the groaning and tearing ship, and the exertion of bringing what could be saved ashore, made even the damp and salty sand a sufficient mattress for some. During the night, the wind calmed and the seas came down a bit, and the men lay contemplating their fate on what felt like an invisible dot in the middle of the Pacific Ocean, ninety-three souls seeking the comfort of a well-earned sleep and some hope for the future.

On Sunday morning, the usual divine service was skipped, and the crew went immediately to work on the more pressing matter of survival. Some were sent out to the wreck to continue to strip what could be recovered from her rigging and spars, and others began to inventory and dry the damaged provisions on the beach. It was clearly apparent to all that, judging by the amount saved, they would be hard-pressed for food, and the discussion quickly turned to the abundance of seals and albatross on the island, and on what fish they could capture in the lagoon. The crew and officers alike immediately went on half rations, and it would only get worse from there.

Saginaw's crew were already familiar with the Hawaiian monk seal from their time at Midway. These large marine mammals, some exceeding 600 pounds, feared only the sharks of the atolls during their feeding forays in the dark ocean at night. On land they fought only among themselves, and barked at the odd human intruders only when they came too close, though males and mothers with pups could prove aggressive. Now, they

Rats about the "Wing Holes"

FIGURE 17. Island rats swarming the dunes around the pits or wing holes dug to trap the albatross. Courtesy of Library of Congress.

regarded the castaways with wary but sleepy glances as they slumbered on the warm sands. With a little caution, they could be killed with clubs. Their meat was so tough, though, that the cook had to parboil it overnight and then fry it again in the morning just to make it palatable.

The albatross, too, had no learned reason to avoid humans. With a wing-span of more than seven feet, they were large and powerful birds. Once at sea, these graceful creatures soared for thousands of miles, on the wing for years at a time. The adults then returned, ultimately, to the atoll sands where they were born, to raise their fledglings on the single spot of land familiar to them. The gooney birds (as they were called) were built for air and sea, but on land their lack of amphibious grace became almost comical. They were unable to get aloft without running a long path on their large webbed feet straight into a good headwind, an ungainly sprint. They could not easily escape. The crew learned to dig pits in the sand, "wing holes," chasing the gooney birds into these, where they were trapped (see fig. 17). They could be decapitated by swords. Even though only a portion of the bird's flesh could be chewed, they were voted more palatable than the seal.

The approachability of these wild creatures so unused to humans meant that, if not checked, Sicard's ever-hungry crew of ninety-three could have eliminated the local population in very short order. The commander there-fore prohibited interference or any actions unnecessarily upsetting the seals and the gooney birds. The extreme west end of Ocean Island, claimed by the majority of the albatross, was placed off-limits without specific permission. And collecting the albatross eggs was forbidden, though the eggs themselves were quite large. Foraging parties took care to maintain a low profile in their culling operations, and limited their take per orders.[21] No one wanted to frighten off the only sources of food on the island, for there was no telling how long they would have to rely on the atoll's inhabitants for survival. All of the sailors were aware that the albatross was a migratory seabird, and once the eggs hatched and the fledglings learned to fly, the population of the island's goonies would depart. But they had months before that fateful day. And surely they would be rescued by then.

Not all appreciated the restraint in the face of so much potential sustenance. Nor did they appreciate the fact that most of the preserved food from the ship had immediately been placed under armed guard. Nor did it seem right that the ship's officers somehow had managed to save more of their belongings than had the men. The inevitable grumbling had begun. Exposure and lack of clothing brought chills and fevers. And, making up for the half rations of ship's provisions, the men were ingesting an unfamiliarly high amount of oil and fat, particularly from the seal meat. This contributed to an outbreak of violent dysentery. Surgeon Frank treated the painful diarrhea as best he could with his limited supply of camphor and opium pills.[22] He had no acetate of lead, or sulphate of copper, his more familiar remedies. The sailors simply suffered, and expressed their unhappiness in the few ways available to them.

There was some dissension in the ranks. Not two days following the wreck, Seaman Daniel Collins was placed in single irons and under a sentry's charge to await court-martial for disobedience and gross disrespect to a superior officer. Similarly, Landsman Solomon Graves and Coxswain William Halford were confined in double irons under sentry's charge for disrespect to a superior officer.[23] Not surprisingly, the ship's shackles or irons were among the important items saved from the sea. In navy fashion, resistance would not be tolerated. The first of a number of summary court-martial proceedings was convened on the beach at 9:00 a.m. Collins was sentenced to twenty days in double irons and half rations of already meager supplies. Seaman Dennis Fitzgerald and Ship's Cook William Edmans were next in line for the atoll's "brig." The summary charges and courts continued. The steady pace of punishments established on board the ship went unaffected by their new circumstances. Strict discipline and more work were to be the twin solutions to the morale problem on Ocean Island. It was no more than the men expected.

FIGURE 18. Montgomery Sicard's improvised tent on the beach with writing table, Ocean Island. From Read, *Last Cruise of the* Saginaw.

And there was plenty of work to keep the survivors busy during the first week ashore. Besides scavenging from the wreck and the sorting and careful storing of the sodden provisions, men were employed with building low tents from the ship's sails and spars among the scrub and dunes. One tent was raised per ship's mess, and a larger one for the wardroom officers. Commander Sicard had his own private accommodation (see fig. 18). Fishing parties took *Saginaw*'s dinghy out into the turquoise lagoon, an easy task preferred by the crew. Other parties were sent out in the ship's cutters along the shore to gather driftwood. All kinds of flotsam and jetsam found its way to the beaches of the Northwestern Hawaiian Islands: parts of *Saginaw*, parts of other shipwrecks like the whaler *Gledstanes*, logs that went adrift and circulated into the North Pacific from Washington Territory and Oregon (see fig. 19).

The most pressing question was water. Like many vessels of the time, USS *Saginaw* had carried most of hers in interior tanks, not in large but portable wooden barrels. It had been impossible to save most of the freshwater; only the smaller kegs and breakers that had been stowed in the ship's boats had been rescued. Men were sent out to find locations to dig wells, but initially they struck only brackish salty liquid, unsuitable for drinking. Rain catchments were a possibility, but the atolls had very little

FIGURE 19. Sicard's sketch of the stern breaking apart on the reef, while crew salvage timbers from the wreckage. From Read, *Last Cruise of the* Saginaw.

FIGURE 20. The donkey boiler condensing freshwater at Ocean Island, which saved the lives of ninety-three men. From Read, *Last Cruise of the* Saginaw.

orographic effect on the surrounding trade winds, for the specks of islands were too low to cause their own uplift and form clouds and rain. Showers passed in random fashion, most seen only from a distance—dark, slanting shadows moving across the far horizon and wasting their sustenance on the sea. Without a reliable source of freshwater, the men would not last more than a handful of days.

The solution came from Townsend's Boston contractors, who had shipped a small boiler to Midway to supply steam power for their hoist. This auxiliary, or "donkey," boiler, being basically a watertight iron cylinder, had survived the wreck, breaking free from its lashings on the aft deck and floating high into the back reef and protection of the lagoon. The men secured it between two boats and pulled it to the shore. There they assembled some copper speaking tubes salvaged from the ship. They also got their hands on a copper distillation coil, which had been retrieved at great peril from the crashing surf and the ruined wheelhouse by Chief Engineer Butterworth. These, along with some canvas hose, allowed the steam from the jury-rigged boiler to run beneath the cooling waters at the edge of the lagoon, making a crude steam condenser (see fig. 20). The experiment provided a slow but steady trickle of freshwater into a bucket on the beach. Cheers broke out at the first appearance of the distilled liquid. By November 1, 50 gallons had been accumulated. The fire for the condenser was kept continually burning, having been started by the one remaining waterproof match preserved by Townsend's chief diver, George Bailey.[24] The condenser watch included three seamen and three of the ship's engineers superintending. No effort was spared in maintaining this improvised contraption; it would save all of their lives.

The immediate problem of water having been tackled for the moment, the crew's other efforts also began to pay off. The pile of canvas and rigging and yards and timbers and hardware grew on the beach, along with crockery and boxes of tinned coffee and sodden blankets and sails and awnings. Certain vital items came up from the surf as well, such as the carpenter's tool box and a cask of sperm whale oil for light. The bow of the ship had vanished completely beneath the waves, along with all the goods in the forward berthing deck or forecastle. Saginaw's stern, pushed higher onto the reef and hard over on her port side, held together for a longer period. This meant a considerable amount of bedding and clothing could be rescued—for the officers, but not the men. That was the social geography of the wreck.

Slowly, with each passing day, the chances of their common survival increased. True, the remaining supplies of familiar hardtack, pork, and potato used to make scouse could not last, and much of the flour saved from the wreck had been turned into a salty hardened crust by the sea. But the men's initial reaction to their oily protein diet eased with time. They continued to sorely miss sugar and bread, and lost weight quickly from this high-protein, high-fat, and low-carbohydrate diet, yet they were able to maintain a minimum of energy for life on the island on the small portions of food strictly controlled by the officers. *Saginaw* herself had, by November 2, been stripped of all movable items, save the timbers of the stern section itself. Continuing attempts to retrieve more were as much to keep the men busy as to assure their physical survival.

Weather for the most part exhibited the benefits of the steady trade winds of the mid-northern Pacific. Infrequently, though, the seas grew to a tremendous size and violent sharp squalls swept over the atoll, the edges of low-pressure systems making their way to the east. On one such occasion, the commander and his boat party (both first and second cutters) were caught on the distant sand spit to the west of the island, having gone there to gather driftwood.[25] The officers remaining at the camp could make out the ship's boats in the glass (telescope), inverted on the beach to protect the trapped party, but were helpless to assist, unable to launch their own boats in the rough seas. Sicard and his team had to literally bury themselves in the sand, beneath their upturned boats, in order to avoid being thoroughly soaked by the showers. Sailors only emerged from the boat shelters to capture several green sea turtles, which had pulled themselves out of the rough surf seeking refuge on shore. They flipped these large creatures on their backs, the next day adding turtle meat and soup to the ever-shrinking larder. (Feeding almost one hundred hungry men was a constant struggle.) At the main camp it was all the crew could do during the squall to keep their own provisions and tents from being torn asunder as the surf rolled to within a few feet of their belongings. The following day, the commander and the cold and sodden boat party returned to their shipmates, having spent a most uncomfortable night.

Fortuitously, the ship's mainmast, having already once served as an impromptu bridge on the reef crest, broke free in the squall and was retrieved from the lagoon by the boats. This was laboriously pulled ashore, and a hole dug and tackle rigged in order to raise it as a lookout platform, the highest natural point of the island being only some 10 feet above sea level. Hopes were dashed and then suddenly raised again when the mast, hoisted upright with improvised ground tackle, ripped out its standing rigging and toppled over. But the hole excavated by the foot of the mast revealed water. It was not freshwater, but pure enough to drink without serious immediate reaction. The men added on more rigging and ground tackle, and the mast, once successfully raised, provided a perch for a look-out and a yard for flying the national flag upside down, a universal sign of distress. But would anyone ever see it? What ships (besides their own) would intentionally pass so close to known navigational hazards?

Meanwhile, from the Navy Department telegrams continued to be sent to the commandant at Mare Island, and to the commander of the Pacific Fleet: "When will the *Saginaw* probably be at San Francisco? Answer."[26] Rear Admiral Winslow's estimate placed the ship at Mare Island around December 1, if not earlier. From the Pacific Mail Steamship Company, he learned that their China steamer had never made contact with his ship, so he guessed that *Saginaw* would be headed directly to San Francisco from Midway Island. These Department inquiries went out to their destinations at the same time that Commander Sicard was drafting the first reports of *Saginaw*'s loss on Ocean Island. They were far from the shipping routes in the middle of an immense emptiness, and the chances of sighting and signaling to another vessel were slim to none. It was time for *Saginaw*'s crew to begin shaping their own rescue.

Preparations

Sicard made the general announcement on November 2 that one of the ship's boats would be modified for the long voyage to the east, and five volunteers were to be chosen. This was a dangerous and necessary deci-sion, and therefore the commander desired to know for the record where each of his officers stood on the matter. Consequently, he ordered each of them to seek an out-of-the-way dune and to write out, on the small scraps of salvaged paper that now served as official documents, their individual opinions of the mission, a kind of poll.

Ensign Arthur Parsons considered the issue as a balance of risks: "we are dependent on the condenser for our supply of water, and should anything occur to it so as to render it unfit for service, the risk of great suffering and loss of life would be much greater than the risk incurred by sending the gig."[27] Parsons was dead right: the ninety-three castaways were hang-ing by a thread when it came to freshwater. The old, corroded boiler could not be expected to hold out more than a couple of months. The tides could eliminate the thin lens of brackish water they had managed to discover. Ensign James Cogswell noted the state of the boiler as well, and also mentioned the devastating effects an outbreak of disease would have on the crew, there being almost no medicines on the island. The gig voyage was "the quickest means of relief" given the scarcity of provisions. "And I take this opportunity to express my desire to be the officer to go in the boat," Cogswell added.[28] Ensign Perry Garst also cited "the almost total lack of medicines and proper food in case of sickness" and optimistically pointed out "the seaworthiness of the gig itself."[29] Paymaster Read calculated the probability of relief from outside sources versus the length of time they could hold out on their current provisions, and found no other alternative than "an attempt be made to obtain relief by sending the gig to the nearest port."[30] Surgeon Frank naturally highlighted "the danger of an epidemic of various diseases arriving in the camp."[31] The consensus was unanimous: no matter the risk, the lengthy boat voyage must be undertaken for the greater good, and the sooner the better.

The captain's gig, a well-crafted, stout whaleboat, was the proper choice for the voyage. One of *Saginaw*'s launches had been lost in the wreck, leaving only the well-worn first and second cutters and the much smaller ship's dinghy. All had been built at the Mare Island small boat shop. The open gig, though, was designed only for close-in work, and would have to be modified on the beach for the blue-water passage. It was hauled inland and set into a cradle for the job. The carpenters made good use of the salvaged timbers from the wreck to this end. The main portion of the hurricane deck, also torn from the stern in the recent squall, came drifting into the lagoon a few days after the mainmast was recovered. The three-inch-thick deck planks would be suitable building material for the gig, but they needed to be split in half. The carpenters dug a pit and built a stage, converting their single bucksaw into a two-man jigsaw, one pulling from above and one from below, to cut the planks down.[32] Spikes and bolts were pulled from the debris, straightened and sharpened, and reused. Copper drift pins were pounded flat and shaped into deck fittings, and patches of the *Saginaw*'s copper sheathing were attached to the gig's hull, reinforcing weak points on the boat. The gunwale or freeboard was raised by some eight inches at the stern and the bow, and the open boat was decked over and covered tightly with canvas. Four hatches were cut in the deck, allowing the small crew to man the tiller, row if need be, and handle the sails. Boards were run fore and aft below the canvassed deck, giving the men a snug place to recline and sleep. Finally, the gig's rigging was changed (two

FIGURE 21. *Saginaw*'s crew on Ocean Island laying out a set of sails for the gig. Courtesy of Library of Congress.

FIGURE 22. Sicard's sketch of the ship's modified gig ready for sea. From Read, *Last Cruise of the* Saginaw.

small masts were stepped) and a new suit of miniature sails laid out and cut from *Saginaw*'s old canvas (see fig. 21). In all the ways possible, the small open whaleboat was ingeniously modified and made ready for sea (see fig. 22).

Meanwhile, life on Ocean Island fell into a monotonous pattern. Men gathered wreckage from *Saginaw*'s stern, now collapsing on the reef.

Fishing parties rowed out of sight of the camp and then drifted in the lagoon. And many were simply ordered to "pick oakum," the meticulous task of disassembling frayed bits of rope and cleaning the fibers for reuse as caulking material. The phrase "picking oakum" was somewhat synonymous with mild punishment or busywork, an assignment to do anything to appear busy. Meanwhile, the commander had plenty of time alone in his own tent, at an improvised writing desk, to complete his final report on the Midway project, and to draft his more immediate report of the loss of his ship to his superiors:

> Sir: I have to report the loss of the United States steamer Saginaw, under my command, on Ocean Island Reef, at about 3 o'clock on the morning of October 29. The vessel left Midway Island late in the afternoon of October 28, bound for San Francisco with the contractor's party. . . .
>
> Thinking to make Ocean Island Reef at daylight, I ordered myself called at 2 a.m., and also that the vessel should not make over four knots per hour, and that the officer of the deck should keep his watch on the forward part of the hurricane-deck, and keep the lookout vigilant. . . . At about 2.20, the officer of the deck having reported, (in obedience to part of the night orders,) that the ship had run by the deck-log thirty-five miles since 5 p.m., (28th) I ordered the mainsail taken in, and the engines stopped (this I thought would reduce her speed to about one and a half knots per hour.) The engines previously had been kept turning over.
>
> At 3 a.m. the officer of the deck reported that the vessel was going two and a half knots, which I did not consider too much, as she still had by the deck-reckoning eleven knots and four fathoms, and by the patent log six knots and seven fathoms, to run to the reef. Almost immediately he hastened to me again, and reported breakers in sight . . . so I ordered the topsails clewed up at once, and the engines backed. The men of the watch appeared paralyzed, and so slow that I had all hands called, and it was only by the greatest exertions of myself and the officer of the deck that the topsails were gotten in finally. The engines were all the time backing slowly, but the pressure of steam was not enough to drive her astern with the topsails set, and just as they were clewed up she struck the reef. She bilged within ten minutes, and flooded the holds at once; and the forward body broke nearly off within an hour of the time of striking. . . .

I worked all the 29th of October saving the necessaries of life; and the next morning I found the after-body of the vessel had been thrown more upon the reef, and then I succeeded in saving a few more articles. The paymaster's money-safe and part of his books were obtained, but no other articles of importance, the guns and all heavy articles sinking in deep water outside the reef and under a heavy sea. The log-book was saved.

I feel thankful to be able to say that all the ship's company and contractor's men were saved. The yeoman's books and stores, (being in the eyes of the ship,) were all lost, and most of the men lost and ruined their clothing. (Lists will be forwarded by the first opportunity, agreeably to regulations.)

A very little of the engine and part of one boiler, with one paddle-wheel, and part of the shaft, protrude still above the water; but it is utterly impossible to approach them, on account of the immense surf that breaks there constantly.

I have decided to send a boat (properly decked and equipped) to Honolulu, with news of our state; she will carry this letter. . . . In the meantime the ship's company is under temporary tents on the island. We have about four month's provisions, (at quarter rations,) but turtle, seal, and fish can be caught, which help us to live, though the men feel the reduction in their food a good deal. . . . I have given Mr. Talbot directions about chartering the vessel and buying provisions, and have done the best I could to economize for the United States. . . . I am, respectfully, your obedient servant, Montgomery Sicard (Lieutenant Commander, Commanding)[33]

These were no doubt very trying moments for Montgomery Sicard, who in his meticulous habit strove to consider all aspects and details for bettering their chances of survival. Sicard felt himself at no specific fault for the loss of his ship, but could not shake the inevitable feelings of guilt, as his was the ultimate responsibility no matter the circumstances. His official report of the event, written to Secretary of the Navy George M. Robeson, included a glimpse of his personal feelings along these lines:

It gives me very great pain to think that I should have lost the vessel but I feel that I exercised my usual vigilance and care in navigation, and that I am habitually vigilant and careful. I believe all those under whom, and over whom, I have served will testify. I regret very much to say that owing to the speedy destruction of the vessel, but little was saved (as will be seen by the enclosed report); but the officers, crew, and contractor's party are all saved. I trust that the Department in this matter will consider that it was solely from a desire to relieve possible distress that I came to this island. . . . These letters are written in haste and under many difficulties.[34]

It had been Sicard's decision to go anywhere near Ocean Island at all.

"With Full Hearts and with Many in Tears"

Other officers surely considered the opportunity and expressed their desire to lead the rescue voyage, but none was quicker or more intent upon volunteering than Lieutenant John Gunnel Talbot. Just a day after the wreck, Talbot informed Sicard that if there were to be a boat voyage, he wanted to be the officer in charge. This was a dedicated and brave decision by one who once had seemed less than enthusiastic about staying in the navy. But Talbot had passed that turning point long ago. Sicard had been impressed with Talbot's actions during the crisis, and he was the one chosen. In Sicard's words, the young lieutenant was "most zealous and spirited through this whole affair, [of] greatest assistance to me."[35] Talbot served as the executive officer, and the decision was an appropriate one (see fig. 23).

As for the other four "volunteers," many may have indicated their desire to go, but few actually volunteered.[36] This was hazardous duty, and the men were debilitated due to the lack of proper food. Seaman Henry D. Vivian and Landsman John R. Miller went back on the sick list from rheumatism, on account of the time spent in the surf salvaging debris near the wreck. Adam Frank noted this in his log as a "disease originating in the line of duty."[37] Steerage Cook Lawrence McCabe's acute rheumatism flared up as well, and he was treated with potassium iodide. Six others officially remained on the list with acute dysentery. Ensign Perry Garst's symptoms included frequent mucus and bloody discharge, and an absolute loathing of food. And the surgeon's opiate pills were running out. Physical robustness would play a large factor in the pending voyage, and many of Saginaw's crew lacked the needed strength.

Both Coxswain William Halford and Quartermaster Peter Francis stepped up and were chosen for the voyage. Both had known each other from their time on board USS Independence at Mare Island, and had signed

Left: FIGURE 23. Executive Officer John Gunnel Talbot. From Read, *Last Cruise of the Saginaw.*

Right: FIGURE 24. Gunner's Mate William Halford. From Read, *Last Cruise of the Saginaw.*

on board *Saginaw* in San Francisco in 1869 for a term of three years. They were strong and excellent seamen and, more importantly, in good health relative to the rest of the crew. William Halford had been born in England in 1841.[38] Choosing to be a sailor had opened the sea lanes of the world to him, and by the time he was twenty-eight years old, he found himself enlisting in the U.S. Navy in New York and soon assigned to duty on the Pacific Station at Mare Island (see fig. 24). Peter Francis was from Manila, a "Manila man" (half Filipino and half Spanish)—"but a white man for all that," in Halford's estimation—and was chosen for the passage despite his recent bout with severe dysentery.[39] And they both had faith in the seaworthiness of the ship's gig.

Surgeon Frank had been charged with making the recommendations on the men's fitness to the commanding officer. Many of his own men were in poor shape, and Sicard was forced to accept two of the contractor's men to complete the boat's crew. Fortunately, thirty-eight-year-old John Andrews and thirty-six-year-old James Muir were, according to Sicard, "men of such fine qualities and endurance, [it was] proper to let them go."[40] The commander enlisted them officially into the U.S. Navy on Ocean Island on November 15 for an unusually short term of one month, signing them on for the dangerous voyage in order that, should they be lost in the line of duty, their families might properly benefit. Andrews was made a coxswain and Muir the captain of the hold. They were Boston hard-hat divers, large men built for donning the standard 200 pounds of copper helmet, heavy canvas, and lead weights of the deep-sea dress and laboring for hours underwater. They were built for the voyage.

By November 18, almost three weeks since the ship had gone onto the rocks, the gig was ready for sea. *Saginaw*'s navigation department, what remained of it, placed on board the boat 1 chronometer, 1 barometer, 1 sextant, 1 compass, 1 boat compass, 1 nautical almanac, a chart, parallel rulers, 1 ensign, 3 Castons signals, 1 logline (235 feet), 1 sea glass, 1 deck lantern, 4 gallons of sperm whale lamp oil, 2 balls of lamp wick, note paper, and three pencils. Paymaster Read took charge of selecting the best of the food provisions for the boat, equal to approximately half rations for five men for thirty-five days, plus about 90 gallons of freshwater in ten breakers. This included five days of hardtack sealed in tin; ten days of the same in canvas bags; two dozen small tins of preserved meat; 5 tins of desiccated potato; 2 tins of cooked beans; 3 tins of boiled wheat grits; 1 ham; 6 tins of preserved oysters; 10 pounds of dried beef; 12 tins of lima beans; 5 pounds of butter; 1 gallon of molasses; 12 pounds of white sugar; 4 pounds of tea, and 5 pounds of coffee.[41] A small cooking apparatus was fashioned and provided in the hope of rendering these provisions more palatable on the small, pitching craft.

Engineer Herschel Main contributed what may have been the most creative tool for the trip. He carefully reconstructed a navigational sextant from parts of what had been one of *Saginaw*'s steam gauges, along with bits of a broken shaving mirror and zinc strips taken from the linings of various fixtures. This instrument, a delicate precision tool, was tested and pronounced "sufficiently accurate for navigating purposes."[42]

The official reports of the ship's loss, as well as a great many personal letters, also went with the gig. The men wrote to wives and sweethearts who, on November 18, might not have yet heard any ill tidings of the voyage, but who would, in a month's time, surely have begun to imagine the worst. Sicard himself was particularly worried about how his wife in New York, Elizabeth, would handle the news of the tragedy, and appealed to a family friend:

My Dear Mrs Browne, you will soon be hearing that the Saginaw has been wrecked on the reef of this place, but I am thankful to say that we have all escaped with life, and with sufficient provisions to last until relief comes. Of course, we have lost most of our own effects, but all that can be repaired. The ship is a total loss, we only saving the boats and provisions. I of course feel very very anxious that my wife should be at once assured of my safety, so I am going to ask you to have the enclosed telegraph sent her at once. I know that you will attend to it for me, and I shall hereafter feel relieved on the source of her anxiety. Lieutenant Talbot (the executive officer) has volunteered with a crew of five men to go to Honolulu in a boat; this letter goes by him. I must close now as I am in great haste.[43]

George Read's letter to his family in Philadelphia included a description of the wrecking event, their situation on the island, the preparations for the boat voyage—and, of course, himself:

If you could see me now you would hardly recognize me: a pair of boots almost large enough for two feet in one, ragged trousers, an old felt hat, and no coat—I keep that for evenings when it is cool. I have my best uniform saved, having rescued it to come ashore in. . . . I hope this will reach you before you get anxious about us, for if the gig should not be successful we may have to stay here until the middle of March.[44]

In an informal procession joined by the whole crew, the ship's gig was bodily lifted and carried down to the water, where she rode in the lagoon while all the provisions and outfit were stowed on her. The crew's dinner that day was a somber affair with little conversation. The risks of the voyage hung over the men like a cloud, though Lieutenant Talbot strove to appear unconcerned by the danger. He had given his last will and testament to Paymaster Read the night before, with instructions to pass it on to his family in Kentucky should anything happen.[45] At 4:00 p.m., Sicard mustered his men at the beach and prayers were read, followed by the final farewells. The fifty-first chapter of Isaiah seemed particularly appropriate: "The isles shall wait upon me and on my arm they shall trust." The crew's emotions were plain: "With full hearts and with many in tears, we gave them three rousing cheers and a tiger, which were responded to with spirit, and we watched them until the boat faded from sight on the horizon."[46] Once again, the boat was departing on a Friday.

Tragedy at Kaua`i

On board the gig, Lieutenant Talbot initially shaped his course northward, seeking the prevailing westerlies at 32 degrees north latitude to push him to the east, where he would find his estimated longitude for O`ahu before he made his turn to the south. This rather large detour would add hundreds of miles to the otherwise direct boat voyage, but there was no other choice; one had to adapt to, rather than fight against, the prevailing wind patterns and currents for success.

Decades earlier, Captain William Bligh had completed what many referred to as the most famous of Pacific open-boat passages following the infamous mutiny on the HMS *Bounty* in 1792. Cast into the ship's boat with only a handful of loyalists and a compass, Bligh succeeded in making his way to the island of Timor in the Dutch East Indies, across an almost unimaginable 3,700 miles of open ocean, in a vessel no bigger than *Saginaw*'s gig. The voyage lasted forty-two days. This was a masterful accomplishment of navigation and boat handling, but Bligh failed to win any sign of appreciation from the men whose lives he had just saved. He may have been an excellent navigator and sailor, but he was an abysmally inept leader of men, and his small, starved crew lost no time filing official charges of mistreatment against him as soon as they touched shore.

Talbot and his own men, however, were united behind a more achievable goal. The gig carried provisions for approximately thirty-five days. Projecting a roundabout course of some 1,600 nautical miles, the boat had to average only 50 miles per day, feasible if granted fair weather. But the North Pacific in winter was not so cooperative; it was a rough passage. Even with the effort to cover the gig in canvas, the small boat shipped a good deal of water across the deck and down the hatches, dowsing the provisions and men and requiring constant bailing. All wooden boats work in a seaway and leak, and the water across the decks simply made things worse. Their tinder was soaked and lamp extinguished after five days at sea, and the small tin oil-filled cooking apparatus was rendered inoperable. The men spent the majority of the voyage cold, wet, and without light or hot food.

The eastward leg was the roughest for the men, forcing them to heave to among the mountainous waves twice, dowsing sail and using the sea anchor, a parachutelike device fashioned on the beach to prevent the small boat from broaching down-swell in the heavy seas. All progress ceased as they fought for survival. The strain on the line broke the sea anchor away, and the wet, miserable men jury-rigged another by crossing and lashing three of the gig's oars. This, too, was broken by the seas, and in desperation the men rigged another drag from the two remaining oars and a bit of the boat's own square sail. This "lasted for three hours of bad weather. The last time it broke adrift and all was lost of it."[47] The loss of the oars, needed for maneuvering the gig, was critical.

By Coxswain Halford's own account, the provisions brought from the camp actually caused a great portion of their suffering. The bread in the canvas bag had spoiled, and the sugar and tea and coffee had all been ruined by seawater. To "the dessicated potato, five five-pound tins of which were given us at the last moment before sailing," Halford wrote, "we attributed the preservation of our lives from starvation. For the last week it was all we had, mixed with a little fresh water."[48]

> The stores that were given us were largely spoiled because someone, thinking to do us a kindness, mixed molasses with the rice and beans. This fermented and spoiled them. I had had experience with this sort of thing before and I warned them what the result would be and strongly advised that it be thrown overboard, which was done. This left us very little. . . . I held my own better than the rest because we had five gallons of Sperm Oil. I buttered my potato liberally with Sperm Oil. The others couldn't "go it." They couldn't keep it down. As it was I lost sixty pounds.[49]

Both Muir and Andrews were sick for the majority of the voyage. Only Halford and Peter Francis remained in relatively good health under the circumstances. The poor diet and conditions on the gig took a toll on the men, who grew more and more lethargic and lost weight. The men etched their names into the hatch coamings of the gig, should the boat itself be the only survivor of the passage. And they tied sealed tins, each containing a letter describing the plight of their shipmates, to their bodies, should their floating corpses be the only signpost found on some distant beach.[50] Talbot was severely struck with diarrhea and was ill and fatigued for more than a week, though he did the most to constantly maintain a positive attitude. To him fell the duties of navigating their craft, and the careful measurement of what little food and water they had available. Talbot had the ultimate responsibility for their voyage. He sang to his men hour after hour to keep their spirits up even as his own voice grew feeble.[51]

They had to physically withstand the rigors of the voyage, and they had to continually believe that they could make it.

In rough weather, it's difficult to see half-submerged navigational hazards from a normal vessel, and from the low cockpit of a tiny whaleboat, it's almost impossible. The world from a small boat extends only the width of the trough between ocean swells, and only momentarily glimpses anything farther when cresting each peak. One night during the passage, Halford was standing in the stern hatch, scudding along before a gale of wind under reefed sail. The seas were sharp, their tops being blown into horizontal spray. The canvas cover, which had been nailed around the hatches in an attempt to keep out the seas, was drawn tight up under his arms. Suddenly, there was a violent crash and the boat stopped nearly dead in the water: "The boat almost capsized, but the next sea lifted her over. I looked astern and saw a great log forty or fifty feet long and four or five feet in diameter, water-logged and just awash. We had jumped clean over it. It was a case of touch and go with us."[52]

Halford was also at the helm when, their provisions finished near the end of their trial, a large seabird landed on the gig. The bird sought refuge on the tiny "island," unfamiliar with the dangers posed by the boat's occupants. The others being "more dead than alive" by this point, Halford caught the bird by hand, "tore off its feathers, cut it up into five pieces, and we all had a good meal. It was raw, but it tasted good."[53] Another stroke of luck brought a handful of sleek flying fish onto the gig's deck, providing their final meager sustenance at sea.

At length, on the twenty-eighth day since leaving Ocean Island, the crew sighted tiny "Kauhulaua" (Kaula) Rock just south of the island of Ni'ihau. They had not run sufficiently east before making their southerly turn after all. In fact, they had almost completely missed the main Hawaiian Islands, and were still downwind from Kaua'i, and more than 100 miles west of Honolulu. Nonetheless, they now knew where they were and, tired but considerably relieved, the men tacked into the wind north by east with Ni'ihau in sight all that Friday. All that night and the following day they continued to stand to the northeast, until on Saturday night the wind veered to the south, and the gig proceeded directly eastward. At sunset before darkness fell, they made out the much larger island of Kaua'i, and the following evening (Sunday) they hove to off the north shore's Hanalei Bay, nearer to salvation, but in large, rough seas that prevented safe approach to their sanctuary. This was the most perilous juncture of the voyage, but the boat's crew were so incapacitated that they were in no shape for their impending landfall. William Halford recalled:

> [T]oward the end everyone but myself was so reduced that they couldn't stand watch or navigate the boat and I blame myself that I didn't insist on keeping up the whole time at the end. We were off Hanalei in the evening; it was bad weather from the N.W., in fact it was the worst weather I have seen in the Pacific the whole way. A heavy squall came up just at dark. We talked it over as to what we had better do. I said "We have stood this sort of thing for over a month, we can stand it one night more. We had better keep off and then try it again in the morning."[54]

Halford finished his watch and was relieved by Talbot, and he crawled under the hatches and dozed off, only to be awakened abruptly later by a totally different motion, the boat beginning to capsize in the surf zone. The inhabitants of Kaua`i's north shore remember seeing the boat fighting for its life on the sea that day, for a small gig near their island under those conditions meant only one thing: distress. Deputy Sheriff A. W. Wilcox remembered, "it was one of those times when there is a heavy swell . . . account[ing] for the strong current running to windward."[55] When currents and winds run contrary to each other, a steep mean sea is produced, one that demands expert navigation. The gig, however, seemed out of control. They had lost the oars, though it seems doubtful that, had they retained them, the men would have had the strength remaining to have pulled themselves to safety that night. Halford roused Muir as the boat drifted into shore and the crashing waves—and then tumbled for the first time.

> I kicked Muir and told him we had better get up as there was trouble in the wind. Talbot called to Francis, who was at the tiller to throw her hard over. . . . I might have been killed in the first upset but fortunately my hand was caught in the loop of a rope attached to the rigging, and that brought me up with a jerk that nearly took my arm out. As soon as I could see I found Talbot trying to climb up by the bilge of the boat. I helped him round to the bow and helped him up there, but the next roller carried her over and over and Talbot lost his grip and disappeared, also Francis and Andrews.[56]

(In an odd coincidence, Peter Francis had also been at the helm when *Saginaw* had gone onto the rocks at Ocean Island.) Both Francis and

Andrews were thrown clear and swept away from the boat by the initial breaker. Masts and rigging went by the board. All of their possessions down below were jumbled into chaos.

Upside down in the rough surf at night, the whole world for the men erupted into an unseen dark and disordered tumult of water and air and sharp coral. There was only one thing to do: hold on to something and survive the impact. Halford had no idea about Muir, who had remained below. Lieutenant Talbot, heavily clothed and already exhausted, attempted to cling to the slippery bottom of the gig, but there was no purchase to be had. Halford tried to help him move toward the bow of the upturned gig, but Talbot didn't have the strength. In the roar of the whitewater and crashing waves, he vanished without a cry. Halford then climbed momentarily onto the bottom of the boat, and stripped off his heavy clothes, tearing them away, when another comber rolled the gig back upright. Clinging to the gunwale, he saw James Muir, who, trapped below, now emerged from the hatch, "exhibiting signs of insanity." Climbing on board, Halford assisted him onto the deck and secured him to the stump of the mast, only to be thrown aside himself by the next wave. The gig rolled completely twice more, and finally rested upright and inside the main break in calmer waters. The landing was over, and several of the crew were missing. The gig had come ashore at a place called Kapapala by the locals, at the western end of Kalihikai, four or five miles to the east of Hanalei Bay.[57]

Halford waded ashore with the tin of dispatches and letters, and then returned to the broken gig. It was approximately 3:00 a.m. The box containing the navigation books and charts, Sicard's instructions to Talbot, discharge papers for Muir and Andrews, and all other documents destined for Mare Island Naval Shipyard, had been broken open by the first breaker and ruined. Exhausted, practically naked, and bleeding from a large splinter from the mainmast projecting from his thigh, Halford nonetheless made five trips to and from the shore, saving the remaining documents and the boat's chronometer, compasses, barometer, and binnacle. He also "assisted Muir to the shore. He was still insane; but said little, incoherently; he groaned a good deal. I was much exhausted, and laid myself down to rest until sunrise."[58] In fact, Halford pulled the splinter of the mast from his leg and passed out from the loss of blood.

On Monday, December 19, Halford regained consciousness to find a local resident, Peter Nowlien, leaning over him. Nowlien knew some English and helped Halford up to check on Muir, who was not where Halford had left him the night before. The men soon located Muir's dead body, his face strangely blackened, at some distance down the beach. Nowlien then fed and clothed Halford and cleaned his wounds at his nearby house, and with a crowd of other locals, they managed to pull the gig ashore.

That same day, now bandaged and his strength restored, Halford accompanied Nowlien on horseback to Hanalei, where they contacted Sheriff Wilcox and Mr. Frank Bindt, manager of the Princeville Plantation. Halford's single priority was to carry word of his stranded shipmates to the American minister in Honolulu as quickly as possible, but Captain Jules Dudoit II and the schooner *Waiola* were not scheduled to sail from Hanalei for O'ahu until the following morning, and the local sheriff insisted on an inquest before Halford went anywhere. In fact, *Waiola*, then at Hanalei harbor unloading lumber, was next bound for Waimea to pick up a cargo of rice, prior to making Honolulu. But Halford convinced Captain Dudoit that the American government would make up the seventy-five-dollar cost of skipping that port.[59]

The group then returned to the beach at Kalihikai, and the coroner's examination was held at the schoolhouse for the bodies of James Muir and John Talbot. Talbot's body had drifted ashore just before Halford's departure for Hanalei. His forehead, like Muir's, was blackened, as well as being considerably bruised. Apparently he had struck his head forcibly on the boat or reef. The bodies were taken to Hanalei, placed in coffins, and buried in a single grave next to that of an American sailor from USS *Lackawanna* who had died in 1867. The Episcopal funeral service was held by Mr. William Kinney, and hymns were sung by the daughters of a local missionary family.[60] On Tuesday morning, Halford went on board *Wainona* and sailed for Honolulu. Before he left, the naked body of James Andrews washed ashore. Either the sea or reef had torn the clothing from it, or Andrews himself had stripped down in a failed attempt to survive the ocean. He was buried several miles from where his shipmates had been interred. The body of Peter Francis, claimed permanently by the sea, was never recovered.

To the great credit of both the American minister and the Hawaiian government, rescue efforts were begun practically the instant that Halford made his report in Honolulu. He arrived at 11:00 a.m. on December 24, Christmas Eve, and went immediately to the United States consul's office, where he relayed his information in sworn statement to both Acting Consul Elias Perkins and Minister Henry A. Peirce. Seven hours later that same evening, the minister chartered, outfitted, and dispatched the 85-ton fast-sailing schooner *Kona Packet*, Captain James A. King, complete and on her way to Ocean Island. He then also chartered the old bark *Comet*. But before *Comet* sailed, he was able to acquire a more suitable vessel for the mission.[61] Duplicate ships and supplies were the safest course—redundancy in the lifesaving effort—and time was of the essence. Peirce made application to the Kingdom and His Royal Majesty Kamehameha V (King Lot Kapuaiwa), via Mr. F. Hutchinson, the minister of the interior, for the use of the old 399-ton wood-screw steamer SS *Kilauea*. This was granted without hesitation for the relief of the stranded crew. Dr. Shipley, formerly of the U.S. Navy, agreed to go on board as well.[62] The steamer had been built in Boston in 1859 specifically for the interisland trade, and carried a fore-and-aft rig. The aging *Kilauea* was a common sight among the islands, and had recently been completely overhauled (her rotten timbers replaced), to serve for years more until being scrapped in 1878. The old steamer was "thoroughly renovated from stem to stern, from truck to keel."[63] She was a workhorse of the islands, having inaugurated profitable interisland steam navigation, and having been adapted to many different roles (decks fitted out for carrying cattle, plantation equipment, passengers, etc.). And, it was said, the ship had touched her bottom on all the reefs of the archipelago. The 1870 passage to Ocean Island was to be her midlife post-refit trial run.

William Halford did not sail with the steamer though he stridently insisted on going, but at the direction of the American minister, he departed on the liner *Moses Taylor* for San Francisco. He was instructed to make his report directly to the rear admiral. Minister Peirce had also sought out the steamship *Moses Taylor* for making the transit to Ocean Island, but Captain Floyd knew his vessel could not carry sufficient coal for that long passage.[64] *Moses Taylor* could make the one-way to San Francisco, but not the two-way trip to Ocean Island. Halford would miss the arrival of his shipmates at Honolulu.

The SS *Kilauea* could make the round-trip voyage, but just barely. The ship's crew coaled the vessel with a total of 156 tons in the bunkers and in sacks, stacked in the hold, between decks forward of the boilers, and even on the quarterdeck, two tiers deep. The ship sailed on the evening of December 26, loaded down to the scuppers, the gangway ports having to be fastened and caulked against the ocean.[65] Fortunately, smooth seas were in the offing, though later an occasional wave was shipped into the fire room through the deck scuttles, or into the cabins on the overloaded steamer. Each vessel, the SS *Kilauea* and the schooner *Kona Packet*, had on board thirty days' full ration for one hundred men, with ample supplies of clothing, medicines, vegetables, tobacco, and all other articles thought to be needed. On board went ham, bacon, flour, corn, salt, tea, crackers, coffee, salmon, sugar, beef, fruit pies, sauces, pickles, cranberries, and more. In the case of *Kilauea*, Captain Thomas Long and the merchants of Honolulu also gathered 12 sheep, 6 beef cattle, and 1 milk cow, and, from the American consulate, "two casks whiskey, one cask brandy, one case port wine, one case ale, and one case porter," a rather respectable supply.[66] Though the schooner had a two-day head start, the vessels would arrive at Ocean Island within hours of each other.

Minister Peirce, once relief was on its way northward, focused on transmitting his information to San Francisco, and from there to the Department of State and the Department of the Navy. All this, of course, took time. Communications moved at a nineteenth-century pace. More than a week after *Kilauea* had departed Honolulu, the commander of the Pacific Station had still not taken any direct action to commence the search for the missing side-wheel steamer, even though Secretary Robeson in Washington, D.C., had already obtained the assistance of the Pacific Mail Steamship Company. Rear Admiral Turner in San Francisco wrote to the Department: "Since the Department has ordered the China Steamer to touch at Midway Islands, with provisions for any party which might have been left on the islands, and the Honolulu steamer [which is] nearly due, will bring account of the *Saginaw*, has arrived at the Sandwich Islands . . . I do not think it advisable to dispatch the *Saranac* in search of her, as after leaving Honolulu no coal can be obtained among the islands further westwards. . . . Should the *Saginaw* however not be heard from, I will order the *St Mary's* to cruise in those latitudes, to ascertain if anything can be learned of the missing vessel."[67]

The Empty Desert of the Pacific

For the castaways on Ocean Island, unaware of the fate of their shipmates and the boat voyage to the southeast, time dragged slowly on, particularly now that the boat had been launched. And due to the length of the gig's journey, all chance of rescue had to be held in abeyance for at least thirty days. Many of the sailors simply did not dwell directly on the topic aloud, or when they did, only briefly mentioned the gig's chances in muted tones, in that superstitious way they had of not speaking about fair weather, not talking about shipwrecks, of not tempting the fates. However, the phrase "when we get home" and fantasy descriptions of various banquets and endless bountiful fare were common, for no one had outwardly given up hope.[68] In the evenings, the officers gathered around the smoking lamp. A box of Manila cigars had been saved from the wreck. The sailors stretched out around their small fires, with the bright blanket of the Milky Way rotating slowly overhead. It was a serene but uncomfortable prison, a tiny speck amidst an endless lonely void. On moonlit nights, the white reflection danced on the waters of the lagoon.

That beautiful but impoverished setting was also marred by a dark plague scurrying through the bushes. Rodents, thousands of them, adapted themselves freely to the presence of their new occupants on the island, and soon competed frantically over the smallest traces of provisions and materials. These were the hardy Polynesian rats (*Rattus exulans*), hitchhikers themselves from some ancient drifting palm, flotsam on the sea. Or perhaps an ancient double-hulled voyaging canoe had carried the travelers among the provisions of breadfruit and gourds, an unwanted component of the Austronesian sailing migrations that peopled the dispersed islands of the Pacific. Today anthropologists theorize that the rats may have been intentionally included in these ancient explorations, their prolific nature making them an excellent food source for remote Pacific colonization. Europeans would later do the same, spreading rabbits and pigs and goats throughout the world. Whatever their true origin, rats swarmed over Ocean Island, and darkened the bright dunes when they fled en masse before the sailors who tried vainly to stamp them out. The men were forced to protect their supplies by constructing an elevated storage hut, placing the posts in tins of water, and doubling the guard against their depredations.

No one had eaten rat yet, but the sailors knew they were possible fare should the seals and gooney birds become exhausted. The constant consumption of food by the remaining eighty-eight survivors on the island stretched the provisions thin. There was never enough for the crowd of men. Small dough balls made from the remaining flour, and a tablespoon of desiccated potatoes or mashed beans here and there, were all that broke the monotony of oily seal meat and stringy gooney bird flesh. A bit of tea or coffee, and some portions of salt beef and salt pork were the only items the sailors had saved for themselves, though the sand spit to the west of the island occasionally supplied a sea turtle or two.

In other small ways, some improvements were made to their condition. By November 21, a recessed tank near the shore had been assembled for the production of salt. And by November 28, a smokehouse had been built

for curing the seal meat.[69] The monk seals, however, were growing noticeably more scarce. Sicard redoubled his guard on the wildlife, his long-term
larder: "I commenced to send parties out to kill seal and birds; but after
about a month I found that, owing to the rapid diminution of the seal, I
was obliged to cut the allowance down, and only killed one seal and twenty
birds per day for the whole crew."[70] By December 11, the sailors had killed
and eaten seventy-five monk seals and some 1,200 albatross.[71]

Shaping the rescue effort and maintaining his crew's morale were the
dual priorities of the commander, and now that the gig's cradle on the
beach was empty, Sicard put the carpenters to work again, this time building a 40-ton, center-board, flat-bottom schooner for the second rescue
party, should it be needed—redundancy in lifesaving efforts. The saw pit
and cutting frame were kept in use, laboriously ripping down timbers
into suitable stock for the frames and hull planks. The keel for the vessel
was hewn from *Saginaw*'s old foremast.[72] In all, some 2,000 linear feet of
planking were produced from wreck material, salvaged by men working
in the surf with hand spikes and crowbars (see figs. 25–27). In this, Sicard
was following a long tradition of sailors stranded in the Northwestern
Hawaiian Islands. The carpenters on board the whalers *Pearl* and *Hermes*
constructed the 30-ton schooner *Deliverance* in 1822. The carpenters of the
Gledstanes built the 38-ton schooner *Deliverance* in 1837. The crew of the
whaler *Holder Borden* launched their beach-built 35-foot schooner *Hope* in
1844. And the whaler *Konohasset* launched their 22-foot sloop *Konohasset*

FIGURE 25. *Saginaw*'s carpenters building the rescue schooner *Deliverance* on the beach
at Ocean Island. From Read, *Last Cruise of the* Saginaw.

FIGURE 26. Sketch of the castaway camp, amidst the low dunes at Ocean Island. From Read, *Last Cruise of the* Saginaw.

FIGURE 27. Photograph of Green (Ocean) Island today, taken from near the same vantage point. Courtesy of NOAA Office of National Marine Sanctuaries.

Jr. two short years later in 1846. Other castaways (as had *Saginaw*'s crew) modified the ship's boats for the necessary passage. Some were so desperate for material that they were forced to rely on the drifting lifeboats that came their way from other shipwrecks to furnish them the means for the passage. All shaped their own salvation; Sicard was in good, if unlucky, company. The proposed name of the schooner being built by *Saginaw*'s carpenters on Ocean Island was *Deliverance*.

Thanksgiving Day came and went. Thirty-five days following the departure of the gig came and went. The men knew that it would take some time after Lieutenant Talbot's projected landfall for the authorities in Honolulu to assemble a rescue mission. Christmas Day came and went, Sicard presiding in the usual Episcopal manner, but the celebration was muted. Paymaster Read donned his best uniform in an attempt to raise his own spirits, but failed: "I could not keep up the deceit, and I slipped out of line before the Service was ended, to change back to the blue sailor shirt and working clothes. I felt that I had been 'putting on airs.' It has been my first really blue day, for the pictures in my mind of the Christmas festivities at home but emphasized the desolation of the life here."[73] Coffee was served up as a common present.

Minor phenomena began to be mistaken for signs of ships passing the atoll; an evening star on the horizon on one night, a coral rock reflecting the rays of the sun on another morning. Eyes and nerves strained upon the horizon, finding only phantom sightings. The lookouts at the mainmast, climbing the rope ladder to the cross trees above the center of the island, faced nothing but the emptiness of the North Pacific: "The loneliness and solitude of the vast expanse of water surrounding us is beyond expression. Truly, it is the desert of the Pacific Ocean, and more dangerous than that upon the land, for there are no trails or guideposts for the weary traveler when the sky is obscured. One might easily fancy that beyond the line of the horizon there exists only infinite space."[74] Depression among the crew grew palpable following each of these sightings and the arousing of false hopes, and Sicard ordered that no one again alarm the camp without first reporting the possibility to the commanding officer.[75]

Passing squalls and wind, and changes in the shape of the sea were the only realities of life on Ocean Island, itself more like a piece of flotsam adrift than firm land. Surgeon Adam Frank—sensitive as always to the exposure and diet of the men, and being forced to tend to their condition without proper supplies—grew progressively more unhappy. He noted in his journal that "the men are worked very hard, the quantity of food is limited, scarcely any vegetables, the bulk being, altogether, seal meat and albatross. There are no cases of dysentery at the moment, the reverse, namely constipation, is the prevailing complaint."[76] He finally approached the commander regarding their workload, and the fact that the critical nourishment needed by the sick lay behind armed guard in the storage hut—being saved there for the planned voyage of the second boat under construction—but found no satisfaction: "I suggested a change to the Commanding Officer, which was disregarded, as are many suggestions of mine."[77] Sicard was not insensitive to the condition of his men, but he was obviously more strict with their remaining resources than the surgeon would have preferred.

> As regards breadstuffs, we were at first on one-eighth rations, but . . . I was obliged to cut this down to one-sixteenth rations. The officers and crew felt the want of bread very much, and for a long time were quite weak; but as they became accustomed to an almost exclusively animal diet, they gradually improved in health and strength, though we always had a good many cases of dysentery, rheumatism, &etc.[78]

Meanwhile, in the face of continuing inquiries as to *Saginaw*'s status, Rear Admiral Winslow telegraphed his concerns to the Navy Department. On December 8, he confessed: "the delay has made me apprehensive that some disaster has happened to her, and she may have put into Honolulu. Should this have been the case, the next steamer due in two or three days will no doubt bring us the news." And again the next day, "*Saginaw* has not yet arrived." And again the next week, "Nothing has been heard from her as yet."[79] Nonetheless, instructions regarding the work to be done for *Saginaw*'s Panamanian cruise continued to be sent out from Washington, D.C.

By now there was very little left still visible of USS *Saginaw*. The sea had broken the stern section, the machinery falling into the coral reef and portions of deck tossed into the lagoon. On December 5, Sicard ordered a survey of the remains of the ship's machinery, which was summarily completed by Ensigns Cogswell and Parsons, and Engineers Blye and Butterworth. Sicard requested the survey in order to confirm that no effort had been spared in the salvage of his vessel, and to determine whether it was "to the advantage of the United States to attempt the recovery of all or part of what remains."[80] His officers replied:

Sir: in obedience to your order of the 5th Inst., we have held a strict and careful survey on the hull, equipment, machinery, boilers, etc. of USS Saginaw as mentioned in your order, and report that in our opinion they are as follows: nothing remains of the hull. The machinery has been broken and injured by the sea, so that it is unfit for use and lies in such a position that it is impossible to obtain it. Only one of the boilers is visible and is unapproachable on account of the sea breaking over it. One bower anchor without stock and part of the cable are visible, but the cable cannot be unshackled, and the state of the sea is generally such that it would endanger the boats, and be impractical to recover the anchor.[81]

By December 20, Sicard's department heads had also each completed written reports (in triplicate—the commanding officer was responsible for keeping his officers busy as well as his men) surveying the entirety of the hundreds of small articles saved from the wreck and their condition. This not only gave him an assessment of material for planning a second boat voyage, but also started the necessary inventory in anticipation of their eventual rescue. Sicard was meticulous by nature, and the U.S. Navy, even on Ocean Island, seemed to run upon a sea of paperwork, in this case small portions of scrap covered on front and back by lightly penciled script.

As time wore on, the officers of the wardroom fell into the habit of meeting daily to discuss the possible alternatives and the timing of Talbot's voyage. Plans were beginning to be shaped regarding the next attempt. The schooner under construction would be able to carry more men and more provisions. They were aware that other groups of castaways from other shipwrecks in the atolls had successfully made the voyage into the prevailing winds and swells—and also that other alternatives existed. From the middle of the North Pacific, the downwind leg would take the boat to Guam, or perhaps an island in the South Seas, crossing the equator. Sicard laid plans to send one of the ship's cutters back to nearby Midway to erect a suitable sign there for passing ships. New Year's Eve came and went. Without any festivities or observances (or even an open eye save that of the sentry posted at the store hut), the men on Ocean Island slipped silently into 1871. The paymaster wrote in his journal: "Talbot has now been away 43 days and it seems almost beyond probability that he should have reached the Sandwich Islands before the food was exhausted."[82]

Jubilation and Then Mourning

Sicard's orders to communicate all possible sightings directly to the commanding officer alone were completely ignored on January 3, when, finally, their certain salvation was at hand. At 3:30 p.m., while at work on the new boat, Mr. Mitchell, one of the contractor's party, caught sight of the merest shadow of dark cloud at the horizon to the northeast, growing very slowly in size and density. Speaking in a low voice to Paymaster Read beside him, Mitchell said: "Paymaster, I believe that is the smoke of a steamer . . . I am sure of it."[83] And then, after both had stared at the object, the plain joyful cry rang out, "Sail Ho!"

The camp erupted in excitement and confused action. Commander Sicard sent Paymaster Read immediately to the lookout station at the crosstrees with the sea glass, from where he could make out the lengthening line of smoke, a steamer moving to the west: "She was not heading directly for us, and I cannot describe the anxiety with which I watched to see if she was going to pass by, my heart was thumping so that one could hear it. I could not believe she would fail to see our signal of distress that waved above me, and pass on to leave us stricken with despair." But when the ship reached a point north of the island, she surely did turn and head their way. The SS Kilauea came in from the north, having run slightly off course due to overcast skies and a lack of the usual meridian navigational fix over the past two days. Captain Long had first sighted the breakers on the atoll's northern edge, and then had picked up the flag staff and distress signal beyond.[84] Only later did the low island lift into sight.

Read confirmed to the men below that the ship had seen them and was headed their way: "Rough looking men—many of them having faced the shocks of storm and battle—all of them having passed through our recent misfortunes without a murmur of complaint—were embracing each other with tears of joy running down their cheeks, while laughing, singing, and dancing."[85] The last and best of the provisions were broken out for their supper, salt pork, flour, and beans, finished off with a cup of coffee. By that time, the steamer had been identified as the Kingdom's own SS Kilauea. The first cutter was quickly outfitted and sent out of the lagoon to communicate with the ship, but darkness forced the boat to return to shore and haul out. As evening was coming on, the steamer would have to stand out to sea for the night, approaching the atoll the next day. Before doing so, however, the steamer's captain brought her alongside the eastern reef, directly abeam the wreck site, and in a touching nautical gesture, lowered (dipped) her flag or colors, before steaming slowly away to the south. To make sure the castaways understood his intentions, Captain Long also fired aerial rockets, fireworks. On shore, Sicard answered in kind, and ordered the fire to be kept high and ablaze, as a beacon in the darkness for their rescuers. The result was a festival throughout the night, the men cavorting around the bonfire and the hard-won hand-built frame of the 40-foot-long, 12-foot-wide schooner (ready for planking up) on the beach. The paymaster crept into the store tent in order to shelter momentarily from the singing, and collect his wits for his regular journal entry:

> It is near an impossibility to sanely and calmly write up my journal to-night—my nerves are shaken and my pencil falters. . . . [N]o one can possibly sleep, for I can see through a rent in the canvas men dancing around a huge fire on the highest point of the island, and hear them cheering and singing while feeding the fire with timbers that we have been regarding as worth their weight in coin. To a looker-on the entire camp would seem to have gone crazy.[86]

In the morning, *Kilauea* moved toward (but not inside) the western entrance to the atoll and dropped anchor, the captain sounding for some time with the ship's boats in the vicinity of the anchorage to assure himself sufficient depth. Fortunately on that day the entrance was calm enough for small boats to safely make the passage into the lagoon. Surgeon Frank wrote, "The camp is in a fearful state of confusion, the men are laboring under a great deal of excitement, and are working hard to get ready to leave this desolate place."[87] The steamer launched a whaleboat, and Sicard brought his officers and crew, tired but happy, to attention in ranks at the edge of the camp. The officers, those who had them, were dressed in their best uniforms. The men stood, emaciated and sunburned, barefoot and literally in rags. The commanding officer alone met the boat at the shore, and conferred for some minutes with Captain Long, whom some now recognized as an old friend, a former whaling skipper in the Pacific. What complication could possibly be delaying matters? At length, both men returned to the crew, but their countenances were somber. Long had delivered letters from the American minister, who was also a good friend to Montgomery Sicard, detailing the tragic event at Kaua'i:

> My dear friend, I wrote you the 24th inst., by the schooner Kona Packet, a vessel of 85 tons, chartered for the rescue and relief of yourself and companions. . . . The gig was upset at Kalihi Kai, about 5 miles from

Hanalei Bay, Island of Kaua`i of this group, 31 days after their leaving you. All perished in the surf except Halford. . . . Poor, gallant, noble, self-sacrificing Talbot! His body and that of Muir were buried in one grave at Hanalei. . . . Your dispatches were saved and go by the steamer's mail tomorrow. Your instructions and requisitions to Talbot were lost when the boat upset. The want of them has caused me to work for your relief somewhat in the dark. . . . How much all our hearts bleed for you and those with you. I hope to see you all in 15 days or about middle of January. Floyd [captain of the *Moses Taylor*] reports that when he left San Francisco December 15th the Naval people were getting very anxious about you and spoke of sending a vessel in search of the Saginaw. I shall telegraph Sec of State, so as to have correct version of your disaster reported to the country. . . . Truly your sincere friend.[88]

Sicard addressed his crew, directly and with his usual bluntness: "Men, I have the great sorrow to announce to you that we have been saved at a great sacrifice. Lieutenant Talbot and three of the gig's crew are dead. The particulars you will learn later; at present, Captain Long is anxious for us to remove to the *Kilauea* as quickly as possible."[89] Sicard bowed his head. The news was hard, but January was no month to linger in the Northwestern Hawaiian Islands. Grief, in an instant, struck the crew like a physical blow, and all of their celebration suddenly seemed to have been "putting on airs." Their suffering had shaped them into a family, and four men had died for their shipmates.

Shortly thereafter, the schooner *Kona Packet* arrived at the atoll, anchoring near *Kilauea* outside the western entrance some several miles distant and sending a boat ashore. Both waited on the orders of Commander Sicard, who now had duplicate bills of articles, provisions, clothing etc., the purchase of which would eventually have to be reimbursed by the United States government. (The consulate in Honolulu had, in this instance, refused payment, this being a navy shipwreck.) He made haste to prepare to remove his men and the property salvaged from the wreck to the steamer, the larger of the two vessels. For Captain Long, however, transporting the equipment to his ship by boat across the intervening five or six miles would be time-consuming, and put them at greater risk from any change in the weather. His priority was to get *Saginaw*'s castaways on board and return to Honolulu, not to economize for the U.S. government by carrying what looked like scrap. Likewise, *Kona Packet*'s captain declined to take his vessel into the lagoon, and his own boats were too small to get the articles off the island. Like Captain Long, he informed Sicard that "he was sent only to save life, and that the value of the articles on shore would scarcely pay for the expense of getting them to Honolulu."[90] Sicard was obliged to leave most of his cache, well-secured under a shelter of boards and canvas. He did admit to the Department in his official report that, had he been in the position of the other captains, he would have recommended the same course of action: "I mention this matter . . . simply to show that I made an effort to bring the articles off with me." Sicard was meticulous to the end.

> The following articles were left on the island under cover, viz (Engineers Dept) 1 drill, 2 copper pipes cocks and valves, 3 wrenches, 2 couplings; (Ordnance Dept) 2 battle axes, grapnels and chains, 2 fire buckets; (Construction and Repair Dept) 1 scuttle butt, wood axes, 5 gallons linseed oil, 1 water tank, 1 wood saw, and 70 blocks various sizes; (Equipment Dept) 1 cabin table, 1 cutter with masts, oars and sails, 1 82 lb, 1 520 lb & 1 1450 lb anchors, 30 fathoms chain cable, 2 scrapers, 1 pick, 1 hoe, 1 grapnel, 1 4-inch hawser, 1 deck tackle, contractor's stores, 1 anvil, 1 grindstone, 1 metallic boat, 3 boat sails, 1 steam boiler, 1 leather bellows, 2 bed screws, 2 breakers, 1 40 gal cask, 1 crow bar; (Navigator's Dept) 1 chest of books, 6 charts, 1 14 foot long union jack, 1 set signals 10 feet, 1 side lamp, 3 deck lanterns, 1 oil can wherein were a quantity of bolts, spikes and old iron left over; the tents and the spars were left lying on the beach all of which were damaged.[91]

Nonetheless, a shorter list of smaller items, some of the many tools and navigation instruments and signal flags, and a few of the carbines and pistols and cutlasses, and even the 12-pounder boat howitzer, found their way off the island and onto the steamer. The paymaster's department even brought the last of the beef and pickles and butter on board.[92] Of course, all of these items were carefully inventoried, and Sicard supplied a detailed breakdown of the conditions of Townsend's property as well.

The SS *Kilauea* seemed sufficient for their needs, so Commander Sicard ordered *Kona Packet* to leave for Honolulu. The schooner's charter, after all, was costing his government twenty-eight dollars per day in coin, and the ship was uninsured. Neither vessel could carry *Saginaw*'s first cutter, so Sicard had the boat hauled up onto the beach and covered in canvas. At 5:00 p.m. on January 5 (a Thursday this time!), *Kilauea*, with all of Sicard's men on board, steamed for Midway Island, arriving there the following day in order to load 60 tons of sandy coal from the Pacific Steamship

Company's depot. Captain Long had decided to proceed as quickly as possible to Honolulu under steam rather than to economize by a much slower transit under sail. (Sicard noted the expense of this option, but decided it would have been inappropriate for him to object.) At Long's suggestion, Sicard left *Saginaw*'s second cutter at Midway, secured near the scow from the dredging effort: "She is an old boat, and of but little value, which is the case also with the boat left on Ocean Island. . . . These cutters (about 27 feet long and 6 feet beam) would perhaps be useful in case work is resumed at Midway Islands."[93]

Meanwhile, on board the steamer, *Saginaw*'s men were adjusting as quickly as they could to some longed-for amenities. They were reunited with the world through recent newspapers, which still carried the breaking news of the Franco-Prussian War (July 1870–May 1871), and other important items. Two months had seemed an eternity, and the men were starved for information of any kind. True, the accommodations on *Kilauea* were small and insufficient for the numbers of debilitated men who were now crowded on board in the cabins and passageways and deck spaces. The vessel remained packed with provisions, clothing, and coal. And though the good weather and smooth seas held, the overloaded ship rolled heavily and proved to be quite wet. But who was going to complain?

At Midway, the former castaways were set ashore on the familiar beach to load the coal themselves, some 1,650 bags of it. Surgeon Adam Frank complained. To him, exposure to the elements of the open sea (again) and these continual labors seemed almost as bad as their imprisonment on the deserted island. Were they not debilitated and starved? But at least he was better provisioned now. Frank thought it all the more proper therefore to recommend that the crew partake regularly of the alcoholic stimulants, whiskey in particular, as a medicinal preventative in the face of their continuing labors and distress.[94] In the nineteenth century, such alcoholic stimulants were considered to prevent disease. And if they didn't prevent it, then they might be part of the cure.

True to form, there was no break in military discipline, even on the rescue steamer bound for Honolulu. For impudence shown to a petty officer, Seaman Edwards was placed on bread and water for four days, and punished again later in the voyage. Nolan and Wallace were confined for five days for disrespect to a superior officer. Kelly and Jordan and Doran were locked up and placed on bread and water for three days for disobedience of orders. Even the apothecary, Henry Clarke, was put on bread and water for five days for smoking on the berth deck.[95] Surely bread and water were disappointing fare for a former castaway, particularly when one's ship-mates were eating fresh mutton and steak. But it was bread of which they had long been deprived. The men, needless to say, were otherwise clothed and cleaned and well fed, and utensils and pots and pans distributed. During the eastward transit, the sheep and cattle on deck disappeared one by one. The SS *Kilauea* arrived at Honolulu and made fast to the wharf on the afternoon of January 14, 1871.

On January 8, the Department finally learned of the fate of USS *Saginaw*. Rear Admiral Winslow telegrammed Robeson: "*Saginaw* was lost on Ocean Island 29 October Lieutenant Talbot with four men reached Sandwich Islands after 30 days by boat to be drowned with three men by surf one survivor left who gave information Hawaiian steamer and schooner sailed for rescue of crew immediately." Robeson replied: "Use all available means for the relief of the survivors of the *Saginaw*. Telegraph what you have done and are doing."[96] The old USS *Nyack*, Commander Henry Glass, was standing by in Honolulu and stood ready to receive the survivors and their stores.

In Honolulu, word of the loss of *Saginaw* and the heroic and tragic voyage of the ship's gig had spread quickly, for life in the islands naturally rotated around maritime activity. Having waited more than two weeks, a crowd of several thousand native and foreign residents gathered at the harbor once the steamer *Kilauea* had been sighted on the horizon by the lookout on the slopes of Diamondhead. The crowd was packed at the water's edge. The throng parted for the entrance of the royal carriage and His Majesty the King (who had taken a lively interest in the rescue expedition), along with his many ministers and foreign officials. Curiosity about the castaways mixed with philanthropic goodwill, and in true aloha spirit an overabundance of island foods of all descriptions arrived to the dock. There was far more than what the survivors could have ever needed, but it was the way the community expressed its concern and care. Bowls of poi, pork laulau, fish (both cooked and raw), chickens, steamed pork buns, jerked beef, and even calabashes filled with a potent mixture of okolehao (a strong liquor made from the fermented root of the ti plant) found their way down to the wharf. There were many mouths at the harbor that day, and if those poor men from Ocean Island had nowhere else to stash the food, it would certainly not go uneaten. And then cheers began to ring out as the steamer slowly came alongside.

The Reverend Hiram Bingham, from horseback, led the crowd in "hurrahs" as hats flew into the air. The king himself could scarcely refrain from joining in. The survivors ("gallant tars") responded as best they could from the deck of the steamer, their voices no match for the multitude as the crowded vessel drew closer to the crowded dock. For many it was the most touching scene of welcome they had ever witnessed. Commander Sicard himself was unable to maintain a dry eye, and as soon as the gangplank was down, the crowd swelled forward to physically embrace the men of the lost *Saginaw*. Their fellow mariners knew what the castaways had been through. The noise and tumult precluded any attempt at speechmaking (there would be time for that later). It was more important for the people to touch the sailors, to give them something, and to cover their heads and shoulders with piles of fragrant flower lei. Only then could they really say that they were safe on shore at last.

The people of O'ahu opened their homes to Sicard's crew and his officers, and the men had never seen such a feast and joyous occasion, lasting well into the night. The wife of Captain John Paty, a well-known figure who had recently passed away, provided the family's spacious and comfortable island home and hospitality to the survivors. With typical naval brevity, though, *Saginaw*'s deck log ends at this moment on January 14, 1871, with only the briefest of notes: "Transferred the crew baggage and all the stores to USS *Nyack*."[97]

Concluding Affairs in the Islands

The steamer *Moses Taylor* was scheduled to sail for San Francisco on January 28, and, having arranged a generous discount price for their passage, Commander Sicard made arrangements for his officers and crew to travel together to San Francisco on board that ship. He had his own doubts about the seaworthiness of the old USS *Nyack* in Honolulu, and about the time it would take for her to make the Pacific crossing. *Nyack* had been in port when the SS *Kilauea* and *Kona Packet* were sent to rescue the castaways, but she was considered unfit and too slow for the mission. *Nyack* had arrived in a disabled condition from San Francisco, and required repairs.[98]

For the next two weeks, the men were treated to a memorable time in Hawai'i. They were heroes, once again racing on horseback through the dirt streets of the town. They were unable to pay for their own grog at the taverns—banana beer, mango cider, or orange cider, whatever it may have been. They had the time of their lives. Sicard, though, was busy. His own duty was to settle the accounts of *Kilauea* and *Kona Packet*, gathering up

FIGURE 28. Photograph of the damaged gig at Honolulu Harbor, after the rescue voyage. From Read, *Last Cruise of the* Saginaw.

all the bills made out against the Navy Department for the water, stores, medicines, clothing, provisions, coal, etc. furnished in support of the castaways. Some of these materials were taken on board USS *Nyack*, some were sold back to the appropriate vendors, and the rest were sold at auction. Selling the excess material, as well as any of the properties deemed no longer useful to the U.S. Navy, was a common way of recouping some of the losses suffered during shipwrecks. Sometimes the money could provide relief for families, or pay for transportation home for the sailors.

The auction to benefit *Saginaw* castaways took place at the wharf on January 25. One item in particular drew curious and melancholy observations from the crowd. The day after the crew made port, the schooner *Fairy Queen* brought *Saginaw*'s gig from Kaua`i to Honolulu. The craft lay on the wharf, with its battered tale of patches and damage, and passersby read into these the story of the heroic rescue voyage and tragic ending (see fig. 28). The modifications completed at Ocean Island were obvious and deserved some proper respect. One old salt observed that he "would feel safe in that boat at sea in any weather."[99] To the great surprise of Commander Sicard and his officers, a group of local residents, led by Mr. Charles Augustus Williams, purchased the gig for eighty dollars and donated it back to the crew, to be conveyed to San Francisco by steamer on January 28, "and will no doubt be an object of much interest there."[100]

The wealth of good feeling following the return of the castaways over-flowed into a long series of letters, those of recommendations and of recognition, and Sicard busied himself with the paperwork. As the young officer in charge of the gig's voyage, Lieutenant Talbot received a special kind of adoration, for there is, after all, something about youth and sacrifice that continually deserves this. The commander praised his fine bearing, cheerfulness, and devotion to duty: "His boat was evidently commanded with the greatest intelligence, fortitude, and gallantry, and with the most admirable devotion. May the service always be able to find such men in time of need."[101] Sicard also recommended that William Halford be awarded the Medal of Honor for his extraordinary heroism during the rescue voyage, and no less than George Robeson himself, secretary of the navy, suggested advancement in rank for his meritorious services.[102] A host of others, including the residents of Hanalei, Captain Long, and selected enlisted men of USS *Saginaw*, also earned specific recognition and honors. Long received a five-hundred-dollar gold watch from Rear Admiral Winslow, and the Hanalei locals were given much smaller cash rewards as well:

> To Mr. Peter Nowlins [Nowlien], for humanity and kindness shown to Wm. Halford, sole survivor of the boat's crew of U.S. steamer Saginaw (Mr. Peter Nowlins took Halford to his house, changed his wet for dry clothing, gave him food, furnished horses, and accompanied him from Kalihikai to Hanalei), the sum of twenty-five dollars. To Kapelehua, who received into his house the bodies of Lieutenant Talbot and Wm. [*sic*] Muir, and watched them overnight, fifteen dollars. To Pupu, Kapahi, Kamaka and Kaelemakule, who found the body of Lieutenant Talbot and brought it to shore, to each ten dollars. To John Hobbs, who found the body of John Andrews and took care of it, ten dollars. To Hailama and Kahanu, who assisted Halford in saving the boat, &c., each five dollars.[103]

But it was the men of the gig who stood out as the highest models of sacrifice and attainment.

> The men were fine specimens of the seaman—cool and brave, with great endurance and excellent physical strength. They were undoubtedly

those best qualified in the whole party on Ocean Island to perform such a service. Both Lieutenant Talbot and his men had very firm confidence in their boat. . . . Such men should be the pride of the Navy, and the news of their death cast a deep gloom. . . . I don't know that I sufficiently express my deep sense of their devotion and gallantry; words seem to fail me in doing justice to my feelings in that respect.[104]

The commander's own diligence came in for high praise, but through no agency of his own. Having read in full the lengthy reports written from Ocean Island, Commodore William Rogers Taylor expressed his admiration for Sicard's "industry, prudence, excellent judgment, and devotion to duty." Sicard had, after all, completed his final report on the Midway project while encamped on Ocean Island, existing on seal meat and gooney birds. "It must not be forgotten that when he made the report just mentioned, together with many of those for the Department and Bureaus, and all the memoranda from which the whole mass was compiled, he was shipwrecked upon a desert island, with but a distant prospect of relief. That he should have found time in the midst of the engrossing and anxious duties devolving upon him, and should have had the inclination to apply himself to such work, however important it might be, is a matter of surprise to me."[105] The commander, in his makeshift tent, wrote his way into the good graces of his superiors. He was that rare human being, an effective officer and an excellent administrator.

Sicard's bureaucratic duties continued in Honolulu. His responsibilities even extended to the items that remained at Ocean Island and Midway. He wrote to the American consul C. S. Mattoon: "Sir: There are a quantity of articles on Ocean Island that were saved from the wreck of the United States Steamer *Saginaw*. These things belong to the United States. . . . What remains of the vessel, her armament, machinery, tackling, &c,. is also under the control and ownership of the United States. It has not been abandoned. Its condition has been reported to the United States Navy Department, and it is for the Government to signify what steps should be taken in the matter."[106] To his own superiors, Sicard was more candid about the practicality of actually recovering anything else. True, small schooners did occasionally visit the atolls to the northwest, and it was perhaps possible that they could recover some of the navy's property—but was it worth it? "The invoice price of the most important of these things . . . is about $350, but their real value is a good deal less. . . . I do not really think that the articles are worth any special effort at recovery."[107] Regarding the machinery of the ship herself, he doubted any amount of salvage work would be warranted in the surf of the eastern reef crest:

> I would say that in my opinion it is not worth while for the United States to attempt to save anything on the outer face of the reef. The sea breaks constantly where the machinery, guns etc. lie. The probability is that the machinery will be greatly damaged and wrenched beyond the possibility of repair—only a very small part of it projects above water—and there are not probably three days during the year when the sea is quiet, or when, in my opinion, it would be possible to work over any part without great danger.[108]

The commander's final responsibility before departing Oʻahu was to provide for the proper burial of his deceased sailors. This was an official and yet also a very personal matter to the men. Saginaw's officers and crew, by their own subscription, raised the funds needed to disinter the bodies of Andrews and Muir from their resting places at Hanalei and bring them to the Nuʻuanu Cemetery in Honolulu. The officers also left sufficient funds with the consulate to bring Talbot's body to Honolulu, and from there to Mare Island, where his family might obtain it in case they so desired. This was a complicated task, and not one to complete in the last rush of days before the steamer's departure, so Sicard left specific directions to wait at least six months before beginning the process of disinterment and transport.[109]

The day before their departure from the islands, an official reception at the royal palace was held in honor of the shipwreck survivors, arranged for by Minister Henry Peirce. Commander Glass (USS Nyack) accompanied Sicard, as did Consul Calvin Mattoon, Minister Peirce, Lieutenant Charles Craven, Lieutenant W. Moore, Ensign James Cogswell, and Ensign A. H. Prescott. Once again, in island fashion, it was a lavish affair, for in Hawaiʻi a little too much food is "just enough." The chancellor of the Kingdom, the cabinet ministers, the governor of Oʻahu, His Majesty's chamberlain, and Colonel Pratt were in attendance, as was the sovereign. This was a chance for Commander Sicard, on behalf of Rear Admiral Winslow commanding the Pacific Fleet, to formally thank His Majesty King Lot (the last ruler of the royal bloodline of Kamehameha) for sending the Hawaiian steamer Kilauea to Ocean Island, and in other ways to attempt to further cement the good relations between the Kingdom and the United States.

It [*Kilauea*] was a most welcome and opportune relief to the company of United States officers and seamen in distress there, and a proof of your Majesty's friendly feeling towards our Navy. . . . On our arrival in port, we were welcomed with the most warm-hearted cordiality, and have received abundant proofs of the kind feelings of the Hawaiian people. One officer and four men, belonging to my vessel, bravely and generously ventured on a long sea-voyage in a small boat, for the relief of their shipmates; and finally, (with one exception,) made sacrifice of their lives upon the shores of the island of Kaua`i. Your Majesty's subjects on that island received the survivor of the boat's crew with great kindness and hospitality, and were most solicitous to recover the remains of my officer and his men, and to inter them in a suitable and Christian manner.[110]

King Lot was not to be outdone in eloquence, and had the last word, of course:

Captain, I am pleased to see you here today, and to congratulate you and the officers of the late United States ship Saginaw upon their delivery from their unpleasant position upon a desolate island. I am glad that my government has been enabled to render you assistance. The officers of your service in this ocean have always shown themselves prompt to go to the assistance of distressed men of all nations. . . . Such interchanges tend to promote personal and national friendship. I sympathize with you, Captain, for the loss of your ship, a misfortune always keenly felt by a sensitive officer, however unavoidable it may have been. I sympathize with you for the loss of a gallant officer and men who, after a long voyage in an open boat, met their death on the shores of Kaua`i. Such examples of devotion to duty are a rich legacy to all men. Permit me, Captain, to express a hope that you and your officers who have shared with you your service in this ocean for some time past, and your peril in your late shipwreck, may live to attain the highest honors in your profession.[111]

These eloquent and heartfelt comments were also part of the diplomatic relationship between the United States and the Kingdom of Hawai`i. Commander Sicard stressed the friendliness and good feelings he observed on the part of his hosts toward the United States, and the king praised the foreign naval officers in a circumspect fashion, without implying any concrete relationship at all. Like Kamehameha IV (his older brother) before him, King Lot was, in fact, friendly but not a great friend of America. He had concerns for his nation's sovereignty, particularly as more and more discussion in 1870 centered on the issues of emerging reciprocity with the mainland and the economic and military dominance of the United States in the Pacific. The king had, in fact, appointed Frenchman Charles de Varigny as minister to his cabinet, who made no secret of his own "uneasiness which the covetousness and the ambition of the United States inspired in me. . . . [T]he only danger which Hawaiian independence could run into would come from the United States, and that an agent of France ought to unite himself closely with the agent of England."[112] The fate of Hawai`i at this time was an intensely local and international issue. At the arrival of the SS *Kilauea*, USS *Nyack* had not been the only warship in port. The French steam gunboat *Hamelin* (Commander Pouthier) had recently come in from Tahiti, bearing two 60-pounders and two 45-pounders and 150 sailors on board. (The officers of the gunboat *Hamelin* had already had their royal reception.) On this occasion, though, Sicard and the king found it easy to be polite. The rescue of shipwrecked survivors was without overt political implications. Almost a year later, with the arrival in Honolulu of Rear Admiral Winslow and his family on board the American flagship, another reception was held at the palace, and the pleasantries regarding the USS *Saginaw* affair were repeated once again.

Following the reception at the palace, the steamship *Moses Taylor* sailed the next day, and for once Surgeon Frank was pleased: "The men are all made comfortable, and appear to be cheerful and very content. They have good sleeping accommodations and an abundance of good food."[113] Also, for the first time in a long period, longer than Frank could remember, there were no sailors on the sick list. *Moses Taylor* arrived in San Francisco on February 7, and the men were home at last, as much at home as enlisted sailors at Mare Island could be.

The Court of Inquiry

Once settled and back at the navy yard, it was a return to regular order and business as usual. The men whose enlistments had not expired were detached from Sicard's command and distributed by the yard in different directions. USS *Saranac* had first choice from the former *Saginaw*'s crew. The rest, thirty-three of their shipmates, found themselves back on board the old receiving ship *Independence*. Orders for the inevitable court of inquiry were issued by Rear Admiral Winslow on February 7 (the day Montgomery Sicard arrived in San Francisco) from his flagship USS *Pensacola*. Commodore W. R. Taylor was appointed president, Captain J. H. Spotts and Captain Paul Shirley members, and Captain P. C. Pope of the Marine Corps judge advocate for the court. A ship had been lost, and there was no choice in this matter. Though not a court-martial, the investigation could lead to that should one be justified. Sicard would have to defend his actions and explain the loss of the vessel under his command.

The board gathered two days later, promptly at 11:00 a.m. on February 9, on board USS *Saranac* for the formal proceedings. The order convening the inquiry was then read over in the presence of the accused (Sicard), who was asked if he had any objection to any member of the court, to which he replied no. The court was then sworn in, in the usual manner. Master Perry Garst was called as the first witness, and also duly sworn. He described his role as officer of the deck, and the events of the night of October 29. In particular, the court wanted to ascertain the nature of the night orders, the written and verbal instructions issued by the commander, the position of the lookouts, etc. The night order book had been lost in the wreck. The court also focused on the orders given immediately after the breakers had been sighted, and the decision made to not alter the ship's course. Lieutenant Commander Sicard had the opportunity to cross-examine the witness:

Question by Lieutenant Commander Sicard: What did I first do when you reported breakers?

Answer: Went on Hurricane deck and remarked that they were surely breakers and gave orders to back the engines and reduce sail.

Question by Lieutenant Commander Sicard: In what way did the crew obey the order to shorten sail and what did I do and say regarding getting in sail?

Answer: In a very slow manner. Said the sail must be gotten in if we wished to save the ship, and I had no opportunity of observing what the Captain did, as my attention was called elsewhere.

Question by Lieutenant Commander Sicard: Do you think it would have been expedient to have altered the helm after the breakers were reported?

Answer: No sir.

Question by the Court: Why would it not have been expedient to change the helm, when breakers were reported?

Answer: In consequence of our proximity to them, if the helm had been changed, I think it would have brought the ship on the reef in a more unfavorable position.

Question by the Court: Do you think that breakers could have been discovered sooner than they were by any better lookout than was kept?

Answer: No sir.[114]

Slowly, piece by piece, the salient points of Sicard's official report on the loss of USS *Saginaw* were borne out from Garst's perspective, proved to the court's satisfaction. This is exactly what they expected.

On the second day of the inquiry, Second Assistant Engineer Jones Godfrey was called to testify, and he described in detail the events as they played out in the engine room up until the point where the reef came through the hull near the keelson and water flooded the lower spaces. He was followed on the stand by First Assistant Engineer James Butterworth. Questions focused on the steam pressure at the time of the wreck and the actions taken to back the engines. The steam log, like the night order book, had also vanished with the ship. Then Mate Gustavus H. Robinson made his appearance. Like that of the others, his testimony seemed to establish due vigilance and observation of duty, as did that of Second Assistant Engineer Herschel Main; Master Arthur H. Parsons; Chief Quartermaster George Sellers; Seamen Dennis Fitzgerald, Michael Jordan, John Daily; and Landsman William Coombs.

Next Ensign James K. Cogswell, as the navigator on the ship, came under detailed examination. The court questioned him on the deviation and variation of the ship's compass. They questioned him on the specific charts he used (North Pacific, Sandwich Island, with Islands and Reefs to the Westward, from the Survey of Lieutenant Brooke USN 1859; Captain Brooks of the Hawaiian Bark *Gambia* 1859; Captain Reynolds, Commander USN *Lackawanna*, 1867; and British Admiralty charts issued by the Hydrographic Office, December 1868). They also brought in Lieutenant Commander Louis Kempff, the navigator of USS *Saranac*, as an additional expert and assurance as to Cogswell's testimony. The ship's chronometer had changed at Midway, so Cogswell had to admit not taking any navigational fixes to determine his longitude. But, nonetheless, his course set for Ocean Island, west by five-eighths north, was correct. Finally, they asked, "Please state what currents you had experienced about those Islands and what means you had of ascertaining them?" Cogswell answered, "Never had any opportunity of ascertaining any currents about those Islands."[115]

The problem facing the court was a simple but persistent one: if Commander Sicard had indeed taken all the proper actions (which it seemed he had), and his officers had been diligent in their duties (which it seemed they were), how then did a ship of the U.S. Navy end up running slowly but decisively aground onto a known navigational hazard? The court, after all, was concerned not only with the career of Lieutenant Commander Sicard, but with the reputation of the service as well. And the matter had been commented on publicly, beginning with commentary in the *Friend*, Hawai`i's local journal: "It was in truth, a remarkable shipwreck. The night had been clear and straight, with a moderate breeze. The ship was heading direct for an island whose position and distance—and that a short one—were known, approximately if not precisely. She was making not over two and a half to three knots, yet she ran directly, without any particular lack of vigilance, on a reef which was above water, and on which the breakers were dashing furiously."[116] Fortunately, Commander Sicard had an answer to that question. George A. Bailey, the agent for the contractor at Midway Islands, was called to the stand. Expert testimony from outside of the service could not have hurt Sicard's cause. And Bailey had discussed his own observations at both Midway and Ocean islands with the commander long before *Kilauea* had come to rescue them from the island.

Question by the Court: Have you had much nautical experience?

Answer: I have been thirty (30) years at sea, off and on.

Question by the Court: Was everything done that, in your opinion, could have been done by a judicious and prudent commander for the preservation of life, provisions and stores, after the striking of the *Saginaw* upon the reef?

Answer: It was.

Question by the Court: Please state whether or not in your opinion if the helm had been put hard a starboard or port, and the engines worked ahead, would she have cleared the reef?

Answer: I do not think she could have cleared.

Question by Lieutenant Commander Sicard: How long before leaving Midway Island do you remember having seen bar buoy number 4?

Answer: Number 4 buoy was there about eight (8) days before leaving the Midway Islands.[117]

This was something of a surprise line for the defendant to take, but he had discovered an important fact regarding the course navigated between the atolls. The many buoys used at Midway in the survey and blasting of the channel had a way of breaking free and ending up at Ocean Island, a fact corroborated by others, namely John Ryan and William Loring.

> Question by the Judge Advocate: Please state your name and rank in the service and where you have lately been serving.
>
> Answer: John J. Ryan, 2nd assistant engineer, United States Steamer *Saginaw*, and was attached to her when she was wrecked at Ocean Island October 29th 1870.
>
> Question by Lieutenant Commander Sicard: After our arrival on Ocean Island, did you see upon the beach a buoy that had been on Midway Island bar, if so, describe it and its situation.
>
> Answer: I had charge of a working party digging for water on Ocean Island and while walking up from the South western point, picked up a small whiskey cask, with painted red hoops, with a large "B" painted in white on the head and about two fathoms of buoy rope attached to it. Saw the keg on board ship, it was brought over from Honolulu, and I saw it on board ship at Midway Island.
>
> Question by the Judge Advocate: Please state your name and position in life.
>
> Answer: William G. Loring, was employed at the Midway Islands as a submarine diver and was on board the Saginaw when she was wrecked at Ocean Island October 19th 1870.
>
> Question by Lieutenant Commander Sicard: While on Ocean Island did you find one of the Midway Island bar buoys, if so describe it, its number and situation.
>
> Answer: The day we landed at Ocean Island I found a buoy on the beach and looked at it, it was number VI, and had seen it at Midway Islands, about a week before we left there.[118]

For any buoy, whether marked #4 or B or VI or whatever, to drift from Midway to Ocean Island indicated the existence of a current setting to the west at that particular time of year. The estimation of a single buoy making the crossing in a matter of a few days seemed to indicate a significant current. And the same thing had occurred with a number of the buoys used at Midway and later confirmed at Ocean Island. But except for some general descriptions of currents in the larger Pacific basin, observations originally begun by Lieutenant Charles Wilkes and the United States

Exploring Expedition in 1838, very little was specifically known about the seasonal currents among the Northwestern Hawaiian Islands. Ensign Cogswell and his commanding officer had no way of knowing that their ship was being set to westward at a dangerous pace, ending up ahead of their projected landfall by several hours. They were carried onto the reef by the sea. This they proved to the court's satisfaction, from empirical evidence on the island.

At the end of the inquiry, as was standard procedure, the court read Sicard's official report of the loss to the assembled officers and all of *Saginaw*'s crew, and asked, "Have you anything to object to the narrative just read to the Court or anything to lay to the charge of any officer or man with regard to the loss of the United States late vessel the United States Steamer *Saginaw*?"[119] Answer: No. Sicard was asked, "Have you any complaints to make against any of the surviving officers and crew of the said vessel on that occasion?" Answer: No. The course ahead was clear; the court's problem had been solved. A culprit had been found for the loss of their ship: the Pacific Ocean itself. On February 15, their inquiry was concluded.

> The Court finds . . . that every measure was taken to ensure vigilance on the part of the lookouts and to prevent the vessel from running too fast . . . that owing to the proximity of the breakers, it would have been useless to attempt to avoid them by changing the helm, which would have thrown the vessel on the reef in a more unfavorable situation. That every step was taken after striking the reef, to preserve life, provisions and property of all kinds. . . . The Court is of opinion that the wrecking of the Saginaw was caused by a current, as the evidence shows care in running the vessel at a safe rate of speed. . . . And that Lieut. Comdr. Montgomery Sicard used due vigilance and care in the navigation of his vessel and after striking upon the reef that he exercised sound judgment and exhibited great skill and prudence.[120]

The matter, as far as the navy was concerned, was closed.

8

Afterword

Legacy and Shipwrecks

Our maritime heritage is that part of our seafaring past that we choose to treasure, that part of ourselves that informs us about our human relationship to the sea. We were all sailors once, no matter where we find ourselves now, so this heritage is made up of many things: charts, oral histories, seafaring superstitions, marine art, sea literature, official reports, museum ships, and more. For the tale of USS *Saginaw* and her crew, maritime heritage falls under three different themes: what we choose to remember from the historical narrative (re-created here from the documentary record); what we have left from the event as artifacts on shore; and what the sea has kept for us hidden beneath the waves. And all of these are associated with specific geographical locations: the National Archives; the Naval Academy at Annapolis; Mare Island, California; and Midway and Kure atolls. The legacy of USS *Saginaw* and all of her Pacific passages lives on in these different ways.

Lieutenant Commander Montgomery Sicard and his crew had been through an amazing experience, and most had come back alive and in fairly reasonable condition. With his men dispersed and the official navy inquiry completed, the story of *Saginaw*'s loss folded into history. The wreck, and the voyage of the ship's gig, became parts of the most famous shipwreck event in the distant Northwestern Hawaiian Islands—a small vessel lost in the world's largest ocean, on its most remote atoll.

Following his return from Ocean Island, Montgomery Sicard was assigned to the New York navy yard, and began to work on designing the navy's first steel breech-loading cannon. In 1876, he published *Description of Naval 3-Inch Breech-loading Howitzers*, and in 1880 *Ordnance Instructions for the United States Navy*. Chiefly, Sicard would be remembered in his capacity as head of the Bureau of Ordnance for ten years, and for his innovative and then-controversial work in the advancement of naval weapon technology, where he made his true mark in the service. He would eventually achieve the rank of rear admiral. At the end of his career, he even took command briefly of the North Atlantic Squadron, at the beginning of the Spanish American War in 1898. Sicard was poised with his squadron at Key West, Florida, when word arrived of the explosion on board USS *Maine*. But recurring malaria forced him to relinquish his position to Captain William T. Sampson. All would fondly recall, though, his uncanny ability to remain calm in the face of hardship and crisis, a natural leader with his even-tempered, meticulous, and unflappable nature. Much later, following his death at his summer home in Westerville, New York, the Department celebrated the respect and esteem he had earned throughout the entire navy: "His courage, coolness and presence of mind in time of danger were proverbial and unquestioned."[1] Sicard was sixty-four years old at the time of his death, and he had spent forty-seven of those years in the service. In many ways, he exemplified some of the best qualities of both the old and new steam navies. The shipwreck of USS *Saginaw* had been his most challenging test early in his career, and he had passed with high recommendations. The Clemson-class destroyer DD-346 was laid down on June 18, 1919, by the Bath Iron Works, Maine, and named in his honor USS *Sicard*.

William Halford, the boat's sole survivor at Kaua'i, was promoted to acting gunner's mate and awarded the Medal of Honor for personal valor demonstrated during the gig's voyage. He remained in the service at Mare Island and San Francisco, as well as on board the ships of the Pacific fleet, for forty-nine more years, ending his days as an acting lieutenant during World War I. In 1914, he again found himself in the Hawaiian Islands, where he met with J. M. Lydgate to discuss the shipwreck and rescue voyage.[2] Halford's retelling of the story, perhaps naturally enough, tended to feature himself in the starring roles. He had, after all, saved the lives of all of his shipmates. His strength and stalwart nature, and his luck, served him well all throughout his sailing career. He had, in fact, been shipwrecked and cast adrift twice in the Atlantic Ocean several years prior to his service on board *Saginaw*, once when the vessel *Nellie F* caught fire and burned, and once when the Portuguese ship *Jova Francisco*'s seams opened up and she sank.[3] Halford died in 1919 in Oakland, California.[4] His descendants still live in the Vallejo area. In 1943, the Fletcher-class destroyer USS *Halford* DD-480 was commissioned in Bremerton, Washington. William Halford's grave is located at the Mare Island Naval Cemetery.

Mare Island, where the slipways used to be covered in wood shavings, later developed into a major shipbuilding facility, prominent during World War II for the construction of numerous Liberty ships and submarines. The naval yard, so long a part of Vallejo life, shut down in 1992, and today townhouses and condominiums are being raised on its grassy slopes, though some of the historic buildings remain. The oldest is the maritime museum, with tales of USS *Saginaw* and images of the old navy yard.

Ensign Cogswell, *Saginaw*'s navigator, went on to have an extended naval career, becoming a specialist in ordnance and torpedo construction. Despite a court-martial in 1873 (charges suspended), certain other accusations of drunkenness while on duty in the Congo in 1876, and the feeling on the part of one of his later commanding officers, such as Commander Schley, USS *Essex*, that Cogswell lacked zeal and professional capability, he continued to climb the ranks.[5] Other officers were supportive and very positive in their assessment, including Sicard. Schley may have had a personal axe to grind. Cogswell, as a lieutenant commander, was on board USS *Oregon* as the ship's executive officer during her historic dash around Cape Horn and long race to join the North Atlantic Squadron for its raid on the Spanish Fleet in 1898. He received promotion for his duty during the Battle of Santiago. Cogswell retired in 1904 after reaching the rank of rear admiral, and he died in Florida in 1908. The general-purpose destroyer DD-651 was launched in 1943 as USS *Cogswell*, named for this hero of the Spanish-American War.

Ensign Perry Garst, officer of the deck that night at Ocean Island, also remained in the navy. Five years after his return to Mare Island and the court of inquiry, Garst was a young officer serving on board USS *Saranac* when she struck hard on a rock near Seymour Narrows, off British Columbia. Unlike in his previous wreck experience, *Saranac* was doing fourteen knots at the time. *Saranac*'s bow hung on the sharp pinnacle, then slipped off, water gaining rapidly in the holds. Fortunately, Garst's luck held out, and he found himself safely ashore once again. The crew camped with what little provisions they had time to get out of the ship.[6] Afterward, Garst served with the U.S. Coast and Geodetic Survey on the Pacific Coast between 1879 and 1882, visiting many of those same waters once traveled by *Saginaw*. Later Garst became commandant of the navy yard at Portsmouth. Following his forty-year service, he retired as Rear Admiral Perry

Garst in 1907, and he died in Florida in 1939, on the eve of another great war.

William Sheffield Cowles, who as a twenty-four-year-old ensign served on board a portion of *Saginaw*'s last cruise as sailing master, departed the vessel before her last passage to Midway, headed for his next duty station at the Naval Observatory. He was promoted to lieutenant in 1872. Subsequently, he served for a long period in East Asia on board the Mohongo-class double-ender gunboat USS *Monocacy* as executive officer. Commander Sumner reported Cowles to be "a natural born Executive, and he is one of the best with whom it has been my pleasure to serve."[7] In later years, Cowles was the first commanding officer of the battleship USS *Missouri* BB-11, on which the articles of surrender were signed by the Japanese government at the end of World War II. He was married to Anna Roosevelt Cowles, sister of President Franklin Roosevelt. Cowles retired from a long career in the navy as a rear admiral. He is buried at Arlington Cemetery.

The kindly and dignified paymaster, George Henry Read, was eventually promoted to the rank of commander, mainly for his meritorious service during the Civil War. His name remains quite prominent in the legacy of USS *Saginaw*, though, because he published in 1912 a short book on his ship's last mission, entitled *The Last Cruise of the Saginaw*, by far the best firsthand account of the struggle for survival on any of the Northwestern Hawaiian Island's tiny atolls. He died in 1924 and was buried in Philadelphia.

Engineer James Butterworth, who fashioned the makeshift still on the beach, providing freshwater on Ocean Island and saving the lives of the entire crew, never fully recovered from the effects of exposure during the incident. He remained, however, a gentleman, and a popular and respected shipmate, serving at the Boston navy yard, and then on a South Pacific cruise on board USS *Narragansett*. He was promoted to chief engineer in 1881, moving to USS *Marion* on the Asiatic Station. He died on October 2, 1891.

Including the hot-tempered Rear Admiral Richard Meade, who commanded *Saginaw* from 1868 to 1869 (commemorated by USS *Meade* DD-274); the stately Rear Admiral James Findlay Schenck, *Saginaw*'s first commander between 1860 and 1861 (commemorated by USS *Schenck* DD-159); the more relaxed Rear Admiral Samuel Rhoades Franklin; and even the eventual Rear Admiral John Elliot Pillsbury, who served as a lieutenant on board *Saginaw* in Alaska (taking part in the raids against the

Kake Indian villages); and the eventual Rear Admiral Charles H. Baldwin, the one-time temporary commander on *Saginaw* for two months on San Francisco Bay—this makes a grand total of at least nine rear admirals to have walked the deck of the small steamship lost at Ocean Island, and a total of seven destroyers named after them (adding to the list USS *Pillsbury* DD-227 and USS *Baldwin* DD-624). This is a rather remarkable record for a tiny fourth-rate gunboat. But these small vessels were, after all, a stepping-stone to greater things for many officers. And the ranks of U.S. Navy officers back then were not that large. It was a different age.

Saginaw's own name lived on for a number of years as the 1179-class landing ship tank (LST-1188), launched and commissioned in 1970 at Long Beach, California. With the subsequent changing roles of the U.S. Navy, though, it was then decided that most of these amphibious ships were no longer needed. USS *Saginaw* LST-1188 was decommissioned and sold to Australia in 1994, to be rebuilt as an amphibious landing platform. The ship is currently an active part of the Royal Australian Navy, christened the HMAS *Kanimbla*. So it goes; will there be another USS *Saginaw*?

For Peter Francis and John Gunnel Talbot, there would tragically be no further entries in their service records. Though Francis's body was never recovered, his name appears on the headstone at Nu`uanu Cemetery in Honolulu, where lie the remains of John Andrews and James Muir, the hard-hat divers with Townsend's Boston company who served their last month on earth as enlisted men in the United States Navy (see fig. 29). Unfortunately, due to the loss of certain papers in the gig, and sometimes inevitable bureaucratic obstacles, assistance was not immediately forthcoming from either the navy pension fund or Mr. Townsend's company to the families of Andrews and Muir. Commander Sicard took up this cause as his own, making sure there was proper compensation, and he developed a true friendship with members of both families. Andrews's eighteen-year-old-son Robert expressed his appreciation to the commander in writing:

> Dear Sir, I take this opportunity to write to you. I hope you will forgive me for not writing to you before. I feel ashamed of myself. I wish I could see you and I could tell you better, I cannot speak in writing how I thank you for your kindness you have done for me and my mother. I was glad to read in your kind letter that my father was a brave man. . . . I feel the loss of him. I told him when he left me that I should never see him again. The last words he said to me, "Remember my son, that a rolling stone never gathers moss."[8]

FIGURE 29. The headstone for Peter Francis, John Andrews, and James Muir in the naval section of Nuʻuanu Cemetery, Honolulu, Hawaiʻi. Photograph by author.

Mrs. Andrews took the loss of her husband hard, becoming inconsolable for a time and later moving into a boardinghouse.

James Muir had originally come from Glasgow, and from there he traveled overseas in Melbourne for an extended length of time prior to his employment as a diver in Boston. His widowed mother, two sisters, and a brother (also a sailor), and his young wife, Mary Jane Muir (formerly Higgins), proved more difficult to locate, and Sicard prevailed upon the services of a detective and a local chief constable to be certain that all was correct. Mary Jane was then working as a live-in servant with a ship-owner's family in Glasgow; Muir's mother and siblings were "in poor circumstances."[9] Sicard arranged for the pension, and donations from the Life Saving Benevolent Association of New York, to be sent to the Muir family. George W. Townsend, the submarine contractor from Boston, fell onto hard times himself in the years following the unfulfilled contract in the Pacific. His company went into insolvency in 1883 with a debt of four-teen thousand dollars.[10]

Young John Gunnel Talbot had never married, but he did have a half-brother who had remained in Kentucky. Lieutenant Talbot's body was eventually claimed by his family and transported back to his hometown of Danville in August 1871, where he was buried in Bellevue public cemetery.[11] A tall, white marble monument was erected over his grave, its inscription aging slowly into obscurity over time.

Peace Returns to Ocean Island and Midway Atoll

The narrative of USS *Saginaw* is an indelible part of some of the most remote and pristine locations in the distant Pacific. Ocean Island—or Kure, as it is now known, although there is no record of the Russian explorer Captain Kure ever having been there—quickly reverted back to what it had been, an unoccupied sandy spit, home only to the gooney birds and the monk seals, the inhabitants of the wind, the sea, and the sun. No doubt these animals felt some kind of relief at the departure of the castaways. The albatross went back to their clacking and dancing, and the seals slept in the sun, unmolested at last. The store hut eventually collapsed, covering the tools and hardware left under its canvas. And the frames and keel of the schooner *Deliverance*, still in the cradle between the dunes, dried and warped in the sun. Even the rats settled down—until 1886, when the next set of castaways fetched up on their shores.

That year the 1,750-ton three-masted iron sailing ship *Dunnottar Castle* was returning from Sydney, Australia, to San Pedro, California, with a cargo of coal. Friendly wagers had been placed between the *Castle* and two other merchant vessels at Sydney, for the British tall ship had a reputation for speed. That speed (and perhaps a course laid recklessly close to the atoll) took the ship onto the southwest curve of the reef at the entrance to the lagoon at Kure Atoll, directly onto a coral shoal. The ship lodged upright, permanently stuck and fatally holed through the turn of the bilge, but in no danger of sinking. The lookouts had little sign of the low reef in the thick darkness of the early morning, but being downwind of the atoll, they had a chance to smell the guano of Ocean Island before they ran aground. Just as they were alerting their captain, the vessel struck head on. The loss was later blamed on faulty chronometers. Anchors were sent out, and they worked the heavy iron yards back and forth, but it was to no avail, and they abandoned the tall ship for land. The chief officer and six seamen took one of the boats and, purposefully retracing Talbot's path, made a long fifty-two-day passage to Kaua`i, coming ashore at Kalihiwai, very near to the same location as *Saginaw*'s gig. Fortunately, the calmer seas this time allowed the boat to land with no loss of life.

The *Waialeale* was soon chartered by the British commissioner in Honolulu and sent on the rescue mission. (The SS *Kilauea* had been scrapped years earlier.) This time, Hawaiian officials feared that the British might use the occasion to annex the island, so they shared the rescue expenses, and Hawaiian commissioner James Boyde accompanied the voyage. Boyde took formal possession of Kure Island on September 20 for His Majesty King David Kalakaua, Kamehameha VII. Upon arrival at the island, however, not a soul was to be seen. There were only the dogs left behind by the crew, which had been terrorizing the bird population. Two fox terriers and a retriever were rescued. The stranded sailors had been picked up from Kure two days earlier by the bark *Birnham Wood* and were by then en route to Valparaiso, Chile. A note left in a bottle explained their fate. The frames of the *Saginaw*'s half-built schooner *Deliverance* still stood in their cradle on the beach.

As an aid to future shipwreck victims, Commissioner Boyde and the crew of *Waialeale* set up a permanent structure, including two 500-gallon water tanks and a rain-gutter drainage system, and established a variety of plants (algerboa, kamani, kukui, ohia, monkey pod, noohui, and coconut) during this trip.[12] The submerged coral heads and unseen reefs were still proving to be too hazardous for vessels. The site was *Saginaw*'s former island camp. Sadly, though, poachers destroyed the castaway facility within a year, but distant Kure had been reconfirmed as part of the Hawaiian Kingdom.[13]

USS *Saginaw* in Hawai`i was, as a navy ship on a modernizing mission, part of a larger economic and political agenda. American domination of the islands, so long a matter of growing concern for the Kingdom of Hawai`i, culminated in the two decades following the ship's voyage. In 1887, King Kalakaua signed the Reciprocity Treaty with the United States, and the mainland market for island sugar was exchanged for military rights at Pearl Harbor. The gates had been opened for the sugar plantation boom. In 1890, the king traveled to the mainland, where unfortunately he died from disease in January of the following year. Queen Lili`uokalani, ascending to the throne, had clear intentions of shifting the Kingdom's constitution back toward greater sovereign and independent power, challenging

American domination. But powerful commercial and political players, men such as Lorrin Thurston, Sanford B. Dole, William Wilder, J. B. Castle, H. P. Baldwin, Alexander Young, J. H. Soper, and William R. Castle—some of the most influential foreigners in Hawai`i—resisted this, and gained public support over time. This annexation clique saw their chance for a successful revolution in January 1893.

Having professed recognition of the Hawaiian Kingdom, in the end the U.S. Navy played a direct role in the overthrow of the sovereign government. Captain G. C. Wiltse, on board USS *Boston*, stood ready to respond to orders from United States Minister John L. Stevens, who (as had previous ministers) approved of the overall aims of the annexation clique. As the actual event played out, Stevens's instructions did not even have time to reach USS *Boston*. But Captain Wiltse had composed his own orders, in accordance with standard navy procedure and past instructions from the American secretary of state. Marines went ashore to "assist in preserving public order," but were warned to remain neutral in any conflict, acting with extreme prudence.

This time, U.S. marines would not provide a balance against other foreign powers in support of the sovereign and independent monarchy—just the opposite. USS *Boston*'s presence alone carried considerable weight; the ship was a 3,185-ton, 283-foot-long Atlanta-class protected cruiser, armed with two 8-inch and six 6-inch guns. One hundred sixty-two blue jackets and marines from USS *Boston* landed at 5:00 p.m. on January 16, ostensibly to protect American lives and property in anticipation of pleas from the annexation group, who were "unable to protect ourselves without aid and, therefore, pray for the protection of the United States forces."[14] The real message was clear; the marines had guns, most others did not. A few were posted at the consulate near the waterfront, others marched up Nu`uanu Street to the American minister's office, and the rest, armed and at the ready, occupied Arion Hall near Iolani Palace. The possibility of bloodshed was very real. On January 17, the queen was forcefully dethroned and placed under house arrest. Lili`uokalani surrendered under protest not to the annexationists, but to the "superior forces of the United States of America, whose minister plenipotentiary . . . has caused United States troops to be landed at Honolulu and declared that he would support the said provisional government."[15] Sanford B. Dole was named president by the annexationists the following day.

The investigation following the action, conducted by U.S. Commissioner James H. Blount, was critical of the illegal overthrow, and later charged that navy troops were landed under a prearranged agreement to intentionally assist in overthrowing the queen.[16] The United States government, faced with this fait accompli, took no immediate or effective action. The United States did not formally recognize the takeover until 1898, when the Spanish-American War and other outside events again made clear the Hawaiian Islands' strategic importance. Very quickly then, the "Republic of Hawai'i" was officially annexed by the United States. The days of American naval commanders like Sicard and Winslow attending receptions at the palace of His Majesty the King and recognizing the Kingdom's inherent sovereign rights were over.

These upheavals in the main Hawaiian Islands had almost no immediate effect on the distant islands to the northwest, but ultimately change was coming. World War II eventually did touch at remote Kure Atoll. Beginning in 1933, massive training flights for Advanced Base operations—squadrons of bi-wing flying boats—were conducted from Ford Island at Pearl Harbor, ranging up and down the entire archipelago. And naval aircraft used the many reefs and rocks around the atolls as training targets. In 1942, advance notice of Japanese plans to invade Midway allowed the American navy to make hasty but critical preparations and position itself appropriately. These preparations included not only Midway but the entire chain of the Northwestern Hawaiian Islands. Prior to June 1942, two PT-boats were stationed at Kure, along with four smaller patrol craft. Had the Japanese invasion at Midway been a success, plans existed for a contingent of 550 men at Kure Atoll, as well as a seaplane and mini-submarine base.[17]

Permanent residence was in the future for Kure. In 1961, the U.S. Coast Guard arrived to erect a LORAN (Long Range Aid to Navigation) station on Green Island, named for the low naupaka shrubs and single tree that clung to life there. The 625-foot tower broadcast its signal far across the ocean, and the 4,000-foot runway eliminated any need for constant boat traffic at the atoll. Unfortunately, the LORAN station seemed to be no help at all to the fishing vessel *Houei Maru*, which drifted onto the northern reef in 1976 and broke up in a severe storm. The initial inspection the following day revealed no signs of the crew, missing at sea with no explanation. But after LORAN came satellite navigation, known as the Global Positioning System (GPS). The Coast Guard left Kure, the tower gone and the runway grown over, and the island is inhabited now only on a part-time basis by the manager of the State of Hawai'i's Kure Atoll Wildlife Refuge and her seasonal research staff.

Midway Atoll

USS *Saginaw* initiated the American naval presence at Midway, or "Naval Station, Midway islands." In the American narrative in the Pacific, Midway Atoll occupies a critical and unique niche, for there has never been another location like it in any way. The small island would more than fulfill the nineteenth-century visions of strategic importance in a number of different ways. The United States was not, however, quick to continue its efforts there. Following the rescue of *Saginaw*'s crew, Midway, like Kure, was left in peace—at least for a while. Between 1870 and 1900, the Midway Islands were a forlorn outpost, known mostly to other unlucky castaways of other ill-fated ships. The huts, built in the hope of someday establishing a coaling depot, crumbled into the sand, and the boards were reused for the rough construction of temporary shacks for stranded castaways. And Midway also continued to accumulate shipwrecks. Immediately following the loss of the *Dunnottar Castle* at Kure, the small 30-ton wooden schooner *General Siegel* sailed from Honolulu on a shark-fishing and opportunistic salvage or wrecking expedition in the Northwestern Hawaiian Islands.[18] The schooner wrecked herself during a storm in November, dragging the anchors and blowing onto the reef at Midway Atoll. Eight survivors established camp on Eastern Island. In May, the castaways began repairing a lifeboat that had drifted to Midway from the wreck of the *Dunnotter Castle* (proving the countercurrent in the summer season?).

The schooner *General Siegel*'s story remains something of a mystery to this day, for only four of the eight survivors left the atoll on the rescue passage to the Marshall Islands. Reportedly, the first mate, Adolph Jorgensen, traveled with Captain Asberdine and Seaman Brown to Sand Island. Jorgensen returned alone, telling the unlikely story of the captain's murder/suicide, the alleged event occurring completely out of sight of the remaining crew. The others then hastened their preparations and left on their repaired boat without Jorgensen, leaving him only an axe, some dried fish, and a few other articles.[19] They later made their way back to Honolulu on board the schooner *Lillian*.

A year later, the 377-ton bark *Wandering Minstrel* departed Honolulu on a similar voyage of opportunity to the productive fishing grounds of the Northwest. The vessel was lost on the reef during a sudden squall while anchored in Welles Harbor in December 1887. Captain Walker and family established their camp on Sand Island, while *Minstrel*'s crew took up residence on Eastern Island, where they found castaway Adolph Jorgensen of the schooner *General Siegel*. Over time, six of these survivors drowned while attempting escape on repaired boats, one or two may have been murdered, and several succumbed to starvation during the long fourteen months that the party was stranded. The schooner *Norma* rescued the remaining castaways on March 17, 1889.[20]

Midway's role as a strategic communications link began in 1903, when the Commercial Pacific Cable Company established its relay station at Sand Island. This was the northern, or "American," route through Midway for the submarine cable, rather than the southern, or "German," route through the Marshall Islands. The station manager's initial impression, that Midway was "unfit for human habitation," quickly led to the importation of hundreds of foreign species of flora and fauna. Midway's environmental makeover had begun. Nine thousand tons of soil from Honolulu and Guam transformed the landscape, and tall ironwood trees took root. This was the only shade in the Pacific for 1,000 miles. Gardens were started. A few of the more optimistic visions of Charles Brooks and William Reynolds were finally being realized. Descendants of the station manager's pet canaries still flutter about the island. The gooney birds, unused to vertical obstacles, occasionally collided against the tree trunks while on their final glide paths for an island touchdown.

The cable station brought permanent occupation to Midway. The first around-the-world message, by President Theodore Roosevelt, was transmitted on July 4, 1903. Occupation also meant that the government could finally crack down on illegal activities in the distant archipelago. Twenty-one marines were stationed on the island, the first permanent military presence. In the late nineteenth century, Midway and other atolls had become popular with bird poachers. Women in Europe at that time were wearing whole stuffed bodies of birds on their heads as part of their hats, a style that had the predictable negative effect on wildlife. Ultimately, President Theodore Roosevelt would designate the entire northwestern atoll area as a Hawaiian Islands wildlife refuge in 1909. USS *Iroquois* conducted regular enforcement patrols of the waters.

This did not mean, however, that the reefs had ceased to be navigational hazards. In 1903, *Julia E. Whalen*, a 101-ton two-masted schooner, was bringing provisions, building materials, and 100 barrels of soil (as well as livestock) to the cable station. The vessel was lost in a gale while attempting passage into Welles Harbor in the predawn hours, beating about looking for the opening until 3:00 a.m.[21] The crew was able to abandon the ship, but no access from the shore was possible for any salvage of the cargo. A wide and marked passage cut through the bar would have been helpful.

In 1906, the American bark *Carrollton*, under the command of Captain Hinrichs, went head on into Midway's southern reef. The ship was en route from New South Wales to Honolulu with coal consigned to W. G. Irwin and Company.[22] *Carrollton* had been built and launched by the prominent Downeast Maine shipbuilding family of Arthur Sewall during the heyday of American wooden sailing vessels, one of the "largest and the best built wooden ships in the world."[23] (Son Harold Sewall later became the U.S. minister to Hawai`i.) The ship's entire career was spent in various trades to and from San Francisco: coal, lumber, and guano—typical cargoes of many large Pacific merchant vessels. A clear channel might have prevented this accident.

Change was literally in the air for Midway. In 1935, Pan American Airways established a flying boat refueling base at Midway Atoll, dredging some of the interior of the lagoon. These were the famous flying clippers of the new age. Guests and mail could now cross the Pacific in comfort and at high speed (five days), island-hopping from San Francisco to Manila via Honolulu, Midway, Wake, and Guam. The flying boats included smoking lounges, full-service dining facilities, and an enviable level of luxury long since vanished in the airline business. The cost of one trip was about three times the annual salary of the average American citizen. Once touched down in the lagoon of lonely Midway Island, travelers rode in "woody" wagons to the PanAm Hotel, also known as the "Gooneyville" Lodge. Cottages, tennis courts, a baseball field, and a nine-hole golf course (players used black golf balls due to the glare from the white sands) sprang up. Pan American terminated its flying clipper operations on December 8, 1941. The attack on Pearl Harbor heralded events that would change the entire Pacific region. The ocean had temporarily become too hazardous for commercial operations.

The zenith of Midway's importance was achieved during its critical role in World War II. Years before the war, Admiral Hepburn had noted that from a strategic perspective, an air facility at Midway Atoll was second in importance only to Pearl Harbor. Three runways had been constructed on Eastern Island. Sand Island featured seaplane ramps and a hangar, shops for ordnance, radio, engine, repair, communication facilities, a naval hospital, and housing. The Naval Air Station was commissioned on August 1, 1941. Midway's character had shifted completely from a civilian enterprise to military operations. As a part of War Plan Orange, the Hawaiian

Islands, including Midway, were the nation's first line of defense for the west coast. Deck guns from scrapped World War I ships were sent to the island, along with old Brewster Buffalo and Vought Vindicator aircraft— all that the navy could spare at the time from the theater in the Atlantic (reminiscent of the Pacific's inferior position during the American Civil War).

The Battle of Midway, June 4–6, 1942, remains a defining moment in the Pacific conflict. The atoll was the military gateway to the Hawaiian Islands, and a successful invasion there would have had the most dire consequences. Planes from an enemy-held Midway would have been within striking distance of O`ahu, where the salvage of the bulk of the Pacific Fleet from the bottom of Pearl Harbor was still under way. But thanks to successful intelligence operations, the planned Japanese invasion of Midway was foiled in a major sea battle, one commonly regarded as the turning point in the Pacific War, the moment when the Japanese Imperial Navy was forced to go on the defensive.

This was the first time that naval aviation alone had decided the outcome between fleets at sea. Four Japanese and one American carrier were sunk as a result of the battle, though the enemy forces had never sighted each other from their own decks. Though the majority of the action took place some 200 miles to the north, a fierce air battle was waged over the atoll itself, and a total of roughly twenty-six aircraft from both sides crashed in the vicinity of Midway, with at least twenty airmen missing in action. The hospital, fuel oil tanks, and the partly completed torpedo shop at the submarine basin were completely destroyed, and the administration buildings, laundry, and seaplane hangar received considerable damage. The base, however, continued operations.

The development of Midway continued after the attack at a renewed pace. By late 1942, the construction battalions had finished building a major submarine refit base. And by 1944, three 471-foot piers, a 769-foot tender pier, and an ARD wharf (auxiliary repair dry dock) had been completed. Montgomery Sicard might have been proud. Private contractors were brought in to dredge 5 million cubic yards of lagoon bottom and create the inner harbor and mooring basin for both submarines and surface vessels. Townsend and the Boston divers would have been impressed with the 300-foot-wide, 35-foot-deep channel and expanded anchorage for six cruisers and five destroyers within the shelter of the new harbor. The channel reached the lagoon from the south, rather than the natural opening on the west side where work focused in 1870. Costs exceeded even

Sicard's most expansive estimates, but it was wartime. The job had finally been completed at Midway seventy-four years after it had begun.

The submarine base was of great strategic importance. Midway added 2,400 miles to the cruising radius of the American subs, which saved eight days transit and precious fuel. U.S. submarines could also refit and repair, taking on ammunition while crews rested and recuperated. This meant sports, USO shows, talent shows, mail, news, movies, fresh fruit, ice cream, real beds in the Gooneyville Hotel, and beer, to a limited extent.

The U.S. submarine force in the Pacific destroyed 1,314 enemy ships, representing 55 percent of all enemy ships lost and a total of 5.3 million tons of shipping. This, of course, was not without cost. The force lost 375 officers and 3,131 enlisted men in fifty-two submarines. Fifteen of these submarines, and some 1,203 submariners, last touched land at tiny Midway Atoll.

USS *Macaw* ASR-11, a deep-sea salvage and submarine rescue vessel, was lost at Midway while supporting operations at the submarine base. The 1,780-ton Chanticleer-class *Macaw* was stranded on the reef on January 16, 1944, during the attempted salvage of the grounded submarine USS *Flier*. Approximately 25 feet of *Macaw*'s stern projected into the narrow channel. Due to the pressing need to maintain an open passage, attempts to refloat *Macaw* began as soon as possible. USS *Clamp* placed a crew on board after *Flier* was freed from the reef. Three separate attempts were made to lift USS *Macaw* from the reef without success. During heavy weather on the night of February 12–13, the ship broached and gradually slipped into deeper water.

The commanding officer, executive officer, and twenty crewmen were on board during that night in February. High surf prevented the crew from safely abandoning the ship before darkness fell. Their best option seemed to be to remain on board. But the ship started to list alarmingly and slide backward into the channel. With conditions deteriorating, they were soon forced to take shelter in the pilothouse. By 2:30 a.m., with 20- to 30-foot waves beginning to break over the entire vessel, the air inside the pilothouse became foul. The crew were forced to jump into the heavy seas in the darkness. The commanding officer, executive officer, and three sailors were lost at sea. Two 33-foot boats from Midway base capsized during rescue attempts, with the loss of three more lives. Search during the following day was conducted by beach patrols, two aviation crash boats, one LCM, plane-rearming boats, and contractor tugs, in addition to aircraft. Seventeen *Macaw* crewmen were recovered finally from the atoll, washed onto beaches, clinging to buoys, and floating in the lagoon.[24] The atolls were continuing to break vessels even though the "perfect harbor" had been established.

Activity at Midway continued after World War II. During the Cold War, three squadrons of Lockheed Super Constellation radar planes, otherwise known as "Willie Victor" aircraft, made up the airborne early-warning wing in the Pacific. These squadrons flew seven days a week, twenty-four hours a day. By 1964, there were thirty-four flight crews of between fifteen and twenty men per crew. The Pacific barrier consisted of continuous fourteen-hour flights between Midway Atoll and Adak Island in the Aleutians, 1,300 miles away. The United States also established a secret underwater listening post at Midway in an attempt to track Soviet submarines. Sand Island had the infrastructure of a small town, supporting thousands of permanent residents. Families lived at Midway, and children who were born and schooled there today remember the distant island as home.

The vision of Midway as a naval and commercial depot of exceeding importance in the middle of the northern Pacific Ocean had been more or less correct. Sicard, Welles, Borie, and Seward had demonstrated a farsighted understanding. They had been, though, some sixty years ahead of the proper moment in time. It was a humble beginning in 1870, placing a single hard-hat diver on the bottom of the reef, with his leaky cans of explosives and a small hoist for the "rock." The nation simply did not have the technical expertise or the logistical commitment to transform the Pacific atoll in the necessary manner. But America did not lack for want of trying. Commander Sicard realized this in his notes from Ocean Island, recognizing the strategic nature of the location even as initial efforts failed at Midway. This is the significance of *Saginaw*'s final chapter, the story of Midway and Kure atolls, and the maritime heritage of all of the Northwestern Hawaiian Islands.

In 1978, the navy downgraded Midway from a naval air station to a naval air facility, and large numbers of personnel and their dependents began leaving. With the conflict in Vietnam over, and the introduction of spy satellites above and nuclear submarines below, Midway's strategic importance to security finally declined. Its major role on the world stage of national defense was over; it was being returned to the birds. In 1992, the naval air facility was closed down under the Base Realignment and Closure Act. Four years later, jurisdiction of Midway Atoll was transferred to the Department of the Interior, and it became a national wildlife refuge. The "key to Midway" (in the shape of an albatross) was handed to the U.S. Fish and Wildlife Service representative in a speech that celebrated "trading guns for goonies."

The heritage of the World War II battle, Midway's historical watershed moment, has been recorded permanently on the island, thanks to the efforts of Dr. James d'Angelo and the International Midway Memorial Foundation. In 1995, several veterans of the battle, as well as noted naval officers and historians, were present at the dedication of a stone memorial to the memory of the Battle of Midway and the atoll's critical role in 1942. In 1999, the Fish and Wildlife Service completed a historic preservation plan for Midway, designating nine World War II–era properties as national historic landmarks.

Today the birds and seals once again claim Midway, the scrub growing over the legacy of the cable station and the Pan American clipper facility and the World War II and Cold War structures. But USS *Saginaw* was there at the very beginning, and will always be part of Midway Atoll.

The Gig's Continuing Voyage

A few traces of *Saginaw*'s story exist today as hallowed artifacts. The improvised sextant, fashioned from a steam gauge and pieces of a shaving mirror by Herschel Main, is encased on display at the U.S. Naval Academy in Annapolis, Maryland. So too is a portion of the gig's boathook, and the original deck log of USS *Saginaw*, and all are not far from the large marble tablet in the Academy's chapel commemorating Lieutenant John Gunnel Talbot, Peter Francis, James Muir, and John Andrews, and the sacrifice they made for their shipmates (see figs. 30–31). But there is no question that the most direct and enduring artifact of the saga is the ship's gig. The fact that it still exists at all is, of course, due entirely to Mr. C. A. Williams and the residents of Honolulu in 1871, who donated it to the ship's crew.

USS *Saginaw*'s gig, once brought back to Mare Island, did indeed attract attention as predicted. The boat arrived in San Francisco on the steamer *A. P. Jordan*, remaining at Mare Island until 1886. From there the gig traveled to the east coast on board USS *Jamestown*, and served as a training boat for naval apprentices. By 1889, the small vessel was preserved on display at the museum of the Naval Academy.[25] The story of USS *Saginaw* and the open-ocean rescue voyage has become part of the living legacy of the U.S. Navy. For years, the gig remained at Annapolis, until it was finally leased to the city of Saginaw, Michigan, and moved into the historic Castle Museum. The 30-foot gig has been on display to the public, alongside panels

FIGURE 30. The sextant built on the beach out of scrap parts by Engineer Herschel Main, now on display at the Naval Academy. Photograph by Tane Casserley.

FIGURE 31. The memorial tablet at the Naval Academy chapel honoring Lieutenant John Talbot and the other *Saginaw* men who lost their lives during the open-boat rescue voyage. Photograph by Tane Casserley.

FIGURE 32. *Saginaw*'s gig on display at the Castle Museum in Saginaw, Michigan. Photograph by Brenda Altmeier.

FIGURE 33. The names of J. Andrews and J. Muir etched into gig's hatch coaming. Photograph by Brenda Altmeier.

featuring information on *Saginaw*'s loss. The craft is in good shape, though some of the original materials, such as the canvas deck and paint, have been replaced over time. The boat still shows the patches and interior and exterior modifications completed on the beach in 1870, the original wear and tear from the voyage. The names of the gig's crew are still etched into the hatch coamings (see figs. 32–33). It is the single most evocative and tangible artifact left from the historic event.

Maritime Resources and the National Marine Sanctuaries Act

Other artifacts remain where they fell, beneath the waves on the reef, and these over time have become important historic maritime resources in their own right. The remoteness of the northwestern atolls has protected this chain of islands from the more negative impacts of population growth and exploitation for years, and fortunately the legacy of conservation begun by Theodore Roosevelt in 1909 has continued. USS *Saginaw* artifacts under the sea exist as a historic "museum" of the real world. And this museum has a special part in the evolving marine protection of the Hawaiian archipelago.

Recognition of the relatively pristine nature of the ecosystems in the Northwestern Hawaiian Islands spurred more than three decades of research and monitoring conducted by federal and state agencies, academic institutions, and other organizations. In 2000, the Coral Reef Conservation Act was passed, providing funds for the area's protection. Then, in 2001, executive orders 13178 and 13196 were signed by President William Clinton, establishing the Northwestern Hawaiian Islands as a coral reef ecosystem reserve. The orders included instructions to the secretary of commerce to initiate the designation of the reserve as a national marine sanctuary, potentially the fourteenth such protected area within the National Oceanic and Atmospheric Administration's (NOAA) Office of National Marine Sanctuaries.

Many people both within and outside the government worked on this public designation process between 2001 and 2006, for the chain of atolls and ocean was potentially one of the largest marine protected areas in the world. The Northwestern Hawaiian Islands reserve encompassed a vast region, approximately 140,000 square miles of the Pacific, a band 100 miles wide and 1,200 miles long, dotted with small islands, islets, atolls, and a complex array of shallow coral reefs, deepwater slopes, banks, seamounts, and abyssal and pelagic oceanic ecosystems supporting a unique diversity of marine life. In 2006, the atoll chain was established not solely as a sanctuary, but as the Papahānaumokuākea Marine National Monument, by proclamation of President George Bush. Today the monument is jointly managed by the State of Hawai`i, NOAA, and the U.S. Fish and Wildlife Service. Thus, the growing appreciation, scientific knowledge, and management efforts ultimately led to permanent protections for a unique area and all of its marine resources, quite a success story for ocean conservation. The survival of our planet depends on such efforts to appreciate and care for our marine resources.

And most notably for the history and the maritime heritage of these atolls, these marine resources include whatever may be left of historic shipwrecks like the *Dunnottar Castle*, and the nineteenth-century whalers *Pearl* and *Hermes*, and USS *Saginaw*. The National Marine Sanctuaries Act (NMSA), an integral part of the conservation groundwork, specifically protects "areas of the marine environment which have special conservation, recreational, ecological, *historical, cultural, archaeological*, scientific, educational, or esthetic qualities" (emphasis added).

In the field of marine survey and resource management, it is a rare thing to find social scientists like historians and archaeologists working side by side with biologists and oceanographers, but that is exactly what has been created by this effort, a more comprehensive and multidisciplinary approach to conservation and preservation. By whatever label these social scientists are known (historians, nautical archaeologists, or cultural resource managers), they are charged by specific state and federal preservation mandates to inventory and assess historic and archaeological resources underwater, and to share this information with the public.[26] This is a way of reconnecting with the human element in the marine environment, gaining an understanding of the history tied to specific marine locations, and of honoring the lives that were tragically lost at sea.

There is no question that the Northwestern Hawaiian Islands possess some of the most unspoiled and productive natural reef systems in the North Pacific Ocean. The isolation of these islands and atolls makes them natural reserves for ecosystem diversity. The Northwestern Hawaiian Islands also possess a rich maritime history and abundant submerged maritime heritage resources. These locations witnessed, for better or worse, a wide variety of Hawaiian and Pacific vessels and activities, such as guano mining, fishing, copra traders, Japanese sampans, transpacific colliers, and the local wreckers or salvage companies from the main Hawaiian Islands. Understanding our past can help us develop a better environment.

Therefore, the conservation of natural resources *and* preservation of historical resources, like USS *Saginaw*, are two sides of the same coin, parts of a growing idea of comprehensive ocean stewardship.

Footprints in the Sea: The Search for USS *Saginaw*

The physical legacy of the past exists outside the walls of museums and libraries; heritage surrounds us. If we could, theoretically, drain the oceans, even if only for a moment, we would find ourselves surrounded by the world's largest real-life maritime museum (although the relics would smell a bit). This is particularly true in a setting like the Hawaiian Islands, which are literally just the visible tops of submerged ancient towering volcanoes, rising up from the unseen floor of the sea thousands of feet below the gentle waves at Waikiki beach. Most of what has crashed, sunk, been dropped or dumped into the ocean still lies there, unseen, in the darkness, settling into the silts of time. Hundreds of shipwrecks and aircraft, and all sorts of debris, line the slopes of these underwater mountains in Hawai`i. It is only the illusion of the surface, the emptiness of the flat, two-dimensional blue sea as seen from above, that fools us into thinking these footprints in the ocean have been lost for good. It is the "out of sight, out of mind" bias, deeply embedded into the popular psyche, that has made it difficult for many to comprehend our true impacts to the marine environment. And it is the illusion of the flat, two-dimensional sea that has masked some of the historical treasures of our own maritime past.

As a direct result of the comprehensive protection for heritage resources in the Northwestern Hawaiian Islands, I found myself in 2002 being pulled through the turquoise water of the lagoon at Kure Atoll on the end of a polypropylene line, like a piece of human bait, visually scanning the bottom for traces of the wreck of USS *Saginaw*. The Coral Reef Ecosystem Reserve had chartered the research vessel *Rapture*, and forty-five ichthyologists, coral reef biologists, oceanographers, invertebrate experts, and others boarded the ship for the thirty-day expedition. Our team consisted of three volunteers: myself, Suzanne Finney (a student from the University of Hawai`i's anthropology department), and Marc Hughes (biologist and diver with an interest in shipwrecks). The 2002 trip marked the first systematic survey for shipwrecks and historic resources to the northwest archipelago.

Maritime archaeologists the world over usually rely on two basic pieces of equipment to find shipwreck sites: the magnetometer and the side scan sonar. The magnetometer is a passive device, a sensitive instrument capable of detecting concentrations of iron in the marine environment. A small torpedolike sensor, or towfish, is pulled behind a boat, back and forth over the search area. The towfish detects the strength of the earth's own magnetic field at two-second intervals. Any heavy iron object, such as a cannon or anchor, creates a disruption in the magnetic field, like dropping an iron marble onto a table of tiny magnetic filings. The towfish can sense these localized changes, and ultimately produce a map of magnetic anomalies. The targets might be ship anchors, a 55-gallon steel drum, an engine block from a car, but usually it is something artificial, something human—something that needs to be checked out.

The side scan sonar is a more active remote-sensing tool. Its torpedo-shaped towfish emits a pulse of high-frequency sound from transceivers mounted on its sides. These "pings" are reflected from the sea floor, captured by the transceivers, and sent back up the cable to the survey boat, where the computer translates the acoustic echo into a visual image. It is a sound image of the bottom, painted in artificial colors, shadows, and vague outlines depicting sand ripples, rocks, and (sometimes) the straight lines and corners of ships, aircraft wings, mooring blocks, etc.

These are useful tools under the proper conditions. Both need to be pulled through the water close to the seafloor to be effective. The magnetometer, however, can be fooled by high concentrations of iron in the natural environment. Hawai`i's basalt lava formations, which are iron-rich, can generate so much natural variation that finding the artificial signals in the data is like looking for a needle in a haystack, or a breeze in a hurricane. The side scan sonar works best when high-profile objects emerge from a relatively flat sea floor. The rough topography of Hawai`i's coral reef atolls, the dramatic gullies and ridges of the spur-and-groove formations, can mask what are often low-profile artifact scatter sites behind the coral heads. And no one wants to tow the expensive sensors into the side of a coral pinnacle or sharp reef.

From the scant bit of historical research completed at that time, I knew that Saginaw was one of the more historic of the archipelago's shipwrecks. If anything remained of the site, it had been resting in a high-energy environment, forgotten at the end of the world for 132 years. And Montgomery Sicard himself had said: "there are not probably three days during the year when the sea is quiet, or when, in my opinion, it would be possible to work over any part without great danger,"[27] so we had our doubts about our ability to work on the exposed eastern reef at Kure Atoll.

Before we could assess the wreck site, we had to find it. The question of using remote-sensing tools like magnetometers and side scan sonars was moot, for we were volunteers, and had no such budget or equipment. We relied on cruder techniques. That's how I found myself being pulled through the lagoon at Kure Atoll like bait, attracting undue attention from occasional Galapagos sharks and large aggressive Trevally jacks (ulua in Hawai`i) chasing my wake. Anyone who has been forced to rely on visual survey in the ocean (and many have) knows the odds are long, and knows the feeling of insignificance that comes from pulling a tiny human through the water in the middle of the North Pacific. Visual search is not the preferred tool, for the ocean is mainly an acoustic world, not a visual one. Marine creatures do not usually rely on sight as their primary sensory mechanism for survival. The boat moved five miles up and five miles down inside the lagoon, and the chances of coming across a part of USS *Saginaw* were slim. I felt small, with hours to think about *Saginaw*'s crew standing up to their waists in the water, carrying provisions to the island (somewhere right over there perhaps). Acres of coral formations and sand patches rolled underneath me. I was aware of the approximate location of the ship's loss from historical documents, but the ocean is a big place nonetheless. One hundred and thirty-two years of currents, surf, and storms could have pushed wreckage almost anywhere within the atoll. Yet no matter the chances, every diver feels within his or her own soul that discovery could be just another fin-kick away. It is our own last frontier, and every dive is a hunt, a "sea hunt." Flashes of Lloyd Bridges as Mike Nelson in the black-and-white television series came back to me in the lagoon. Or was that just exhaustion?

The ship *Rapture* paused at Kure Atoll for only two days. We surveyed the crash site of a World War II Corsair. We began the site map of the nineteenth-century American whaler *Parker* from New Bedford, lost in 1842. We went ashore to Green Island, talking with refuge manager Cynthia Vanderlip about USS *Saginaw* castaways and walking between the dunes near the survivor's camp. Outside the atoll, huge breakers rolled against the reef crest. No one worked outside the eastern crest in 2002, for the ocean was not cooperative, as Sicard predicted. But that was where the heavier material probably lay. Sicard knew: "I succeeded in saving a few more articles . . . but no other articles of importance, the guns and all heavy articles sinking in deep water outside the reef and under a heavy sea."[28] We rolled the dice, and we towed inside the lagoon; it was all we could do. And we lost. No trace of *Saginaw* was found that year.[29]

Like the truly obsessed, initial failure only whetted our appetite for more survey. In 2003, we had an opportunity to return to Kure and continue the search. This time the team consisted of myself, Dr. Bradley Rodgers (East Carolina University's Program in Maritime Studies), Andy Lydecker (Panamerican Consultants Inc.), and Kelly Gleason (a graduate student at ECU). The Coral Reef Ecosystem Reserve's 40-foot research vessel *Manacat* and crewmen Don Moses and Tony Sarabia were already at nearby Midway Atoll in support of ongoing coral reef and marine mammal research projects. *Manacat* provided a lift for us to and from Kure Atoll and functioned as our diving platform. On August 9, we loaded our equipment and provisions onto a G-1 turboprop aircraft for the five-hour flight and arrived at Midway, cautiously silent in our optimism, unwilling to jinx the effort.

This time we came equipped with a magnetometer, on contract with Panamerican Consultants in Memphis, Tennessee. All we needed was calm seas on the east side to allow us to pull the towfish close to the reef. After two days of weather delay at Midway, we made the crossing and navigated through the western entrance toward the beach landing at Green Island. Research vessels calling at Kure always brought critical provisions, for facilities at the small cinderblock (former Coast Guard) buildings were simple and primitive. Two pit toilets, a small propane stove, solar oven, and some photovoltaic cells that provide a trickle charge to a series of batteries make up the infrastructure. An Iridium satellite phone was the only link with the outer world. Water came in jerry cans (no rusty condenser on the beach). Except for *Manacat*'s temporary duty in the northwestern atolls, there was no vessel at Midway capable of making the run to Kure at all. Both locations were far beyond the range of any helicopter from the main Hawaiian Islands. And the runway on Kure from the atoll's Coast Guard days was long out of commission. If there were a medical emergency, or a powerful storm approaching, the refuge staff would be as trapped as Commander Sicard and his men had been in 1870. We offloaded water and a variety of fresh, canned, and dried foods, and received a warm welcome. Green Island is one of the most peaceful places on earth, and the extraordinary beauty of the wildlife, the lagoon, and dark blue sea beyond is a phenomenon that ultimately cannot be captured in any photograph or description. The low scrub has reclaimed most of the changes made to the island over time, and the birds and seals and wind render the setting not at all unlike that which greeted the sodden *Saginaw* crew. To visit the atoll is to go far back in time. No visible trace of the 1870 castaway camp remained on the surface of the sands, but this was the spot.

We rigged the magnetometer and navigation equipment. We swam the inside reef border, seeking a debris trail leading toward the north point of the island. We documented the crash site of a Sikorsky helicopter. And we waited for the seas to come down on the east side. From the island we could see distant geysers of white water jumping skyward as the huge ocean swells impacted the reef. They leapt upward from the horizon like silent flashes of white diamonds in the sunshine. Distant but forceful, they were the teeth that guarded the wreck site. Sicard's assessment was beginning to look all too correct.

Soon enough, though, the seas did calm down, and the magnetometer towfish splashed into the water at the start of the first and most crucial survey lane closest to the reef. Through the clear water we could see the multicolored coral heads in profusion. Rather than a linear feature, the reef crest was actually a reef crest zone, the contours of which seemed random and fractal. There was no firm outline. The path twisted and curved in and out of fissures and crevices, and constantly the large swells, rising precipitously as the bottom shoaled, broke over the shallow points. Any attempt to pull the magnetometer too close to the reef itself would assuredly put *Manacat* aground and break her. We were looking for a shipwreck, and so had to go into the places where shipwrecks happen, but we didn't need to become one ourselves.

Discovery in 2003

The magnetometer anomaly map, depicting targets in gamma or magnetic force, showed no trace of any heavy iron artifact, though we had covered the search area to the best of our abilities for two miles north and south of the historic position of the wreck. It did not appear that the boilers, or engines or other heavy material had moved seaward at all, the atoll slope perhaps rolling artifacts into deeper water, as we had conjectured. This was, to say the least, a disappointment, for we were counting on some signal to indicate the proper position of the site, and serve as the starting point for the search on scuba. We guessed that the wreckage must have been pounded into the fissures of the reef crest zone itself, too far in to the coral maze for the towfish to detect. As in 2002, we fell back on the old standby method. We splashed the divers.

It seems to be a cliché, but nonetheless it's the truth: Discoveries seem to always occur at the last possible moment. The weather was beginning to fall apart. Dark North Pacific clouds rolled in on the horizon. And there we were, donning dive gear and jumping into the seaward swell at the northern limit of our search zone. The plan was to move reefward from our drop-off point, hug the bottom in the surge, and head south, investigating every spur and groove in that tortuous contour for any trace of the wreck. It was a long shot again, but the plan was simple, and simple is good. We were visually searching for traces of the past. *Manacat* stood off to seaward, farther from the breakers, following our towed buoy southward. The underwater topography was beautiful but rugged. Clearly, the reef zone was an immense and permeable structure, over which the ocean swells filled the lagoon with water, and then through which, in a series of tunnels and passages, the water flowed back outside to sea. It was a maze.

This was the exposed side of the atoll, and only the strongest corals and largest fish existed here in the powerful surge. Pairs of Galapagos and white-tip reef sharks came and went, eying us and moving on. The ulua were more persistent, dogging our fin tips like packs of dogs, and instinctively we tucked in our fingers to avoid the potential bite. The ulua struck our red, torpedo-shaped buoy in large vertical arcs, shooting up like silver bullets and hitting the plastic float. We worked our way in toward the reef to the 15-foot contour, where the horizontal movement of the ocean swell began to take on a vertical component. Shallower than that, diving became too dangerous under the conditions and our progress to the south would become impossible. Even this close inspection within the contour of the maze would be hit-or-miss.

We covered more than two miles in this fashion. And just as we were beginning to run low on air at the end of our dive, we crossed the first indication of a wreck site. Ironically, the first trace consisted of some of the smallest artifacts remaining from the ship. These were tiny brass nails, sheathing tacks, once used to secure the sheets of copper to the wooden hull planks. Over the years, the loose tacks had been swept into a small bowl-like depression in the reef. Kelly signaled to Brad and me. These were the most beautiful sheathing tacks we had ever seen. At the same time, Tony saw two large iron anchors framed at the entrance to a cavern. These were lying on top of one another and unshackled (see fig. 34). Too small to be the main bower anchors, they may have been secondary stream anchors stored in the hold. Very quickly the underwater camera and folding

FIGURE 34. USS *Saginaw*'s anchors near the initial impact site, the area discovered in 2003. Courtesy of NOAA Office of National Marine Sanctuaries.

ruler came out for some quick documentation. And then we heard Tony's dive signal buzzing excitedly. Near the anchors lay a small encrusted iron cannon, which couldn't have been more than four or five feet in length, similar to a 24-pounder short howitzer (see fig. 35).

We were scientists; we were supposed to remain calm and systematic in our documentation of the resource. That did not really happen. My heart was pounding in my chest, and I made a conscious attempt to control my breathing and save some air. Judging from the clouds of bubbles pouring from the other members of the team, we all were doing the same. We were being pushed back and forth against the reef by a 10-foot surge with each wave. And we were carefully watching our air supply, needing to save a 500 psi reserve for absolute emergencies only. Cameras were out, photo scales were out, and we did our best to hold on in the surge and capture photographs of the wreckage at the same time. Near the site lay a heavy bronze gudgeon strap, the hardware that held the rudder to the ship's sternpost. More spikes, and copper drift pins (the fasteners for the timbers of a wooden hull) were scattered on the bottom. A second deteriorated iron cannon, shaped like the first, lay in a crevice. And, one

FIGURE 35. An encrusted 24-pdr broadside cannon, one of two located. Four were carried on board the ship. Courtesy of NOAA Office of National Marine Sanctuaries.

of the most ironic artifacts found on wreck sites, the ship's sounding lead lay on the coralline substrate. This was the heavy lead that the crew had unfortunately not been using to sound the depths, for in their estimation they were nowhere near any navigational hazard.

These few things were only a scattered portion of the wreck site. All were consistent with the remains of USS *Saginaw*, but what we had seen was only a tantalizing piece of the whole, and it was time to go. We gathered together and kicked into the swells for deeper water, leaving the torpedo float to mark the wreck's position. At the surface the ocean had kicked up appreciably. Don shouted to us to make it quick, and we swam for the dive ladder. *Manacat* pulled away from the breakers after retrieving the float and taking a GPS fix, and we were out of there. The dive on the site had lasted approximately ten minutes. We spent our remaining time at Kure Atoll watching the white geysers jump skyward on the eastern crest, prevented by the passing storm from returning to the seaward site.

Of course, we could approach the location from the west, from the lagoon side, now that we had the coordinates of the initial artifacts. The vessel's draft was less than two feet, but the back reef lagoon on the atoll's eastern side is extremely shallow. The boat took us within a quarter mile of the breakers, and from there we swam and pulled ourselves into the current, the water coming in over the top of the reef from the east, flowing constantly like a river across a broad table. The corals in the back reef, more protected than those found outside, are both more abundant and more fragile, and it took careful navigation to make the trip to the site while avoiding contact. Before we reached the emergent reef crest, though, we came across a debris trail, scattered rigging hardware, davits, pipes, fasteners, and of course a plethora of unidentifiable pieces, all of which had been blown inside the lagoon by the prevailing seas. This was the area where the men stood on October 30, 1870, loading the ship's boats with provisions and passing weary jokes up and down the line about the nonedible nature of their provisions. We used hand-held GPS units, carried in waterproof cases, and underwater cameras, to begin to document the back reef scatter. At the crest zone, we hauled ourselves onto the tough coralline substrate, patches of an irregularly shaped surface bordered by the towering surf that now was a constant roar in our ears. We could only search a portion of the crest area. The noise and the proximity of the breakers made it a little like looking for artifacts next to a waterfall. One particularly angular-looking piece, though, caught our eye. A broken iron boiler face, torn from its brass tubes, lay on the reef. This was a feature that we could measure and sketch in place, matching its design eventually to the triple-grate Martin Company water-tube boilers carried by USS *Saginaw* (see fig. 36). And then our time was over. With another break in the weather, *Manacat* made the run back to Midway, and we flew home to Honolulu.

A certain amount of site assessment could be completed, even though the amount of time spent on the site in 2003 had been fairly brief. There were two general areas of dispersed artifacts. The first consisted of two cannon, two anchors, gudgeon, fasteners, tacks, and sounding lead lying immediately seaward, and underneath, the reef crest itself. The second area was approximately 550 feet south of the first and consisted of the boiler face, anchor fragments, fasteners, and rigging hardware, and other remains. These were scattered on top of the reef crest and in the adjacent back reef zone within the lagoon. The nature of the artifact collection was consistent with that of a wooden hull navy steamship, battered and broken in the high-energy environment of a windward reef setting. There were no other similar vessels reported lost at Kure, and the location of the wreck site coincided with historical reports. Furthermore, these two distribution areas seemed to confirm the historical report of *Saginaw*'s loss.

FIGURE 36. The author standing near the Martin boiler face on the reef. Courtesy of NOAA Office of National Marine Sanctuaries.

The ship initially went aground bow first onto the reef. Then, while being reoriented bow to seaward, at some point the stern broke away (moving south) and fell over on the reef, while the bow remained in deeper water. The location, the cannon, and the type of boiler face confirmed the site's identity. USS *Saginaw* had been found, a little bit of the world of 1870.

Completing the Survey

Finding a ship capable of crossing 1,200 miles of open ocean, conducting diving survey, and returning safely to port was not easy then, and is not easy today. Fortunately, in 2004, NOAA dedicated an entire research vessel to the growing effort to monitor the resources of the atolls, a ship specifically fitted out for conducting scientific diving operations at remote Pacific sites. The NOAA ship *Hi'ialakai* (Pathways to the Sea) is a former navy ship, a renovated T-AGOS–class submarine hunter that once spent long weeks and months at sea towing a sonar array and listening for Russian and Chinese submarines. She now carries a complete recompression chamber, numerous dive lockers, showers, rinse tanks, computer and wet labs, etc. The ship is 220 feet in length, and provides the scientists with a professional crew of officers, deckhands, and coxswains—and the chief steward serves up the best chow in the fleet. In all ways, the ship is exactly suited for science in the Pacific, so time and space on board are precious commodities, and the process for allocating science missions and choosing destinations and assembling collaborative multidisciplinary working teams begins years in advance of the actual cruise.

In 2004, there was no opportunity for archaeologists to return to Kure Atoll and the wreck site. In 2005, the team was on board *Hi'ialakai*, but by the time we got to Kure, the white geysers on the reef had returned, prohibiting all access to the main wreck site. That year we focused on surveying the nineteenth-century whaling ships discovered at Kure and at Pearl and Hermes atolls. It was not until 2006 that we had a chance again of getting back to the wreck of USS *Saginaw*, three years after our initial exciting ten minutes on site. And despite Sicard's warning, in early July of that year we finally found our "three days" when, as he predicted, it would be safe enough to work on the wreck. And even then the site provided some of the most dynamic conditions we've ever encountered.

Once again, we had applied for the appropriate research permit through the Papahānaumokuākea Marine National Monument, meaning our project had been reviewed by State of Hawai'i, U.S. Fish and Wildlife, NOAA resource managers, and the public. We had cleared our proposed noninvasive survey through the Naval Historical Center's Underwater Archaeology Branch, for as a navy ship, the wreck of USS *Saginaw* remains property of the federal government. These were important steps, for cultural material can be a significant resource, and the site is protected by the Abandoned Shipwreck Act, the Sunken Military Craft Act, the Antiquities Act, and other archaeological preservation legislation. And who is more bound to obey the preservation mandates than the resource managers themselves? Our goal was to complete the in situ survey of USS *Saginaw*, retrieving data from the field prior to proposing the careful recovery of any of the historic artifacts.

Our 2006 team consisted of myself and fellow NOAA divers Tane Casserley, Robert Schwemmer, Kelly Gleason, and Brenda Altmeier. Lindsey Thomas joined the team as a maritime archaeology intern via NOAA's Hollings Scholarship summer program. As we were again a "piggyback" mission on a multidisciplinary expedition, we had the opportunity to conduct work at a series of other sites prior to arriving at Kure Atoll. At Pearl and

Hermes, the maritime heritage team completed the in situ survey of the British whaler *Pearl*, discovered in 2004 by the NOAA Fisheries Service marine debris divers. The try pots, anchors, cannon, tools, and other scattered artifacts of the British whaler lay in a shallow sand groove. Their distribution told the story of a ship grounding hard into the reef (pressing the keel and garboard strakes into the substrate beneath the sand) and falling apart in place, the heavy iron cauldrons used to render the whale oil falling through the ship and trapping the copper sheathing in crumpled pieces beneath them against the reef. Additionally, the team investigated an unidentified wreck site (also discovered by NOAA Fisheries divers) called the "Oshima" site, after the style of anchors diagnostic to the wreck. The in situ survey of the American whaler *Parker* at Kure Atoll was also completed. All surface artifacts were mapped and inventoried, and surveys of the surrounding areas revealed the wreckage trail right through the reef crest, where the whaling vessel came through during a violent storm relatively intact, losing only the topside tryworks and try pots at the passage before coming to settle in the shallows of the lagoon.

At Kure, the refuge manager's staff had suddenly discovered the site of the ship *Dunnottar Castle*, crossing a shoal area on the western side of the lagoon in their skiff and coming across a field of large iron debris. We conducted a preliminary survey, using cameras and rough sketches to capture the early outlines of this large site. But our priority was set on USS *Saginaw* and, as the weather permitted, we worked the site as much as was physically possible.

That year an odd short stretch of extremely calm weather coincided with Hi'ialakai's research schedule, and we ended up at Kure Atoll looking with disbelief at a mirror-flat sea, our ship barely rolling over its glassy surface. The winds had dropped, and the constant ocean swells relaxed. It seemed ominously calm, like the eye of a hurricane, as if the Pacific were just waiting to come roaring back. But we lost no time in taking advantage of the weather and headed directly to the eastern reef crest.

Beginning with the known site coordinates, we relocated the anchors and small cannon, and confirmed that the small collection of features found in 2003 comprised everything in that particular location. We completed our documentation there, noting a large encrusted feature, an amorphous shape covering numerous other objects, and showing patches of active rust corrosion. We'd seen these iron humps before near the bows of wreck sites, piles of chain, released from their triangular lockers as the wood deteriorates over time. Could this be the remains of the ship's chain locker? *Saginaw*'s lockers had been located a little farther aft, not in the forepeak of the ship.

To be thorough, we then worked our way over and into several of the adjacent grooves to the north, swimming over the ridges during a lull in the swells, and then hugging the bottom of the valley or groove, moving reefward into the shallows, ultimately going under the whitewater of the surf zone. The atoll is ringed by an alternating miniature ridge and valley system. These spurs and grooves channel the water back to sea. At their deeper open ends, they flatten onto the atoll slope. Toward the reef they end in the complicated maze of shallow tunnels and crevices. No artifacts were found north of the initial site. The boiler face found in 2003 lay to the south, so the spurs and grooves between the anchors and boiler then became our main search area. Even with the calm seas, the swells still built at the heads of the channels and broke into surf, tumbling into the lagoon at the wreck site. As with the *Manacat* in 2003, *Hi'ialakai*'s jet-drive dive boat dropped our team near the reef, then moved seaward away from the surf to stand by for the pickup. Live-boating was the best alternative, for there was not a bit of sand or holding ground on the flat-swept substrate on that east side, and there was no need to drop anchor and possibly damage the bottom.

After investigating several of the grooves to the south, we again picked up the debris trail. Pieces of broken copper and brass items appeared firmly embedded into the bottom. Naturally, this location was called "Brass Alley." Working our way up this groove in teams, we pressed reefward to the surge limit, to the point where it was all we could do to brace against the rushing water, bubbles from our regulators streaming alternately into the tunnel to the lagoon or out to sea. Just out of reach lay a large piece of heavily encrusted equipment, a square block of some type with large bolt heads on one side. There was no way to climb over it and reach the other side. The next day, though, the seas and surge had dropped a bit, and we could creep forward a little more. The block was one end of a large trunnioned cylinder, one of *Saginaw*'s oscillating steam engines; its connecting rod emerged intact from the far end. The rough measurements matched the historic descriptions of *Saginaw*'s machinery. And rough measurements were all we could manage. We had taped off sections of PVC pipe in 10-centimeter intervals, and filled these pipes with heavy sand for weight, their ends sealed with epoxy. These scales were the only tools with a chance of holding their position on the bottom; all other tools were simply too light and subject to being blown away in the surf. Cameras and

FIGURE 37. A diver searching the surge channels near the reef crest and surf zone. Courtesy of NOAA Office of National Marine Sanctuaries.

photo scales were the main tools used to document features and artifacts in the dynamic reef maze. Almost all other measurements proved impossible in the surging waters beneath the surf.

"Brass Alley" was renamed "Engine Alley," leading to more copper and bronze artifacts closer to the reef. The thin brass tubes found in so many different locations seemed to be boiler tubes. The brass piston for the bilge pump lay between the ridges. Some of *Saginaw*'s wreckage emerged directly from the walls of the ridges themselves. The reef-formation process, which involved calcium carbonate sediments being trapped by the tough reef coralline algae, had overgrown the wreck, and there was no telling how much of the site was completely inside the reef itself. The search continued. At times, we were uncertain if we were seaward of the reef crest, under the reef crest itself, or even somewhere on the lagoon side of the tunnels (see fig. 37). Our greatest difficulty was estimating a position for any of these major features toward the reef. We were safe enough at the surface over deeper water, but no one could chance getting to the surface for a fix with a GPS unit anywhere near the main features in the surf. And these GPS units were only accurate to an approximate position at best, rendering a location within, perhaps, a circle some 30 feet in diameter.

Over the divers closer to the reef crest was the tumbling whitewater, like violent storm clouds at ceiling level. In other words, the standard accurate site plan, produced from careful measurements using grids and baselines, would not be possible on this site. We were there to simply do the best we could.

More artifacts appeared in adjacent grooves. Brass engine parts had been trapped in crevices (see fig. 38). At the head of another groove, locked into the reef and covered with tough coralline algae, lay one of the large, heavy, Parrott rifled cannon. Needless to say, this groove became "Gun Alley." One by one, we took turns attempting to brace near the breech end, waiting for the moment to snap a picture—a moment the water wasn't

FIGURE 38. Brass and bronze steam engine components pushed into crevices within the reef crest. Courtesy of NOAA Office of National Marine Sanctuaries.

FIGURE 39. The ship's bell discovered underwater 136 years after the loss of the ship. Courtesy of NOAA Office of National Marine Sanctuaries.

filled with aeration—and then make our escape. Deck fittings were scattered in the fold near the cannon. Also, the breech end of what looked like a brass 12-pounder, a boat howitzer, was discovered nearby. (A second 12-pounder? One 12-pounder was recorded as being salvaged and carried by SS *Kilauea* back to Honolulu.) And, in a small cave, the ship's bell lay upside down and half buried with reef cobbles, the crown of the bell cracked (see fig. 39). This, to us, was a sight both touching and rare, unquestionably an object of some reverence.

Nearby, we found the heavy solid iron paddle-wheel shaft and hubs. They were immense, a testimony to nineteenth-century steam power. And yet the shaft had snapped in midsection, between the webs for the connecting rods. The shallow cove in the reef was accessible only from the lagoon side, the seaward edge being sealed by whitewater. In "Paddle Wheel Cove" also lay the second Parrott rifled cannon, along with components of its pivot carriage, and a small anchor and one of the pintles, or hinges, from the rudder (see fig. 40). Undoubtedly, the second of the steam cylinders and the heavy components of the engine's A-frame were located somewhere in this area, as well as pieces of the second Martin boiler. Perhaps they would be the target of some future survey, though the chances of meeting with such excellent weather again are slim, and we found no sign of them in 2006.

In these difficult conditions under the surf zone adjacent to the seaward reef crest, the 2006 team discovered and photographed all of the remaining and accessible major elements of the navy steamer USS *Saginaw*, including bow and stern Parrott rifled pivot guns, 24-pounder broadside howitzers, steam oscillating engine, port and starboard paddle-wheel shafts, rim of paddle wheel, anchors, brass steam machinery, boiler tubes, boiler face, rigging components, ship's bell, fasteners, rudder hardware, davits, sounding lead, and other material remains (see fig. 41). No major wood components were located on the wreck site. If they exist at all, they are perhaps buried by sediments inside the lagoon, protected from the hungry teredo ship worm. The majority of credit for this survey work goes to my fellow members of the 2006 maritime team, for putting themselves into some amazing and difficult positions and literally going (safely) into

FIGURE 40. One of the two 30-pdr Parrott rifled pivot guns. Both were found by the divers. Courtesy of NOAA Office of National Marine Sanctuaries.

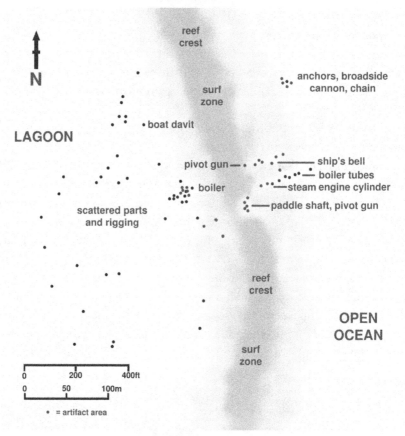

FIGURE 41. Distribution of artifacts and major features at the wreck site, eastern reef crest of Kure Atoll. Courtesy of NOAA Office of National Marine Sanctuaries.

harm's way in order to record the historic wreck within the reef crest (see fig. 41). At this point, the survey of the wreck site represents all that can be expected to be safely achieved on scuba under normal conditions.

The ocean is a powerful force, capable of breaking and scattering the heaviest pieces of our nineteenth-century warships. USS *Saginaw*, once aground, didn't have a chance. The location of the sheet anchors (and possibly the chain locker) and two of the 24-pounder howitzers confirms the report of the loss of the bow. Could these items have been heaved overboard, the anchors and chain and cannon and all, in an attempt to lighten the ship and bring it off the reef? Possibly, but there is no record of that having happened, and the navy documents go into every action that occurred that night. This location is, then, the initial impact site. The heavy bronze gudgeon, hardware from the stern of the ship, rests near these

FIGURE 42. The 2006 NOAA site survey team on board the NOAA ship *Hi`ialakai*. *Left to right:* Lindsey Thomas, Kelly Gleason, Tane Casserley, Hans Van Tilburg, Brenda Altmeier, and Robert Schwemmer. Courtesy of NOAA Office of National Marine Sanctuaries.

items from the bow, but this is not that unusual. *Saginaw* locked her bow in the reef and pounded her stern in this location, breaking off the rudder and tearing away the gudgeon strap from the sternpost and hull. On several other sites, we have seen rudder hardware located near bow components. They are usually the first things to go. The rudder itself came off this site and either drifted south or remained partially attached to the ship's stern as it moved. One of the rudder's pintles, or hinges, was found at "Paddle Wheel Cove." A second pintle was found inside the lagoon.

The components of the midships section, including the engine room, were carried farther south after the broken vessel pivoted and turned broadside on the reef. There the stern section fell apart, dropping its heavy equipment into the fissures of the reef crest. Portions of the boiler and paddle wheels remained above the water for some time, as recorded by the ship's officers, but have since then been reduced over the course of 135 years. The majority of the back reef debris scatter is lagoon-ward of this midships and stern location, and this is where *Saginaw*'s crew risked their lives working over the remains of the wreck. Some of the debris in the lagoon, however, including what appears to be a boat davit, is farther north, inward from the initial impact site. During the early minutes of the wreck, the ship's launch was carried away by a wave, davits and all, and swept into the lagoon. This davit and debris may be from that loss.

No wreck site survey is complete without its mysteries and unanswered questions, and the most obvious of these is simply: How did the forward Parrott rifled pivot gun end up hundreds of feet away to the south from the bow section? It's no surprise that the aft gun lies in "Paddle Wheel Cove," but the forward gun is in "Gun Alley," near the oscillating steam cylinder. The position of the Parrott pivot, from the deck plans, is forward of the main mast and forward of the chain locker below, right up on the foredeck. When the bow section breaks off just forward of the hurricane deck, according to the historical record, how does the 3,500-pound cannon move itself south? Did a portion of the bow (buoyant enough to carry the gun) drift off on its own?

If the ocean, in its capriciousness and power, ever allows us to return and continue work on the USS *Saginaw* site, perhaps more of the wreck's features may be located, or those already found in the surge-tossed gullies might be more accurately fixed in position (though it's hard to imagine how). For now, the site has been documented to the point where the archaeological data can contribute to the story. These physical resources capture a portion of our maritime heritage, items associated with the history of Midway, a heroic open-boat voyage, and the stepping-stones of a young navy in the Pacific. For the site, the next step is to investigate the potential for a nomination to the National Register of Historic Places. Given the necessary budget, selected artifacts from the site can be recovered, properly conserved, and shared with the public as a way of remembering the men and officers of *Saginaw* and our own seafaring past in the Pacific.[30]

Early Pacific Passages and the Museum of the Sea

In a way, these artifacts at Kure Atoll are like the single Boston hard-hat diver blasting his own way through the coral reef at Midway in 1870. The artifacts tell the story of a single small step in what was to become a much larger national project. Back in the nineteenth century, America was a young and bold—some would say brash—nation making its first real strides into the Pacific, and it did so with the ships and tools of an antiquated steam navy, for the country was a self-acknowledged second-rate power seeking its place in the world. America was not then what it was to later become. U.S. Navy officers had been trained in the Mexican-American War and the American Civil War, and were then sliding (some gracefully, others less so) into their postwar peacetime careers. Navy ships could barely carry enough coal to get them from point A to point B, and commanders were uncertain if, when they got there, there would be any fuel available for them to be able to get back. The navy was working to put sail back into service, and penalized commanders for raising steam. America had a fuel-hungry and budget-poor navy then. The need for coal, and supplies of it in the proper locations, drove much of the political and territorial agenda in the Pacific.

But, with these small steps, the nation seemed intent on conducting itself on the world's stage at least as an equal member to all others, if not better. Americans may have been brash, but they certainly were early, and had begun implementing their national vision for the Pacific in many cases before the U.S. Navy could truly see it through to completion. America moved forward with individual vessels, small ships like the third-class, fourth-rate USS *Saginaw*. The days of the modern steam navy and the concentration of the great fleets, as promoted by strategist Captain Alfred Thayer Mahan, had yet to arrive. Nonetheless, the United States refused to be left out of events in places like China, though the nation was clearly on the sidelines of the Opium War conflict and not a direct combatant in that empire's confrontation with the West. Americans rode the coattails of its allies into the treaty ports of the South China coast. No doubt that was a difficult position for commanders like James Findlay Schenck, Josiah Tattnall, and others. And then, with the American Civil War, the U.S. flag temporarily vanished from the South China Sea as the United States could not at that time sustain its presence in East Asia.

In Mexico, the U.S. secretary of state walked a tightrope with his hands tied behind his back during the nation's internal conflict. Fortunately, France's plans for Maximilian I and their New World empire collapsed on their own, and the U.S. Navy in the Pacific remained focused only on access to the isthmus at Panama. Again, America was on the fringe of someone else's war. Commanders William Hopkins and Robert Scott fought the tropical diseases there more than they did any Mexican revolutionary or French mercenary. And just as well, because the Pacific Fleet was not in any condition to challenge any navy on the Pacific coast at the time. Two harsh realities dictated life in the Pacific Squadron between 1860 and 1870:

the primary role of the wartime blockade for the eastern and Gulf states, and the massive downsizing of the U.S. Navy in the years following the conflict. And still, the handful of navy vessels spread over thousands of miles of ocean were somehow able to fulfill their assigned missions.

Following the Civil War, attention was focused on Reconstruction, and no new funds were available from Congress for supporting an overseas navy. America was a domestic power, with its eyes set on harbor and coastal defense. The American merchant marine that had existed prior to 1861, scattered in ports like Hong Kong and Shanghai and Nagasaki, had been lost to foreign registries, and navy ships were being laid up. *Saginaw*, though, was fortunate enough to find a reason to continue service. The nation stood at the doorway of the former Russian territory of Alaska, and was just beginning to realize the resources possessed by the Far North. The steamer's duties there were not easy, for the government did not commit the necessary resources to challenge the freewheeling smuggling trade for many years. Commanders John Mitchell and Richard Meade did what they could, but USS *Saginaw* could not be everywhere at once. Conflicts erupted, for America was not yet a presence there to be respected.

The national relationship with the Kingdom of Hawai`i was different. Certainly, as with the cases above, *Saginaw*'s attempt to transform Midway into a strategic depot in the middle of the Pacific was far ahead of its time. Midway would become that critical location, but the curtailed 1870 project to open the harbor was followed by three decades of inactivity. In hindsight, the importance of the major events played out at Midway is clear, and *Saginaw* will forever be tied to that history at the remote atoll, and the shipwreck and rescue voyage part of the maritime heritage of the Northwestern Hawaiian Islands.

For the main Hawaiian Islands, USS *Saginaw*'s presence was only one part of a larger trend in emerging American dominance as a whole, one that was plain for all to see. And it was a trend that led to the overthrow of the islands and ultimately the annexation of the Kingdom in the decades following *Saginaw*'s tour. Had the Midway project been, in part, an attempt to establish a depot that would have bypassed the Kingdom as the foreign merchants in Honolulu feared, obviating any need for a permanent naval presence at Honolulu or Pearl Harbor? Commander Montgomery Sicard provided the Navy Department with a more accurate estimate of what such an undertaking at Midway might require, and more importantly, a more precise description of the nature of Midway Atoll than what they had been led to believe.

Many great changes were on the horizon in the mid-nineteenth century, and USS *Saginaw* was a part of these coming changes, in as bold and brash a manner as a small fourth-rate gunboat could be. Therefore it is only fitting that her bones rest in the geographic middle of the North Pacific, and are still on the site of the ship's tragic loss. If she had been sent to an unfamiliar breaker's yard for dismantling and salvage, a part of the nation's common maritime heritage would have ceased to exist. Better that the sea claim *Saginaw* and she rest in peace, for that is where the ship belongs. The pristine waters of the world's most remote atoll are a fitting place for her tomb.

For the small gunboat USS *Saginaw*, the sea was a highway, and over the years of her service she crossed thousands of miles of open ocean. But the sea was also a barrier, a kind of ever-present test. And it only took one small mistake, one miscalculation involving an unknown current, to end the ship's career in a slow-motion instant. This is the way it has always been, no matter if the ships are built from California laurel trees or welded in steel. Bad things happen on the oceans; shipwrecks happen. They always have, and they always will. *Saginaw*'s story, though, remains intact. For the archaeologists and historians whose stock in trade is the business of inventorying and assessing these kinds of resources, these sites contain a record of the past like no other, to be shared with the public. They open the door on a maritime legacy in the Pacific Ocean, like an underwater museum of the real world.

Notes

Chapter 1. A New Ship for a New Ocean

1. Hayward, "A Gazetteer of the United States of America."

2. Delgado, *To California by Sea*, 48.

3. Canney (quoting Schufeldt report, April 1870), *Old Steam Navy*, 282.

4. Barnes (quoting Hegel), *A History of Historical Writing*, 196.

5. Franke (quoting von Ranke), *China and the West*, 142.

6. Canney, *Old Steam Navy,* 71.

7. *Report of the Secretary of the Navy*, 1858.

8. Norris and Griffiths to Toucey, June 18, 1858, U.S. Navy Subject File, Record Group 45, NAB (National Archives Building, Washington, D.C.).

9. Cunningham to Bureau of Construction, July 17, 1858, U.S. Navy Subject File, Record Group 45, NAB.

10. McCleary, "Nineteenth-Century Building Instructions," 142.

11. In 1863, following refit, *Saginaw*'s armament expanded to include one Dahlgren 50-pounder rifle, one 32-pounder, and two 24-pounder rifled cannon (see *Saginaw* ZB file, Naval Historical Center, Washington, D.C.). At the time of the ship's loss in 1870, *Saginaw* carried two Parrott 30-pounder rifled cannon and four 24-pounder broadside cannon (see Baldwin, "Narrative of William Halford," 1287).

12. *Saginaw* ZB file, Naval Historical Center, Washington, D.C.

13. Donahue, January 10, 1859, Records of the U.S. General Accounting Office, Navy Contracts 1795–1893, Record Group 217, NAB.

14. Canney, *Old Steam Navy*, 88.

15. McCleary, "Nineteenth-Century Building Instructions," 149.

16. Hubbard, *Vallejo*, 348.

17. Zadwick, "The Early Days of Mare Island's Naval History," 2.

18. "A Visit to Mare Island," December 13, 1857, History Subject File, Naval District 12, Record Group 181, NARA—Pacific Region (San Francisco).

19. Ibid. The writer for the *Daily Alta California* was taken on a tour of the shipyard by naval constructor Isaiah Hanscom, the builder of *Saginaw*.

20. *Milwaukee Daily Sentinel*, August 4, 1869.

21. *New York Herald*, January 15, 1860.

22. Ibid.

23. Ibid.

24. *San Francisco Daily Evening Bulletin,* January 30, 1860.

25. Cunningham to Toucey, January 31, 1860, excerpt in *Boston Daily Advertiser,* March 9, 1860.

26. *Pacific Commercial Advertiser,* March 22, 1860.

27. Teng, *Americans and the Taiping Rebellion.*

28. Ward to Cass, February 13, 1860, Despatches from United States Ministers to China (National Archives Microfilm M92, roll 20), Record Group 59, NAB.

Chapter 2. Seasoning on the China Station

1. Toucey to Stribling, June 10, 1859, Confidential and Other Letters, Telegrams, and Cablegrams, 1843–1886, Record Group 45, NAB.

2. Franklin, *Memories of a Rear Admiral,* 14.

3. Spence, *The Search for Modern China,* 180.

4. December 15, 1869, Confidential and Other Letters, Telegrams, and Cablegrams 1843–1886, Record Group 45, NAB.

5. Johnson, *Far China Station,* 107.

6. Ward to Cass, February 18, 1860, Despatches from United States Ministers to China (National Archives Microfilm M92, roll 20), Record Group 59, NAB.

7. *Pacific Commercial Advertiser,* March 22, 1860.

8. August 19, 1860, Medical Journals of Ships, 1813–1910 (*Saginaw*), Record Group 52, NAB.

9. Ibid., March 21, 1860.

10. Stribling to Walloch, May 9, 1860, Squadron Letters 1841–1886 (National Archives Microfilm M89), Record Group 45, NAB.

11. Smith to Cass, April 26, 1860, Despatches from United States Ministers to China (National Archives Microfilm M112, roll 5), Record Group 59, NAB.

12. Ibid., November 3, 1860.

13. Ward to Cass, September 3, 1860, Despatches from United States Ministers to China (National Archives Microfilm M92, roll 20), Record Group 59, NAB.

14. Teng, *Americans and the Taiping Rebellion,* 223.

15. Spence, *God's Chinese Son,* 279.

16. October 15, 1860, Medical Journals of Ships, 1813–1910 (*Saginaw*), Record Group 52, NAB.

17. Ibid.

18. Stribling to Toucey, September 1, 1860, Squadron Letters 1841–1886 (National Archives Microfilm M89), Record Group 45, NAB.

19. September 25, 1860, Medical Journals of Ships, 1813–1910 (*Saginaw*), Record Group 52, NAB.

20. Stribling to Toucey, October 3, 1860, Squadron Letters 1841–1886 (National Archives Microfilm M89), Record Group 45, NAB.

21. Harris to Cass, December 27, 1860, Despatches from United States Ministers to Japan (National Archives Microfilm M133), Record Group 59, NAB.

22. Stribling to Toucey, September 18, 1860, Squadron Letters 1841–1886 (National Archives Microfilm M89), Record Group 45, NAB.

23. Ibid.

24. Harris to Cass, February 14, 1860, Despatches from United States Ministers to Japan (National Archives Microfilm M133), Record Group 59, NAB.

25. Ibid., August 1, 1860.

26. Mayers, Dennys, and King, *The Treaty Ports of China and Japan*, 596.

27. Harris to Cass, March 10, 1861, Despatches from United States Ministers to Japan (National Archives Microfilm M133), Record Group 59, NAB.

28. Ibid., February 13, 1861.

29. Harris to Cass, November 7, 1860, Squadron Letters 1841–1886 (National Archives Microfilm M89), Record Group 45, NAB.

30. Finlay (surgeon) to Stribling, November 28, 1860, Squadron Letters 1841–1886 (National Archives Microfilm M89), Record Group 45, NAB.

31. Records of General Courts Martial and Courts of Inquiry of the Navy Dept., 1799–1867 (National Archives Microfilm M273), Record Group 125, National Archives Building, Washington, D.C. Prior records indicate that Commander Schenck lacked marines on board in Shanghai; a contingent may have been added to the Japan cruise.

32. Westcott to Stribling, December 10, 1860, Squadron Letters 1841–1886 (National Archives Microfilm M89), Record Group 45, NAB.

33. Ibid.

34. Schenck to Toucey, December 28, 1860, Squadron Letters 1841–1886 (National Archives Microfilm M89), Record Group 45, NAB.

35. Ibid.

36. Lowndes to Stribling, December 19, 1860, Squadron Letters 1841–1886 (National Archives Microfilm M89), Record Group 45, NAB.

37. Stribling to Toucey, December 14, 1860, Squadron Letters 1841–1886 (National Archives Microfilm M89), Record Group 45, NAB.

38. Day to examining board, July 9, 1864, Records of the Office of the Judge Advocate General, Examining Board Files, 1861–1903, Record Group 125, NAB.

39. Stribling to Schenck, January 11, 1861, Squadron Letters 1841–1886 (National Archives Microfilm M89), Record Group 45, NAB.

40. Stribling to Toucey, March 13, 1861, Squadron Letters 1841–1886 (National Archives Microfilm M89), Record Group 45, NAB.

41. Stribling miscellaneous papers, Area File of the Naval Records Collection 1775–1910 (National Archives Microfilm M625), Record Group 45, NAB.

42. Ibid.

43. Spence, *God's Chinese Son*, 290–91.

44. McCarter (translating Taiping response), May 28, 1861, Despatches from United States Ministers to China (National Archives Microfilm M92, roll 20), Record Group 59, NAB.

45. Ibid.

46. Teng, *Americans and the Taiping Rebellion*, 189.

47. Spence, *God's Chinese Son*, 303.

48. Ibid., 304.

49. *Saginaw* Deck Log, May 15, 1861, Record Group 24, NAB.

50. Stribling to Toucey, May 28, 1861, Squadron Letters 1841–1886 (National Archives Microfilm M89), Record Group 45, NAB.

51. June 8, 1860–June 10, 1861, Medical Journals of Ships, 1813–1910 (*Saginaw*), Record Group 52, NAB.

52. Stribling to Schenck, June 26, 1861, Squadron Letters 1841–1886 (National Archives Microfilm M89), Record Group 45, NAB.

53. Schenck to Stribling, July 5, 1861, Squadron Letters 1841–1886 (National Archives Microfilm M89), Record Group 45, NAB.

54. Stribling to Lowndes, June 30, 1861, Entry 608 (subentry 92), Journals and Remark Books of George C. Remey (June 14, 1859–November 30, 1861), Record Group 45, NAB.

55. *San Francisco Daily Evening Bulletin*, October 9, 1861.

56. Merchants to Engle, August 3, 1861, Squadron Letters 1841–1886 (National Archives Microfilm M89), Record Group 45, NAB.

57. Engle to Welles, August 5, 1861, Squadron Letters 1841–1886 (National Archives Microfilm M89), Record Group 45, NAB.

58. Schenck to Welles, August 8, 1861, Letters Received from Commanders 1804–1886 (National Archives Microfilm M147), Record Group 45, NAB.

59. June 21, 1861, Medical Journals of Ships, 1813–1910 (*Saginaw*), Record Group 52, NAB.

60. Schenck to Welles, August 17, 1861, in Rush and Woods, *War of the Rebellion*, 1:68.

61. Schenck to Welles, November 27, 1861, Letters Received from Commanders 1804–1886 (National Archives Microfilm M147), Record Group 45, NAB.

62. Ibid, December 13, 1861.

63. "Affairs at Hong Kong," *New York Times*, March 29, 1862.

64. Mallory to Bulloch, January 20, 1862, in Rush and Woods, *War of the Rebellion*, 2:133–34.

65. Bulloch to Mallory, April 11, 1862, in Rush and Woods, *War of the Rebellion*, 2:183–85.

66. Schenck to Welles, February 12, 1862, Letters Received from Commanders 1804–1886 (National Archives Microfilm M147), Record Group 45, NAB; Welles to Schenck, February 13, 1862, Letters Sent to Officers 1798–1868 (National Archives Microfilm M149), Record Group 45, NAB.

67. Welles to Gardner, February 15, 1862, Letters Sent to Officers 1798–1868 (National Archives Microfilm M149), Record Group 45, NAB.

68. Welles to Schenck, March 24, 1862, Letters Sent to Officers 1798–1868 (National Archives Microfilm M149), Record Group 45, NAB.

69. Schenck to Welles, March 28, 1862, Letters Received from Commanders 1804–1886 (National Archives Microfilm M147), Record Group 45, NAB.

70. *San Francisco Daily Evening Bulletin*, February 22, 1862.

71. Carr, *Devil Soldier*, 191.

72. McDougal to Welles, April 13, 1862, in Rush and Woods, *War of the Rebellion*, 1:373.

73. Seward to Adams, April 16, 1862, in *Claims against Great Britain Transmitted to the Senate of the United States*, vol. 1.

74. Ibid., August 14, 1862.

75. Watkins to Welles, May 10, 1862, in Rush and Woods, *War of the Rebellion*, 1:387.

76. Franklin, *Memories of a Rear Admiral,* 203

77. *Emancipator and Republican*, April 11, 1850.

78. *San Francisco Daily Evening Bulletin,* July 5, 1862.

79. Welles to Watkins, August 8, 1862, excerpt in *Boston Daily Advertiser*, November 5, 1862.

80. *San Francisco Daily Evening Bulletin,* January 2, 1868.

Chapter 3. The Civil War on the Pacific Coast

1. *Daily National Intelligencer,* March 16, 1846.

2. Ibid.

3. Welles to Bell, January 8, 1862, Confidential and Other Letters, Telegrams, and Cablegrams, 1843–1886, Record Group 45, NAB.

4. Bissell to Welles, April 14, 1862, in Rush and Woods, *War of the Rebellion*, 1:379.

5. Welles to Gardner, August 20, 1862, Letters Sent to Officers 1798–1868 (National Archives Microfilm M149), Record Group 45, NAB.

6. Selfridge to Bell, February 20, 1863, in Rush and Woods, *War of the Rebellion*, 2:95.

7. Hopkins, ZB File, Naval Historical Center, Washington, D.C.

8. Welles to Montgomery, April 27, 1861, Confidential Letters and Telegrams Sent, 1861–1876, Record Group 45, NAB.

9. Wasserman, *Everyday Life and Politics in Nineteenth Century Mexico,* 125.

10. Bell to Welles, February 25, 1863, Squadron Letters 1841–1886 (National Archives Microfilm M89), Record Group 45, NAB.

11. Callahan, *American Foreign Policy in Mexican Relations*, 301

12. *Saginaw* Deck Log, March 23, 1863, Record Group 24, NAB.

13. Johnson, *Thence Round Cape Horn,* 130.

14. www.legendsofamerica.com/CA-Alcatraz.html.

15. Hunt, "The Pacific Squadron of 1861–1866," www.militarymuseum.org/Pac%20 Sqdn.html. Excerpt from Hunt, *Army of the Pacific,* 2004.

16. Dunn, *The Diplomatic Protection of Americans in Mexico,* 4.

17. Selfridge to Hopkins, March 26, 1863, in Rush and Woods, *War of the Rebellion*, 2:141.

18. Selfridge to Welles, April 2, 1863, in Rush and Woods, *War of the Rebellion*, 2:140.

19. *Saginaw* Deck Log, March 28–29, 1863, Record Group 24, NAB.

20. Selfridge to Hopkins, April 23, 1863, in Rush and Woods, *War of the Rebellion*, 2:165.

21. Francis to Hopkins, May 13, 1863, in Rush and Woods, *War of the Rebellion* 2:260.

22. Ibid.

23. *Saginaw* Deck Log, May 3–30, 1863, Record Group 24, NAB.

24. Bell to Welles, May 25, 1863, in Rush and Woods, *War of the Rebellion*, 2:215.

25. *Saginaw* Deck Log, June 24–July 6, 1863, Record Group 24, NAB.

26. Valley, *Rocks and Shoals*, 83.

27. Wilson to Seward, July 29, 1863, General Records of the Department of State (National Archives Microfilm T395), Record Group 59, NAB.

28. *Saginaw* Deck Log, August 31–September 7, 1863, Record Group 24, NAB.

29. Ibid., September 29, 1863.

30. Welles to Bell, October 13, 1863, Confidential and other Letters, Telegrams, and Cablegrams, 1843–1886, Record Group 45, NAB.

31. Ibid., January 14, 1864.

32. http://freepages.misc.rootsweb.com/~ssgoldengate/.

33. Bell to Welles, January 20, 1864, Squadron Letters 1841–1886 (National Archives Microfilm M89), Record Group 45, NAB.

34. Ibid.

35. *San Francisco Daily Evening Bulletin*, January 27, 1864.

36. Blake to Seward, April 23, 1864, General Records of the Department of State (National Archives Microfilm M295), Record Group 59, NAB.

37. Whelan, January 25, 1864; Records of General Courts Martial and Courts of Inquiry of the Navy Dept., 1799–1867 (National Archives Microfilm M273), Record Group 125, NAB.

38. Court of Inquiry, January 25, 1864, Records of General Courts Martial and Courts of Inquiry of the Navy Dept. 1799–1867 (National Archives Microfilm M273), Record Group 125, NAB.

39. Ely to Seward, September 19, 1863, General Records of the Department of State (National Archives Microfilm M143), Record Group 59, NAB.

40. Court Martial, January 13, 1864, Records of General Courts Martial and Courts of Inquiry of the Navy Dept. 1799–1867 (National Archives Microfilm M273), Record Group 125, NAB.

41. Blake to Seward, January 28, 1864, General Records of the Department of State (National Archives Microfilm M295), Record Group 59, NAB.

42. Bell to Welles, February 3, 1864, Squadron Letters 1841–1886 (National Archives Microfilm M89), Record Group 45, NAB.

43. Ibid., March 19, 1864.

44. Ibid.

45. Ibid, February 3, 1864.

46. Bell to Hopkins, February 15, 1864, Squadron Letters 1841–1886 (National Archives Microfilm M89), Record Group 45, NAB.

47. Carman to Corwin, April 13, 1864, General Records of the Department of State (National Archives Microfilm M159), Record Group 59, NAB.

48. Bell to Welles, July 6, 1864, Squadron Letters 1841–1886 (National Archives Microfilm M89), Record Group 45, NAB; Ely to Seward, June 5, 1864, General Records of the Department of State (National Archives Microfilm M143), Record Group 59, NAB; *Saginaw* Deck Log, June 3, 1864, Record Group 24, NAB.

49. Bell to Hopkins, October 10, 1864, Squadron Letters 1841–1886 (National Archives Microfilm M89), Record Group 45, NAB.

50. *Saginaw* Deck Log, September 24, 1864, Record Group 24, NAB.

51. Mallory to Hogg, May 7, 1864, in Rush and Woods, *War of the Rebellion*, 3:356.

52. Savage to McKee, October 1, 1864, General Records of the Department of State

(National Archives Microfilm M139), Record Group 59, NAB; Dow to Arrizer, November 6, 1864, in Rush and Woods, *War of the Rebellion*, 3:360; McKee to Seward, November 14, 1864, General Records of the Department of State (National Archives Microfilm M139), Record Group 59, NAB.

53. McKee to Seward, November 14, 1864, General Records of the Department of State (National Archives Microfilm M139), Record Group 59, NAB.

54. Ibid., November 5, 1864.

55. Davenport to Pearson, November 12, 1864, in Rush and Woods, *War of the Rebellion*, 3:355.

56. Dow to Hoadley, November 15, 1864, in Rush and Woods, *War of the Rebellion*, 3:363–64.

57. Ibid.

58. McLane to Seward, January 17, 1865, in Rush and Woods, *War of the Rebellion*, 3:409–10.

59. Pearson the Welles, November 24, 1864, in Rush and Woods, *War of the Rebellion*, 3:364.

60. McLane to Seward, January 17, 1865, Rush and Woods, *War of the Rebellion*, 3:409–10.

61. Allen to Seward, January 3, 1865, in Rush and Woods, *War of the Rebellion*, 3:411.

62. *Saginaw* Deck Log, December 6–7, 1864, Record Group 24, NAB.

63. Ibid., November 24, 1864.

64. Poor to Pearson, November 25, 1864, in Rush and Woods, *War of the Rebellion*, 3:392.

65. Miller, *Mexico: A History*, 19.

66. Hanna and Hanna, *Napoleon III and Mexico*, 299.

67. Carman to Seward, January 12, 1865, General Records of the Department of State (National Archives Microfilm M159), Record Group 59, NAB.

68. *Daily Dramatic Chronicle*, April 17, 1865.

69. Welles to Pearson, August 3, 1865, Confidential and Other Letters, Telegrams, and Cablegrams 1843–1886, Record Group 45, NAB.

70. William Whittle, August 2, 1865, in *The Voyage of the CSS Shenandoah*, 182.

71. Minor to Seward, March 11, 1865, in Rush and Woods, *War of the Rebellion*, 3:484–85.

72. Wasserman, *Everyday Life and Politics in Nineteenth Century Mexico*, 74.

Chapter 4. Hard Times on Coastal Patrol

1. www.rudyalicelighthouse.net/CalLts/MareIs/MareIs.htm.

2. Elmer to Seward, June 6, 1865, General Records of the Department of State (National Archives Microfilm M282), Record Group 59, NAB.

3. Dabbs, *The French Army in Mexico*, 143.

4. Ibid., 152.

5. Ibid., 165.

6. Miller, *Mexico: A History*, 246.

7. *New York Times*, February 12, 1886.

8. *Saginaw* Deck Log, August 21, 1865, Record Group 24, NAB.

9. Pearson to Welles, September 15, 1865, Squadron Letters 1841–1886 (National Archives Microfilm M89), Record Group 45, NAB.

10. Cole to Seward, October 10, 1865, General Records of the Department of State (National Archives Microfilm M143), Record Group 59, NAB.

11. Stevenson, *Maximilian in Mexico,* 78.

12. Cole to Seward, February 17, 1866, General Records of the Department of State (National Archives Microfilm M143), Record Group 59, NAB.

13. Conner to Seward, November 3, 1865, General Records of the Department of State (National Archives Microfilm M284), Record Group 59, NAB.

14. *San Francisco Daily Evening Bulletin,* January 16, 1866.

15. Ibid.

16. McDougal to Pearson, November 17, 1865, Letters Sent to the Commander in Chief and Officers of the Pacific Squadron 1863–1907, Mare Island Navy Yard 1854–1940, Record Group 181, NARA—Pacific Region (San Francisco).

17. Welles to Pearson, November 17, 1865, Confidential and Other Letters, Telegrams, and Cablegrams 1843–1886, Record Group 45, NAB.

18. Ibid., January 27, 1866.

19. *New York Times,* February 12, 1886.

20. *Saginaw* Deck Log, January 5–6, 1866, Record Group 24, NAB.

21. Wilson and Fiske, *Appleton's Cyclopedia of American Biography,* 536.

22. Franklin, January 20, 1885, Records of the Office of the Judge Advocate General, Examining Board Files, 1861–1903, Record Group 125, NAB.

23. Franklin, *Memories of a Rear Admiral,* 203.

24. McDougal to Pearson, April 7, 1866, Letters Sent to the Commander in Chief and Officers of the Pacific Squadron 1863–1907, Mare Island Navy Yard 1854–1940, Record Group 181, NARA—Pacific Region (San Francisco).

25. Ibid., April 28, 1866.

26. Franklin, *Memories of a Rear Admiral,* 205.

27. Welles to Thatcher, May 22, 1866, Confidential and Other Letters, Telegrams, and Cablegrams 1843–1886, Record Group 45, NAB.

28. *Saginaw* Deck Log, April 16, 1866, Record Group 24, NAB.

29. Ibid., July 18, 1866.

30. Ibid., July 19–20, 1866.

31. www.eh.net/bookreviews/library/0434.shtml.

32. Gough, *The Royal Navy and the Northwest Coast of North America,* 207.

33. Thatcher to Welles, November 1, 1866, Squadron Letters 1841–1886 (National Archives Microfilm M89), Record Group 45, NAB.

34. Franklin, *Memories of a Rear Admiral,* 211.

35. Ibid.

36. Ibid., 214.

37. www.arlingtoncemetery.net/ttcraven.htm.

38. Stevenson, *Maximilian in Mexico,* 130.

39. Parker to Russell, October 10, 1867, Letters Sent to Officers of Naval Vessels at the Yard 1865–1868, Mare Island Naval Yard 1854–1940, Record Group 181, NARA—Pacific Region (San Francisco).

40. www.sfgenealogy.com/sf/history/hbtbc9.htm.

41. Elmer to Seward, July 3, 1866, Despatches from United States Ministers to China (National Archives Microfilm M282), Record Group 59, NAB.

42. *Saginaw* Deck Log, January 5, 1868, Record Group 24, NAB.

43. Francis, *A History of World Whaling*, 122.

44. Scanlan (testimony), February 6, 1868, Squadron Letters 1841–1886 (National Archives Microfilm M89), Record Group 45, NAB.

45. Ibid.

46. *Saginaw* Deck Log, February 20, 1868, Record Group 24, NAB.

47. Welles to Mitchell, March 16, 1868, Letters Sent to Officers 1798–1868 (National Archives Microfilm M149), Record Group 45, NAB.

48. *Saginaw* Deck Log, March 13, 1868, Record Group 24, NAB.

49. Sprout and Sprout, *The Rise of American Naval Power*, 166.

50. Buhl, "Mariners and Machines," 722.

51. Sprout and Sprout, *The Rise of American Naval Power*, 173.

52. Franklin, *Memories of a Rear Admiral*, 203–4.

Chapter 5. Exploring Seward's Icebox

1. http://en.wikipedia.org/wiki/Alaska_Purchase.

2. Ibid.

3. Lain, "North of Fifty-three," 13.

4. Ibid., 27.

5. Ibid., 121.

6. *Saginaw* Deck Log, April 14–18, 1868, Record Group 24, NAB.

7. DeArmond, *USS Saginaw in Alaska Waters*, 1.

8. Ibid., 3.

9. April 17, 1868, Medical Journals of Ships, 1813–1910 (*Saginaw*), Record Group 52, NAB.

10. Ibid., April 29 and May 3, 1868.

11. DeArmond, *USS Saginaw in Alaska Waters*, 116.

12. Lain, "North of Fifty-three," 135.

13. Ibid., 118.

14. Ibid., 19.

15. DeArmond, *USS Saginaw in Alaska Waters*, 9–10.

16. *Port Townsend Weekly Message*, May 7, 1868, quoted in DeArmond, *USS Saginaw in Alaska Waters*, 11.

17. DeArmond, *USS Saginaw in Alaska Waters*, 13.

18. Ibid.

19. Ibid., 14.

20. Teichmann (report), quoted in DeArmond, *USS Saginaw in Alaska Waters*, 15.

21. Meade, quoted in DeArmond, *USS Saginaw in Alaska Waters*, 129.

22. DeArmond, *USS Saginaw in Alaska Waters*, 19.

23. Ibid., 20–21.

24. Lain, "North of Fifty-three," 137.

25. DeArmond, *USS Saginaw in Alaska Waters*, 24.

26. Meade, quoted in DeArmond, *USS* Saginaw *in Alaska Waters*, 128.

27. DeArmond, *USS* Saginaw *in Alaska Waters*, 118.

28. Ibid., 24.

29. Ibid.

30. Meade to Craven, December 26, 1868, Squadron Letters 1841–1886 (National Archives Microfilm M89), Record Group 45, NAB.

31. Lain, "North of Fifty-three," 142.

32. July 12, 1868, Medical Journals of Ships, 1813–1910 (*Saginaw*), Record Group 52, NAB.

33. Ibid., July 5, 1868.

34. Ibid., July 9, 1868.

35. Ibid., September 12, 1868.

36. Craven to Welles, October 3, 1868, Squadron Letters 1841–1886 (National Archives Microfilm M89), Record Group 45, NAB.

37. *Alaska Herald*, November 1, 1868.

38. Alden to Welles, November 2, 1868, Copies of Letters Sent to the Secretary of the Navy from the Commandant's Office, Mare Island Naval Yard 1854–1940, Record Group 181, NARA—Pacific Region (San Francisco).

39. Meade, Records of the Office of the Judge Advocate General, Examining Board Files, 1861–1903, Record Group 125, NAB.

40. Ibid.

41. Ibid.

42. DeArmond, *USS* Saginaw *in Alaska Waters*, 35.

43. Ibid., 40.

44. November 8 and 20, 1868, Medical Journals of Ships, 1813–1910 (*Saginaw*), Record Group 52, NAB.

45. Meade to Craven, December 26, 1868, Squadron Letters 1841–1886 (National Archives Microfilm M89), Record Group 45, NAB.

46. DeArmond, *USS* Saginaw *in Alaska Waters*, 47.

47. Meade to Craven, December 26, 1868, Squadron Letters 1841–1886 (National Archives Microfilm M89), Record Group 45, NAB.

48. Ibid.

49. Craven to Welles, January 6, 1869, Squadron Letters 1841–1886 (National Archives Microfilm M89), Record Group 45, NAB.

50. Welles to Craven, December 5, 1868, Confidential and Other Letters, Telegrams, and Cablegrams, 1843–1886, Record Group 45, NAB.

51. Meade to Craven, December 26, 1868, Squadron Letters 1841–1886 (National Archives Microfilm M89), Record Group 45, NAB.

52. Ibid., January 2, 1869.

53. Ibid., February 1, 1869.

54. Ibid.

55. Ibid.

56. Meigs, quoted in DeArmond, *USS* Saginaw *in Alaska Waters*, 83.

57. January 31, 1869, Medical Journals of Ships, 1813–1910 (*Saginaw*), Record Group 52, NAB.

58. Meade to Craven, February 24, 1869, Squadron Letters 1841–1886 (National Archives Microfilm M89), Record Group 45, NAB.

59. Ibid.

60. Pillsbury to Meade, February 16, 1869, Squadron Letters 1841–1886 (National Archives Microfilm M89), Record Group 45, NAB.

61. Bridge to Meade, February 16, 1869, Squadron Letters 1841–1886 (National Archives Microfilm M89), Record Group 45, NAB.

62. Meade to Craven, February 24, 1869; Squadron Letters 1841–1886 (National Archives Microfilm M89), Record Group 45, NAB.

63. DeArmond, *USS* Saginaw *in Alaska Waters,* 95.

64. Meade to Craven, February 24, 1869, Squadron Letters 1841–1886 (National Archives Microfilm M89), Record Group 45, NAB.

65. Borie to Craven, March 17, 1869, Confidential and Other Letters, Telegrams, and Cablegrams 1843–1886, Record Group 45, NAB.

66. Ibid., March 15, 1869.

67. Craven to Borie, March 23, 1869, Squadron Letters 1841–1886 (National Archives Microfilm M89), Record Group 45, NAB.

68. Sprout and Sprout, *The Rise of American Naval Power,* 165–66.

69. *Daily Cleveland Herald,* December 18, 1868.

70. *Irish World and American Industrial Liberator,* May 25, 1895.

71. *Milwaukee Sentinel,* May 21, 1895.

72. *Hawaiian Gazette,* May 28, 1895.

73. Ibid.

Chapter 6. Hawai`i and the End of the Archipelago

1. Sicard to Craven, April 14, 1869, Squadron Letters 1841–1886 (National Archives Microfilm M89), Record Group 45, NAB.

2. Borie to Craven, April 23, 1869, Confidential and Other Letters, Telegrams, and Cablegrams, 1843–1886, Record Group 45, NAB.

3. Porter to Turner, June 11, 1869, Confidential and Other Letters, Telegrams, and Cablegrams, 1843–1886, Record Group 45, NAB.

4. *Saginaw* Deck Log, June 24, 1869, Record Group 24, NAB.

5. Turner to Borie, June 30, 1869, Squadron Letters 1841–1886 (National Archives Microfilm M89), Record Group 45, NAB.

6. Landauer and Landauer, *Pearl: The History of the United States Navy in Pearl Harbor,* 60.

7. Taylor, "The American Navy in Hawai`i," 916.

8. Landauer and Landauer, *Pearl: The History of the United States Navy in Pearl Harbor,* 96.

9. Taylor, "The American Navy in Hawai`i," 917.

10. www.history.navy.mil/docs/wwii/pearl/Hawai`i.htm. Texts at this site are excerpts from *Administrative History of the Fourteenth Naval District and the Hawaiian Sea Frontier.*

11. Taylor, "The American Navy in Hawai`i," 917.

12. www.history.navy.mil/docs/wwii/pearl/Hawai`i.htm.

13. Brooks, "Our Furthest Outpost," 828.

14. Ibid.

15. *Pacific Commercial Advertiser*, January 28, 1871.

16. Whitney, *Scribner's Monthly*, April 1871.

17. Read, *Last Cruise of the* Saginaw, 10.

18. *Report of the Secretary of the Navy*, 1868.

19. Brooks, "Our Furthest Outpost," 828.

20. Kuykendall, *Hawaiian Kingdom*, 2:169.

21. Robeson to Turner, October 12, 1869, Confidential and Other Letters, Telegrams, and Cablegrams 1843–1886, Record Group 45, NAB.

22. Brooks, "Our Furthest Outpost," 828.

23. Sicard to Robeson, December 1, 1869, Officers Letters 1802–1884 (National Archives Microfilm M148), Record Group 45, NAB.

24. *Galveston Daily News*, June 28, 1877.

25. Turner to Robeson, February 6, 1870, Squadron Letters 1841–1886 (National Archives Microfilm M89), Record Group 45, NAB.

26. *Saginaw* Deck Log, February 10, 1870, Record Group 24, NAB.

27. *Saginaw* muster roll, January 1, 1870, Records of the Bureau of Naval Personnel, Record Group 24, NAB.

28. *Independent Statesman*, August 4, 1879.

29. Entry 232, Records of the Accounting Officers of the Treasury of the United States, Records of the U.S. General Accounting Office, Navy Contracts 1795–1893, Record Group 217, NAB.

30. Ibid.

31. Brooks, "Our Furthest Outpost," 828.

32. Much of the following biographical information is gleaned from: ZB File, Naval Historical Center; Records of the Office of the Judge Advocate General (Examining Board Files, 1861–1903), Record Group 125; Officers Promotion and Retirement Board Files, Record Group 125; and Abstracts of Service Records of Naval Officers, 1829–1924 (National Archives Microfilm M1328), Record Group 24, NAB.

33. Read, *Some Descendants of John Read, Senior*, 56.

34. Talbot, Officers Promotion and Retirement Board Files, Record Group 125, NAB.

35. Ibid.

36. *Saginaw* muster roll, January 1, 1870, Records of the Bureau of Naval Personnel, Record Group 24, NAB.

37. Putney, *Black Sailors*, 12.

38. *Pacific Commercial Advertiser*, March 12, 1870.

39. *Saginaw* Deck Log, March 12, 1870, Record Group 24, NAB.

40. *Pacific Commercial Advertiser*, June 18, 1870.

41. *Friend*, October 1864, 76.

42. Ibid., November 1864, 32.

43. *Hawaiian Gazette*, March 23, 1870.

44. *Pacific Commercial Advertiser*, April 10, 1869.

45. Turner to Sicard, February 14, 1870, Collection 777, Floyd Family Papers, Division of Rare and Manuscript Collections, Cornell University Library.

46. *Saginaw* Deck Log, March 25–27, 1870, Record Group 24, NAB.

47. Ibid, April 7–May 7, 1870.

48. *Pacific Commercial Advertiser,* January 21, 1871.

49. Sicard to Turner, April 16, 1870, Squadron Letters 1841–1886 (National Archives Microfilm M89), Record Group 45, NAB.

50. Blye (Townsend Construction Journal), Squadron Letters 1841–1886 (National Archives Microfilm M89), Record Group 45, NAB.

51. Sicard to Turner, April 16, 1870, Squadron Letters 1841–1886 (National Archives Microfilm M89), Record Group 45, NAB.

52. *Saginaw* Deck Log, May 14, 1870, Record Group 24, NAB.

53. Ibid., June 18, 1870.

54. Sicard to Turner, July 21, 1870, Officers Letters 1802–1884 (National Archives Microfilm M148), Record Group 45, NAB.

55. Ibid.

56. Sicard to Winslow, September 22, 1870, Officers Letters 1802–1884 (National Archives Microfilm M148), Record Group 45, NAB.

57. Sicard to Turner, July 21, 1870, Officers Letters 1802–1884 (National Archives Microfilm M148), Record Group 45, NAB.

58. *Pacific Commercial Advertiser,* January 28, 1871.

59. *Idaho Daily Avalanche,* April 11, 1876.

60. *Saginaw* Deck Log, September 29, 1870, Record Group 24, NAB.

Chapter 7. The Castaways of Ocean Island

1. October 21, 1870, Medical Journals of Ships, 1813–1910 (*Saginaw*), Record Group 52, NAB.

2. Blye (Townsend Construction Journal), Squadron Letters 1841–1886 (National Archives Microfilm M89), Record Group 45, NAB.

3. Robeson to Winslow, October 5–6, 1870, Confidential and Other Letters, Telegrams, and Cablegrams, 1843–1886, Record Group 45, NAB.

4. Winslow to Robeson, November 8, 1870, Squadron Letters 1841–1886 (National Archives Microfilm M89), Record Group 45, NAB.

5. Robeson to Goldsborough, October 17, 1870, Copies of Letters Sent to the Secretary of the Navy from the Commandant's Office, Mare Island Naval Yard 1854–1940, Record Group 181, NARA—Pacific Region (San Francisco).

6. *Report of the Secretary of the Navy,* 1871, 207.

7. Beck, *Folklore and the Sea,* 6.

8. Read, *Last Cruise of the* Saginaw, 13.

9. Garst, February 7, 1871, Court of Inquiry Records (*Saginaw*), Case no. 4643, Record Group 125; NAB.

10. Ibid.

11. Ibid.

12. Robinson, February 7, 1871, Court of Inquiry Records (*Saginaw*), Case no. 4643, Record Group 125, NAB.

13. Ibid.

14. Main, February 7, 1871, Court of Inquiry Records (*Saginaw*), Case no. 4643, Record Group 125, NAB.

15. Parsons, February 7, 1871, Court of Inquiry Records (*Saginaw*), Case no. 4643, Record Group 125, NAB.

16. Halford, cited in Lydgate, "Halford Interview."

17. Most of the details of the actual wreck of USS *Saginaw* come from: Report of the Secretary of the Navy 1871, 208–9; Read, *The Last Cruise of the Saginaw*, 19–30; *Saginaw* Deck Log, Record Group 24 (October 29, 1871); and Medical Journals of Ships, 1813–1910 (*Saginaw*), Record Group 52.

18. Halford, in Lydgate, "Halford Interview."

19. *Pacific Commercial Advertiser,* January 28, 1871.

20. Read, *Last Cruise of the* Saginaw, 27.

21. Ibid., 34.

22. *Saginaw* Deck Log, November 10, 1870, Record Group 24, NAB.

23. Ibid., October 31, 1870.

24. Read, *Last Cruise of the* Saginaw, 35.

25. *Saginaw* Deck Log, November 3, 1870, Record Group 24, NAB.

26. Robeson to Winslow, November 11, 1870, Confidential and Other Letters, Telegrams, and Cablegrams, 1843–1886, Record Group 45, NAB.

27. Parsons, November 12, 1870, Collection 777, Floyd Family Papers, Division of Rare and Manuscript Collections, Cornell University Library.

28. Cogswell, November 13, 1870, Collection 777, Floyd Family Papers, Division of Rare and Manuscript Collections, Cornell University Library.

29. Garst, November 12, 1870, Collection 777, Floyd Family Papers, Division of Rare and Manuscript Collections, Cornell University Library.

30. Read, November 13, 1870, Collection 777, Floyd Family Papers, Division of Rare and Manuscript Collections, Cornell University Library.

31. Frank, November 13, 1870, Collection 777, Floyd Family Papers, Division of Rare and Manuscript Collections, Cornell University Library.

32. Read, *Last Cruise of the* Saginaw, 47.

33. Sicard to Winslow, November 15, 1870, *Report of the Secretary of the Navy*, 1871, 187, 207–8.

34. Sicard to Robeson, November 16, 1870, Squadron Letters 1841–1886 (National Archives Microfilm M89), Record Group 45, NAB.

35. Sicard to Winslow, November 16, 1870, Squadron Letters 1841–1886 (National Archives Microfilm M89), Record Group 45, NAB.

36. Halford, cited in Lydgate, "Halford Interview."

37. November 18, 1870, Medical Journals of Ships, 1813–1910 (*Saginaw*), Record Group 52, NAB.

38. Halford's official record of service reports England as his place of birth; the *Saginaw*'s muster roll reports New York.

39. Halford, cited in Lydgate, "Halford Interview."

40. Sicard to Winslow, November 16, 1870, Squadron Letters 1841–1886 (National Archives Microfilm M89), Record Group 45, NAB.

41. Read, *Last Cruise of the* Saginaw, 62.

42. Ibid., 61.

43. Sicard to Brown, November 17, 1870, Papers of Montgomery Sicard, 1800–1948, Manuscript Division, Library of Congress, Washington, D.C.

44. Read, *Last Cruise of the* Saginaw, 66.

45. Ibid., 63.

46. Ibid., 67.

47. Halford, December 27, 1870, quoted in *Report of the Secretary of the Navy*, 1871, 213.

48. Halford, quoted in Read, *Last Cruise of the* Saginaw, 101–2.

49. Halford, quoted in Lydgate, "Halford Interview."

50. *Pacific Commercial Advertiser*, December 10, 1906.

51. Ibid.

52. Read, *Last Cruise of the* Saginaw, 111.

53. Ibid., 112.

54. Halford, quoted in Lydgate, "Halford Interview."

55. Lydgate, "The Wreck of the *Saginaw*."

56. Halford, quoted in Lydgate, "Halford Interview."

57. Lydgate, "The Wreck of the *Saginaw*"; and Paul Nitchman, communication with author, September 27, 2007.

58. Halford, December 27, 1870, quoted in *Report of the Secretary of the Navy*, 1871, 214.

59. Halford, quoted in Lydgate, "Halford Interview."

60. Halford, August 10, 1870, quoted in *Report of the Secretary of the Navy*, 1871, 214.

61. Peirce to Sicard, December 26, 1870, Collection 777, Floyd Family Papers, Division of Rare and Manuscript Collections, Cornell University Library.

62. Ibid.

63. Kuykendall, *Hawaiian Kingdom*, 2:167.

64. Peirce to Sicard, December 26, 1870, Collection 777, Floyd Family Papers, Division of Rare and Manuscript Collections, Cornell University Library.

65. *Kilauea* Logbook, December 26, 1870, Log 232, Manuscripts Collection, G. W. Blunt White Library, Mystic Seaport Museum.

66. January 7, 1871, Medical Journals of Ships, 1813–1910 (*Saginaw*), Record Group 52, NAB.

67. Turner to Robeson, January 6, 1871, Squadron Letters 1841–1886 (National Archives Microfilm M89), Record Group 45, NAB.

68. Read, *Last Cruise of the* Saginaw, 59.

69. *Saginaw* Deck Log, November 21 and 28, 1870, Record Group 24, NAB.

70. Sicard to Winslow, February 9, 1871, *Report of the Secretary of the Navy*, 1871, 217.

71. *Pacific Commercial Advertiser*, January 28, 1871.

72. Sicard to Winslow, February 9, 1871, *Report of the Secretary of the Navy*, 1871, 217.

73. Read, *Last Cruise of the* Saginaw, 76.

74. Ibid., 79.

75. Ibid., 75.

76. December 2, 1870, Medical Journals of Ships, 1813–1910 (*Saginaw*), Record Group 52, NAB.

77. Ibid., December 16, 1870.

78. Sicard to Winslow, February 9, 1871, *Report of the Secretary of the Navy*, 1871, 218.

79. Winslow to Robeson, December 8, 9, and 16, 1870, Squadron Letters 1841–1886 (National Archives Microfilm M89), Record Group 45, NAB.

80. Sicard, December 5, 1870, Collection 777, Floyd Family Papers, Division of Rare and Manuscript Collections, Cornell University Library.

81. Parsons, Butterworth, Blye, Cogswell, December 5, 1870, Collection 777, Floyd Family Papers, Division of Rare and Manuscript Collections, Cornell University Library.

82. Read, *Last Cruise of the* Saginaw, 83.

83. Ibid., 86.

84. *Pacific Commercial Advertiser*, January 21, 1871.

85. Read, *Last Cruise of the* Saginaw, 87–88.

86. Ibid., 85.

87. January 4, 1871; Medical Journals of Ships, 1813–1910 (*Saginaw*), Record Group 52, NAB.

88. Peirce to Sicard, December 26, 1870, Collection 777, Floyd Family Papers, Division of Rare and Manuscript Collections, Cornell University Library.

89. Read, *Last Cruise of the* Saginaw, 91.

90. Sicard to Winslow, February 9, 1871; *Report of the Secretary of the Navy*, 1871, 219.

91. *Saginaw* Deck Log, January 5, 1871, Record Group 24, NAB.

92. Cogswell et al., January 7, 1871, Squadron Letters 1841–1886 (National Archives Microfilm M89), Record Group 45, NAB.

93. Sicard to Winslow, February 9, 1871, *Report of the Secretary of the Navy*, 1871, 219.

94. January 5, 1871, Medical Journals of Ships, 1813–1910 (*Saginaw*), Record Group 52, NAB.

95. *Saginaw* Deck Log, January 7–13, 1871, Record Group 24, NAB.

96. Winslow to Robeson, January 8, 1871, and Robeson to Winslow January 11, 1871, Squadron Letters 1841–1886 (National Archives Microfilm M89), Record Group 45, NAB.

97. *Saginaw* Deck Log, January 14, 1871, Record Group 24, NAB.

98. *Chicago Tribune*, January 16, 1871.

99. *Pacific Commercial Advertiser*, January 18, 1871.

100. Ibid., January 28, 1871.

101. Sicard to Robeson, January 18, 1871, *Report of the Secretary of the Navy*, 1871, 212.

102. Sicard to Winslow, February 13, 1871, Squadron Letters 1841–1886 (National Archives Microfilm M89), Record Group 45, NAB; Robeson to Winslow, February 13, 1871, Confidential and Other Letters, Telegrams, and Cablegrams 1843–1886, Record Group 45, NAB.

103. *Pacific Commercial Advertiser*, June 3, 1871.

104. Sicard to Robeson, January 18, 1871, *Report of the Secretary of the Navy*, 1871, 212.

105. Taylor to Winslow, February 11, 1871, *Report of the Secretary of the Navy*, 1871, 211.

106. Sicard to Mattoon, January 21, 1871, *Report of the Secretary of the Navy,* 1871, 216.

107. Sicard to Winslow, January 27, 1871, *Report of the Secretary of the Navy,* 1871, 215–16.

108. Sicard to Winslow, January 27, 1871, Squadron Letters 1841–1886 (National Archives Microfilm M89), Record Group 45, NAB.

109. Sicard to Winslow, January 27, 1871, *Report of the Secretary of the Navy,* 1871, 215.

110. Excerpt from *Hawaiian Gazette,* quoted in *Report of the Secretary of the Navy,* 1871, 209.

111. Ibid.

112. Kuykendall, *Hawaiian Kingdom,* 197.

113. February 1, 1871, Medical Journals of Ships, 1813–1910 (*Saginaw*), Record Group 52, NAB.

114. Court of Inquiry Records (*Saginaw*), Case no. 4643, Record Group 125, NAB.

115. Ibid.

116. *Friend,* March 1871, 12.

117. Court of Inquiry Records (*Saginaw*), Case no. 4643, Record Group 125, NAB.

118. Ibid.

119. Ibid.

120. Ibid.

Chapter 8. Afterword: Legacy and Shipwrecks

1. Special Order No. 4, included in Sicard, ZB File, Naval Historical Center, Washington, D.C.

2. Lydgate, "The Wreck of the Saginaw."

3. Paul Nitchman, communication with author, September 29, 2009.

4. Much of the following biographical information is gleaned from: ZB File, Naval Historical Center, Washington, D.C.; Records of the Office of the Judge Advocate General (Examining Board Files, 1861–1903), Record Group 125; Officers Promotion and Retirement Board Files, Record Group 125; and Abstracts of Service Records of Naval Officers, 1829–1924 (National Archives Microfilm M1328), Record Group 24, NAB.

5. Cogswell, Records of the Office of the Judge Advocate General (Examining Board Files, 1861–1903), Record Group 125, NAB.

6. *Daily Evening Bulletin,* June 22, 1875.

7. Cowles, Officers Promotion and Retirement Board Files, Record Group 125, NAB.

8. Robert Andrews to Sicard, November 22, 1871, Collection 777, Floyd Family Papers, Division of Rare and Manuscript Collections, Cornell University Library.

9. M. Dall to Sicard, October 26, 1871, Collection 777, Floyd Family Papers, Division of Rare and Manuscript Collections, Cornell University Library.

10. *New York Times,* November 27, 1883.

11. Paul Nitchman, communication with author, February 20, 2007.

12. Thrum, *Hawaiian Annual,* 1915; Gibbs, *Shipwrecks in Paradise,* 53–55; *Pacific Commercial Advertiser,* September 14, 15, and 30, 1886.

13. Apple, *Prehistoric and Historic Structures in the Hawaiian Islands,* 18.

14. Daws, *Shoal of Time,* 273; Kuykendall, *Hawaiian Kingdom,* 594.

15. Daws, *Shoal of Time,* 276.

16. Kuykendall, *Hawaiian Kingdom,* 594–95.

17. Rauzon, *Isles of Refuge,* 180.

18. Gibbs, *Shipwrecks in Paradise,* 53.

19. Rauzon, *Isles of Refuge,* 150; Gibbs, *Shipwrecks in Paradise,* 53–54; *Pacific Commercial Advertiser,* December 7, 1887.

20. *Pacific Commercial Advertiser,* June 12, 1888, and June 13 and 14, 1889.

21. Ibid., October 23, 1903.

22. Ibid., December 27, 1906.

23. *National Cyclopedia of American Biography.*

24. Fleet Salvage Officer to Commander Service Force, U.S. Pacific Fleet, February 15, 1944, Bureau of Ships General Correspondence 1940–45, USS *Macaw,* Record Group 19, National Archives, College Park, Md.

25. *Chicago Daily Inter Ocean,* January 29, 1889.

26. Information on many of the NOAA maritime heritage projects is available at: http://sanctuaries.noaa.gov/maritime/.

27. Sicard to Winslow, January 27, 1871, Squadron Letters 1841–1886 (National Archives Microfilm M89), Record Group 45, NAB.

28. Sicard to Winslow, November 15, 1870, *Report of the Secretary of the Navy,* 1871, 207–8.

29. Van Tilburg, "Maritime Cultural Resource Survey."

30. In 2008, a NOAA research team recovered the ship's bell and deep-sea sounding lead for conservation and public display at the NOAA Discovery Center in Hilo, Hawai'i.

References

Primary Sources

Bernice P. Bishop Museum: Henry M. Whitney letter, February 1871; various files and correspondence; Journal of Robert W. Andrews (SS *Kilauea*).

Brooks, Charles Walcott. "Our Furthest Outpost." *Old and New* (June 1870): 828–38.

Busk, Hans. *The Navies of the World: Their Present State and Future Capabilities*. London: Routledge, Warnes, and Routledge, 1859. Reprint, Annapolis: Naval Institute Press, 1973).

Cornell University Library Division of Rare and Manuscript Collections: Collection 777, Floyd Family Papers.

Franklin, Samuel R. *Memories of a Rear Admiral, Who Has Served for More Than Half a Century in the Navy of the United States*. New York: Harper and Brothers, 1898.

Hawai`i State Archives Interior Department Books.

Hayward, John. "A Gazetteer of the United States of America." Hartford: Case, Tiffany and Company, 1851. http://cprr.org/Museum/California_1851.html.

Library of Congress: Papers of Montgomery Sicard.

Lydgate, J. M. "Halford Interview" (notes). August 10, 1914. Kaua`i Historical Society Papers.

———. "The Wreck of the *Saginaw*: Notes on Halford's Story." Kaua`i Historical Society Papers, May 22, 1914.

Mayers, William Frederick, Nicholas B. Dennys, and LT Charles King. *The Treaty Ports of China and Japan: A Complete Guide to the Open Ports of Those Countries, Together with Peking, Yedo, Hongkong and Macao*. London: Trubner and Co., 1867.

McCleary, J. R. "Nineteenth-Century Building Instructions: USS *Saginaw*." *Nautical Research Journal* 45 (2000): 141–53.

McKee, Andrew. "The Wreck of the *Saginaw*." Manuscript, n.d. Vallejo Maritime Museum.

National Archives and Records Administration, College Park, Md., Record Group 19: Bureau of Steam Engineering, ship and equipment plans; *Saginaw* machinery contract Peter Donahue; Bureau of Ships General Correspondence 1940–45.

National Archives and Records Administration, Pacific Region (San Francisco), Record Group 181: Letters to Commandant Mare Island from Commander Pacific Squadron; Letters to Commander Pacific Squadron from Commandant Mare Island; Letters

Sent to Officers of Naval Vessels at the Yard from the Commandant's Office, Mare
Island Naval Yard 1854–1940; Letters Sent to the Secretary of the Navy from Commandant Mare Island; Letters Sent to the Commander in Chief and Officers of the
Pacific Squadron 1863–1907; Mare Island Navy Yard 1854–1940; shipyard logs; Reports Received and Forwarded Subject File: Mare Island Shipyard History.

National Archives and Records Administration, Washington, D.C., Record Group 24:
Deck logs USS *Saginaw;* Records of the Bureau of Naval Personnel.

———. Record Group 45, Office of Naval Records and Library: M-1328 service record abstracts; M-625 area files 9 and 10; M-149 letters sent by the secretary of the navy to officers; M-125 captains letters; M-147 commanders letters; M-148 officers letters; M-89
squadron letters; Correspondence 1798–1918; Confidential and Other Letters, Cablegrams, and Telegrams, and Cablegrams Sent to Commanding Officers of Squadrons
and Vessels; Confidential Letters and Telegrams Sent; Journals and Remark Books of
Midshipmen; Telegrams Sent to Naval Officers; Subject File Design and Construction
Letters (Isaac Toucey); Letters Received by the Secretary of the Navy from Captains
("Captains' Letters"); Letters Received by the Secretary of the Navy from Commanding Officers of Squadrons ("Squadron Letters"); Letters Received by the Secretary
of the Navy from Commanders, 1804–1886 ("Letters Received from Commanders");
Letters Sent by the Secretary of the Navy to Officers, 1798–1868 ("Letters Sent to
Officers"); Letters Received by the Secretary of the Navy from Commissioned Officers below the Rank of Commander and from Warrant Officers ("Officers' Letters,")
1802–1884.

———. Record Group 52, Medical Journals of Ships, 1813–1910: (*Saginaw*).

———. Record Group 59, General Records of the Department of State (U.S. consular despatches): M-143 Acapulco; M-159 Mazatlan; M-139 Panama; T-395 La Union; M-295
Manzanillo; M-282 La Paz; M-284 Guaymas; M-112 Shanghai; M-92 U.S. Ministers
to China; M-131 Nagasaki; M-133 U.S. Ministers to Japan; M-108 Hong Kong; M-144
Honolulu.

———. Record Group 125: Records of General Courts Martial and Courts of Inquiry of
the Navy Dept., 1799–1867 (National Archives Microfilm Publication M273); Records
of the Office of the Judge Advocate General; Examining Board Files, 1861–1903.

———. Record Group 217: Records of the Accounting Officers of the Treasury of the United States; Records of the U.S. General Accounting Office; Navy Contracts 1795–1893.

Naval Historical Center: ZB files (various commanders, officers, crew, ship data); Ships'
history file; Reports of the Secretary of the Navy, various years.

Read, George H. *The Last Cruise of the* Saginaw. Boston: Houghton-Mifflin, 1912.

———. *Some of the Descendants of John Read, Senior, of Newport, Rhode Island and
Freetown, Massachusetts, 1646–1924.*

Rush, Richard, and Robert H. Woods. *Official Records of the Union and Confederate Navies
in the War of the Rebellion.* Washington, D.C.: Government Printing Office, 1894.

Selfridge, Thomas O. *Memoirs of Thomas O. Selfridge Jr., Rear Admiral, USN.* New York:
G. P. Putnam's Sons, 1924.

J. Porter Shaw National Maritime Museum Library: *Saginaw* file.

Stevenson, Sara Yorke. *Maximilian in Mexico: A Woman's Reminiscences of the French*

Intervention, 1862 to 1867. New York: Century, 1899. Reprint, Whitefish, Mont.: Kessinger, 2004).

Thrum, Thomas G. *Hawaiian Annual* (various years). Bishop Museum.

United States Patent Office: Foster and Townsend Rock Drill.

Vallejo Naval and Maritime Museum: Bureau of Construction letter to Mare Island, detailing design and construction of USS *Saginaw*, 1858.

Welles, Gideon. *Diary of Gideon Welles*. Edited by Howard K. Beale. New York: Norton, 1960.

G. W. Blunt White Library at the Mystic Seaport Museum: SS *Kilauea* log.

Whittle, William C., Jr. *The Voyage of the CSS* Shenandoah: *A Memorable Cruise*. Tuscaloosa: University of Alabama Press, 2005 (modern publication of original journal).

Secondary Sources

Aiman, Eliece. "American Acquisition and Development of Minor Pacific Islands." Master's thesis, University of Chicago, 1944.

———. *National Cyclopedia of American Biography*. Clifton, N.J.: J. T. White, 1926.

Alden, Carroll S., and Allan Westcott. *The United States Navy*. Chicago: Lippincott, 1943.

Anonymous. "Middlebrook Islands Discovered." *Paradise in the Pacific* 48, no. 10 (1936): 23.

Apple, Russell A. *Prehistoric and Historic Structures in the Hawaiian Islands National Wildlife Refuge*. Honolulu: National Park Service, 1973.

Armon, Yehuda. *Ports around the World*. New York: Crown, 1980.

Baldwin, Hanson W. "Narrative of William Halford." *U.S. Naval Institute Proceedings* (July 1935): 1287–97.

Barnes, Harry Elmer. *A History of Historical Writing*. Norman: University of Oklahoma Press, 1938.

Beck, Horace. *Folklore and the Sea*. Edison, N.J.: Castle Books, 1999.

Bennett, Frank M. *The Steam Navy of the United States*. Pittsburgh: Warren and Co., 1896.

Brooke, George M., Jr. *John M. Brooke: Naval Scientist and Educator*. Charlottesville: University Press of Virginia, 1980.

———, ed. *John M. Brooke's Pacific Cruise and Japanese Adventure, 1858–1860*. Honolulu: University of Hawai`i Press, 1986.

Buhl, Lance C. "Mariners and Machines: Resistance to Technological Change in the American Navy, 1865–1869." *Journal of American History* 61, no. 3 (1974): 703–27.

Cable, James. *Gunboat Diplomacy: Political Applications of Limited Naval Force*. New York: Praeger, 1971.

Callahan, James Morton. *American Foreign Policy in Mexican Relations*. New York: Macmillan, 1932.

Canney, Donald L. *The Old Steam Navy: Frigates, Sloops, and Gunboats, 1815–1885*. Annapolis: Naval Institute Press, 1990.

Cardwell, Robert. "Pirate Fighters of the South China Sea." *National Geographic*, ser. 6, 89 (May 1946): 787–92.

Carr, Caleb. *The Devil Soldier*. New York: Random House, 1992.

Cole, Allen B. *Yankee Surveyors in the Shogun's Seas: Records of the United States Surveying*

Expedition to the North Pacific Ocean, 1853–1856. Princeton: Princeton University Press, 1947.

Dabbs, Jack Autrey. *The French Army in Mexico 1861–1867*. The Hague: Mouton, 1963.

Davids, Jules, ed. *American Diplomatic Public Papers: The United States and China*. Ser. 2, 1861–1893. Wilmington: Scholarly Resources, 1979.

Davis, William C. *The Last of the Conquistadores: The Spanish Intervention in Peru and Chile, 1863–1866*. Athens: University of Georgia Press, 1950.

Daws, Gavin. *Shoal of Time: A History of the Hawaiian Islands*. Honolulu: University of Hawai`i Press, 1968.

Day, A. Grove. "Strong Man of the Saginaw." *American Heritage* 2, no. 3 (1951): 13–16.

DeArmond, Robert N. *The USS Saginaw in Alaska Waters 1867–1868*. Fairbanks, Alaska: Limestone, 1997.

Delgado, James P. *To California by Sea: A Maritime History of the California Gold Rush*. Columbia: University of South Carolina Press, 1990.

Dominguez, Jorge, and Rafael Fernandez de Castro. *The United States and Mexico: Between Partnership and Conflict*. New York: Routledge, 2001.

Dunn, Frederick Sherwood. *The Diplomatic Protection of Americans in Mexico*. New York: Columbia University Press, 1933.

Eng, Robert Y. "The Transformation of a Semi-Colonial Port City: Shanghai, 1843–1941." In *Brides of the Sea*, edited by Frank Broeze. Honolulu: University of Hawai`i Press, 1989.

Farrell, Andrew. "Island Wrecks." Pts. 6–8. *Pacific Marine Review* (October–December 1920).

Fitch, R. F. "Life Afloat in China." *National Geographic* 51 (1927): 665–86.

Francis, Daniel. *A History of World Whaling*. Ontario: Viking, 1990.

Franke, Wolfgang. *China and the West*. Columbia: University of South Carolina Press, 1967.

Gibbs, Jim. *Shipwrecks in Paradise: A Maritime History of Hawai`i*. Seattle: Superior, 1977.

Gilbert, Benjamin Franklin. "Naval Operations in the Pacific, 1861–1866." Ph.D. diss., University of California, 1951.

Gleason, Duncan. *The Islands and Ports of California*. New York: Devin Adair, 1958.

Gough, Barry M. *The Royal Navy and the Northwest Coast of North America, 1810–1914: A Study of British Maritime Ascendancy*. Vancouver: University of British Columbia Press, 1971.

Hanke, Lewis, ed. *Benito Juarez and the French Intervention in Mexico*. Cambridge: Armon Books, 1971.

Hanna, Alfred Jackson, and Kathryn Abbey Hanna. *Napoleon III and Mexico: American Triumph over Monarchy*. Chapel Hill: University of North Carolina Press, 1971.

Henson, Curtis T. *The United States Navy and China, 1839–1861*. Ann Arbor: University Microfilms, 1965.

Hiroaki Kani. *A General Survey of the Boat People in Hong Kong*. Hong Kong: Chinese University, 1967.

Hubbard, Harry D. *Vallejo*. Boston: Meador, 1941.

Hunt, Aurora. *The Army of the Pacific: Its Operations in California, Texas, Arizona, New*

Mexico, Utah, Nevada, Oregon, Washington, Plains Region, Mexico, etc. 1860–1866. Mechanicsburg, Pa.: Stackpole Books, 2004.

Johnson, Robert Erwin. *Far China Station: The US Navy in Asian Waters 1800–1898*. Annapolis: Naval Institute Press, 1979.

———. *Rear Admiral John Rodgers 1812–1882*. Annapolis: Naval Institute Press, 1967.

———. *Thence Round Cape Horn*. Annapolis: Naval Institute Press, 1963.

Kern, James. *Vallejo*. San Francisco: Arcadia, 2004.

Kuykendall, Ralph S. *The Hawaiian Kingdom: 1854–1874: Twenty Critical Years*. Honolulu: University of Hawai`i Press, 1953.

Lain, Bobby Dave. "North of Fifty-three: Army, Treasury Department, and Navy Administration of Alaska, 1867–1884." Ph.D. diss., University of Texas at Austin, 1974.

Landauer, Lyndall, and Donald Landauer. *Pearl: The History of the United States Navy in Pearl Harbor*. Lake Tahoe: Flying Cloud Press, 1999.

Langley, Harold D. *Social Reform in the United States Navy, 1798–1862*. Chicago: University of Illinois Press, 1967.

Lemmon, Sue, and E. D. Wichels. *Sidewheelers to Nuclear Power: A Pictorial Essay Covering 123 Years at the Mare Island Naval Shipyard*. Annapolis, Md.: Leeward, 1977.

Lott, Arnold S. *A Long Line of Ships: Mare Island's Century of Naval Activity in California*. Annapolis: Naval Institute Press, 1954.

Lydgate, J. M. "Wrecks to the Northwest." *Thrum's Hawaiian Annual and Standard Guide* (1915): 133–44.

MacDonald, Scot. "Saga of the *Saginaw* Gig." *Surface Warfare* (November 1980): 10–16.

Mack, William P., and Royal W. Connell. *Naval Ceremonies, Customs, and Traditions*. Annapolis: Naval Institute Press, 1980.

Malone, Dumas, and Basil Rauch. *Crisis of the Union 1841–1877*. New York: Appleton-Century-Crofts, 1960.

McKee, Christopher. *Sober Men and True: Sailor Lives in the Royal Navy, 1900–1945*. Cambridge: Harvard University Press, 2002.

McMaster, John. *Sabotaging the Shogun: Western Diplomats Open Japan, 1859–69*. New York: Vantage, 1992.

Miller, Robert R. "Arms across the Border: United States Aid to Juarez during the French Intervention in Mexico." *Transactions of the American Philosophical Society* 63, pt. 6 (1973): 1–68.

———. *Mexico: A History*. Norman: University of Oklahoma Press, 1985.

Offutt, Milton. *The Protection of Citizens Abroad by Armed Forces of the United States*. Baltimore: Johns Hopkins University Press, 1928.

Parker, Torrance R. *20,000 Jobs under the Sea: A History of Diving and Underwater Engineering*. Palos Verdes Peninsula, Calif.: Sub-Sea Archives, 1997.

Putney, Martha S. *Black Sailors: Afro-American Merchant Seamen and Whalemen Prior to the Civil War*. New York: Greenwood, 1987.

Rauzon, Mark J. *Isles of Refuge: Wildlife and History of the Northwestern Hawaiian Islands*. Honolulu: University of Hawai`i Press, 2001.

Rawlinson, John J. *China's Struggle for Naval Development, 1839–1895*. Cambridge: Harvard University Press, 1967.

Revere, Joseph Warren. *Naval Duty in California*. Oakland, Calif.: Biobooks, 1947.

Ringle, Dennis J. *Life in Mr. Lincoln's Navy*. Annapolis: Naval Institute Press, 1998.

Shelmidine, Lyle S. "The Early History of Midway Islands." *American Neptune* 8, no. 3 (1948): 179–95.

Silverstone, Paul. *Civil War Navies, 1855–1883*. Annapolis: Naval Institute Press, 2001.

Slocum, Victor. "The Saginaw's Gig." *Rudder*, January 1933, 7–10.

Spence, Jonathan D. *God's Chinese Son: The Taiping Heavenly Kingdom of Hong Xiuquan*. New York: W.W. Norton, 1996.

———. *The Search for Modern China*. New York: Norton, 1990.

Sprout, Harold, and Margaret Sprout. *The Rise of American Naval Power 1776–1918*. Princeton: Princeton University Press, 1939.

Steinbeck, John. *The Log from the Sea of Cortez*. New York: Viking, 1951.

Stevens, Sylvester K. *American Expansion in Hawai`i, 1842–1898*. Harrisburg, Pa.: Archives, 1945.

Still, William, Jr. *American Sea Power in the Old World: The United States Navy in European and Near Eastern Waters, 1865–1917*. Westport, Conn.: Greenwood, 1980.

Taylor, Albert Pierce. "The American Navy in Hawai`i." *U.S. Naval Proceedings* August (1927): 907–33.

Taylor, John M. *William Henry Seward: Lincoln's Right Hand*. Washington: Brassey's, 1991.

Teijuhn Wada. *American Foreign Policy towards Japan during the Nineteenth Century*. Tokyo: Toyo Bunko, 1928.

Teng, Yuan-chung. *Americans and the Taiping Rebellion: A Study of American-Chinese Relationship, 1847–1864*. Taipei: China Academy, 1982.

Tolley, Kemp. *Yangtze Patrol: The U.S. Navy in China*. Annapolis: Naval Institute Press, 1971.

Valley, James E. *Rocks and Shoals: Naval Discipline in the Age of Fighting Sail*. Annapolis: Naval Institute Press, 1980.

Van Slyke, Lyman P. *Yangtze: Nature, History, and the River*. Stanford: Stanford Alumni Association, 1988.

Van Tilburg, Hans. "Maritime Cultural Resource Survey: Northwestern Hawaiian Islands, NOWRAMP." National Marine Sanctuary Program, 2002.

———. "US Navy Shipwrecks in Hawaiian Waters: An Inventory of Submerged Naval Properties." Manuscript submitted to the Underwater Archaeology Branch, Naval Historical Center, 2003.

Wasserman, Mark. *Everyday Life and Politics in Nineteenth Century Mexico: Men, Women, and War*. Albuquerque: University of New Mexico Press, 2000.

Welsh, Frank. *A Borrowed Place: The History of Hong Kong*. New York: Kodansha International, 1993.

Whitney, Henry M. Unpublished draft article to *Scribner's Monthly*, February 1871. (Bishop Museum).

Wilder, Gerrit P. "A Short Trip to the Midway Islands with Captain A. P. Niblack in the USS *Iroquois*." *Hawaiian Forester and Agriculturist* 2, no. 12 (1905): 390–96.

Wilson, James Grant, and John Fiske, eds. *Appleton's Cyclopedia of American Biography*. New York: Appleton, 1888. Reprint, Detroit: Gale Research, 1968.

Zadwick, Kenneth A. "The Early Days of Mare Island's Naval History." *Mare Island Historic Park Foundation Newsletter* 3, no. 2 (2002).

Index

Abandoned Shipwreck Act, 311
Acapulco. *See* Mexico
Alabama, CSS (commerce raider): Thomas Hogg to coordinate with, 108–9; prizes taken by, 146; sunk by USS *Kearsage* (Winslow commanding), 219–20
Alaska: Alcohol smuggling along Alaskan coast, 160; Chilcat-kon, confrontations with, 168–69; Chinook language, Mitchell lexicon of, 160; *Growler* wreck, investigation of, 156–58; Haida Indians, 150, 156; illness, rheumatism among crew, 152, 170, 174–75; Inuit Indians, 150; Kake/Kake-kon (*see* Kake War); "kon," defined, 154; Kootznahoo, coaling operations at, 161; Lynn Canal, 159–60; need for *Saginaw* in (Craven note), 175–76; North Pacific Squadron resupply problems, 153–54; Peril Straits, near grounding at, 170; purchase of, 4, 148; Sitka, events at (*see* Sitka); slipshod administration of, 149–50; sovereignty transferred to U.S., 149; tension between Navy and natives, 161; Tlingit Indians, 149–50, 154–55, 160. *See also* Coal/coaling; Kake War
Albatrosses, Laysan. *See* Gooney birds
Alcatraz, fortification of, 84
Alcohol/alcohol abuse: aboard *Saginaw,* 55, 91, 94–95, 98, 106, 183, 197; aboard schooner *Louisa Downs,* 159–60; James Campbell accidental drowning, 48; daily whiskey ration (U.S., British), 88; drunkenness, punishment for, 33, 91, 94–95, 98; as escape from conditions of service, 55, 94–94; grog and "Bob Smith," 88; Schenck charged with, 55; smuggling aboard and concealment of, 98;

smuggling along Alaskan coast, 4, 155, 160; "sucking the monkey," 98; U.S. Army experience at Sitka, 155; Lt. Westcott, drunkenness of, 54–55
Anaconda Plan (naval blockade of Confederacy), 80–81
Andrews, John: coxswain on rescue gig, 245–46; lost as rescue gig capsizes, 251–52; body washed ashore (at Kapapala, Hawai`i), 253; interred at Nu`uanu Cemetery, 272, 284, 285*i*; son's letter to Sicard, 284–85; U.S. Naval Academy memorial, 296; name cut on rescue gig coaming, 298*i*
Antiquities Act, 311
Arrow war. *See* Opium War, second
Atlantic cable, 126–27, 134

Baldwin, Cmdr. Charles H.: relieves Hopkins as *Saginaw* commander, 116; leaves *Saginaw,* returns to Mare Island, 121; rear admiral commanding *Saginaw,* 284
Baldwin, USS (DD-624), 284
Black Flag Decree, 124–25
Bligh, Capt. William, 248
Boston, USS, 288
Britain/British: attack on Taku (Peiho) Forts, 38, 43–44; attempt to annex Hawai`i, 186; and devastation of Nanjing area, 60–61; humiliation of Meade by (Victoria BC), 167; hydrographic surveys of Hawai`i, 185; ransom of Shanghai by, 42; surrender of *Shenandoah* to (1865), 118, 126; *Trent* incident, response to, 70–71
Brockway, Ensign J. H., 114
Brooks, Charles W., 188

Brooks Island: Brooks's accolade for, 194; Brooks lands on, claims, 188; Captain Daggett description of, 188–89; Pacific Mail station on, 192–93; Reynolds possession of (for U.S.), 193. *See also* Midway Island/ Midway Atoll

Brunel, Isambard Kingdom, 19, 134

Burditt, Capt. Henry, 192

Butterworth, James: biographical sketch of, 199; post-*Saginaw* career of, 283

California: Baja, grey whales at, 140–41; Baja, mining activity at, 139; Channel Islands, 90, 121; coastal forts, 81–82; French/British designs on, 128–29; gold shipments, importance of, 82; Gulf of California, *Saginaw* ordered to, 123; Lower California, Confederate interest in, 69, 86; passage to (Cape Horn, Panama), 10–11; San Francisco (*see* San Francisco); Santa Barbara, 29, 90, 122; Southern sympathizers in, 83–84. *See also* Mare Island Naval Shipyard

Cape Horn, passage around: difficulties of, 10; by Pacific Squadron, 126; USS *Oregon*, 282; by Yankee merchant vessels, 185

Carrollton (bark), 292

Casserley, Tane, 297*i*, 311, 319*i*

Central America: Confederate threat to, 85, 94, 113–14; Nicaraguan incursions in, 96; "piratical hordes" in (Pearson note), 96, 331n59; political instability of, 96; *Saginaw* on station in, 97–98, 119; Noel Wilson ill health in, 96. *See also* Panama

Changmao (long hairs). *See* Taiping Rebellion

Channel Islands, 90, 121

China: Chinese civilians, employment of (by U.S. Navy), 47–48; civil war in (*see* Taiping Rebellion); foreign concessions, granting of, 38; Nanjing, diplomatic negotiations at, 58–60; Nanjing area, devastation of, 60–61; opium trade, prohibition of (by Taiping), 59; Qing Dynasty, disintegration of, 77; Shanghai, privateer fitting out at, 68; Shanghai, *Saginaw* arrives at, 41; Shanghai, *Saginaw* defense of, 44–45; Shanghai waterfront, perils of, 48; southern China climate, crew illness from, 41–42, 47; Treaty of Tianjin, 38; treaty ports, 13; Union commerce with, protection of, 69; U.S. commercial interest in, 78–79; Yangtze River, *Saginaw* ascent of, 57–58, 60–62; Yangtze River, Western trade on, 13, 59–61. *See also* Cochin China; Opium; Opium Wars

Chinook language, Mitchell lexicon of, 160

Cholera, 48, 68, 96, 167, 211

Civil War, U.S.: Anaconda Plan (naval blockade of South), 80–81; anti-draft riots (NYC), 165; Atlantic and Gulf states, importance of, 81; Guadalupe, secret Confederate base on, 89–90; General Lee, surrender of, 116; Lincoln *vs.* McClellan (vote aboard *Saginaw*), 114; Mare Island shipyard, planned attack on, 90–91; Mexico and Central America, importance of, 85; neutral countries, sovereign rights of, 90; notice to American ships of war, 65, 328n54; Pacific Theater, secondary importance of, 81–82; Thomas Hogg Affair, 108–13, 113–14, 115; Union commerce, effect on, 68–69, 81–82, 83, 118. *See also* Commerce raiders; Confederate States of America; Panama

Cleary, Judge, 69

Coal/coaling: Acapulco, importance of, 102; Brooks (Midway) Island, coal pit at, 192–93; coal, cost of, 67, 167, 170, 181; coaling, unpleasantness of, 33–34, 57; coal passers/ coal heavers, 32, 52, 54, 201; coal supplies, importance of, 15, 145, 150, 158; coal use, logistics of (Sicard analysis), 182; French gift to *Saginaw*, 123–24; Hamilton coal, burning qualities of, 158; Honolulu harbor, coaling station at, 202; Kootznahoo coal, burning difficulties with, 161, 167, 169–70; Midway coaling station, attempted establishment of, 4–5, xii; mining of, by Alaskan natives, 159, 161, 168; mining of, by *Saginaw* crew, 158, 159; navy contracts for (British Columbia), 158; *Saginaw* coal capacity, 18, 20, 24; steam propulsion, inefficiency of, 20

Cochin China (Vietnam): gun battle at Qui Nhon Bay, 64; *Saginaw* posted to, 63–64

Coffin, Capt. Horace ("Tom"), 156

Cogswell, James K., 198, 282; biographical sketch of, 198; evaluation of small-boat voyage risks, 240; post-*Saginaw* career of, 282, 341n5

Cogswell, USS (DD-651), 282

Commerce, U.S.: California gold shipments, importance of, 3, 82, 85; importance of (*see* Pacific Ocean, expansion into); protecting

(*Report of the Secretary of the Navy*, 1858), 16; threat to (*see* Civil War, U.S. Commerce raiders; Privateers); whaling (*see* Whaleships and whaling). *See also* Alaska; China; Japan; Mexico; Panama

Commerce raiders: Chinese trade, threat to, 69, 72; Confederate monitors on Pacific coast, 133–34; CSS *Alabama*, 81, 108, 145–46, 218–19; CSS *Florida*, 146; CSS *Shenandoah* (*see Shenandoah*, CSS); foreign-built, Confederate purchase of, 81; *guerre de course*, 68, 82; Havana, Confederates assembling in, 119; historical note regarding, 68–69; *J.M. Chapman*, USS *Cyane* capture of, 89–90; Pacific commerce raids planned, 72, 83, 119, 331n64. *See also* Letters of marque; Pirates/ piracy; Privateers

Commercial Pacific Cable Company, 291

Confederate States of America: Anaconda Plan (naval blockade of), 80–81; CSA commissioners removed from *Trent*, 70; naval weakness of, 69, 80; Thomas Hogg Affair, 108–13, 113–14, 115; Waddell resigns commission, joins CS Navy, 66. *See also* Civil War, U.S. Commerce raiders

Coolies: coolie trade, abuses of, 34; employment of, by *Saginaw*, 47; kidnapping of, by rogue American sailors, 39

Copper ingots, theft of (Topolocampo), 142

Cowles, William Sheffield, 283

Craven, Cmdr. Tunis A. M.: death at Battle of Mobile Bay, 135

Craven, Rear Adm. Thomas T.: biographical sketch, 135; commandant of Mare Island, 135; command of North Pacific Squadron, 153; court-martial of (as commodore), 135–36; objection to laying-up *Saginaw*, 175–76; uncommunicative character of, 168

Crew, ship's. *See Saginaw*, officers and crew

Crimean War, 81

Crimps and Shanghaied sailors, 138

Cunningham, Comdt. Robert B.: first commander of Mare Island shipyard, 17; instructions for *Saginaw* design, construction, 18, 20; response to criticism of *Saginaw* construction, 25, 30, 326n24; *Saginaw* commissioning speech, 30, 32

Dacotah, USS, 57

Dahlgren cannon, armament of: on *Saginaw*,

16, 84, 132, 325n11; on shallow-draft armed steamers, 16

Daily routines. *See Saginaw*, life aboard

Darwinism, social: von Ranke commentary on, 14

Davis, Gen. Jefferson C.: established as territorial governor (Alaska), 149; difficulties in administering territory, 150; Fort Wrangell established, 153

Desertion: of foreign nationals in Pacific Squadron, 89; from *Saginaw*, 57–58, 62, 91, 92–93, 94, 95, 150, 163, 166, 196; in time of war, penalties for, 101–2. *See also Saginaw*, discipline aboard

Discipline, shipboard. *See Saginaw*, discipline aboard

Dole, Sanford B., 288

Draft riots (NYC), 165

Dunnottar Castle (iron sailing ship), 286–87, 290, 300, 312

East India Squadron: Cornelius Stribling, commanding, 37; Japanese visit by (USS *Niagara*), 49; *John Adams* reluctance to serve in, 39, 326nn4–5; *Saginaw* assignment to, xi; *Saginaw* to (Shanghai, 1860), 41; weakness of, 37, 38

El Salvador: La Union, *Saginaw* at, 95–96, 97, 98–99

Engle, Capt. Frederick: relieves Stribling, 63, 66; requests *Saginaw* remain on station, 67, 68

Farragut, Adm. David G., 17, 25

Finney, Suzanne, 301

Fire Dart (steamer), 61

Food, shipboard: provisioning (typical), 33; spoilage of, 97, 114, 119, 209, 249

Fowler, William: illness, derangement of, 162–63

France, 38, 43–44; blockade/control of Mexican ports, 87, 103–4, 105–7, 114, 115; contraband for Mexican Liberal forces, 115; control of Manzanillo, 103–4; Maximilian I, French support of (*see* Maximilian I); Mexico, French-Austrian intervention in, 4, 85–87, 102, 106–7; Mexico, withdrawal of forces from, 105, 136; Napoleon III, Mexican intervention of, 4, 85–87; Treaty of Miramar, 105; and *Trent* incident, 70–71; war with U.S., Seward threat of, 87

Francis, Peter: chosen for ship's gig voyage, 244–45; drowned, body not recovered, 253; headstone at Nuʻuanu Cemetery (Honolulu), 284, 285

Franklin, Cmdr. Samuel: biographical note, 128, 129; command of *Saginaw*, 130; at Mare Island (*Saginaw* repair/refit, 1866), 130–31; Monterey, abortive capture of, 128–29

Fusi Yama, 91

Gardner, Capt. William H., 83

Garst, Perry: biographical sketch of, 199; evaluation of small-boat voyage risks, 199, 240; post-*Saginaw* career of, 282–83

General Siegel (schooner), 290

Gig, *Saginaw*. See Rescue gig, *Saginaw*

Gledstanes (whaleship), 221, 229, 235, 257

Golden Gate (schooner): burning, grounding of, 99; contraband aboard, 103–4; gold specie, salvage/disappearance of, 99, 100–101

Gooney birds: colliding with tree trunks on landing, 291; comparison with seal meat, 233; "Gooneyville Lodge" (Pan Am Hotel), 292, 294; native to Midway Island, 5, 191, 286; need to conserve (by *Saginaw* crew), 233, 256; shipwrecked sailors surviving on, 221, 256, 271, 291; ungainly behavior, ease of capture, 233. See also Seals/sealing

Great Eastern, SS, 19, 127

Green Island (formerly Ocean Island): beauty of, 304; LORAN station on, 289; photograph of, 258i; Van Tilburg on (2003), 303, 304–5. See also Kure Atoll; Ocean Island, *Saginaw* crew on

Griffith, John W., 15

Growler (schooner), loss of, 156–58

Guadalupe, secret Confederate base on, 89–90

Guano: Chincha (guano) Islands, 113; Guano Act (1856), 188; guano trade, *Carrollton* in, 292; guano trade (in Northwest Hawaiian Islands), 300; on La Perouse Pinnacle, 205; smell of (on Ocean Island), 231, 286

Guerre de course, 68, 82

Haida Indians, 150, 156

Halford, USS (DD-480), 282

Halford, William: evaluation of Peter Francis, 245; Peter Knowlien kindness to, 252–53, 270; rescue gig voyage, 244–45, 251–53; post-*Saginaw* career of, 281–82

Hartford, USS: at Hong Kong, 38, 41, 57, 64–65; Commander Li Xiucheng address to, 46; Nanjing, diplomatic negotiations at, 58–60; Shanghai, defense of, 44–45

Hawaiʻi/Hawaiian Islands: Advanced Base operations (flying boats) at, 289; American dominance of, 185, 187, 188; annexation, British attempt at, 186; annexation (by U.S.), 287–89; commercial privileges (to U.S.), 186–87; foreign diseases, devastating effects of, 187; geology of, 220; Hawaiian Islands, map of, 206i; Hawaiian sailors/whalemen, skills of, 143; Honolulu (see Honolulu); hydrographic surveys of, 185; Kamehameha IV, pro-British sentiments of, 187; Kamehameha VII (David Kalakaua), 287; Kure Atoll (see Kure Atoll); marine resources at, 299–301; plantation, agricultural boom in, 187; Queen Liliʻuokalani, 287, 288; reciprocity, commercial, 190, 203, 274; Reciprocity Treaty (with U.S.), 287; Williams Reynolds affection for, 190; satellite image of, 230i; shipwrecks on, 220–21; strategic/logistical importance of, 184–86; underwater debris, artifacts at, 301; USS *Boston* lands troops on, 288; Daniel Webster position regarding, 186. See also Hawaiian Islands marine resources; Midway Island/Midway Atoll; Ocean Island, *Saginaw* crew on

Hawaiian Islands marine resources: Coral Reef Conservation Act, 299; coral reef ecosystem reserve (Clinton order), 299; National Marine Sanctuaries Act (NMSA), 300; Papahānaumokuākea, 300

Heavenly Army (Taiping), 43, 45

Heavenly Capital of Perfect Peace (Nanjing), 58

Heavenly Kingdom of Great Peace, 35

Hegel, Georg Wilhelm Friedrich: Western progress, inevitability of, 14

Heusken, Charles, 51

Hiʻialakai (research vessel), 310–11

Hogg, Thomas. See Thomas Hogg Affair

Hong, Xiuguan. See Taiping Rebellion

Hong Kong: Capt. Engle relieves Schenck, 73; *Saginaw* arrives at (1861), 52; *Saginaw* decommissioned at, 72; *Saginaw* ordered from (by British), 74–74; USS *Hartford* on station at, 38–39; USS *Niagara* ordered to, 49; Thomas Walker dies at, 47

Honolulu: damaged rescue gig at, 269*i*; growing importance of, 202; Honolulu Harbor, coaling station at, 202; Japanese ambassadors feted at, 39–40; opium dens in, 204; rescued *Saginaw* crew arrives at, 267–68; *Saginaw*, residents' pride in, 40. *See also* Hawai`i/Hawaiian Islands

Hopkins, Lt. Cmdr. William E.: assumes command of *Saginaw*, 85; biographical sketch of, 84–85; condemned by Navy medical board, 115–16; relieved by Hopkins as *Saginaw* commander, 116

Hydrographic surveys. *See* Surveys, hydrographic

Illness. *See Saginaw*, illness aboard
Independence, USS: at Mare Island Naval Shipyard (as razee), 26*i*, 27, 27*i*

Japan: anti-Western violence in, 12–13, 34, 51–52; Dutch sea captains slain (Yokohama), 51–52; first embassy to U.S., 39–40; Secretary Heusken attacked, slain, 51; inland sea, 52; Japanese ambassadors feted (Honolulu), 39–40; Kanagawa, *Saginaw* at, 49–51, 70; kobang (gold coins), selling of, 50; need to adopt Western ways, 13–15; Adm. Matthew Perry opening of, 13; Russians slain (Yokohama), 34; *Saginaw* at, 3, 50–52; samurai, 51; Schufeldt manifest destiny remark regarding, 14; Simonoseki Straits (battle at), 115; Tokugawa Shogunate, 34; uneasy conditions for Americans at, 3, 34; USS *Niagara* at, 49; Yedo (Tokyo), 50, 51, 70; Yokohama, USS *Niagara* at, 49

Jiacampo: *Saginaw* brief grounding off, 143
J.M. Chapman (Confederate privateer), 89–90, 91
John Adams, 39, 41
John L. Stevens (PMC steamer), 115
Johnston, Col. A. S., 84
Juarez, Benito: acquires *John L. Stevens*, 115; Black Flag Decree, 124–25; guerilla war of, 87; Maximilian I, execution by, 87; progressive/liberal aspects of, 86; U.S. military surplus, Union veterans to, 13; U.S. support for, 86, 105, 122. *See also* Mexico
Julia E. Whalen (schooner), 291–92

Kake War: Kake attack on garrison guard, 168–69; Kake-kon confrontations with Russians, 158; Kake settlement shelled (Meade), 172; Meade final report on, 173–74; Midshipman Bridge landing party, 173; Midshipman Pillsbury landing party, 172–73; remains of murdered traders sent to Sitka, 171–72; summary and analysis of action, 173–74, 178. *See also* Alaska

Kanakas (Hawaiian seamen), 143
Kate Piper (schooner), 196, 197
Kidnapping: of coolies (by rogue Americans), 39; impressed seamen (British navy), 137; Shanghaing seamen (San Francisco), 138
Kilauea, SS, 254–55, 262–63, 264–65, 267
Knowlien, Peter, 252–53, 270
Kon, defined, 154
Kona Packet, 253–54, 263–64, 265
Kure Atoll: grounding of *Dunnottar Castle* on, 286; Hawaiian possession of, 287; Kure Atoll Wildlife refuge, 289; LORAN station at, 289; in Northern Hawaiian Island chain, 206*i*, 221; PT boats at, 289; *Saginaw* grounding on (*see Saginaw*, grounding and loss of); satellite image of, 230*i*; *Waiaieale* rescue mission to, 287; wreckage of whaler *Gledstanes* on, 229. *See also* Green Island; Ocean Island; Ocean Island, *Saginaw* crew on

Lackawanna, USS, 188
Law, Capt. William C., 89–90
Letters of marque: Confederate, 69, 89; *guerre de course*, 68, 82; merchants' note to Engle regarding, 67, 328n56; *vs.* piracy, 68–69. *See also* Commerce raiders; Privateers
Li Xiucheng, 46
Lorcha, 55
Louisa Downs (schooner), 159–60, 175

Macaw, USS (ASR-11), 294–95
Manchu: defeat of (by British, French), 44; Hakka uprising against, 34, 35; Qing Dynasty, disintegration of, 77; rulers, origins of, 35; traditions, constraints of, 35. *See also* China
Manifest destiny, Western. *See* Racial preeminence, philosophy of
Manzanillo: Confederate agents at, 89; description of, 99–100; French military takes control of, 103–4; *Golden Gate* at, 99, 103–4; *Saginaw* at, 100–101

Mare Island Naval Shipyard: construction of
Saginaw, 17–18; David G. Farragut, commanding, 25; floating dry dock at, 27–28;
David McDougal commandant of, 115; ori-
gins, history of, 25–27; planned rebel attack
on, 90–91; questions of employee loyalty to
Union cause, 83–84; Saginaw repair/refit at
(see Saginaw, construction/configuration of;
Saginaw, topical history of); USS Indepen-
dence at (as razee), 26i, 27, 27i
Marines, imperial (French), 103, 107
Marines, U.S.: aboard Saginaw, 53, 201; to
control NYC draft riots, 165; at Hawai`i, 288;
rounding up deserters, 217; at Shanghai, 45
"Marsh fever" (malaria), 96
Maui fever, 40
Maximilian I: capture, execution of, 87, 136;
Empress Carlota, 126; and John L. Stevens,
115; promulgates Black Flag Decree, 124–25;
puppet regime of, 4, 85–87, 124; Treaty of
Miramar, 105; U.S. opposition to, 105, 107,
127. See also France; Mexico
Mazatlan: American occupation of, 29, 105; as
European-style city, 105; French shelling of,
106; as haven for deserters, 107; Saginaw at,
104, 123, 139, 143. See also Mexico
McDougal, Lt. Cmdr. Charles J.: assumes com-
mand of Saginaw, 121; death of, 121
McDougal, Capt. David S.: commandant of
Mare Island, 115; Simonoseki, Straits of
(battle at), 115
McDougal, Kate, 121
Meade, Capt. Richard W., Sr.: biographical
sketch of, 164–65; insanity of, 177
Meade, Richard W., Jr.: assumes command of
Saginaw, 166; biographical sketch of, 164–66,
177; cashiering of (by President Cleveland),
177; court-martial of, 165; frugality of, 167,
168; hot temper of, 165–66, 177, 178, 283;
humiliation of, by British (Victoria BC), 167;
illness of (cholera morbus), 167; life after
Saginaw, 177; suppresses NYC draft riots,
165; U.S. Naval academy appointment, 167
Meade, USS (DD-274), 283
Melville, Herman, 129
Merrill, Edwin, 68
Messenger (ship): attempted kidnapping of
coolies by, 39
Mexico: Acapulco, importance of, 102;

Acapulco, Saginaw shore guard at, 124;
Acapulco, unrest and violence in, 106–7;
Confederate sympathizers in, 84–86, 122;
disruption, instability of, 86; French-Austrian intervention in, 4, 85–87, 102, 106–7;
French withdrawal from, 105, 136; Juarez
administration in (see Juarez, Benito); Manzanillo, 89, 90, 99–100, 103, 184; Maximilian
I, regime of (see Maximilian I); Mazatlan
(see Mazatlan); Mexican-American War, 81;
Mexico and Central America, importance of,
85; Monterey, abortive capture of, 128–29;
Treaty of Miramar, 105; War of the Reform
period, 86
Middle Brook Island. See Midway Island/Mid-
way Atoll
Midway channel, cutting of (1870): chart of
channel (partial), 212i; contractor's stores
(for project), 196–97; coral, difficulties working with, 213–14; cost overruns, charges
of fraud, 215–17; expedition party, names
of, 210; Navy contract with Townsend for,
193–94, 197–98; Saginaw returns to San
Francisco, 5; Saginaw support of, 194, 208–9,
211; Sicard trouble reports, 211, 215; submarine rock-drilling machine, 197, 213, 214i;
surge and current, diver's problems with,
210, 213; termination of project, 218–19;
Welles Harbor entrance, lagoon, 208
Midway channel, dredging of (WWII), 293–94
Midway Island/Midway Atoll: bark Carrollton
grounds on reef, 292; barrenness, unrealistic
assessment of, 189, 191–92, 336n18; coal
pit on, 192–93; coaling station, importance
of, 4–5; Cold War activity at, 295; Captain
Daggett description of, 189–90; designated
a Hawaiian Islands Refuge, 291; downgrad-
ing of (post-WWII), 295; first marines
stationed on (ca. 1903), 291; geology, coral
reef, 190–91; gooney birds on, 191, 216, 221,
233, 256, 271, 291; as Middle Brook Island,
4, 5, 188; Midway, Battle of, 293; as national
wildlife refuge, 295–96; Navy hydrographic
survey of, 188–89; Pan American Airways
flying boats at, 216, 292, 296; Capt. Reynolds
takes possession of, 189; as Sand Island (see
Sand Island); Sand Island (current name),
210; shipwrecks on, 189–90, 286–87, 289,
290–92, 294–95; strategic importance of,

292–93; structures at, 209, 209*i*; submarine base at, 293, 294; submarine cable relay station, 291; Welles Harbor, Seward Roads, 189, 291; in WWII, 216, 289, 292–94. *See also* Kure Atoll; Ocean Island, *Saginaw* crew on

Miramar, Treaty of, 105

Mitchell, Cmdr. John: biographical sketch of, 136–37; as disciplinarian and "hard driver," 143; hydrographic survey off Cerralvo Island, 139–40; lexicon of Chinook language, 160; murder of, 164

Monadnock, USS, 126, 132

Monk seals, capture and cooking of, 232–33

Moses, Don, 304

Moses Taylor (steamer), 217, 254, 264, 268, 274

Muir, James: biographical, family sketch, 285; captain of hold on rescue gig, 245–46; headstone at Nuʻuana Cemetery (Honolulu), 284, 285; illness during rescue gig voyage, 249; rescue gig capsize, 251–53; rescue gig coaming, name on, 298*i*; Sicard pension for, 285; U.S. Naval Academy memorial, 296

Myrtle and crew, search for, 63–64

National Marine Sanctuaries Act (NMSA), 300

Navy, U.S. *See* U.S. Navy

Neutral countries, sovereign rights of, 90

Neva (topsail schooner), 69

Niagara, USS: blockade of CSS ram *Stonewall*, 136; to Hong Kong, 49; at Yedo, 50; at Yokohama, 49, 50

Nicaragua, incursions by, 96

Nicaragua Co., 10, 11

Ningpo: capture, pillaging of (by Taiping), 70; *Saginaw* ordered to, 47, 48; as treaty port, 13

North Pacific Squadron: composition, mission of (1866), 131; Rear Adm. Craven commanding., 153; resupply problems (Craven report), 153–54; Rear Adm. Thatcher commanding., 131, 151

Nuʻuanu Cemetery (Honolulu): *Saginaw* crewmen headstone, 285

Nyack, USS, 267, 268, 269

Ocean Island (later Green Island): *Saginaw* grounding on (*see Saginaw*, grounding and loss of; Wreck site, survey of). *See also* Green Island; Kure Atoll; Sand Island

Ocean Island, *Saginaw* crew on: albatrosses,

capture and cooking of, 233–34, 257; captain's tent, 235*i*; castaway camp, Sicard sketch of, 258*i*; crew arrives at Honolulu, feted, 267–70, 271–72; deceased sailors, burial of, 272; discipline, courts-martial, 234; donkey boiler (for freshwater), 236*i*, 237; dysentery, rheumatism among, 234, 244, 260; food, need for, 232; freshwater, need for, 228, 235, 237; Green (Ocean) island today (photo), 258*i*; improvised sextant, creation/display of, 246, 297*i*; inventory of items left on island, 265; limited rations, weight loss, weakness, 234, 238, 256–57, 269; mainmast salvaged, raised on beach, 238–39; medicines, lack of, 240, 244; monk seals, capture and cooking of, 232–33, 257; morale, difficulty in maintaining, 259; officers' written reports, meetings, 261; rats, plague of, 233*i*, 256; rescue gig, construction/voyage of (*see* Rescue gig, *Saginaw*); rescue gig, report of loss, 263–64; rescue schooner, construction of, 257, 257*i*, 259; rewards and acknowledgments, 270–71; salvaged material on beach, 237; ship's machinery surveyed, 260–61; squalls and storms at, 238; work parties, 235; rescue effort mounted (Hawaiian/American), 253–55; SS *Kilauea* arrives, removes crew, 262–63, 264–65

Officers, ship's. *See Saginaw*, officers and crew

Opium: aboard *Fire Dart*, 61; Honolulu, opium dens in, 204; as medicinal, 42, 68, 163; opium trade, legalization of, 38; opium trade, origins of, 12–13; opium trade, prohibition of (by Taiping), 59. *See also* Opium Wars

Opium War, first, 13

Opium War, second (Arrow War): beginning of, 13; Taku (Peiho) forts, British attacks on, 38, 43; Treaty of Tianjin, 38

Ordnance, naval. *See* Dahlgren cannon; Parrott rifled cannon; *Saginaw*, armament of

Pacific Mail Steamship Company: Acapulco offices defended (by *Saginaw*), 124; arming steamers of, 83; Confederate plans against, 89–90; creation of, 10–11; *Golden Gate*, burning/grounding of, 99, 100; *John L. Stevens* (as gun runner), 115; Panama Route of, 10–11; treasure-laden steamers of, 3–4; Capt. J. L. Watkins, 73, 75, 76–77, 329nn76–78

Pacific Ocean, expansion into: comparison with British Empire, 14; as expression of manifest destiny, 14; Japan, opening of (by Adm. Perry), 13; origins of, 9–10; Panama Route (to San Francisco), 10–11; U.S. Navy role in, 15–17; U.S. commercial interest in, 11–12, 15; whaling, importance of, 11–12. *See also* Cape Horn, passages around; Racial preeminence, philosophy of

Pacific Republic (rebel), 84

Pacific Squadron: Cape Horn passage by, 126; protection of commerce by, 81–82; special service squadron joins, 126

Panama: Confederate raiders, base for, 85; Confederate sympathizers in, 113–14; Federal steamers, planned seizure of, 108–9; gold shipments to, 82, 85; Isthmus of Panama, threat to, 4, 82, 83, 118–19; Japanese embassy to, 50; maritime communication, importance to, 82, 83, 85, 94; Panama Canal, De Lessep's failed attempt, 86, 220; Panama Route (to San Francisco), 10–11; *Saginaw* at, 95–97, 114; Thomas Hogg Affair, 108–15. *See also* Central America

Parrott rifled cannon: aboard *Saginaw*, 132, 172, 183, 325n11; in *Saginaw* wreckage, 315, 316, 317, 320

Parsons, Arthur H.: evaluation of small-boat voyage risks, 239–40

Paulet, Lord George, 186

Peichili, Gulf of: John Ward diplomacy at, 43

Perry, Admiral Matthew: opening of Japan to Western trade, 13

Pillsbury, J. E.: raid on Kake settlements, 172–73

Pirates/Piracy: American vessel, seizure of, 49; Central America, "piratical hordes" in, 94, 96; impossibility of controlling, 79; letters of marque, 67, 68–69, 89; by rogue American seaman, 39, 49; *Saginaw* antipiracy patrol, 55–56; suppression of (by East India Squadron), 37; suppression of (by Frederick Ward), 46. *See also* Commerce raiders; Privateers

Port Townsend (Washington Territory), 91, 92

Powhattan, USS, 39

Privateers: American licensing of (against British), 69; at British Columbia, 91–92; Central America, potential refuge for, 94; Channel Islands, fitting out at, 90; Confederate, American merchants' concerns about, 66–67; Confederate, Navy concerns about, 69; at Guadalupe, 89–90; *guerre de course*, 68, 82; historical background, 68–69; *J.M. Chapman*, 89–90, 91; merchants' note to Engle regarding, 67. *See also* Commerce raiders; Letters of marque; Pirates/Piracy; *Shenandoah*, CSS

Qui Nhon Bay (Vietnam), 64

Racial preeminence, philosophy of: Hegelian attitude toward, 14; Leopold von Ranke and social Darwinism, 14; Schufeldt comments on, 9, 14. *See also* Pacific Ocean, expansion into

Redoubt St. Dionysius, 153

Rescue gig, *Saginaw*: arrival at Kaua`i, capsize in surf, 251–53; captain's gig, sails for, 241, 241*i*; damaged gig at Honolulu Harbor, 269*i*; funeral services for gig seamen, 253; gig purchased, donated to crew, 269–270; Halford saved; Talbot, Andrews buried, 253; history of gig after rescue, 296, 298*i*, 299; improvised sextant, creation/display of, 246, 297*i*; modification of, 240–41, 241*i*; rescue voyage, Sicard analysis of, 239–40; rescue voyage, volunteers and crew for, 244–46; rescue voyage, personal letters on, 246–47; rescue voyage, narrative of, 248–50; report to Sicard on loss of, 263–64; small-boat voyage risks, evaluation of, 239–40

Reynolds, William: biographical sketch of, 190; Hawai`i residence of, 190; Midway Island, possession of, 189

Richardson, William L. (schooner), 122

Rock-drilling machine, 197, 214*i*

"Rocks and Shoals" (disciplinary code), 95, 122

Russia: Alaskan fur trade of, 148; Crimean War, 81; friction with Kake Indians, 158; purchase of Alaska from, 4, 133, 148; Russian American Company, 148, 149, 150, 156; Russian/American Telegraphic Expedition, 132; Russian frigate at Yedo, 50; Russian Plenipotentiary General (China), 43; Russians slain in Yokohama, 34

Saginaw, armament of: after refit/rebuild at Mare island (1869–70), 196; Dahlgren cannon, 84, 132; original design, 17–18; Parrott rifled cannon, 132, 162–63, 172, 183, 315, 316, 317i, 320; prior to Midway dredging voyage, 182; rearming during refit/rebuild (1862), 84, 325n11; rearming during repairs (1866), 132; at the time of her loss (1870), 325n11

Saginaw, construction/configuration of: as auxiliary (sail-assisted) steamship, 19, 145; broadside aspect (photo), 17i; coal bunkers on, 24; construction, accolades for, 30–31; construction, criticism of, 31–32; cost of, 19; deck plans and elevation, 23i; design compromises in, 19–20; interior spaces, arrangement of, 20, 24; laurel wood, questions regarding use, 75, 84; paddle boxes, 24; paddle wheels, construction of, 18; rebuild and re-rig (Mare Island, 1862), 84; repair and refit (Mare Island, 1865), 115; repair and refit (Mare Island, 1866), 130–31; repair and refit (Mare Island, 1868), 163, 166; repair and rebuild (Mare Island, 1869–70), 195–97; sail plan, 22i; specifications and arrangements, 20, 24; steam engines, description of, 18–19, 24; Union Iron Works (machinery contract), 18–19; unseaworthy condition (Schenck report), 62, 71, 328n61; waterline and internal details, 21i; wood species, selection and application of, 28, 75

Saginaw, discipline aboard: captain's mast, 95; courts-martial (specific), 53–54, 94, 95, 97, 103; desertion, incidents of (see Desertion); discipline, courts-martial (after shipwreck), 234; drunkenness, punishment for, 33, 91, 94, 98; insolence/insubordination, incidents of, 94–95, 97, 103, 210; by Capt. Mitchell, 161–62; punishments allowed, proscribed (Rocks and Shoals), 95, 122; shackles/irons, placing crewmen in, 93, 95, 98, 103, 139, 210, 234; sweatbox, use of, 97–98, 143. See also Alcohol/alcohol abuse; Saginaw, life aboard; Saginaw, officers and crew

Saginaw, grounding and loss of (listed sequentially): Kure Atoll, satellite image of, 230i; Sicard decision to round Ocean Island, 222; Friday departure deemed unlucky, 222; Adam Frank premonition regarding, 222–23; night orders, deck watch ("bright lookout"), 223–24; breakers seen, engines backed, 224–25; Saginaw drifts onto reef,

225–26; Saginaw hard aground on reef (Sicard sketch), 226i; crew attempts to save vessel, 226–27; Joseph Ross anecdote, 228; ship breaks up, stores, material salvaged, 227–29, 231; boats lowered, Ocean Island sighted, 229; salvaged material transferred to island, 229, 231; crew on island, discipline established, 231–32, 234; timbers salvaged from wreck (Sicard sketch), 235, 236i; Navy Department initiates inquiries re Saginaw, 239, 260; Sicard initial report of loss, 242–44; court of inquiry proceedings, 275–79, 341nn114–20; buoys drifting free, testimony regarding, 277–79; dismissal of charges, 279. See also Ocean Island, Saginaw crew on; Wreck site, survey of

Saginaw, illness aboard: off Acapulco, 125; accidental shooting of Ensign Brockway, 114; in Alaskan waters, 152, 170, 174–75; coolies, employment of, 47; William Fowler, illness and derangement of, 162–63; and long in-harbor duty, 125; "marsh fever" (malaria), 96; Edwin Merrill, death of (cholera), 68; "seasoning" of crew, 48, 49, 62; Albert Smith, death and funeral of, 97; and southern China climate, 41–42, 47; Stribley comment on (1860), 37; treatments, nineteenth-century, 40, 96–97; tropical diseases, summary of, 37, 96–97; venereal disease (see Venereal disease); Lt. Westcott, illness of, 40–41. See also Saginaw, life aboard

Saginaw, life aboard: alcohol, use of (see Alcohol/alcohol abuse); coaling, unpleasantness of, 33–34; crew (see Saginaw, officers and crew); daily routines, typical, 33; food and provisioning, 33, 97, 114, 119, 209, 249; on-board drills, 33, 125; provisioning and diet, 33, 97, 143; Sunday divine services, 33; uncleanness of (1868), 163. See also Saginaw, discipline aboard; Saginaw, illness aboard

Saginaw, officers and crew: blacks and persons of color in, 201; coolies, employment of, 47; enlisted men, typical (1870), 200; hierarchy of, 24; initial ship's complement (1860), 32–33; marines aboard, 53, 201; multinationality of, 32–33, 88–89, 151, 201; nine rear admirals commanding, 283–84; officers, typical (1870), 200. See also Saginaw, discipline aboard; Saginaw, life aboard

Saginaw, seaworthiness of: fails survey, decommissioned as rotten (1862), 72; poor sailing qualities, inadequate canvas of, 145, 181; Schenck assessment of, 32; sea trials, 30; a "wet ship," 41. *See also Saginaw*, construction/configuration of; Storms

Saginaw, topical history of (listed sequentially): *Saginaw's* ports of call (map), 7i; launch (as USS *Toucey*), 28–29; commissioning of, 29; Schenck takes command, 29; sea trials, 30; ship's complement: officers and crew, 32–33; East India Squadron, assignment to, 39; Shanghai, initial arrival at (1860), 41; Shanghai, defense of, 44–45; Li Xiucheng address to *Saginaw* and *Hartford*, 46; Chinese coolies, employment of, 47; ordered to Japan (1860), 50; courts of inquiry aboard, 53; Schenck complaint about *Saginaw* size, armament and crew, 54–55, 79; Yangtze River ascent, 57–58, 60–62; Nanjing, diplomatic negotiations at, 58–60; Qui Nhon Bay, bombardment of, 64; Schenck senior officer on station (1861), 69–70; return to Japan (1861), 69–70; decommissioned (Hong Kong, 1862), 72; Watkins survey of *Saginaw* (1862), 75; recovery from China by Watkins, 73–76; ordered from Hong Kong (by British), 74; rebuild and re-rig (Mare Island, 1862), 84; San Francisco, guard duty at, 84; Hopkins assumes command, 84–85; recommissioning of (1863), 88; Mare Island shipyard, defense of, 90–91; at Port Townsend (Washington Territory), 91, 92; desertion, discipline (typical), 92–93, 94–95, 97, 101–2; at Panama, 95–99; *Golden Gate*, attempted salvage of, 99; at Acapulco, 102–4; at Mazatlan, 104–5; return to Acapulco, 105–7; Thomas Hogg affair (1864), 114, 115; General Lee, surrender of, 116; repair and refit (Mare Island, 1865–66), 115; McDougal takes command, 121; removed from naval service (1865), 122; Scott takes command, 123; repair and refit (Mare Island, 1866), 130–31; severe storm damage, 132–33; at Vancouver Island, 133–35; hydrographic surveys, 139–40, 151, 183–84, 220; at Alaska, 150–53, 155–63; Mitchell slain, Beardslee commands (1868), 164; Meade assumes command (1868), 166; repair and refit (Mare Island, 1868), 163, 166; repair and rebuild (Mare Island,

1869–70), 195–97; decommissioned (Mare Island, 1869), 176; Midway channel cutting (1870), 194, 208–9, 211; grounding and loss of (1870), 221–36; rear admirals who commanded her, 283–84; epilog and historical summary, 3–5, 320–23

Saginaw, USS (LST-1188), 284

Saginaw Bay (Alaska), 153, 155, 159, 172

Sand Island (was Midway Island): Commercial Pacific Cable Company at, 291; environmental makeover of, 291; and *General Siegel* survivors, 290; *Julia E. Whalen* grounds on, 291–92; seaplane ramps, facilities at, 292; Townsend's men on (for channel dredging), 210; underwater listening post at, 295; *Wandering Minstrel* grounds, 290. *See also* Midway Island/Midway Atoll

Sandwich Islands. *See* Hawai`i/Hawaiian Islands

San Francisco: climate of, 25, 73; contraband at (French), 115; desertion at, 89, 90–91, 140; early history of, 10; passage to, 10–11; pleasures, dangers of, 137–38; *Saginaw*, civic pride in, 30–31; *Saginaw* crew liberty at, 33, 72–73, 150, 176; *Saginaw* guard duty at, 84, 90–91; Shanghaied sailors at, 138; Southern sympathy at, 89, 90–91; violence at end of Civil War, death of Lincoln, 116; as Yerba Buena, 10, 84, 130

Santa Barbara area: Channel Islands, 90, 121; description of, 122; Schenck raises flag at, 29. *See also* California

Scammon, Charles M., 141

Schenck, Cmdr. James F.: admonition of (by Welles), 73; assigned command of *Saginaw*, 29, 30; biographical sketch of, 29–30; bombardment of Qui Nhon Bay, 64; command of USS *St. Lawrence*, 55; complaint about *Saginaw* size, armament, crew, 54–55, 79; court-martial of, 53–54; post-*Saginaw* career, 74; returns to Mare Island (aboard *Swordfish*), 72–73; *Saginaw* unseaworthy condition report, 62, 71, 328n61; senior officer on station (1861), 69–70

Schenck, Woodhul S., 32

Schufeldt, Robert W., 9, 14

Scott, Robert W.: assumes command of *Saginaw*, 123; biographical sketch of, 123; illness, death of, 127–28; shore guard at Acapulco, 124

Seals/sealing: fur seals, trade in, 148, 149, 181; monk seals, conserving (by *Saginaw's* crew), 257; monk seals (on Midway Island), 191, 205, 211, 232–33, 286; monk seals (seamen surviving on), 221, 233

"Seasoning" (of crew on China station), 48, 49, 62

Seward, William Henry: Alaska purchase, 4; Pacific Ocean commerce speech, 11–12

Shackles/irons: placing crewmen in, 93, 95, 98, 103, 139, 210; saving from *Saginaw* wreck (by officers), 234. *See also Saginaw*, discipline aboard

Shanghai: commercial importance of, 42; defeat of Taiping army at, 44–45; ransom of (by British), 42; Shanghai waterfront, dangers of, 48

Shanghaied sailors, 138

Shenandoah, CSS: as commerce raider, 81, 117; informed of Confederate surrender, 118; origin, armament of, 117; ships taken by, 145–46, 187; as stateless pirate (after Confederate surrender), 118; surrender to Royal Navy (1865), 118, 126; U.S. navy search for, 118, 124; James Waddell captain of, 66, 117; Gideon Welles comment on, 80; whalers, attacks on, 117–18

Sheridan, James, 62

Sicard, Lt. Cmdr. Montgomery: as lieutenant commander (photo), 180i; loss of *Saginaw*, court of inquiry proceedings, 275–79, 341nn114–20; pension for James Muir, 57; post-*Saginaw* career of, 280–81; as rear admiral (photo), 180i; sailing master of USS *Dakotah*, 57. *See also* Ocean Island, *Saginaw* crew on; *Saginaw*, grounding and loss of

Sicard, USS (DD-346), 281

Simonoseki, Straits of, 115

Sitka: Adm. Craven negative evaluation of, 153–54; Army garrison at, 4, 148–49; Chilcatkon confrontation with garrison guard, 168–69; description of, 148; difficulties of life aboard at, 161–62; *Saginaw* passage to (Capt. Meade), 167–68; Sitka-kon, minor confrontations with, 162; Tlingit Indians at, 149–50; U.S. Army alcohol abuse at, 155

Slaves/slavery: *Amistad* incident, 164–65; capture of two slavers (by *Yorktown*), 82–83; Spanish vessel, slaves taking control of, 164

Steam power: command difficulties, conflicts with, 145; expense of maintaining, 145; steam engines, description of, 18–19, 24. *See also* Coal/coaling

Storms: Alaska (loss of *Growler*), 156–58; Alaska (*Saginaw* in), 175; *General Siegel, Wandering Minstrel* lost, 290–91; *Houei Maru* lost, 289; and Midway Atoll, 191, 207, 208–9, 289, 290, 291; on Ocean Island, 238; *Saginaw* damaged (1866), 132–33, 135; whaleship *Parker* lost, 221, 312. *See also Saginaw*, seaworthiness of

Stribling, Cmdr. Cornelius K.: appeal for greater forces, 38, 79; biographical sketch of, 37–38; commander, East India Squadron, 37; commendation letter on leaving Hong Kong, 65–66; comment re alleged capture of American bark, 49; and court-martial of Cmdr. Schenck, 54–55; defense of Shanghai, 44–45; diplomatic negotiations at Nanjing, 58–60; note to Toucey re *Saginaw's* fitness, 47, 325n18; relieved by Capt. Engle, 63, 66

Submarine cables: Asia-America (proposed), 126, 134; Atlantic cable, 126–27, 134; Midway Island relay station, 216, 291

"Sucking the monkey," 98

Sunken Military Craft Act, 311

Surveys, archaeological. *See* Wreck site, survey of

Surveys, hydrographic: of Hawai`i (by British), 185; of Hawai`i (by USS *Lackawanna*), 188; of Japanese ports, need for, 49–50, 52; of Midway Island/Midway Atoll, 188–89; off Cerralvo Island, 139–40; by *Saginaw*, 139–40, 151, 183–84, 220

Sweatbox, use of, 95, 97–98, 127, 143, 161

Swordfish: Schenck return to San Francisco aboard, 72–73

Taiping Rebellion, 34–35; Americans permitted Yangtze River trade, 59–60; Changmao (long hairs), 35; defeat of (at Shanghai), 44–45; Heavenly Army, 35; Heavenly Capital of Perfect Peace (Nanjing), 58; Heavenly Kingdom of Great Peace, 35; Hong Xiuquan, biographical sketch of, 34–35; Li Xiucheng address to *Saginaw* and *Hartford*, 46; Nanjing capital of, 58; origins of, 34; rebel restraint regarding Westerners, 45; refusal of audience with American officers, 58; Taiping armies, size/characteristics of, 35; John Ward appeal for U.S. support, 34. *See also* China; Manchu

Taku (Peiho) forts, British attacks on, 38, 43–44

Talbot, John G.: headstone at Nu`uanu Cemetery (Honolulu), 284, 285; memorial tablet to (Naval Academy), 297*i*; U.S. Naval Academy memorial, 296

Tattnall, Cmdr. Josiah, 39

Thatcher, Rear Adm. Henry K.: biographical sketch of, 131; North Pacific Squadron, command of, 131, 151; relieved by Rear Adm. Craven, 153; *Saginaw* ordered to survey harbors, anchorages, 151

Thomas, Lindsey, 311, 319*i*

Thomas Hogg Affair, 108–15

Tianjin, treaty of, 38

Tlingit Indians: Chinook language of, 160; Tlingit Nation, description of, 149–50, 154–55. *See also* Alaska; Kake War

Toucey, Isaac, 15

Toucey, USS (later *Saginaw*), 29

Townsend, George: contract for Midway Island channel, 197–98. *See also* Midway channel, cutting of (1870)

Treaty ports (China), 13. *See also* China; Opium Wars

Treaty ports (Japan), 13. *See also* Japan

Trent incident, 70–71, 74

Union Iron Works (Union Foundry), 18–19

U.S. Navy: decline of (post–Civil War), 144, 175, 176; midshipmen, early training, education of, 38; modernization, expansion of, 15–16; Naval Academy, opening/expansion of, 37; naval vessels, difficulty in manning, 33; shallow-draft vessels, need for, 15–16; steam, post–Civil War prohibition against, 144–45. *See also* Civil War, U.S. Commerce, U.S. Pacific Ocean, expansion into; *Saginaw*, life aboard

Venereal disease: after Sitka, visits to, 162, 170; on China station, 47, 52, 62; gonorrhea, occurrences of, 40, 162, 170; as "Maui fever," 40; nineteenth-century treatments for, 40; syphilis, occurrences of, 52, 62, 166. *See also Saginaw*, illness aboard

Vietnam. *See* Cochin China

von Ranke, Leopold: commentary on social Darwinism, 14

Waddell, James I.: commands CSS *Shenandoah*, 66, 117; resigns commission (1861), 66

Wandering Minstrel (bark), 290–91

Ward, Frederick Townsend: defense of Shanghai, 46; ravaging of Chinese countryside by, 60, 69; suppression of pirates by, 46

Ward, Minister John: growing illness of, 47; at Gulf of Peichili, 43; to Kanagawa, 49; re coolie kidnapping by American ship, 39; re rebel restraint regarding Westerners, 45; warning re danger to U.S. citizens in China, 35

Water, fresh: improvised donkey boiler for (on beach), 236*i*

Watkins, Capt. J. L.: biographical sketch of, 76, 329nn76–77; death of, 77, 329n78; recovery of *Saginaw* from China, 73–76

Welles, Gideon: comment on CSS *Shenandoah*, 80; to lead Navy Department during Civil War, 29

Welles Harbor (Midway Atoll), 189, 208, 291

Westcott, Lt. Bayse R.: brings charges against Schenck, 53–55; reports unfit for duty, 40–41

Westward movement, American. *See* Cape Horn, passage around; Pacific Ocean, expansion into; Racial preeminence, philosophy of

Whaleships and whaling: Aleutian whaling fleet, *Shenandoah* depredation of, 117; American whalermen, protection of, 15, 37, 144; American whaling industry, decline of, 142–43; brief history of, 140; copper ingots, theft of (Topolocampo), 142; grey whales, 140–41; *Harrison* (bark), 141–42; Hawaiian sailors in, 143; Seward speech about, 11–12; shipwrecks of, 221–22; whaling grounds, exhaustion of, 141

William L. Richardson (schooner), 122

Wilson, Noel L., 96

Wiltse, Capt. G. C., 288

Winslow, Rear Adm. John A.: biographical sketch of, 219–20; death of, 220

Wreck site, survey of, 301; Brass Alley/Engine Alley, 314; *Dunnottar Castle* site survey, 312; engine components, cluster of, 315*i*; first dive, 306–8; forward Parrott gun, mysterious location of, 320; GPS units, 309, 314; Gun Alley, 315–16, 317*i*, 320; magnetometer survey, 301–2, 305; NOAA research vessel *Hi`ialakai*, 310–11; "Oshima" site survey, 312; paddle-wheel shaft and hubs, 316; protective legislation, 311; reef geology, configuration, 313; *Saginaw* artifacts, distribution of, 318*i*; *Saginaw* debris trail, 309; secondary stream anchors, 306, 307*i*; sheathing tacks, 306; sheet anchors, 24-pdr. howitzers, 318; ship's bell, 316, 316*i*; side-scan sonar, 302; site assessment, preliminary, 309–10; summary of items found, photographed, 317; surge, effects of, 307; surge channel, diver in, 314*i*; team members (2003), 304; team members (2006), 311; 24-pdr cannon, 307, 308*i*; ulua (fish), 306; Van Tilburg on reef, 319*i*; whaler *Pearl*, survey of (2006), 311–12; whaling ship survey (2005), 311

Yangtze Steam Navigation Company, 56, 61
Yellow fever ("yellow jack"), 96
Yokohama. *See* Japan
Yorktown, USS: capture of two slavers, 82–83
Yurba Buena, 10, 84, 130. *See also* San Francisco

Hans Konrad Van Tilburg, maritime heritage coordinator for the National Oceanic and Atmospheric Administration, is the author of *Chinese Junks on the Pacific*.

The Maritime Heritage of the Cayman Islands, by Roger C. Smith (2000; first paperback edition, 2001; second paperback edition, 2019)

The Three German Navies: Dissolution, Transition, and New Beginnings, 1945–1960, by Douglas C. Peifer (2002)

The Rescue of the Gale Runner: *Death, Heroism, and the U.S. Coast Guard*, by Dennis L. Noble (2002; first paperback edition, 2008)

Brown Water Warfare: The U.S. Navy in Riverine Warfare and the Emergence of a Tactical Doctrine, 1775–1970, by R. Blake Dunnavent (2003)

Sea Power in the Medieval Mediterranean: The Catalan-Aragonese Fleet in the War of the Sicilian Vespers, by Lawrence V. Mott (2003)

An Admiral for America: Sir Peter Warren, Vice Admiral of the Red, 1703–1752, by Julian Gwyn (2004)

Maritime History as World History, edited by Daniel Finamore (2004; first paperback edition, 2004)

Counterpoint to Trafalgar: The Anglo-Russian Invasion of Naples, 1805–1806, by William Henry Flayhart III (paperback edition, 2004)

Life and Death on the Greenland Patrol, 1942, by Thaddeus D. Novak, edited by P.J. Capelotti (2005; first paperback edition, 2014)

X Marks the Spot: The Archaeology of Piracy, edited by Russell K. Skowronek and Charles R. Ewen (2006; first paperback edition, 2007)

Industrializing American Shipbuilding: The Transformation of Ship Design and Construction, 1820–1920, by William H. Thiesen (2006)

Admiral Lord Keith and the Naval War against Napoleon, by Kevin D. McCranie (2006)

Commodore John Rodgers: Paragon of the Early American Navy, by John H. Schroeder (2006)

Borderland Smuggling: Patriots, Loyalists, and Illicit Trade in the Northeast, 1783–1820, by Joshua M. Smith (2006; first paperback edition, 2019)

Brutality on Trial: "Hellfire" Pedersen, "Fighting" Hansen, and the Seamen's Act of 1915, by E. Kay Gibson (2006)

Uriah Levy: Reformer of the Antebellum Navy, by Ira Dye (2006)

Crisis at Sea: The United States Navy in European Waters in World War I, by William N. Still Jr. (2006)

Chinese Junks on the Pacific: Views from a Different Deck, by Hans K. Van Tilburg (2007; first paperback edition, 2013)

Eight Thousand Years of Maltese Maritime History: Trade, Piracy, and Naval Warfare in the Central Mediterranean, by Ayse Devrim Atauz (2008)

Merchant Mariners at War: An Oral History of World War II, by George J. Billy and Christine M. Billy (2008)

The Steamboat Montana *and the Opening of the West: History, Excavation, and Architecture*, by Annalies Corbin and Bradley A. Rodgers (2008)

Attack Transport: USS Charles Carroll *in World War II*, by Kenneth H. Goldman (2008)

Diplomats in Blue: U.S. Naval Officers in China, 1922–1933, by William Reynolds Braisted (2009)

Sir Samuel Hood and the Battle of the Chesapeake, by Colin Pengelly (2009)

Voyages, the Age of Sail: Documents in American Maritime History, Volume I, 1492–1865, edited by Joshua M. Smith and the National Maritime Historical Society (2009)

Voyages, the Age of Engines: Documents in American Maritime History, Volume II, 1865–Present, edited by Joshua M. Smith and the National Maritime Historical Society (2009)

HMS Fowey *Lost and Found: Being the Discovery, Excavation, and Identification of a British Man-of-War Lost off the Cape of Florida in 1748*, by Russell K. Skowronek and George R. Fischer (2009)

American Coastal Rescue Craft: A Design History of Coastal Rescue Craft Used by the United States Life-Saving Service and the United States Coast Guard, by William D. Wilkinson and Commander Timothy R. Dring, USNR (Retired) (2009)

The Spanish Convoy of 1750: Heaven's Hammer and International Diplomacy, by James A. Lewis (2009)

The Development of Mobile Logistic Support in Anglo-American Naval Policy, 1900–1953, by Peter V. Nash (2009)

Captain "Hell Roaring" Mike Healy: From American Slave to Arctic Hero, by Dennis L. Noble and Truman R. Strobridge (2009; first paperback edition, 2017)

Sovereignty at Sea: U.S. Merchant Ships and American Entry into World War I, by Rodney Carlisle (2009; first paperback edition, 2011)

Commodore Abraham Whipple of the Continental Navy: Privateer, Patriot, Pioneer, by Sheldon S. Cohen (2010; first paperback edition, 2011)

Lucky 73: USS Pampanito's *Unlikely Rescue of Allied POWs in WWII*, by Aldona Sendzikas (2010)

Cruise of the Dashing Wave: *Rounding Cape Horn in 1860*, by Philip Hichborn, edited by William H. Thiesen (2010)

Seated by the Sea: The Maritime History of Portland, Maine, and Its Irish Long-shoremen, by Michael C. Connolly (2010; first paperback edition, 2011)

The Whaling Expedition of the Ulysses, *1937–38*, by Lt. (j.g.) Quentin R. Walsh, U.S. Coast Guard, edited and with an introduction by P.J. Capelotti (2010)

Stalking the U-Boat: U.S. Naval Aviation in Europe during World War I, by Geoffrey L. Rossano (2010; first paperback edition, 2021)

In Katrina's Wake: The U.S. Coast Guard and the Gulf Coast Hurricanes of 2005, by Donald L. Canney (2010)

A Civil War Gunboat in Pacific Waters: Life on Board USS Saginaw, by Hans Konrad Van Tilburg (2010; first paperback edition, 2023)

The U.S. Coast Guard's War on Human Smuggling, by Dennis L. Noble (2011)

The Sea Their Graves: An Archaeology of Death and Remembrance in Maritime Culture, by David J. Stewart (2011; first paperback edition, 2019)

CPSIA information can be obtained
at www.ICGtesting.com
Printed in the USA
JSHW040529140223
37575JS00005B/18